JUDGE BAO 包拯 AND THE RULE OF LAW

Eight Ballad-Stories from the Period 1250–1450

JUDGE BAO 包拯 AND THE RULE OF LAW

Eight Ballad-Stories from the Period 1250–1450

Wilt L Idema

Harvard University, USA

NEW JERSEY · LONDON · SINGAPORE · BEIJING · SHANGHAI · HONG KONG · TAIPEI · CHENNAI

Published by

World Scientific Publishing Co. Pte. Ltd.
5 Toh Tuck Link, Singapore 596224
USA office: 27 Warren Street, Suite 401-402, Hackensack, NJ 07601
UK office: 57 Shelton Street, Covent Garden, London WC2H 9HE

British Library Cataloguing-in-Publication Data
A catalogue record for this book is available from the British Library.

JUDGE BAO AND THE RULE OF LAW
Eight Ballad-Stories from the Period 1250–1450

ISBN-13 978-981-4277-01-3
ISBN-10 981-4277-01-0
ISBN-13 978-981-4304-45-0 (pbk)
ISBN-10 981-4304-45-X (pbk)

Typeset by Stallion Press
Email: enquiries@stallionpress.com

Printed in Singapore.

Contents

Acknowledgments   vii

Introduction   ix

Note on the Translations   xxxv

Chapter One: The Tale of the Early Career of Rescriptor Bao   1

Chapter Two: Judge Bao Selling Rice in Chenzhou   31

Chapter Three: The Tale of the Humane Ancestor Recognizing   67
                 his Mother

Chapter Four: Dragon-Design Bao Sentences the White Weretiger   105

Chapter Five: Rescriptor Bao Decides the Case of the   133
                 Weird Black Pot

Chapter Six: The Tale of the Case of Dragon-Design Bao   197
                 Sentencing the Emperor's Brothers-in-law Cao

Chapter Seven: The Tale of Zhang Wengui. Part One   277

                 The Tale of Zhang Wengui. Part Two   309

Chapter Eight: The Story of How Shi Guanshou's Wife Liu Dusai   347
                 on the Night of the Fifteenth, on Superior Prime,
                 Watched the Lanterns. Part One

                 The Story of the Judgment of Dragon-Design   375
                 Bao in the Case of Prince Zhao and
                 Sun Wenyi. Part Two

Glossary   403

Bibliography   411

Acknowledgements

First of all it is my pleasure to thank the staff of the Library of the Sinological Library at Leiden University and the staff of the Harvard–Yenching Library at Harvard University for their assistance in locating and acquiring the materials on which these translations and their introduction are based. Throughout the years they have been unfailingly helpful.

I owe a special debt of gratitude to Nancy Hearst. She not only carefully edited my English but also corrected the proofs, saving me from many mistakes and malapropisms. Gustavo Espada produced the scans of the artwork included in this volume.

Last but not least I would like to thank the production staff at World Scientific. Their attention to detail has greatly enhanced the quality of the final product.

All remaining shortcomings of this book are irrevocably and completely my own.

Wilt L. Idema

Introduction

For almost a thousand years now, Judge Bao (Bao gong) has served as the preeminent embodiment of justice in China.[1] But Judge Bao is far more than an astute judge. Pure, orthodox and incorruptible in his own behavior, he unfailingly establishes the true nature of the crime and its culprit, either through his native intelligence or by supernatural means, but, more importantly, once he has done so, he sees to it that the criminal, irrespective of his or her position and connections, will be punished. It is especially this latter quality that has endeared Judge Bao to Chinese audiences for centuries. The court cases of Judge Bao were popular with storytellers and actors, and were adapted as ballads and stories, novels and plays.[2] Materials

---

[1] Bao gong might also be translated as Lord Bao. Other common designations for Judge Bao are "Rescriptor Bao" (Bao daizhi), "Dragon-Design Bao" (Bao Longtu) and "Clear-sky Bao" (Bao qingtian). The first two of these designations are derived from functions that the historical Judge Bao held at one time or another during his career; the third designation is a reference to his purity.

[2] The development of the legend of Judge Bao has been studied repeatedly. Some of the most important pioneering studies are Hu Shi (1980). "*Sanxia wuyi* xu," reprinted in his *Zhongguo zhanghui xiaoshuo kaozheng*, Shanghai: Shanghai shudian, pp. 393–435; Sun Kaidi (1985). "*Baogong an* yu *Baogong an* gushi," reprinted in his *Cangzhou houji*, Beijing: Zhonghua shuju, pp. 67–150; Zhao Jingshen (1937). "Baogong chuanshuo," in his *Xiaoshuo xianhua*, Shanghai: Beixin shuju, pp. 104–137; and Y. W. Ma (1971). "The Pao-kung Tradition in Chinese Popular Literature," PhD dissertation, Yale. More recent Chinese studies are Ding Zhaoqin (2000). *Suwenxue zhongde Baogong*, Taipei: Wenjin chubanshe; Xu Zhongmin (2002). *Baogong gushi: Yige kaocha Zhongguo falü wenhua de shijiao*, Beijing: Zhongguo zhengfa daxue chubanshe; Zeng Yongyi (2003). *Suwenxue gailun*, Taipei: Sanmin shuju, pp. 569–590; and Zhu Wanshu (1995). *Baogong gushi yuanliu kaoshu*, Hefei: Anhui wenyi chubanshe. In Japanese, by far the most wide-ranging and ambitious survey is Y. Abe (2004). *Hōkō densetsu no keizei to tenkai*, Tokyo: Kyūko shoin, which collects and summarizes the author's many studies on the subject. This latter work contains an extensive bibliography of Judge Bao materials and studies on pp. 546–573. Zhu Wanshu provides a chronological survey of the development of the legend of Judge Bao, whereas Ding Zhaoqin treats the subject by genre, starting from the folktales about Judge Bao that have been collected in the twentieth century, proceeding to fiction and drama. Abe chooses a thematic approach and is especially thorough in his coverage of plays on Judge

that had become popular in one genre were bound to be reworked into other genres, a process that may well have started as early as the twelfth century and continues into the present — for instance, the Taiwan-made television series on the court cases of Judge Bao was a huge hit when it was shown in the People's Republic of China in the 1990s. Judge Bao enjoyed both official and popular veneration, and many of the temples in his honor that had been destroyed during the Cultural Revolution (1966–1976) have been rebuilt in more recent and prosperous times.

Judge Bao is only the most prominent representative of the "pure official" (*qingguan*) in Chinese popular literature. Every age has added new figures to this gallery of saintly and heroic bureaucrats. Popular tradition turned historical officials who had distinguished themselves by their probity, purity, daring and stubborn steadfastness in the pursuit of justice into figures of legend. Once that happened, cases easily moved from one pure official to the next as their legends were further embellished by subsequent generations. In their efforts to maintain the proper social order and to eliminate all crime, these pure officials, if need be with the support of divine powers, do away with thieves and murderers, lecherous monks and adulterous wives, corrupt officials who disregard the law, and thousand-year-old animals that charm gullible young men. Elites and commoners in both traditional and modern China viewed these pure officials as the staunch defenders of the highest spiritual and social values of Chinese culture.[3] It was only in the early months of 1966 leading up to the Cultural Revolution and during the Cultural Revolution itself that these pure officials, beginning with Judge Bao, were condemned by Marxist critics as the most vicious representatives of the old ruling class. As they gave rise to the expectation that justice might be obtainable in individual cases, they were deceptively hiding, these critics argued, the true class nature of "feudal society" and all its attendant structural suffering and injustice. However, as soon as the Gang of Four was toppled and the government of the People's Republic of China adopted a policy to

---

Bao in the many varieties of regional drama. He also includes an extensive section on the veneration of Judge Bao as a deity (pp. 457–538). Both Ding Zhaoqin (pp. 2–9) and Abe (pp. 14–16) provide a brief survey of the development of the study of the legend of Judge Bao.

[3] See Yu Tieqiu (2004). *Qingguan chongbai tan: Cong Bao Zheng dao Hai Rui*, Ji'nan: Ji'nan chubanshe.

establish "a rule of law," the pure officials of pre-modern times once again became figures of inspiration.[4]

The character of the Judge Bao of legend was based on that of the Song dynasty official Bao Zheng (999–1062). Bao Zheng was born into an official family from Luzhou (modern Hefei),[5] and passed the national exams in 1027. However, he initially declined an official appointment and returned home to take care of his parents. When he set out on his official career ten years later, he quickly established a reputation as an astute judge and an incorruptible official. He served in a wide variety of functions in the provinces and in the capital. Most of his active service coincided with the uneventful last decade and a half of the reign of the fourth Song emperor Renzong (the Humane Ancestor; reg. 1022–1063).[6] In his functions at court Bao Zheng fiercely and fearlessly criticized a wide range of officials, including eunuchs and relatives of Emperor Renzong's favorite concubine, for a wide variety of offenses.

---

[4] For a condemnation of pure officials in the national newspaper targeting intellectuals, see, for example, Liu Yongnian and Shi Peiyi (1966). "Jianjue dangdi fengjian wenyi de wuzhuo: Ping Yuan zaju zhong jige 'Baogong xi' he dui ta de chuibang." *Guangming ribao* May 15, p. 4. For a rehabilitation of the pure officials in the same newspaper twelve years later, see, for example, Li Ping (1978). "Shilun qingguanxi de jiji yiyi." *Guangming ribao* November 14.

[5] The grave of Bao Zheng for many centuries has been one of the sights in Hefei. When the grave was destroyed during the Cultural Revolution, after Bao Zheng and other "pure officials" were stridently condemned, archaeological inquiry revealed that the original grave must have been destroyed rather soon following the original funeral (perhaps during the disturbances of the Jürched conquest?). The current grave of Bao Zheng was built in the 1980s. See Chen Guidi and Chun Tao (2007). *Baogong yigu ji*, Taipei: Jiujing chubanshe.

[6] The most detailed survey of the reign of Renzong in English is M. McGrath (2009). "The Reigns of Jen-tsung (1022–1063) and Ying-tsung (1063–1067)," in *The Cambridge History of China*, Volume 5: *The Sung Dynasty and its Precursors*, D. Twitchett and P. J. Smith (eds.), Cambridge: Cambridge University Press, pp. 279–346. McGrath characterizes the last decade and a half of the reign of Renzong as a period of "inertial administration," which he passes over in a few pages (without mentioning Bao Zheng at all). As the Northern Song court and bureaucracy later would suffer from intense factionalism, and society as a whole would be deeply affected by the implementation of the New Policies, their retraction and reinstatement, one can well imagine how in the popular imagination the second half of Renzong's reign in retrospect could become a period of stability and prosperity. The major disturbance during these years was the short-lived rebellion of Wang Ze in early 1048, which by the sixteenth century was written up as the twenty-chapter *San Sui pingyao zhuan* (The Three Sui Pacify the Sorcerers). In this novel, Bao Zheng anachronistically appears as the prefect of Kaifeng in the years before the outbreak of the rebellion, but in a rather lackluster role.

In 1056, Bao Zheng was appointed to the position of prefect of the capital prefecture of Kaifeng, a position in which he served for barely over a year. When he took on that position, he changed the procedures of justice — from then on everyone who wanted to lodge a complaint would be able to directly address the prefect himself, thereby bypassing the clerks, who were widely believed to be corrupt and in the pay of powerful local families. Despite his relatively short tenure as capital prefect, this change, in combination with his probity, established his reputation. The years following his tenure as prefect of Kaifeng were filled with controversy, and at times Bao himself did not escape criticism. For instance, when he secured the dismissal of Zhang Fangping (1007–1091) who had been concurrently appointed to three different important positions, he was appointed to these same positions as Zhang's successor, which earned him the rebuke of Ouyang Xiu (1007–1072).[7]

Bao Zheng and his wife had only one son, who also became an official but died at a relatively young age, as did the boy who had been adopted as his heir. The continuation of the family line was ensured by the birth of a son to a maid of the Bao family — the maid was dismissed by Bao Zheng when it was found out she was pregnant, but his daughter-in-law took care of the infant, and presented the boy to his father when he was one year old.[8]

---

[7] The basic sources for the life of Bao Zheng are the (heavily damaged) grave inscription by his contemporary and colleague Wu Kui; a brief account of his life by Zeng Gong (1019–1083), entitled "Xiaosu Baogong zhuan"; and his biography in the dynastic history of the Song, the *Songshi*. A more detailed account may be constructed on the basis of his collected writings (reprinted for instance as Yang Guoyi [ed.] [1989]. *Bao Zheng ji biannian jiaobu*, Hefei: Huangshan shushe) and the other rich sources from this period. For modern biographies, see for instance Cheng Rufeng (1994). *Baogong zhuan*, Hefei: Huangshan shushe; Kong Fanmin (1986). *Bao Zheng nianpu*, Hefei: Huangshan shushe; Kong Fanmin (1998). *Bao Zheng yanjiu: Lishi yu yishu xingxiang zhongde Baogong*, Beijing: Zhongguo shehui kexue chubanshe; Qu Chunshan and Li Liangxue (1994). *Baogong zhengzhuan*, Zhengzhou: Zhongzhou guji chubanshe; and Zhang Huasheng and Fu Tengxiao (1985). *Bao Zheng*, Hefei: Anhui jiaoyu chubanshe. The content of some of these monographs is conveniently summarized by Ding Zhaoqin in her *Suwenxue zhongde Baogong*, pp. 40–68. Also see Wang Jiaxin (2007). "Songshi Bao Zheng zhuan shuzheng," in his *Chang'e, Li Shangyin, Bao Zheng tanze*, Taipei: Wenshizhe chubanshe, pp. 129–174. A brief account in English of the life of Bao Zheng is provided by Zhang Furui (1976), in H. Franke (ed.). *Song Biographies*, Wiesbaden: Franz Steiner Verlag, pp. 823–832. A detailed German account of his life is provided by B. Schmoller (1982). *Bao Zheng (999–1062) als Beamter und Staatsmann*, Bochum: Brockmeyer.

[8] The daughter-in-law is greatly praised in the official sources for her devotion to the preservation of the family line, and the story was very influential in the formation of the legend of Judge Bao's birth and youth.

In the decades following his death, Bao Zheng was remembered for his probity, sternness and incorruptibility, and from early on, he was compared to King Yama, the highest judge in the underworld.[9] Later, the rapacious Jürched officials administering North China following their conquest of that region in 1126 were ironically referred to as "Best o'luck Rescriptor Baos" (*wanfu Bao daizhi*) by the local population.[10] By the thirteenth century, people in North China believed that Bao Zheng had been appointed the presiding judge in the Court of Swift Retribution, one of the seventy-two courts in the infernal bureaucracy judging the dead and headed by the Great Thearch of the Eastern Marchmount (Dongyue dadi), the widely venerated god of Mt. Tai.[11] The streams of fugitives who fled North China following the Jürched conquest will have taken the legend of Judge Bao to the South, and it is quite possible that the professional storytellers of Hangzhou included tales featuring Judge Bao when narrating tales of court cases.[12] Judge Bao is featured in three vernacular tales (*huaben*) which are dated by Patrick Hanan to the "early period" (ca. 1250–ca. 1450) and "middle period" (ca. 1400–ca. 1550) of *huaben* composition,[13] but as at least one of

---

[9] Early anecdotes on Bao Zheng have been collected in Ding Chuanjing (1981). *Songren yishi huibian*, Beijing: Zhonghua shuju, pp. 414–416.

[10] This phrase is recorded by Lou Yue in his *Beixing rilu*, an account of his trip to Jin territory in late 1169; see Wang Minxin (ed.) (1981). *Nan Song guoxin yulu sizhong*, Taipei: Wenhai chubanshe, p. 33.

[11] Yuan Haowen (1986). *Xu Yi Jian zhi*, in Yuan Haowen et al., *Xu Yi Jian zhi*; *Huhai xinwen Yi Jian xuzhi*, Chang Zhenguo and Jin Xin (eds.), Beijing: Zhonghua shuju, pp. 2–3, "Bao nü de jia" (A Woman of the Bao Family Succeeds in Being Married Off).

[12] Luo Ye (1940). *Zuiweng tanlu*, Tokyo: Bunkyudo, which is often taken to reflect the repertoire of Southern Song storytellers but which is only preserved in a Yuan-dynasty printing, includes a number of summaries of tales featuring Judge Bao; it also lists the title "San xianshen" (Triple Apparition) but does not specify that this is a Judge Bao case.

[13] These three *huaben* are *Hetong wenzi ji* (The Contract), *Nao Fanlou duoqing Zhou Shengxian* (The Passionate Zhao Shengxian Creates Havoc at the Fan Tower), and *San xianshen Bao Longtu duan yuan* (Triple Apparition: Dragon-Design Bao Solves a Case of Injustice). *Hetong wenzi ji* was included by Hong Bian in his *Qingping shantang huaben* of ca. 1550. Hanan argues that this *huaben* most likely was based on a *zaju*, and dates it to his "middle period." See P. Hanan (1973). *The Chinese Short Story: Studies in Dating, Authorship, and Composition*, Cambridge MA: Harvard University Press, pp. 135–136. An anonymous *zaju* entitled *Hetong wenzi* on the same theme but with a somewhat more complicated plot has been preserved in Zang Maoxun's *Yuanqu xuan*; it was rewritten as a vernacular tale by Ling Mengchu in his *Chuke Pai'an jingqi* (no. 33: "Zhang Yuanwai yifu minglingzi; Bao Longtu zhizhuan hetongwen"). A *huaben* entitled *Nao Fanlou duoqing Zhou Shengxian*, dated by Hanan to his "early period," was included by Feng Menglong as no. 14 in his 1627 collection *Xingshi hengyan*; he had earlier included *San xianshen Bao Longtu duan yuan*, dated by Hanan also to

these tales is based on a *zaju* play of the Yuan dynasty (1260–1368), it is very
unlikely that these tales were composed as early as the Southern Song
dynasty, as is often stated in Chinese scholarship. In these vernacular stories
Judge Bao only has a small part near the very end as the wise judge who
brings the plot to a fitting conclusion.

Playwrights of the Yuan and early Ming (1368–1644) showed a growing
interest in the character of Judge Bao, who increasingly displaced other
"pure officials" from the stage and increasingly made their feats his own.[14]
Unfortunately, only two of these plays have been preserved in more or less
contemporary editions, and in both plays Judge Bao is only briefly featured
at the very end.[15] All plays of the Yuan and early Ming in which Judge Bao
plays a more substantive role have been preserved in manuscripts and printed
editions of the late sixteenth and early seventeenth centuries.[16] Chinese
scholarship, in general, treats these texts as reflections of widespread popular

---

his "early period," as no. 13 in his *Jingshi tongyan*. In the second half of the eighteenth century,
this story was developed by the Yangzhou storyteller Pu Lin as *Qingfengzha* (Clear Breeze
Lock), and a novel with the same title was also published in 1819.

[14] For an English–language study of Judge Bao in the drama of the Yuan and early Ming, see
G. A. Hayden (1978). *Crime and Punishment in Medieval Chinese Drama*, Cambridge MA:
Harvard University Press. Hayden identifies twenty-seven *zaju* as courtroom dramas, but only
ten of these feature Judge Bao. Also see Perng Ching-Hsi (1978). *Double Jeopardy: A Critique
of Seven Yüan Courtroom Dramas*, Ann Arbor: University of Michigan, Center for Chinese
Studies. For a detailed survey of known titles of Judge Bao plays, starting even before the Yuan,
see the three-part article by Huang Bingze (2002). "Baogong xi yuanliu xulu zhi yi," *Ningbo
zhiye jishu xueyuan xuebao* 2(2), 41–54; "Baogong xi yuanliu xulu zhi er," *Ningbo zhiye jishu
xueyuan xuebao* 2(3) (2002), 40–43; and "Baogong xi yuanliu xulu san," *Ningbo zhiye jishu
xueyuan xuebao* 2(4) (2002), 37–42.

[15] These plays are an anonymous *zaju* entitled *Gengzhi Zhang Qian tishaqi* (Straightforward
Zhang Qian Kills his Friend's Wife), which has been preserved in a fourteenth-century printing,
and an anonymous *xiwen* entitled *Xiao Sun tu* (Little Butcher Sun), which was included in the
Yongle dadian. In *Gengzhi Zhang Qian tishaqi* the role of Judge Bao is played by the *wai* (extra),
so no text is provided for his role.

[16] The first Judge Bao *zaju* to be translated into a Western language was Li Xingdao's *Huilan
ji* (The Chalk Circle), no doubt because Judge Bao's judgment in a case of two women who
fight over a child shows a remarkable similarity to the biblical King Solomon's judgment in a
comparable case. See S. Julien (trans.) (1832). *Hoei-lan-ki, ou l'Histoire du cercle de craie:
Drame en prose et en vers*, London: Oriental Translation Fund. Julien's version has since been
retranslated and adapted a number of times, most notably by Klabund as *Der Kreidekreis. Spiel
in fünf Akten nach dem chinesischen*; and by Bertold Brecht as *Der Kaukasische Kreidekreis*. Also
see Zhao Jingshen (1937). "Suoluomen yu Bao Zheng," in his *Xiaoshuo xianhua*, Shanghai:
Beixin shuju, pp. 138–152.

(anti-Mongol) sentiment of the Yuan period, despite the fact that some of these texts may well date from the Ming dynasty[17] and that all of these texts passed through the Ming imperial palace, where they were heavily revised before they were deemed fit for performance in front of the emperor.[18] Most readers only know these plays from their editions in Zang Maoxun's *Yuanqu xuan* (Selection of Yuan-dynasty Songs) of 1616 and 1617 (some of the best-known Judge Bao plays are only preserved in that anthology). Zang Maoxun too is well known for the heavy-handed editing of the texts he included in his collection.[19] As a result, it is very unclear to what extent we can trust these late Ming editions as reliable guides to the image of Judge Bao on the Yuan-dynasty stage. Some scholars have noted that the plot of a number of Judge Bao *zaju* is not reencountered in the late Ming compendia of Judge Bao lore such as *Baijia gong'an* (One Hundred Court Cases) and *Longtu gong'an* (The Court Cases of Dragon-Design), and that even if the story is retained, it does not follow the plot of the play.[20] This becomes less

---

[17] Cf. Hayden, *Crime and Punishment*, p. 15, "The courtroom plays of northern drama ceased to be written by known playwrights by the early-Ming period, although the plays by anonymous authors may date from this time and after."

[18] On the rewriting of Yuan-dynasty *zaju* at the Ming court see Sun Kaidi (1953). *Yeshiyuan gujin zaju kao*, Shanghai: Shangza chubanshe, pp. 149–153; K. Komatsu (1991). "Naifukei shohon kō," in *Tanaka Kenji hakase sōshu kinen Chūgoku koten gikyoku ronshū*, Tokyo, Kyūko Shoin, pp. 125–150; W. L. Idema (1996). "Why You Never Have Read a Yuan Drama: The Transformation of *Zaju* at the Ming Court," in S. M. Carletti *et al.* (eds.). *Studi in onore di Lionello Lanciotti*, Napoli: Istituto Universitario Orientale, Vol. 2, pp. 765–791. Fan Chenjia (2006), however, in the introduction to his recently published annotated edition of the Judge Bao *zaju* entitled *Yuan zaju Baogongxi pingzhu*, Ji'nan: Qi Lu shushe, pp. 1–19, presents all Judge Bao plays as works of the Yuan dynasty, without drawing any attention to the possibility of later extensive editing.

[19] On Zang Maoxun's heavy-handed editing practices, see for instance Zheng Qian (1972). "Zang Maoxun gaiding Yuan zaju pingyi," in his *Jingwu congbian*, Taiwan: Zhonghua shuju, Vol. 1, pp. 408–421; N. Akamatsu (1991). "*Genkyoku sen* ga mezashita mono," in *Tanaka Kenji hakase sōshu kinen Chugoku koten gikyoku ronshu*, Tokyo, Kyūko Shoin, pp. 161–186; S. H. West (1991). "A Study in Appropriation: Zang Maoxun's Injustice to Dou E," *Journal of the American Oriental Society* 101, 282–302; and S. H. West (2003). "Text and Ideology: Ming Editors and Northern Drama," in P. J. Smith and R. von Glahn (eds.). *The Song-Yuan-Ming Transition in Chinese History*, Cambridge MA: Harvard University Press, pp. 329–373.

[20] Throughout the Qing dynasty the most popular work presenting the cases of Judge Bao was *Longtu gong'an* (The Court Cases of Dragon-Design; also known as *Baogong an*) of the very beginning of the seventeenth century. In its earliest editions this work contained 100 cases, but later reprints in the nineteenth century often limited the number of cases (to 72, 62, or 58).

of a puzzle once we realize that these plays for most of the Ming dynasty were kept in the palace and only became available to a wider audience when these compendia already enjoyed a wide circulation.[21]

Our knowledge of the early development of the legend of Judge Bao was greatly enhanced by the 1967 discovery of a set of "ballad-stories for narrating and singing" (*shuochang cihua*) that had been printed in Beijing by the Yongshuntang during the Chenghua period of the Ming dynasty (1465–1487). These *shuochang cihua* derive their name from the fact that they tell their stories through an alternation of prose, which is intended to

---

See W. Bauer (1974). "The Tradition of the 'Criminal Cases of Master Pao' *Pao-kung-an* (*Lung-t'u kung-an*)," *Oriens* 23–24, 433–449; Y. W. Ma (1973). "Themes and Characterization in the *Lung-t'u kung-an*," *T'oung Pao* 59, 179–202; and Y. W. Ma (1975). "The Textual Tradition of Ming *Kung-an* Fiction: A Study of the *Long-t'u kung-an*," *Harvard Journal of Asiatic Studies* 35, 190–220. The only original section of *Longtu gong'an* would appear to be the thirteen stories portraying Judge Bao as a judge in the underworld. The collection derived about forty percent of its material from various collections of court cases of the Ming (changing the name of the judge in each case to Judge Bao), and about another fifty percent from the late sixteenth century *Baijia gong'an* (full title *Xinkan jingben tongsu yanyi zengxiang Bao Longtu pan Baijia gong'an* in the 1594 edition) by An Yushi. This latter work also presents 100 cases, but in the manner of a 100-chapter novel. It is known from rare copies of a 1594 and a 1597 edition preserved in Japan and Korea and was inaccessible to scholars for most of the twentieth century. See P. Hanan (1980). "*Judge Bao's Hundred Cases* Reconstructed," *Harvard Journal of Asiatic Studies* 40(2), 301–323. *Baijia gong'an* nowadays is readily available in photographic reprint and modern typeset versions. Hanan discerns three authors at work in *Baijia gong'an*, of which the earliest one relied heavily on the ballad-story texts translated in this volume showing Judge Bao in conflict with the emperor. "Although the later anthologists of Ming courtcase fiction retained these stories, they did not add to their number, but turned their attention instead to the criminal acts of private citizens" (p. 313). Whereas the criminals in the stories of Hanan's Author A are often motivated by greed, the criminals in the stories by his Author B are more often motivated by lust. It is these stories that especially appealed to the compiler of *Longtu gong'an* (Hanan deems the stories by Author C to be of inferior quality). Abe, *Hōkō densetsu*, pp. 215–242 identifies a source of *Baijia gong'an* overlooked by Hanan, and questions Hanan's hypothesis of triple authorship, suggesting that the collection was put together in batches of ten stories. For a recent monograph on this novel, see Yang Xurong (2005). *Baijia gong'an yanjiu*, Shanghai: Shanghai guji chubanshe. For a German selection of twenty stories from *Baijia gong'an* and *Longtu gong'an*, see W. Bauer (1992). *Die Leiche im Strom. Die seltsame kriminalfälle des Meisters Bao*, Freiburg: Herder. The several available general surveys of *gong'an* fiction tend to limit their coverage strictly to prose narrative and ignore developments in drama and early prosimetric literature.

[21] Personally I am quite willing to entertain the notion that some anonymous Judge Bao *zaju* were written for performance at court and were never performed outside the court.

be spoken, and (seven-syllable rhyming) verse, which is intended to be chanted (a few texts also contain one or more sections in ten-syllable verse).[22] While scholars were aware that ballad-stories were widely performed in Yuan and early Ming times, no actual texts from this period were known until the 1967 discovery and its subsequent publication in 1973. The texts were found in a Ming official's grave outside Shanghai, when that grave was destroyed by his modern descendants who wanted to preclude the Liberation Army from occupying their land by turning it into a pigsty. Once these texts had been sold to the Shanghai Zhongguo Shudian (the state-run second-hand bookshop) in 1972, their unique value was quickly discovered, and the complete set was restored and printed in facsimile by the Shanghai Museum in 1973.[23] This edition was reissued in the PRC in 1979, and also in Taiwan,[24] while a typeset edition was prepared by the well-known

---

[22] This continuous alternation of prose and verse is found in many narrative texts intended for performance (and the literary works imitating that format), from the ninth- and tenth-century *bianwen* discovered at Dunhuang down to many genres that are still practiced today. All of these many genres may therefore be equally characterized as a kind of *chantefable*. In order to distinguish *cihua* from other comparable genres I prefer to use the clumsy and perhaps overly literal translation "ballad-story." A more precise translation would be "a story with passages in seven-syllable verse," as *ci* in this compound refers to the seven-syllable line that was (and is) the preferred medium for narrative verse in China's oral performative traditions. For a general survey of the development of Chinese prosimetric literature, see W. L. Idema (forthcoming). "Prosimetric and Verse Narrative," in K.-I. Sun-Chang and S. Owen (eds.). *Cambridge History of Chinese Literature*, Cambridge: Cambridge University Press.

[23] *Ming Chenghua shuochang cihua congkan*, Shanghai: Shanghai bowuguan, 1973; reprint 1979. For a convenient summary of the content of each of the ballad-stories and other treatments of the same stories, see Tan Zhengbi and Tan Xun (1985). *Pingtan tongkao*, Beijing: Zhongguo quyi chubanshe, pp. 347–381. The Judge Bao ballad-stories were separately reprinted as *Baogong an cihua bazhong Shi lang fuma zhuan* in *Guben xiaoshuo congkan* Ser. 22, Vol. 4, Beijing: Zhonghua shuju, 1991.

A fifteenth-century printing of the well-known *chuanqi* play *Baitu ji* was discovered at the same time and also reprinted in the *Ming Chenghua shuochang cihua congkan*. A critical edition of this play was published as *Ming Chenghua bian Liu Zhiyuan huanxiang Baitu ji*, Yangzhou: Jiangsu guangling guji keyinsuo, 1980.

[24] *Ming Chenghua shuochang cihua congkan*, Taipei: Dingwen shuju, 1979. This edition is different from the Mainland publication in including on pp. 209–288, following *Xue Rengui kuahai zheng Liao gushi* (The Story of Xue Rengui Crossing the Sea and Subjugating Korea), a reprint of *Xue Rengui zheng Liao shilüe* (A Brief Account of Xue Rengui's Subjugation of Korea) from the *Yongle dadian* as edited by Zhao Wanli and originally published by Gudian wenxue chubanshe (Shanghai, 1957).

vernacular fiction specialist Zhu Yixuan and published in 1997.[25] No less than eight of the sixteen *shuochang cihua* deal with Judge Bao, but up till today, scholarship on the *shuochang cihua* has mostly focused on other stories,[26] and a closer look at the ballad-stories on Judge Bao in their own right is long overdue.[27]

To the extent that surveys of the development of the Judge Bao legend deal with these materials, they often insert a discussion of these texts between a discussion of the *zaju* plays on Judge Bao, deemed to date from the Yuan, and the *chuanqi* plays and court-case fiction of the sixteenth century and beyond, suggesting a strict chronological development.[28] Some scholars even go so far as to characterize the *cihua* texts as rewritings of *zaju*.[29] This may well be misleading. Even if these ballad-stories may only have been printed in the second part of the fifteenth century, many or all of

---

[25] Zhu Yixuan (ed.) (1997). *Ming Chenghua shuochang cihua congkan*, Zhengzhou: Zhongzhou guji chubanshe; Zhu Wanshu, *Baogong gushi yuanliu kaoshu* (pp. 235–250) provides a critical edition of *Early Bao*.

[26] The most comprehensive study on *shuochang cihua* in English is A. McLaren (1998). *Chinese Popular Culture and Ming Chantefables*, Leiden: E. J. Brill. She discusses the Judge Bao texts primarily in her chapter on "Orthodoxy and Popular Interpretations: Stock Materials in the Chantefables," pp. 154–191. In studies of the *shuochang cihua* most attention is devoted to the four texts that together recount the heroic life of Hua Guan Suo, because this figure is featured in some early editions of the *Sanguo yanyi* (Romance of the Three Kingdoms). These texts have been translated into English, by G. O. King (1989), as *The Story of Hua Guan Suo*, Tempe: Center for Asian Studies, Arizona State University; also see T. Inoue *et al.* (1989). *Ka Kan Saku den no kenkyū*, Tokyo: Kyūko shoin. W. L. Idema (1999) has written about the *Yingge xing xiaoyi zhuan* (The Tale of the Filial Parrot) in "Guanyin's Parrot: A Chinese Animal Tale and its International Context," in A. Cadonna (ed.). *India, Tibet, China: Genesis and Aspects of Traditional Narrative*, Firenze: Leo S. Olschki Editore, pp. 103–150, and about the *Xue Rengui kua hai zheng Liao gushi* (W. L. Idema [2007]. "Fighting in Korea: Two Early Narratives of the Story of Xue Rengui," in R. E. Breuker [ed.]. *Korea in the Middle: Korean Studies and Area Studies*, Leiden: CNWS, pp. 341–358).

[27] The only two articles exclusively devoted to a discussion of the Judge Bao *cihua* are Yang Zhihua (1993). "Yan wei shuochang, jiwang kailai. Ming Chenghua kan Baogong gushi shuochang cihua bazhong shuping," *Henan daxue xuebao* 33(2), 75–80, and Zhang Dengwen (1986). "Lianxuti gong'an lei jiangchang wenxue de xianqu — Ming Chenghua ben 'Bao Longtu gong'an cihua' chutan," *Dongyue luncong* 5, 71–74. P. Hanan "*Judge Bao's Hundred Cases* Reconstructed" pays considerable attention to these *cihua* as sources for the *Baijia gong'an*.

[28] See for instance Zhu Wanshu, *Baogong gushi yuanliu kaoshu*, pp. 63–78.

[29] Abe, *Hōkō densetsu* (p. 10) flatly states that the ballad-stores on Judge Bao were written during the Chenghua period.

them may well have been composed at an earlier date, as has been pointed out by a number of scholars, for instance Zhao Jingshen in one of the earliest articles on the newly discovered texts.[30] Whereas Zhao Jingshen suggests the "Yuan and early Ming" as the general period of composition of the ballad-stories, Tu Xiuhong argues in favor of the slightly earlier period of the late Southern Song and early Yuan dynasties (ca. 1200 to ca. 1300).[31] One obvious reason to assume a date of composition earlier than the date of printing is that the rhymes suggest that some *cihua* texts actually were composed in the Wu-dialect area of Suzhou and surroundings,[32] and the texts must have acquired some popularity there before they were printed in the northern capital. While a precise dating of the composition of the individual *shuochang cihua* eludes us, it seems safe to treat them as works of the preceding two centuries, roughly the same period that was identified by Patrick Hanan as the early period for the composition of *huaben* and that also saw the flourishing of dramatic genres such as *zaju* and *xiwen*.[33] This is a period when officials rode on horseback, not in sedan chairs, and when the most widely venerated deity was the Great Thearch of the Eastern Marchmount. As products of the period from the mid-thirteenth to the mid-fifteenth century, these ballad-stories are a world apart from the literature produced during the last century of the Ming dynasty, such as

[30] Zhao Jingshen (1972). "Tan Ming Chenghua kanben 'shuochang cihua'," *Wenwu*, November issue, 19–22. More detailed general discussions of the ballad-stories are provided by Zhou Qifu (1982). "Tan Ming Chenghua kanben 'shuochang cihua'," *Wenxue yichan* 2, 120–127, and Li Shiren (1986). "'Cihua' xinzheng," *Wenxue yichan* 1, 72–78.

[31] Tu Xiuhong (1997). "Baogong xi yu Baogong xiaoshuo de guanxi," Part 1, *Fujian shifan daxue xuebao* 2, 77–78. Unfortunately, most of her arguments are rather circumstantial. She makes the sensible suggestion, however, that it is much more probable that the *zaju* were adapted from the ballad-stories than the other way around. Liangyan Ge in an unpublished paper, "Narrative Affinities between *Shuihu zhuan* and the Judge Bao *cihua* Cluster: In Search of a Common Storehouse of Convention," p. 10, also compares the relation between *cihua* and *zaju* and reaches the following conclusion: "Without completely barring the possibility of mutual influence, one may consider Judge Bao *cihua* and Judge Bao *zaju* as separate and parallel lines of development following an earlier stage of the popular Judge Bao tradition."

[32] Furuya Akihiro in *Ka Kan Saku den no kenkyu*, pp. 326–346. *Weird Black Pot* is very precise in its description of geographical details for the journey from Shaoxing to Zhenjiang, but is very poorly informed about other parts of China.

[33] Hayden, *Crime and Punishment* (p. 16) stresses the changes in the Judge Bao legend from the late Ming period onwards: "The late-Ming period, although producing popular literature on Pao in some quantity, seems to have been ignorant of previous contributions to the legend. It indeed might be said to form a separate, although related, tradition."

Baijia gong'an and *Longtu gong'an* or the *chuanqi* plays on Judge Bao. The tendency one may observe in some Chinese studies to treat all these works together as products of the Ming dynasty (as if the Ming dynasty were a unified period in cultural terms!) can only obscure the major differences between the various works and genres and diminish our appreciation of the specifics of the *shuochang cihua*.

All ballad-stories were printed in large, easily readable characters, and were richly decorated with full-page or half-page woodblock illustrations. While the quality of the printing and the illustrations cannot compare with that of the 1498 edition of the *Romance of the Western Wing* (*Xixiang ji*), we would be well advised not to jump to the conclusion that we are dealing with popular literature, primarily catering to a barely literate audience.[34] While the texts might be recited and chanted for a listening audience (including women), they were probably primarily printed for reading, and the only positive evidence we have for ownership and readership is the fact that our texts were discovered in a low-ranking official's grave. In general, the texts have been preserved quite well, but occasionally one finds missing characters, missing lines, or even missing pages. The ballad-stories' highly formulaic language,[35] however, makes it possible to reconstruct many of the missing passages with a high degree of probability. In addition, it is not only the text that has suffered occasional damage, but the illustrations as well.

The eight Judge Bao texts here may be divided into two groups on the basis of length and other features. On the one hand, we have four relatively short texts. The first three are closely interrelated. *The Tale of the Early Career of Rescriptor Bao* (*Bao daizhi chushen zhuan*; hereafter *Early Bao*) tells the story of the birth and youth of the later Judge Bao. As an infant, Bao is so ugly that he is rejected by his own father and brought up by his elder brother's wife.[36] The story proceeds to describe his success in the examinations and his first appointment, and then fast-forwards to his appointment as prefect

---

[34] The quality of the printing of the *shuochang cihua* is much better than that of the *Baitu ji* which was discovered at the same time.

[35] D. T. Roy (1981). "The Fifteenth-century *Shuo-ch'ang tz'u-hua* as an Example of Written Formulaic Composition," *Chinoperl Papers* 10, 97–128. Also see McLaren, *Chinese Popular Culture*, pp. 154–166.

[36] This legend obviously derives from the widely published feat of Bao Zheng's daughter-in-law in saving Bao Zheng's son who was born to a maid. Also see Xu Zhongmin, *Baogong gushi*, pp. 224–236.

of Kaifeng following his term of service in Chenzhou. *Judge Bao Selling Rice in Chenzhou (Bao daizhi Chenzhou tiaomi ji*; hereafter *Selling Rice in Chenzhou*) tells the story of Judge Bao's mission to Chenzhou after he has been reinstated in office in order to relieve the misery of the local population which is suffering from a famine.[37] *The Tale of the Humane Ancestor Recognizing his Mother (Renzong renmu zhuan*; hereafter *Recognizing his Mother*) tells how Judge Bao on his return from Chenzhou to the capital meets with a beggar-woman who tells him she is the birth-mother of Emperor Renzong, and how he ensures upon his arrival at court that the truth is revealed and she is given her rightful position.[38] These three stories also may well be the earliest texts of the eight Judge Bao *cihua*. While these stories reflect a well-developed legend which may have taken some generations to develop, they also appear to reflect certain exclusive features

---

[37] Bao Zheng's collected works contain one memorial related to a famine in Chenzhou in 1043, but Song-dynasty sources do not contain information on a trip by him to the famine-stricken area (the sources do record that he was dispatched to other problem spots). It is, however, interesting to note that the final decades of the reign of Renzong witnessed a significant development of the ever-normal granary system. Later, local sources from Chenzhou, explaining the continued veneration Judge Bao enjoyed there, claim he visited the region and executed an imperial relative by marriage surnamed Cao, but *Selling Rice in Chenzhou* does not mention any Cao among the evil-doers. The local legend probably reflects the popularity of *The Emperor's Brothers-in-law Cao* and its rewritings in the Ming and Qing.

On the members of the imperial family in Song times, see J. W. Chaffee (1999). *Branches of Heaven: A History of the Imperial Clan of Song China*, Cambridge MA: Harvard University Asia Center. Until the end of the reign of Renzong, the descendants of Taizu, Taizong and their brother lived secluded in imperially provided housing, supported by large stipends, and Chaffee concludes: "This policy of seclusion goes a long way towards explaining the virtual invisibility of clansmen in the political, social, intellectual, and cultural worlds of K'ai-feng. ... imperial clansmen had little if any impact on their elite contemporaries" (p. 61). But he also quotes the early grand councilor Song Qi (917–996) as writing: "All those in the imperial clan generally have drowned in wealth and honor, are recklessly proud and boastful, and do not know propriety and righteousness" (p. 63). Even as the financial burden of maintaining the members of the imperial clan in style greatly increased, Emperor Renzong remained extremely indulgent towards his kin.

[38] According to the *Songshi*, Renzong was raised by Empress Liu, who acted as a regent during the final years of Emperor Zhenzong and the early years of Renzong. Renzong only became aware of the identity of his birth-mother following the death of Empress Liu, when his birth-mother had already passed away. Renzong was extremely distraught when he was informed of the true state of affairs and went to great length to honor his birth-mother. As there was never a reunion of mother and son, Bao Zheng did not bring it about. An anonymous *zaju* on this affair entitled *Bao zhuanghe* (Carrying the Cosmetics Box) and included in *Yuanqu xuan* has no role for Judge Bao. In later centuries this tale would

of Song society. The fourth short text, *Dragon-Design Bao Sentences the White Weretiger* (*Bao Longtu duan baihujing zhuan*; hereafter *The White Weretiger*) is actually not categorized as a *cihua* on its title page but as a verse narrative (*ciwen*),[39] which means that it is fully narrated in verse. It shows a Judge Bao who is not only able to persevere against his own father, and to impose his will on criminal imperial relatives in the provinces and traitors inside the palace, but whose authority extends even to the other world and the animal kingdom, as he captures and subdues a wily female weretiger.[40]

---

continue to collect gruesome details and would eventually provide the subject matter for the opening chapters of the nineteenth-century novel *Sanxiu wuyi*. The earliest modern study on the development of this particular legend is Hu Shi (1980). "*Sanxia wuyi* xu," reprinted in his *Zhongguo zhanghui xiaoshuo kaozheng*, Shanghai: Shanghai shudian, pp. 393–435, esp. pp. 402–418. For a more detailed account of the many adaptations of this grisly tale, see Sun Kaidi, "*Baogong an* yu *Baogong an* gushi," pp. 103–125.

The novel *Sanxia wuyi* was based on the *Longtu erlu* (A Record by Ear of the Tale of Dragon-Design), which had been compiled on the basis of the prosimetrical narratives on the adventures of Judge Bao and his underlings by the mid-nineteenth century Beijing performer Shi Yukun and his followers. See S. Blader (1977). "A Critical Study of *San-hsia wu-yi* and its Relationship to the *Lung-t'u kung-an* Songbook," PhD Dissertation, University of Pennsylvania. The *Sanxia wuyi* would later be edited by the famous philologist Yu Yue (1821–1907) as *Qixia wuyi* (Seven Heroes and Five Gallants). For translations, see Shi Yukun and Yu Yue (1997). *The Seven Heroes and Five Gallants*, trans. Song Shouquan, Beijing: Panda Books; and Shih Yü-k'un (1998). *Tales of Magistrate Bao and his Valiant Lieutenants: Selections from* San-hsia wu-i, trans. S. Blader, Hong Kong: Chinese University Press.

At about the same time as the preserved ballad-stories were printed, the Chenghua emperor learned in 1475 that one of his concubines had borne him a son five years earlier, but that he had not been informed of this fact because of the jealousy of his favorite, Concubine Wan. The mother of the child died one month later, and foul play was widely suspected. See McLaren, *Chinese Popular Culture*, p. 175.

[39] This genre is already encountered under this name among the Dunhuang manuscripts.

[40] This tale of a shape-shifting animal with great magical powers that preys on young men in order to rob them of their vital essence is somewhat of an anomaly among the ballad-stories on Judge Bao, but the motif, which has a long history in Chinese lore, recurs much more frequently in *Baijia gong'an* and *Longtu gong'an* (which, however, do not include this specific tale). On Chinese tiger lore, see the following articles by C. E. Hammond (1991). "An Excursion into Tiger Lore," *Asia Major* Third Series 4(1), 87–100; "Sacred Metamorphosis: The Weretiger and the Shaman," *Acta Orientalia* 46 Fasc. 2–3 (1992–1993), 235–255; "The Demonization of the Other: Women and Minorities as Weretigers," *Journal of Chinese Religions* 23 (1995), 59–80; and "The Righteous Tiger and the Grateful Lion," *Monumenta Serica* 44 (1996), 191–211.

For a general discussion of the theme of the love between a student and a shape-shifting animal in Judge Bao stories, see Abe, *Hōkō densetsu*, pp. 198–214, which focuses on the tale of a goldfish that takes on the shape of a young man's fiancée. The most versatile shape-shifters Judge Bao

While of limited length, *The White Weretiger* is thematically linked to the second set of texts, as it starts with the departure from home of a student who wants to participate in the examinations at the capital, a motif we reencounter in three of the four remaining texts.[41] These four remaining texts are roughly twice as long as the texts we discussed above, and two of them are formally divided into two "scrolls" (*juan*). Three of them feature a student who leaves home to travel to the capital Kaifeng, and all four of them focus on a cruel murder case. In *Rescriptor Bao Decides the Case of the Weird Black Pot* (*Bao daizhi duan wai wupen zhuan*; hereafter *The Weird Black Pot*),[42] the case is complicated by the absence of a corpse, but in the three other cases the main complication consists of the powerful connections of the murderer — in *The Tale of Zhang Wengui* (*Zhang Wengui zhuan*; hereafter *Zhang Wengui*) the murderer enjoys the protection of the empress-dowager whose life he has saved with the student's treasures,[43] in *The Tale of the Case of Dragon-Design Bao Sentencing the Emperor's Brothers-in-law Cao* (*Bao Longtu duan Cao guojiu zhuan*; hereafter *The Emperor's Brothers-in-law Cao*) the murderer is one of the emperor's brothers-in-law,[44] and in *The Story of How Shi Guanshou's Wife Liu Dusai on the Night of the Fifteenth, on Superior Prime, Watched the Lanterns* (*Shi Guanshou qi Liu Dusai shangyuan shiwu ye kandeng zhuan*; hereafter *Liu Dusai*) yet another murderer is the emperor's own younger brother.[45] The last two titles share the plot element of the kidnapping

---

would encounter in his career, however, were a set of five rats, which would create havoc in Kaifeng by taking on the appearance of high officials, of the empress and even of the emperor! This tale is included in *Baijia gong'an* and *Longtu gong'an*, but it is also encountered elsewhere and was circulated as an independent novel in the late Ming. See A. Lévy (1971). "Le motif d'Amphitryon en Chine: 'Les cinq rats jouent mauvais tours à la capitale orientale'," in his *Études sur le conte et le roman chinois*, Paris: École Française d'Extrême Orient, pp. 115–146.

[41] See McLaren, *Chinese Popular Culture*, pp. 156–157 for a detailed discussion of this stock motif. Curiously enough, the students who set out for the capital to sit for the examinations seem to do so without ever having passed any examination at a lower level.

[42] See Sun Kaidi, "*Baogong an* yu *Baogong an* gushi," pp. 95–103 for a discussion of a number of other adaptations of these materials.

[43] For a discussion of the theme of a student who is given great treasures for which he is later murdered, see Abe, *Hōkō densetsu*, pp. 175–197.

[44] If we can trust our historical sources, the younger brothers of Empress Cao actually served the court with distinction. See Yang Xurong, *Baijia gong'an yanjiu*, p. 57, and McGrath, "The Reigns of Jen-tsung (1022–1063) and Ying-tsung (1063–1067)." For a discussion of a number of other adaptations of this tale, see Sun Kaidi, "*Baogong an* yu *Baogong an* gushi," pp. 126–150.

[45] Chinese scholars have failed to identify any specific source for this story.

of a married woman by an imperial relative, but Liu Dusai's husband Shi Guanshou is a rich weaver, not a traveling student.[46] These longer ballad-stories may well date from somewhat later than the shorter tales. The number of cases said to have been solved by Judge Bao increases from thirty-six to seventy-two to one hundred and eight;[47] *Liu Dusai* would appear to reflect in its description of the duties of craftsmen the institutions of the early Ming; and while *The Emperor's Brothers-in-law Cao* in many ways seems to echo and parody *Selling Rice in Chenzhou*, *Liu Dusai* may well have been written in an attempt to outdo both *The Emperor's Brothers-in-law Cao* and *Zhang Wengui* in the enormity of the crime, the status of the criminal, and the ingenuity of Lord Bao in bringing the criminal to justice.

Each of these ballad-stories tells its tale in simple prose and functional verse. While the author(s) relied heavily on formulaic lines in these *cihua*, he/they is/are also capable of quite striking lines, and they leave little to be desired in their plotting. Each text clearly has its own atmosphere. *Early Bao* combines myth and trickster tale; *Selling Rice in Chenzhou* is a social exposé, while *Recognizing his Mother* has gothic elements in its description of the weird behavior of the beggar-woman, its evocation of sordid palace intrigue, and its performance of an underworld interrogation of a fiendish eunuch by the emperor and Judge Bao in disguise. *The White Weretiger* introduces the element of the uncanny; the first half of *Zhang Wengui* resembles a fairy tale; and *The Weird Black Pot* is the ultimate murder mystery. *The Emperor's Brothers-in-law Cao* develops the characterizations of its major antagonists: if the youngest Cao brother is an undiluted villain, his elder brother is a more cautious bureaucrat, and the snobbishness of their mother is countered by the vindictiveness of Judge Bao.[48] The social criticism of the highest nobility

---

[46] See McLaren, *Chinese Popular Culture*, pp. 164–166 for a brief discussion of "Two Topoi: The Beautiful Woman and the Dangers of the City."

[47] In *The White Weretiger* and *The Weird Black Pot* Judge Bao is credited with solving thirty-six difficult cases, but in *Zhang Wengui* with solving 108 problematical cases.

[48] Anne McLaren (1996). "Women's Voices and Textuality: Chastity and Abduction in Chinese *Nüshu* Writing," *Modern China* 22(4), 382–416 has compared the *cihua* version of this tale to a version preserved in the women's script of Jiangyong, Hunan (and translated into English by me in my *Heroines of Jiangyong: Traditional Narrative Ballads in the Women's Script*, Seattle: University of Washington Press, 2008, pp. 98–118). She stresses that in the latter version the female victim has a much more active role than in the *cihua* version. It may also be pointed out that in this version in women's script it is the father of Empress Cao who is the villain, not her brother. However, the same Cao guojiu (Imperial In-law Cao) is also one of the Eight Immortals. The *cihua* version solves this problem: the youngest brother is executed, but the elder brother becomes a hermit and joins the Eight Immortals as Cao guojiu.

is continued in *Liu Dusai* in the characterization of the emperor's younger brother, who despises Judge Bao for his protection of the common people.

Even the brief introduction to the subject matter of the ballad-stories presented above should suffice to show how different they are in content from the *zaju* plays. The only case in which the *cihua* (*The Weird Black Pot*) and the *zaju* (the anonymous *Pen'er gui* [The Ghost in the Pot]) stay relatively close in their treatment of a crime (apart from the formal differences imposed by genre)[49] is the case of the missing murder victim. When evil potters murder a rich traveler, they pulverize the corpse and mix it with the clay they use in making their pots. The crime comes to light when the ugliest pot starts to complain to its new owner, who then takes the pot to Judge Bao, who eventually through guile and torture forces a confession out of the evil potters.[50] But it is perhaps no accident that the victim is a student on his way to the examinations in the ballad-story, but a traveling merchant in the play.[51] The Ming palace censors may not have liked the suggestion that it could be dangerous to travel to the capital to sit for the examinations.[52] The differences become far more conspicuous when we compare the treatment of Judge Bao distributing rice in Chenzhou. In the ballad-story *Selling Rice in Chenzhou*, the distribution of government rice to the starving population of Chenzhou is bungled by corrupt imperial relatives. When an angry crowd of Chenzhou citizens appears before the imperial palace, Emperor Renzong is at first incredulous, but eventually he

---

[49] A number of Judge Bao *zaju* stand out for their comic treatment. In many courtroom plays, the final judgment is preceded by an episode in which a corrupt or foolish judge bungles the case. See Perng Ching-Hsi, *Double Jeopardy*. Such reversals of judgment are not encountered in the ballad-stories on Judge Bao, with the exception of *Recognizing his Mother*. In a number of Judge Bao plays, it is Judge Bao himself who plays the part of the befuddled judge. See Hayden, *Crime and Punishment*, p. 8. These stage versions of the fumbling Judge Bao may well have contributed to his portrayal in *San Sui pingyao zhuan*, one of our earliest preserved vernacular novels, which deals with the rebellion of Wang Ze.

[50] For an English translation of this play, see Hayden, *Crime and Punishment*, pp. 79–124. This play is best liked for its second act in which the ghost in the pot scares its new owner, who uses him as a chamber pot, and its third act in which the old man takes the pot with him to court but the ghost is scared off by the door gods and initially does not dare enter the yamen.

[51] For a detailed comparison of the ballad-story version and the *zaju* adaptation, see McLaren, *Chinese Popular Culture*, pp. 181–183.

[52] Students are hardly if ever the victims of crimes in courtroom plays. In these plays the victim is "usually a peasant, servant, or small tradesman." Hayden, *Crime and Punishment*, p. 5.

is persuaded to recall Judge Bao to court and to give him full authority to deal with the situation. In order to emphasize that the local problems stem from the inability of the emperor to run his own household properly, the ballad-story includes an episode of Judge Bao imposing a hefty fine on the emperor's favorite concubine when he encounters her on the streets of Kaifeng while traveling with the full set of honor guards, a prerogative of the empress.[53] When Judge Bao travels to Chenzhou disguised as an ordinary student, he discovers a society in which local bullies ride roughshod over their fellow villagers, local magistrates allow their sons to abuse the local population, and imperial relatives line their own pockets with the money they extort from starving farmers and townspeople. In the anonymous *zaju*, also entitled *Selling Rice in Chenzhou* (*Chenzhou tiaomi*), no emperor makes an appearance, and the source of the crime is not the imperial palace, but a single official, who has his son and son-in-law appointed to the lucrative job of distributing government grain.[54] In this way, this play exemplifies a general characteristic of the preserved Judge Bao *zaju*: the criminal is a local and individual nuisance, and the problem they (he) present(s) is quickly and efficiently dealt with by Judge Bao as the representative of the central government.

Unfortunately, we have no examples with which we can compare a Judge Bao *zaju* in a Yuan-dynasty printing with a late Ming manuscript or a late Ming print. But we have numerous other plays for which such comparisons are possible. Judging from the changes one can observe in these plays the preserved Judge Bao *zaju* show all the hallmarks of extensive revision at the hands of the imperial censors, who wished to stress the final authority in all matters of the central government and wanted to downplay the seriousness of social problems portrayed in plays intended for performance before the emperor. Even when existing Judge Bao *zaju* such as *Lu Zhailang* and

---

[53] The *Songshi* informs us that concubine Zhang (1024–1054) once had obtained the permission of Empress Cao (a granddaughter of the statesman Cao Bin [931–999]) to make a trip outside the palace with her honor guard and regalia, but was dissuaded from doing so by Emperor Renzong. See Yang Xurong, *Baijia gong'an yanjiu*, pp. 91–92 (note 10).

[54] For an English translation of this play, see Hayden, *Crime and Punishment*, pp. 29–78. This plays features a rarely seen elderly Judge Bao who is only too eager to retire but is persuaded to go on one last mission. The play is best liked for its third act in which Judge Bao travels to Chenzhou in the disguise of a down-on-his-luck peasant and ends up as the mule-driver of the prostitute who is patronized by the two villains of the piece. In the *cihua* the corresponding episode is much less developed. For a detailed comparison of the play and the ballad-story, see McLaren, *Chinese Popular Culture*, pp. 179–181.

Butterfly Dream (*Hudie meng*) (both usually ascribed to Guan Hanqing but better treated as anonymous works) feature a villain who boasts of his connections in high places,[55] such connections are never specified and the patron never interferes in the action, in contrast to the ballad-stories in which powerful eunuchs, high ministers, empress-dowagers and the empress herself do not hesitate to interfere on behalf of their protégés — only to be forcefully put in their place by Judge Bao.[56]

Whenever a *cihua* version and a *zaju* adaptation of the same story are found, it is the *cihua* version that was continued in later retellings and rewritings. However, whereas in the *cihua* corpus the conflict between Judge Bao and the emperor and his family is a major theme in the majority of the texts, that theme is drowned out in the later compendia by their multitudinous accounts of lurid crimes. While in *Liu Dusai* the emperor's younger brother decries Judge Bao as a champion of the common people of Kaifeng, one can well imagine that the figure of a Judge Bao who insists that the laws and institutions of the dynasty apply as much to the emperor and his family as to his subjects may not only have appealed to ordinary citizens, but also to members of the bureaucracy. After all, good students had learned early on from Confucius that "women and small men are hard to deal with," and what the Sage had in mind must have been the ruler's womenfolk, male relatives, and other assorted hangers-on. With their heavy emphasis on a rule of law that excludes no one from its application, these *cihua* may well be of special relevance even to contemporary times.[57]

---

[55] English translations of these two plays are provided in Yang Xianyi and G. Yang (trans.) (1979). *Selected Plays of Guan Hanqing*, Beijing: Foreign Languages Press, as "The Wife-Snatcher" (pp. 38–66) and "The Butterfly Dream" (pp. 67–91).

[56] The *zaju* which comes closest to the *cihua* in this respect is actually *Chenzhou tiaomi*, in which we first observe the corrupt official Liu Yanei securing the commission to sell rice in Chenzhou for his son and son-in-law, and later observe him as he tries to save them from punishment by appealing to his colleagues — while they are willing to help him out, the wily Judge Bao still has the two villains executed.

McLaren, *Chinese Popular Culture*, following the conclusions of Y. W. Ma, states that "Bao is much more wary of outright confrontation with the emperor" (p. 174) in the *zaju* than in the *cihua*, but does not provide an explanation for the phenomenon.

[57] A number of recent studies mine the Judge Bao tradition for the contemporary project of the institution of "rule of law" in the PRC.

Judge Bao is often invoked in post-Cultural Revolution fiction from the PRC dealing with the struggle against crime and corruption. See J. C. Kinkley (2000). *Chinese Justice, The Fiction*, Stanford: Stanford University Press, esp. pp. 55–88.

All of the ballad-stories on Judge Bao are set during the long reign of the fourth ruler of the Song dynasty, Emperor Renzong. Each story starts with a set piece in praise of the peace and prosperity of his reign, the superior quality of his officials, and the supernatural signs of Heaven's grace.[58] But there is a problem. Just as the knights of the Round Table can only prove their mettle if there are threatening monsters to be killed and damsels in distress to be rescued, Judge Bao can only display his qualities if there are crimes to be solved and villains to be punished. We do not have to worry, as it soon turns out that the peace and prosperity of the reign of Renzong is only a thin veneer. At the very moment the emperor intends to celebrate his achievements with his court officials in *Selling Rice in Chenzhou,* starving subjects clamor for his attention at the gate of the palace. It turns out that the emperor's virtue does little to curb the lust and greed of his subjects, even within his own family.[59] Robbers prey on travelers and imperial relatives kidnap pretty women. Nor do these criminals shirk from murder and they will commit their crimes in the imperial capital itself.

For a crime case, we need a criminal act, a villain, a victim, and a judge. Of the eight *cihua* texts, only the one on the youth of Judge Bao is not focused on crime. The text on Judge Bao's visit to Chenzhou features a whole range of transgressions — a favorite imperial concubine usurps the honors befitting the empress; a local bully privately ties up suspected thieves; a local magistrate allows his son to ride roughshod over the local population while hunting and kidnapping the daughter of a commoner; other local bullies charge artificially high prices for tea and double ferry fees; local officials charge too much for alcohol; and the special commissioners in charge of the sale of government rice to a starving population at fixed low prices double the prices to benefit themselves. *Recognizing his Mother* recounts how Judge Bao on his way back to the capital from Chenzhou is approached by a beggar-woman who claims to be the birth-mother of Emperor Renzong. According to her story, her baby had been stolen by concubine Liu, who had raised the infant as her own and tried to have her killed. Upon his return to court, Judge Bao confronts the emperor, who

---

[58] See McLaren, *Chinese Popular Culture*, pp. 166–170, "Singing of the Virtuous Emperor."

[59] Apart from the five ballad-stories that focus on the crimes of imperial relatives, the ballad-stories mention two other stories in which Judge Bao sentences an imperial relative. The introduction of *Recognizing his Mother* mentions Judge Bao's condemnation of the imperial relative Zeng, and in *The Emperor's Brothers-in-law Cao* we encounter a reference to his condemnation of "the emperor's in-law Tao."

believes the now empress-dowager Liu to be his mother, and eventually succeeds in extracting a confession from her accomplice, the eunuch Guo Huai.

In each of the other cases, the primary crime is a murder most foul. In *The White Weretiger* the seductive monster kills a Daoist priest who disclosed her true nature to a student who met her on his road to the capital; in *The Weird Black Pot*, potters kill a student who is traveling to the capital in order to rob him of his money and goods; in *Zhang Wengui*, yet another student is killed when he arrives at the capital by the innkeeper who covets the three magical objects this student has received from the daughter of the robber king who had captured him — the innkeeper goes on to use these objects to save the life of the emperor's mother and achieve a high position; in *The Emperor's Brothers-in-law Cao*, one of the younger brothers of Empress Cao kills the husband and son of a beautiful woman who has followed her husband to the capital; and in *Liu Dusai*, the emperor's own younger brother not only kills the husband of the beautiful wife he has kidnapped but also more than one hundred members of his household. These murders most foul cry out to Heaven. Whereas *Selling Rice in Chenzhou* and *Recognizing his Mother* contain hardly any supernatural elements, these last five stories do. Judge Bao is alerted to the crime by some kind of supernatural action, and may be informed of the true nature of the event through other supernatural means.[60] What remains to be done is for Judge Bao to arrest the criminal, prove the facts of the case, extract a confession, and ensure that the culprit is punished.

In view of the supernatural nature of the culprit or the high connections of the villains, these cases require a very special judge. *Early Bao* sets out to explain the exceptional background and the peculiar characteristics of Judge Bao. Judge Bao is often said to be an incarnation of the Astral God of Civil Arts (*Wenqu xing*), sent down to earth together with the Astral God of Military Arts (*Wuqu xing*) to assist Renzong, who is said to be the reincarnation of a heavenly deity (the Barefoot Immortal).[61] At other times,

---

[60] Abe, *Hōkō densetsu*, pp. 26–42; 79–102.

[61] The incarnation of the Astral God of Military Arts is often said to be Di Qing (1008–1057). Di Qing, who distinguished himself in the wars against the Xixia kingdom in the northwest and the suppression of the rebellion of Nong Zhigao in the extreme south, had become a character on the stage by Yuan-dynasty times, and in the Qing dynasty would become the hero of three novels: *Wanhua lou* (Tower of Myriad Flowers), *Wuhu pingxi* (The Five Tigers Pacify the West) and *Wuhu pingnan* (The Five Tigers Pacify the South). Judge Bao has a major role in these, especially

Judge Bao is said to be an incarnation of the White Tiger Star, and as such is paired with the emperor, who is of course a dragon. In contrast to the historical Bao Zheng who was born as the son of an official, our Judge Bao is said to have been born as the third son of a farmer, who spent a large part of his younger days herding cows and cutting wheat. Despite his father's wealth, this lowly origin continues to haunt Judge Bao throughout his life. In *The Emperor's Brothers-in-law Cao*, their mother curses Judge Bao by elaborating on his lowly background,[62] and in *Liu Dusai*, Judge Bao fears that one of his actions may be interpreted as a sign of his rural background.[63]

Judge Bao is not only described as a farm boy, but also as extremely ugly, so ugly indeed that his father refuses to accept the child — the infant only survives because the wife of his eldest brother takes care of him. Not only does she feed him, she later sends him to school. When he eventually goes to the capital to sit for the examinations, he is, thanks to divine intervention, taken care of by a top-class courtesan who, like him, hails from Luzhou.[64] When he returns home upon passing the examinations, he manifests himself very much as a trickster. Judge Bao's ugliness reminds one of Zhong Kui, who, according to legend, committed suicide when Emperor Xuanzong (reg. 713–756) refused to grant him his degree after he had passed the examinations because he was so ugly, and from that day on became a ghostly demon-queller.[65] While some texts state that Judge Bao judges the living during the day and the dead at night, the ballad-stories do not describe such

---

in *Wanhua lou*. In some texts, Yang Wenguang, a scion of the Yang family, is identified as the incarnation of the Astral God of Military Arts. For the early novels on the generals of the Yang family, see W. L. Idema (2006). "Something Rotten in the State of Song: The Frustrated Loyalty of the Generals of the Yang Family," *Journal of Song-Yuan Studies* 36, 57–77.

[62] This passage reminds one strongly of the way in which Ji Bu effectively curses Liu Bang by spelling out his rural background in the *Zhuo Ji Bu zhuanwen* (The Text of the Tale of the Capture of Ji Bu), a ninth or tenth century *ciwen* discovered at Dunhuang.

[63] See McLaren, *Chinese Popular Culture*, pp. 171–172.

[64] The courtesan ended up in her profession because she had been kidnapped on the night of the Lantern Festival. This motif will be reencountered in *Liu Dusai*, where the heroine is separated from her servants in the crowd on the same occasion. Cf. McLaren, *Chinese Popular Culture*, pp. 168–170. In her "Revels of a Gaudy Night," *Chinese Literature Essays Articles Reviews* 4(2), 213–231, an analysis of the role of the Lantern Festival in the sixteenth-century novel *Jin Ping Mei*, V. Cass writes, "The Primal Night holiday is a nightmarish scene of eroticism and death fantasies in which human society loses its order and is seen as swarms of life and surges of energy. Creation is seen as chaotic and indiscriminate" (p. 215). On pp. 220–227 she proceeds to discuss the imagery of the lantern, spring and crowds.

[65] Cf. Abe, *Hōkō densetsu*, pp. 3–25; Yang Xurong, *Baijia gong'an yanjiu*, pp. 239–240.

behavior. However, Judge Bao may orchestrate a night performance of an underworld judgment in order to scare an exceptionally stubborn villain, such as the eunuch Guo Huai, into a confession.[66] He may also on occasion order the local city god to do his bidding and his prayers to the gods for support are always answered. Judge Bao's trickster nature will serve him well in his later career, during which he will lie and connive, feign and dissemble for the cause of justice.[67]

Guile and trickery, exceptional ugliness, high offices and extreme moral standards, however, are not enough to operate effectively in the complex bureaucracy of imperial China. Judge Bao needs both the full confidence of the emperor and the backing of the highest officials. Judge Bao has the backing of the emperor, as is demonstrated by a wide variety of objects that are bestowed on him as a sign of his authority.[68] However, the emperor, though described as virtuous, is also a rather weak-spined man when confronted by women, such as his mother, his mother-in-law, his empress and his favorite concubine. Judge Bao's institutional basis is provided by his guarantors (eight when he is appointed prefect of Kaifeng in *Early Bao*, and ten when he is dispatched to Chenzhou in *Selling Rice in Chenzhou*), who represent the highest civil authorities, military officers, and members of the imperial nobility. It was not an empty gesture to act as guarantor for a junior colleague in the bureaucracy — the historical Bao Zheng was demoted at least once for the malfeasance of one of the officials for whom he served as a guarantor.[69] The strongest supporter of Judge Bao at the legendary court of the Humane Ancestor is the Chancellor "Black Wang from Qingzhou." This fictional character must have been based on the historical Wang Zeng (978–1038). Wang Zeng lost his parents at a young age and was raised by an uncle. He became a national celebrity in 1002 when he passed both the metropolitan and palace examinations at the top of the list, and went on to achieve the highest offices under Zhenzong and Renzong, earning wide respect for his honesty and probity.[70] Among the guarantors of

---

[66] In *Recognizing his Mother*. Cf. McLaren, *Chinese Popular Culture*, pp. 115–116.

[67] McLaren, *Chinese Popular Culture*, pp. 116–117; Abe, *Hōkō densetsu*, pp. 63–78.

[68] Yang Xurong, *Baijia gong'an yanjiu*, pp. 250–251.

[69] See B. Schmoller, *Bao Zheng*, pp. 235–250, "Die strafrechtliche Mitverantwortlichkeit des empfhelenden Beamten für das Versagen seines Protégés" (The legal co-responsibility of the recommending official for the failure of a recommended official).

[70] For a brief biography of Wang Zeng (in German), see H. Franke, *Song Biographies* 3, pp. 1159–1161. For early anecdotes on Wang Zeng, see Ding Chuanjing, *Songren yishi huibian*, pp. 260–262. The historical Bao Zheng was recommended for his first position at court (in 1043) by Wang Gongchen (1012–1085).

Judge Bao we also encounter a character who may be called either the Sixth Prince or the Eighth Prince. This character is based on Zhao Yuanyan (987–1044), the eighth and longest surviving son of Emperor Taizong, and a very prominent presence at court throughout his life.[71] Judge Bao's antagonists, of course, may try to bolster their positions by collecting powerful guarantors too.

In these ballad-stories, the law is described as fixed and clear. No law code is ever quoted, as the crimes are so blatant that no such formalities are needed. Nowhere is there the suggestion that the law might be changed (by the emperor or his bureaucrats) or that its interpretation could change in any way. The notion of the law is not limited, however, to criminal acts, but seems to include all fixed norms and rules that have been in existence since the beginning of the dynasty — Judge Bao fines the empress for leaving her palace without good cause. As such, the laws and rules apply equally to all members of the polity, even the emperor himself. While that may be so, it does not mean that punishments are the same for all. High officials as well as commoners (including the emperor's brothers-in-law and his younger brother) may be condemned to death, by strangulation, beheading, and even by a thousand cuts, but the emperor and his wife are excluded from such extreme punishments. They are only fined hefty sums by Judge Bao when he finds them in transgression of the rules (these fines are distributed to the troops as bonuses).

In these ballad-stories, there is little notion of due process. There is no idea that the accused is supposed to be innocent until tried and found guilty by a jury of his peers. No lawyers are present to defend the suspects, and the suspects can be locked up for any period of time. As soon as Judge Bao is convinced of a villain's guilt (and of course his probity ensures that his conviction is always well-founded), he will use all the tricks in his book to prove that person's guilt and extract a confession. As criminals are only all too aware that no case can be concluded without a confession, they often refuse to confess even when their guilt has been established beyond any doubt. In order to extract a confession Judge Bao may resort to scare tactics and extreme torture, in the courtroom and in prison. The common tendency of the villains to refuse to confess to their crimes provides ample opportunity to progress from caning to the application of the finger press and worse

---

[71] On Zhao Yuanyan, see J. W. Chaffee, *Branches of Heaven: A History of the Imperial Clan of Song China*, p. 45.

punishments.[72] These descriptions of the bastinado and forms of torture are so conspicuous that one is tempted to provide the anonymous author of these texts with the sobriquet the "Master of Judicial Torture."

For Judge Bao the primary issue often is not how to extract a confession, but how to attract the villain to his yamen, and to separate the powerful villain from his armed guards. In order to achieve his ends he will not only feign to be ill and dying, but even fake his own death. He will also use his own wife Lady Li as an accomplice in his occasionally quite elaborate schemes. Once he has laid his hands on the villain, his authority inside his own yamen would appear to be practically limitless. High officials, and even the empress, who come to his office to plead the cases of their protégés are brusquely told to get lost, and thereupon quickly leave.

As the villains in these ballad-stories are so stubborn or well-connected, Judge Bao plays a major role in each of these stories. He is the major character from the very beginning in the three shorter *cihua*, and while he is absent in the first half of the five other texts, he takes the central role once the crime has been brought to his attention. In this way, the ballad-stories are quite different not only from the contemporary *huaben* and *zaju*, but also from the cases in *Baijia gong'an* and *Longtu gong'an*, in which Judge Bao more often than not only makes a brief appearance at the very end of the tale — not to mention from the late nineteenth-century *Sanxia wuyi* (Three Heroes and Five Gallants), in which Judge Bao's underlings take central stage after the opening chapters.

The ballad-stories on Judge Bao provide us with the most complete and unexpurgated reflection of the legend of Judge Bao in the earliest phase of its development in written literature (1250–1450). While it is quite possible that some *huaben* and *zaju* were composed earlier than some or all of the ballad-stories, these texts have only been preserved in much later printings, and the *zaju* especially appear to have been subjected to extensive revision. This revision turned Judge Bao into an instrument of central state power, dealing with local and individual instances of corruption and crime. In the ballad-stories, however, Judge Bao's main antagonists are members of the

---

[72] Yang Xurong, *Baijia gong'an yanjiu*, pp. 251–254 notes the exceptional harshness of Judge Bao in the ballad-stories and lists the various forms of torture applied (many of which are not found in the codes and statutes). The description of court procedures in the ballad-stories provides a stark contrast to the legal procedures described by T. Brook, J. Bourgon and G. Blue (2008). *Death by a Thousand Cuts*, Cambridge MA: Harvard University Press, pp. 37–50.

imperial family who abuse their privileged positions in order to give free rein to their lust and greed. As a result, Judge Bao cannot be the *deus ex machina* who appears at the very end of the story to dispense justice and restore order, but has to be a major character in each of the ballad-stories. Dealing with outrageous crimes, he is both an exemplar of moral rectitude and a low-born trickster, who at times even seems vindictive enough to enjoy the opportunity to inflict pain on the high and mighty who have strayed from the straight and narrow. As the elder brother of Empress Cao warns his mother, "He loves to sentence the emperor's kin and relatives."

Note on the Translations

The following translations are, for all practical purposes, based on the critical edition of the ballad-stories by Zhu Yixuan in his *Ming Chenghua shuochang cihua congkan* of 1997. Whereas Zhu Yixuan makes no attempt to fill in missing characters or missing lines, I have restored these missing passages as much as possible. Such added words and phrases and clauses are placed within brackets.

In my translations of the verse passages, one line of translation in principle corresponds to one line of verse. I have not tried to rhyme my translations of verse passages, nor have I attempted to impose a metrical pattern on each line of verse. Within each verse passage, however, I have tried to maintain a roughly equal line length. As a result, I have had on some occasions to pad my translations, and on other occasions to shorten my lines somewhat. Identical lines in the original are as much as possible translated in the same manner each time they occur, but changing contexts and a failing memory preclude absolute consistency in this respect.

In general, the texts of the ballad-stories present few problems. Nevertheless, each translation involves considerable guesswork, and these texts are no exception. In those few cases where my translation is nothing but guesswork, the line or passage is followed by a (?).

The Tale of the Early Career of Rescriptor Bao

Newly Printed, Completely Illustrated, in Prose and in Verse

Let's not sing about the Three Lords or the Five Thearchs,[1]
But of the Humane Ancestor, a ruler embodying the Way.
For a period of forty-two years he was the Son of Heaven,
Repeatedly he thanked Heaven for Its Grace in the suburbs.

  Ten times he sacrificed in the suburbs: that is thirty years;
Four times he sacrificed in the Bright Hall — that's twelve.[2]
For forty-two years he ensured the flourishing of the state,
Relying on the civil officials and military officers at court.

  Among officials there was pure magistrate Rescriptor Bao;
Among officers you had Generalissimo Di of Hexi fame,[3]

---

[1] The Three Lords (*sanhuang*) and Five Thearchs (*wudi*) are a general reference to the earliest rulers who established civilization.

[2] The Song emperors offered sacrifices to Heaven once every three years. They initially did so on a suburban altar outside the city walls of Kaifeng. In 1050, Renzong decided that from then on the sacrifices would be conducted in the Bright Hall. The Bright Hall (*mingtang*, also translated as Hall of Light or Hall of Enlightenment) is a ritual edifice that is mentioned in the Classics, but its precise design and function are much debated by scholars. During Renzong's lifetime no Bright Hall was constructed — on the occasion of the sacrifice, one of the palace halls was designated as the Bright Hall. The Bright Hall sacrifices were an exceedingly grand affair as hundreds of deities were included in the sacrifices. By the end of the Northern Song over 18,000 people took part in the ceremony.

[3] Generalissimo Di is Di Qing (1008–1057), who rose from the ranks to the highest offices in the land because of his courage on the battlefield in the wars of 1038–1044 against the Xixia. Hexi refers to the area of Gansu to the west of the Yellow River, which in the eleventh century was controlled by the Xixia.

And it was thanks to all civil officials and military officers
That the Humane Ancestor could establish Great Peace.

Listen as I sing about that pure magistrate, Rescriptor Bao:
He hailed from Baoxin Garrison in Luzhou prefecture —
From Little Bao Village, by the side of the Phoenix Bridge,
Eighteen miles outside the capital of Luzhou prefecture.
    His father was Millionaire Bao who was loaded with money,
His mother was addressed by the title of "Her Ladyship."
The family owned three-thousand *qing* of irrigated fields,
And constantly employed several hundreds of farm-laborers.
    They kept several hundreds of water buffaloes for plowing:
The sounded gong was the signal for those who herded cows.
Millionaire Bao had been blessed with the birth of three sons,
And the two sons who had been born first were outstanding.
    But it happened that his youngest Third Son was very ugly:
For eight parts he looked like a ghost, for two parts a man.
From birth he had three-cornered eyes with three eyebrows:
As soon as the old man saw this, his rage turned to anger.

Speak:

As soon as Mr. Bao saw that his third child was born so ugly and repulsive,
he ordered his servant to take it to the foot of the southern hill and
drown it in the mountain brook so as to avoid later harm for a thousand
years.

Sing:

If this had startled other people, it would have been a minor matter,
But this startled, in that mansion, his great personal benefactor.
It startled his great personal benefactor, his eldest brother's wife;
She stepped forward and addressed Mr. Bao in the following way.

Speak:

When his eldest brother's wife saw that Mr. Bao wanted to drown the third
boy, she begged him with a bow not to drown the child.

Sing:

His sister-in-law presented herself in front of the steps of the hall,
And making a deep bow, she addressed her father-in-law as follows:
"Even though your third boy may have been born very ugly indeed,
And even though his eyebrows and eyes are both equally strange,
    The hair on his head is sturdy and thick and resembles black clouds,
His two earlobes reach to his shoulders, and his teeth are like silver.
His nose is straight, his mouth square, his heavenly storehouse full,[4]
And his face shows the lines of bringing law and order to the nation.
    Father-in-law, if you are determined you don't want this third boy,
I beg you, please give him to me, so he can be my son or grandson."
    She looked after him and raised him in her own room for ten years,
And by and by he had grown up and turned into an adult man.
Then one day he left her room and passed in front of the hall,
Where he was spotted by Millionaire Bao — now listen to the story!

Speak:

When Mr. Bao saw that his Third Son had turned ten, he said: "You
bastard! You have eaten rice for ten years in the room of your eldest
brother's wife, but today your father will give you a job to do!" When
Third Son heard this, he ran to his sister-in-law to tell her: "Today my father
will assign me a job to do." When his eldest brother's wife heard this, her
heart was filled with joy: "If he doesn't order you to study the books, he
will definitely dispatch you to the southern farm to become a cowherd."

Sing:

When Third Son came to hear the words of his father,
Tears streamed down his cheeks in great profusion.
At the door of her room Third Son [cried:] "Dear sister,
My father sends me away with the job of a cowherd."
    [Hearing this, she then said to the third] brother:
"[Don't be worried] on any account at this juncture.
Your good fortune has not yet come, so please accept,
[And wait for the moment that your luck will arrive.]"

---

[4] The heavenly storehouse refers to the forehead.

Third Son thereupon did as his father had told him to do,
And went to the farm to be a cowherd for the time being.
[He thought he might be gone for only a] few months —
Little did he know he would be gone for a full five years!
    But this day it was the thirtieth night of the final month,
So he went home for a while to celebrate the old year.

Speak:

Third Son thought to himself: "I am a full son of Mr. Bao! But when I return home tonight, I don't dare greet my father and mother — I will go and see my eldest brother's wife!" When his eldest brother's wife saw Third Son, she was overcome by joy, and asked him: "How are you doing now you have come back home tonight?" Third Son told her: "If you have the clothes, allow me to borrow some so I can wear them when I wish people a happy new year." She asked him: "Whom do you intend to wish a happy new year?" Third Son then asked her: "Whom do you want me to wish a happy new year?"

Sing:

"First bow in front of your father and your mother,
And secondly bow in front of your two elder brothers.
Thirdly you must bow in front of your sisters-in-law,
And finally you can make your bows to other relatives."
    Third Son thereupon did exactly as she had told him,
And went off the next morning to make all his bows.
When the fifth watch had arrived and the sky was bright,[5]
Five hundred farm laborers all had arrived at the gate.
    After he had bowed to his benefactor, his sister-in-law,
She then set out a large banquet and served him wine.
But before he was able to drink only a few cups,
Mr. Bao, in the hall, gave out his orders to his sons.

Speak:

Mr. Bao dispatched his eldest son to the houses of the relatives who were living far away to congratulate them in turn, and he dispatched his second son to the houses of the relatives who were living closer by to congratulate them in turn, but the third, that bastard, was sent nowhere!

---

[5] In traditional China, the night was divided into five watches of equal length.

Sing:

"Take off all those fine clothes you are wearing for now,
And go off to the southern farm to be a buffalo plowboy.
If you cannot finish plowing the southern farm's rice fields,
You are not allowed to go back to the farm after sunset."
    When Third Son, timid as he was, had heard this in person,
He lowered his head and his tears flowed down in profusion.
Carrying a plow on his shoulder and leading a buffalo he left,
Going to the southern farm to become a buffalo plowboy.
    Upon arrival at the southern farm, he [sat down] in the fields.
And this startled the Star of Great White up in the clouds.[6]
He immediately dispatched a god down to the world below
To go and become a buffalo plowboy, replacing Third Son.

Speak:

Third Son was very tired, and resting his head on his plow, he laid down in
the fields and soon fell asleep. When he woke up, he saw that the fields had
all been plowed. He thought to himself: "This must have been my eldest
brother's wife — because she saw how much I am suffering, she had the
plowing done for me."
    Leading his buffalo he went back, [and ran into] a fortuneteller.
When Third Son had greeted him, the latter asked: "May I ask you for
your surname?" Third Son replied: "My surname is Bao and I am [the
third] of us brothers." [When the fortuneteller] then asked: "How far is
it from here to the prefectural capital of Luzhou?" he replied: "That is
one hundred and eighty miles." The fortuneteller then said: "Don't
you want to know your future?" Third Son said: "My father has
condemned me to be a buffalo plowboy here on the southern farm, so
what good would it do me? And I have no money to pay you for your
computations." The fortuneteller said: "You told me the distance to
Luzhou, so I will read your future. What are the year, month, and day of
your birth?" Third Son told the fortuneteller: "I was born on the hour of
mao of the fifteenth day of the Second Month of the third year of the
Chunhua reign period."[7]

---

[6] Great White is the planet Venus. In popular literature, the astral god of the Great White often
comes down to earth in various guises, for instance as an old man, to help people in need.
[7] The Chunhua reign period lasted from 990 to 995.

Sing:

When the fortuneteller had heard what Third Son said,
He did not say a single word for more than a full hour, so
Third Son crossed his arms and stepped forward, asking:
"Dear Mr. Fortuneteller, you're some cheating charlatan!"

Speak:

Third Son said: "I told you to read my future, so why don't you say a word?" The fortuneteller said: "Dear sir, don't be so hasty!"

Sing:

Not only were you born in a *mao* year and also in a *mao* month,
But you were also born on a *mao* day and also at a *mao* hour.
[You've been born] under a combination of four *mao* characters,
[And this rare combination predicts a brilliant official career.][8]
    At thirty-two you will become a district magistrate in Haozhou,
At thirty-four you will then rule the common people in Chenzhou.
[At thirty-six] you next will rule the capital prefecture of Kaifeng,
Judging at daytime the world of light, at night the world of shade."
    When Third Son heard this, he at first did not know what to say,
[But then he cursed] the fortuneteller: "You must be fooling me!
If I have to be a civil official, I don't even know a single character;
If I have to be a military officer, I'm not trained in martial arts."
    The fortuneteller again stepped forward and spoke as follows:
"Dear sir, on no account should you be worried about such details.
And please remember the fortuneteller who figured out your fate
Once later you will have risen to that noble rank and great glory."

Speak:

Third Son told the fortuneteller: "I have no other thing for identification but this handkerchief which I will give to you for that purpose. When I have obtained an office, come and see me, bringing this handkerchief, and I will pay you for telling my fortune." The fortuneteller then said goodbye and left.

---

[8] The rhymes indicate that one line here must be missing in the original.

Sing:

After he had said goodbye to Third Son, he went a few steps,
Then rode on a cloud and sauntered off to the gate of heaven.
From the top of his cloud he cried out at the top of his voice;
Calling to him, he said: "Literature Star, man surnamed Bao,
    I am not some common mortal [from the world here below,]
I am the god of the Great White Star of the southern regions."
When Third Son heard this, his heart was filled with great joy;
Lifting both his hands high, [he bowed down before the god.]
    "How grateful I am that the divine immortal told my fortune,
Later I am bound to become an official at some future date.
So I will not plow these fields anymore, but go back home,
Go and see my personal benefactor, my eldest brother's wife."
    As soon as she saw him, she was filled with greatest joy:
"My dear brother-in-law, you should be [quite happy] today.
Today is New Year, the very first day of the whole new year,
Why did your father condemn you to be a buffalo plowboy?"

Speak:

His eldest brother's wife said: "Dear little brother-in-law, every day you came
back home you were annoyed, but today you are happy and joyful. You must
have found some rare treasure!" "Dear sister-in-law, I met a fortuneteller,
who told me my fate, and said that I would pass the examinations at the age
of twenty-nine as Top-of-the-List, and become a district magistrate in
Haozhou Prefecture, that next I would become governor of Chenzhou, and
that later I would be promoted to be prefect of the capital prefecture of
Kaifeng." Hearing this, the eldest brother's wife was very pleased. But when
she told it to the second brother's wife, the latter said: "If he obtains an
office, they really must have no official left to send down to Huaixi!"[9]

Sing:

Hearing this, his eldest brother's wife was annoyed in her heart,
She told her little brother-in-law diligently to study the books.
"We will not spend any of your father's money or treasure,
But find you a teacher who will teach you in his classroom."

---

[9] Huaixi here probably is short for Huainan xilu, the Song administrative region which
included both Luzhou and Haozhou.

Fig. 1.1

Upper picture: Mr. Bao orders his son to go and plow the fields.

Lower picture: Third Son meets a fortuneteller while plowing the fields.

During the day he plowed the fields, at night he went to school,
After three years of study ready to jump across the Dragon Gate![10]
"How grateful I am to you, my brother's wife, my benefactor,
For your support today of me, now I have become a student!"

Speak:

His eldest brother's wife thought to herself: "My little brother-in-law has
no one to look after him at school. I will take some presents to the teacher,
so he will choose him a fitting name as a scholar." She then ordered the
farm laborers to carry her sedan chair, and off she went to the school at the
southern farm with her serving girls and female servants following behind
her. When the teacher saw the Missus, he came out to welcome her, and
after they had drunk a cup of tea, he asked her: "Dear Mrs. Bao, what
business brings you here?" She replied: "I hope you will provide my
nephew with the proper instruction. I have brought [some small presents
as a gift to] you, because I would like to ask you to choose a fitting name
for him as a scholar."

Sing:

"The name he will use for official [purposes will be Bao Zheng],
And his studio name will be Civilized and Right, surnamed Bao."
The teacher had chosen an official name and a scholarly name —
[His sister-in-law then tested Third Son's talent at composition.]

Speak:

His eldest brother's wife said: "Little brother-in-law, why don't you compose
a poem now you are studying the books?" Third Son said: "Please [look
around you and select] an object as my topic."
    The poem reads:

> *If you set to work with a steel ax, everything will be accomplished;*
> *Even though it may be lowly and mean, it has a lofty reputation,*

---

[10] Fishes that could jump across the rapids of the Dragon Gate in the Yellow River were believed
to become dragons. This became a common image for passing the state examinations and
becoming an official.

> *Because as soon as it will be picked up and is selected for use,*
> *The empire's mountains and rivers will be pacified at one stroke.*[11]

[*Sing:*

When she heard this poem, she was extremely pleased;]
When the teacher had seen it, he was very happy indeed.

Speak:

The teacher also told his student [to compose a poem, and pointed to a] tree. Scaring him he said: "I assign these reeds to you as a topic."
    The poem reads:

> *The pine tree, still small, hasn't yet shown its nature,*
> *So my teacher scares me by taking me for reeds.*
> *But if one day in the future I will rise to glory,*
> *I will be able to be a new pillar that supports the sky!*[12]

Sing:

"As a civil official [he will become a minister or a chancellor,]
As a military officer he'll be the commander-in-chief or a general.
'Civilized and Upright', he will be a pillar that supports heaven,
And no other officials will be able to even stand in his shadow."
    When the eldest brother's wife heard this, she was filled with joy,
And after taking her leave of the teacher, she returned home.
Upon her return home, she prepared all he needed for the journey,
And thereupon told Third Son to leave in order to seek office.
    When Third Son heard this, he was filled with joy in his heart;
He was overcome with gratitude towards his great benefactor.
"I will leave for the Eastern Capital to earn high status and glory;[13]
Allow me to thank you upon my return, I'll never forget your help."

---

[11] The text of the original is too damaged here to make sense, and the quatrain translated here is the one found in "Bao daizhi chushen yuanliu" (The Origin of the Career of Rescriptor Bao) as printed in the *Baijia gong'an*. An Yushi (1999). *Baijia gong'an*, ed. Shi Lei, Beijing: Qunzhong chubanshe, p. 7.

[12] This quatrain, like the preceding quatrain, is too damaged to make sense in the original, so I have again relied on the text of "Bao daizhi chushen yuanliu" of the *Baijia gong'an*. An Yushi (1999). *Baijia gong'an*, ed. Shi Lei, Beijing: Qunzhong chubanshe, p. 7.

[13] The Eastern Capital is Kaifeng, the capital of the Northern Song dynasty.

While on the road he traveled on and on, for a number of days,
And one day the sky was turning dark — dusk had already fallen.
"Ahead of me I see no village, there's nowhere an inn in sight —
Where will I be able to lodge tonight so I can sleep in peace?"

Speak:

Third Son then saw a temple of the Eastern Marchmount.[14] "Tonight I can
only sleep here." At midnight, in the third watch, he saw an associate judge
who entered, holding a register. The temple supervisor then asked: "Who will
be next year's Top-of-the-List?" The associate judge replied: "The number
one will be a person from Huaixi; the number two will be a person from
Hanshang in the Western Capital prefecture; and the number three will be a
person from Fujian." The supervisor next asked: "There are forty districts in
the nine prefectures in Huaixi, so who is he?" The associate judge replied: "It
will be Wenzheng, the Third Son of Millionaire Bao of Little Bao Village in
Hefei district of Luzhou prefecture. That man will be the Top-of-the-List."

Sing:

[Before] the fifth watch [had ended], while the sky was still dark,
Third Son had already set out on his journey, making large steps.
He had heard that the Eastern Capital was rich in glorious sights:
It had twenty-four establishments offering musical entertainment.
   All day long he did nothing but take in the many fine sceneries,
Without noticing that the red sun was slowly sinking in the west.
When our student noticed that the sky was already getting darker,
He realized he should find a place to lodge as quickly as possible.
   The big inns did not take in those who had no companions at all,
The smaller inns did not take in those who were traveling all alone.
Our student at this moment had no place where he could stay —
"Where will I be able to lay down my head and rest for the night?"

---

[14] The Eastern Marchmount is Taishan, in Shandong. From early on, it was believed to be the
abode of the dead. By Song times, the god of Taishan was widely venerated as the Great
Thearch of the Eastern Marchmount, and his temples were found all over China. Many of
these temples sported paintings or three-dimensional depictions of the courts of the
underworld in which the underworld judges and their associates judged the dead and
determined the fate of the living.

Speak:

Standing on the bridge across the Bian River, Third Son heaved three heavy sighs. This startled the Great King of the City Walls,[15] who said to his subordinate: "The Star of Literature has come here to seek office, but there is nobody in the Eastern Capital who is willing to take him in for the night. Guide him to the house of Top Courtesan Zhang on Misty Flowers Lane so he can stay there." His subordinate said: "He is a recommended scholar of the state — that would ruin his reputation!" The Great King said: "She is an immortal maiden from the world above, who has been sent down to the world below because of her worldly longings." When the subordinate heard this, he feigned to be a night watchman of the mortal world, and went to the bridge across the Bian River, where he asked Third Son: "Who are you?" The latter replied: "I am a state student." "Why don't you stay at an inn if you are a student?" "There is nobody who is willing to take me in." The subordinate then asked: "Who are you?" "I am the Third Son of Millionaire Bao." The subordinate then guided him to the establishment of Top Courtesan Zhang.

Sing:

When the little servant lit the lamp and came to the gate to look,
His frightened soul fled his body — his gall was shaking with fear.
"Now the night has come to its end and the watches are finished,
The first thing that enters the house as I open the gate is a ghost!"
  When he told Bao to leave and depart, he refused to leave again,
So the servant got his cudgel from inside and started to beat him.
Our student who got such a terrible beating cried out for mercy,
And this startled the top courtesan, the person surnamed Zhang.

Speak:

The top courtesan asked: "Who is crying for mercy?" Little servant Wang informed the courtesan: "There was a student who was knocking on the gate for a room, but when I opened the gate to let him come inside and lit a lamp to have a look, he was so revoltingly ugly it was scary. I refused to let him in, and then he cried for mercy." The courtesan said: "There's

---

[15] The Great King of the City Walls is the city god of Kaifeng. The city god is often seen as a local representative of the Great Thearch of the Eastern Marchmount.

no harm in letting him have a room. Where is he from?" Her little servant said: "He is from Luzhou."

Sing:

When the courtesan heard this, her heart was filled with joy:
"He hails from the same province and same prefecture as I do,
So I will allow him to stay here at my place for the moment,
And I'll deal with any problems first thing tomorrow morning."
　　When the fifth watch had passed and the sky had turned bright,
The top courtesan dressed herself to see her hometown visitor.
Third Son at this time also made haste to get dressed properly;
His head was wrapped in a "free and easy straight-line turban".
　　Third Son wore a white and unlined gown covering his body.
As soon as the top courtesan had the opportunity to see him,
She saw that Third Son was indeed extremely ugly, but that he
In the future, favored by fortune, would rise to be an official!
　　"The Third Month of the next year, at the peach-blossom exams,"
She thought to herself, "Nobody else will be the Top-of-the-List."
On the eastern side was seated the host, Top Courtesan Zhang;
On the western side was seated the guest, the man surnamed Bao.
　　When the boiled water was served and the tea had also arrived,
The courtesan asked the visitor from her own home province:
"In which prefecture were you born and in which district?
And in which local village have you been living since birth?"
　　Third Son at that time answered her in the following manner:
"I was born and raised in Little Bao Village, in Hefei district.
My father is Millionaire Bao who is loaded with money,
And my mother is addressed by the title of 'Her Ladyship'."
　　When the courtesan heard this, her heart was filled with joy
Because she had now met a person from her own hometown!
"I am a daughter of Eldest Son Zhang. [When a few years ago]
We went out in the First Month to watch the red lanterns,
　　In the crowd on Nine Masters Bridge I lost my companions,
And I was abducted by some people to the Eastern Capital.
[There I fell into] the windy dust and became an entertainer,
Acquainted with the eight gentlemen of the southern court.
　　May I ask you, my hometown friend, how old you are?"
Third Son thereupon answered her in the following manner:

"This year I just happen to have turned twenty years of age."
Thereupon they swore friendship as full brother and sister.
　"Thank you very much, dear sister, Top Courtesan Zhang,
For enabling me to again continue my study of the books."
She escorted him to his study, where he stayed for six years;
Overcome by longings for home, he then shed many tears.

Speak:

The serving girl reported to the courtesan: "That student in his study does not answer any questions. Why is his brow always furrowed? Why does he never smile?" "Could it be that the serving girl does not serve you in the proper manner, that your teacher does not teach you all you need to know, or that I am in any way deficient?" "Dear sister, how could that be? You have been so kind as to become my sister because we are from the same hometown, and you have me study the books, so I am overcome by gratitude. But yesterday I went for a spring walk. I have been away from home for many days and would like to go back home. That's why I am so unhappy."

Sing:

When the courtesan heard these words of her younger brother,
She lowered her head and her tears poured down in profusion.
"If you are thinking of your relatives, close like flesh and bone,
You make me feel even worse, adding frost on top of snow."

Speak:

"If you would write a letter and on the Bian River Bridge would give it to a traveler from Huaixi to deliver it to your family on your behalf, that would be the same as if you would go home." Third Son wrote a letter and went to the Bian River Bridge to find a traveler who could deliver the letter to his family.

Sing:

All rivers flow to the east, but the Huai goes to the west —[16]
He went to the Bian River Bridge to have his letter delivered.

---

[16] A little bit of untranslatable wordplay: *Huai xi qu* may be rendered both as "Goes to Huaixi (West of the Huai)" or "The Huai goes to the west."

Before he had called out once, he had already found his man:
A yamen runner carrying letters sped away like a cloud.
  But he dropped a heaven-sealed document from his bag,
Which Third Son picked up, holding it in his hands.

Speak:

Third Son said: "I've picked this up but it has no use for me, but the runner will be in trouble, so I will wait here for his return." When the runner arrived in front of the temple to the God of the City Walls, he noticed he had lost that document, so he prayed to Sharp Eyes and Keen Ears: "Because of my own carelessness I have lost a document, and I have no idea who may have found it." Sharp Eyes and Keen Ears told him: "A student clad in white on the Bian River Bridge has picked it up." When he went back with the speed of fire, he saw that student, and bowed to him with lowered head. Third Son asked him: "Why do you bow to me?" "Dear sir, because of my own carelessness I lost a document." Third Son then said: "I indeed picked up a document, but how do I know it is yours? Let's open it and have a look, and then I will give it back to you." The runner said: "You are not allowed to open it, because that would expose the secrets of Heaven. It's against the regulations of Heaven, I'm afraid. It is a communication of the upper world to the Great King of the City Walls — you are not allowed to open it!" Third Son said: "I cannot give it back to you unless I open it." So they could only open it to take a look.

Sing:

When the student saw the contents of the heavenly-sealed document,
It wrote out the truth, clear and without any chance of mistake:
The man who was to pass the exams as the number one, Top-of-the-List,
Was a person hailing from Baoxin Garrison in Luzhou prefecture.
  The man who was to pass the exams as the number two on the list,
Hailed from one of the fifty-four prefectures of Xichuan province.
The man who was to pass as the number three, the Flower-Snatcher,
Was a person hailing from Fujian district in Huaidong province.[17]
  So he told the runner to put the document back into the envelope,
And to deliver it to the Prefectural Lord and Ruler of the City Walls.

---

[17] This combination of place names does not make sense to me.

But let's not sing about how the student picked up this document,
Let's sing about the Humane Ancestor, a ruler embodying the Way.
    "During last night, [We] had a dream,
Dear ministers, now please listen to Us.
Last night at midnight We had a dream,
But We [don't know] what it might mean."

Speak:

In front of the steps (leading up to the palace hall) Grand Tutor Black
Wang stepped forward, and holding his tablet of office in front of his
breast, he approached and said: "Your Majesty, what did you see in your
dream last night?" "In Our dream we saw a boat that arrived in Luzhou;
on that boat there was a golden peck, and in that peck appeared the
character 'Bao'." The Grand Tutor replied: "If Our King arrived in
Luzhou, there is a Luzhou within the passes. If there is a golden peck
(*jindou*) on that boat, it is because Jindou is most powerful among the
local notables.[18] And if there is a character 'Bao' in that peck, it must mean
that the student who passes when the examinations are held will be
surnamed Bao." The Humane Ancestor nodded in agreement.

Sing:

And when after three years the capital examinations were held,
The imperial brush declared the selection of the man surnamed Bao.
At his first attempt he passed the exams as the Top-of-the-List,
And he appeared before the golden steps, greeting the emperor.
    For one question he had ten answers in front of the golden steps,
For a hundred questions a thousand solutions — such intelligence!
    First of all he received three thousand strings of cash as a gift,
And secondly he received a sedan chair for free and easy roaming.
Thirdly he received a three-tiered pure and cool parasol as a gift,
To go and parade through the six streets and the three markets.
    And next the imperial brush of the Humane Ancestor appointed him
As the district magistrate of Dingyuan to rule the common people.
Three years he was to stay there as the magistrate of the district —
After properly bowing to the Humane Ancestor, he left the palace.

---

[18] The translation of this line is utterly tentative. In *zaju*, Judge Bao is often said to hail from
Lao'er village in Siwang township in Jindou commandery.

He went and saw his sworn sister, Top Courtesan Zhang,
And when the top courtesan saw him, she was overcome by joy.

Speak:

His sister asked him: "Top-of-the-List, how many people will you take with you when you go home now that you have been appointed as the district magistrate of Dingyuan?" He answered: "I will not take anyone. I will tell you, sister: my father does not know that I studied the books and will not believe that I obtained an office, so I will only take little servant Wang with me when I go home." So they called for the little servant, and he did not know what it was about. The top courtesan told him she loaned him out [to Third Son] to go to Huaixi. When the little servant heard this, [he said:] "I don't dare to go! I am afraid he will take revenge for the beating I gave him in the beginning!" When the courtesan heard this, she informed the Top-of-the-List, but he said: "Sister, don't worry! A gentleman does not punish a person of limited understanding. My father is the richest man of all of Huaixi, and is called the Millionaire — he is the Tathagata of Many Treasures from the world above![19] It will not be to his disadvantage if he accompanies me!" The Top-of-the-List said to the little servant: "While on the road you cannot address me as Top-of-the-List or Mr. District Magistrate." The little servant asked: "So how should I address you?" "Just address me as Third Son Bao." His sister then asked: "Why does he have to call you this way?" "My father does not know that I obtained an office. We'll scare him — just call me Third Son Bao."

Sing:

When the Top-of-the-List was addressed like this, he was pleased,
And together with the little servant he set out to return to his home.
After saying goodbye to his elder sister, Top Courtesan Zhang,
He headed straightaway for Baoxin Garrison in Luzhou prefecture.
  But let's not sing of the Top-of-the-List on his way back home,
Let's rather sing of the runners announcing the examination results.
  Coming to the Bao mansion, they loudly announced their arrival,
And the scared Mr. Bao was shaking with fright all over his body.
With the speed of fire he ran away from the gate, back inside,
Calling out to his daughter-in-law: "We're attacked by bandits!

---

[19] Tathagata is one of the many designations of a Buddha.

Speak:

The bandits of Purple Brush Mountain are in front of the gate and demand admittance!" When the wife of the eldest son heard this, she said to her father-in-law: "No problem, let me go and take a look." It turned out these men were runners announcing the examination results, who presented themselves to request a reward: "Madam, we have come here from the Eastern Capital: the Third Son of this family has passed the examinations as the Top-of-the-List! We have come here on purpose to inform you of this happy news." The wife of the eldest son then said: "Father-in-law, little third brother has passed the exams!" He promptly asked: "Whose Third Son?" "Dear father-in-law, your own Third Son!" Mr. Bao laughed heartily: "Now you are fooling me! He never studied the books and has always been a simpleton, so how could he become an official?" "Dear father-in-law, I had him study the books. I've also heard that in the Eastern Capital he became the sworn younger brother of Top Courtesan Zhang, who also had him study the books. So now he has become an official." Hearing this, Mr. Bao was very pleased, and said: "If he has become an official, then matters can be arranged." After the elder son's wife had again inquired with her father-in-law, he invited the runners to the western hall for a banquet, and he rewarded them for their exertions on the long journey.

Sing:

For three days he treated those messengers to a banquet,
And now he liberally rewarded them with precious gifts.
Let's not sing of the messengers, who brought the news,
Let us rather sing of Mr. Bao and his nine hundred men.

Speak:

But later Mr. Bao thought to himself: "I have had my two eldest sons study the books from their earliest age but without any success. And now this simpleton, who has never studied the books, achieves the rank of Top-of-the-List!" So he ordered his two eldest sons to come back home. One of them managed a pawnshop in Luzhou, and the other managed a pawnshop in the Southern Capital, but he told them to come back. Mr. Bao then cursed them out: "You two are my eldest sons, but you are only good for the show, not for the eating. You have wasted my money studying the books, and went to the Eastern Capital to seek office, but you've only written essays that fell to the ground. Now look at your younger brother: he obtained the rank of Top-of-the-List!" The two of them thereupon asked: "Which younger brother?" "That simpleton, Third Son! He obtained the rank of Top-of-the-List. Messengers came here with the news. I had to reward them before they left." The two of them laughed heartily: "Dear father, you know his behavior — how could he become an official? He must have been staying at an inn in some distant place and have owed the owner of the inn quite a lot of money, so he has connived with the owner of the inn to put on this charade as if he had obtained an office and they brought you the news to cheat you out of your money and to divide it between them." Mr. Bao said: "You must be right!" He promptly wrote out a notification, offering one hundred strings of cash as a reward for whoever arrested his simple son and brought him back home.

Our story goes that Third Son while on the road told the little servant: "Never call me Top-of-the-List. My father will not believe it. Today we will go and stay for the night at the house of old Mr. Wang. He is the manager of our farm, we can safely lodge there." Late at night, [in the third] watch, they arrived outside the gate of old Mr. Wang. Mr. Wang was soundly asleep, so it was his son Wang Wu who came out to the gate and opened it. When he saw that it was the simple son of his boss with some other guy standing in front of the gate, he said to his father: "One hundred strings of cash have arrived in our house!" Mr. Wang said: "What do you mean by saying that one hundred strings of cash have arrived in our house?" Wang Wu told his father: "The boss has issued a notification offering a reward of one hundred strings of cash for the arrest of his simpleton son. He has now arrived at our gate, so let's arrest him and claim the reward!" When Mr. Wang heard this, he cursed him: "You oaf! The wife of the eldest son treasures him like a pearl in the palm of her hand, and expects us to get up and welcome him in." As soon as Mr. Wang saw the Top-of-the-List, he bowed down. "You are so old you should not bow to me!" Mr. Wang said: "You are the parent who provides me with food!" Third Son smiled sarcastically: "How could I obtain that office?" "Your father has issued a notification offering a reward of one hundred strings of cash for your arrest." [Mr. Wang] also asked: "Who is that guy there with you?" "That is the little servant of an inn in the Eastern Capital who has accompanied me here, because I owe him three hundred strings of cash, so he has come here to claim that amount." When Mr. Wang heard this, he said: "Master, please speak softly. Let the little servant stay here, then you can go home and see the wife of your elder brother, get the money and send him off!"

Sing:

Let's not sing about Mr. Wang, what happened at his place —
Third Son set out on his journey and traveled all by himself.
    When he arrived in the flower garden of his elder sister-in-law,
He called out to her: "Dear sister-in-law, please open the door!"
When his eldest brother's wife heard her little brother-in-law,
She went out and saw her little brother-in-law, that plowboy:
    The headscarf that covered his crown was torn on the edges,
And the hemp sandals on his feet lacked a heel at the back.
He was dressed in an unlined gown that was torn to tatters —
His appearance like this was quite terrifying, to say the least.
    "I had hoped you would become an official, pass the exams,
I had hoped that you would establish your name in the world.
Earlier, people came to report that you were Top-of-the-List.
So now let your sister-in-law know the facts of the matter."
    "You were so kind as to give me much money and treasure,
Which I used indeed to go and travel to the Eastern Capital.
But today, after all that time, all that money is fully spent —
My gown and my shirt are worn and torn, a saddening sight!"

Speak:

The eldest brother's wife asked her little brother-in-law: "Where is your luggage? Is this all your luggage?" Third Son said: "Please get me something to eat." As his eldest brother's wife went to the kitchen to prepare some tidbits, Third Son took his green gown and ivory tablet, and his black hat and fitting headscarf, and hid them all in the room of his elder sister-in-law. "Dear little brother-in-law, just refresh yourself for a while. But it is not safe for you to stay here in my room. I will loan you three thousand strings of cash, so you can go to the Western Capital and open a pawnshop there. You'd better not stay in the Eastern Capital. Your two elder brothers will go to the Eastern Capital once every three years to take the exams. If they see you, I am afraid they will want to take a share of your goods. When your father has lived to the age of a hundred,[20]

---

[20] That is, after your father's death.

I will send someone to fetch you back home, so you can have a fair share of the inheritance. But don't stay here at home. Tomorrow fifty laborers will be cutting wheat at the southern farm. You better go there and supervise them. I will get the money together, and in a few days send it over to you." When Third Son heard this, he was deeply grateful to his sister-in-law. "Tomorrow morning I will go to the southern farm to cut wheat!"

When he arrived at the gate of Mr. Wang, he called the little servant out, and said: "I have borrowed some money from my sister-in-law, and she will send you on your way." The little servant said goodbye to Mr. Wang, and the two of them left. When they had walked for about half a mile, the little servant asked Third Son: "When will you go to Haozhou to assume your post?" The Top-of-the-List replied: "My official gown is now in the room of my sister-in-law. As long as I cannot get it out of there, we'll have to go to the southern farm to cut wheat."

Sing:

They cut wheat from the early morning till the morning break,
They cut wheat from the morning break till the hour of noon.
Then the runners dispatched by Dingyuan in Haozhou arrived,
And asked the wheat cutters at the southern farm for directions:
    "To which township must we go to find District Magistrate Bao?
We have come here on purpose to welcome His Excellency!"
The Top-of-the-List pointed with his hand and shouted loudly:
"Ask for your magistrate at that big mansion down the road!"
    The forty-two people in that party were all very much pleased,
This morning they would be able to see their new superior!
When they arrived before the gate building of the Bao mansion,
They loudly shouted three times, roaring just like thunder!
    When Mr. Bao heard this, he was overcome with trepidation,
Bumping with his head into everything, he ran like a cloud!
When he had run back to the main hall of the house, he shouted:
"The bandits and robbers of Purple Thorn Mountain are here!"
    When his daughter-in-law heard him shouting in this manner,
[She asked:] "My dear father-in-law, what may be going on?"
The father-in-law then replied to his daughter-in-law, saying:
"They are all violent thugs who rob people of their wealth!"

Speak:

Old Mr. Bao said: "The robbers of Purple Thorn Mountain are standing outside our gate!" His daughter-in-law said: "No problem! Let me go out and have a look!" When she saw the men, they were no robbers at all, so she asked them: "What are you people doing here?" The people who had come to welcome the new magistrate told her: "We have been dispatched by the prefect of Haozhou to welcome the district magistrate of Dingyuan." She replied to them: "There is no district magistrate in our house." "Madam, it's the Third Son in this family, the Top-of-the-List, who received his appointment as district magistrate in the Eastern Capital." "Dear father-in-law, here are people who have come all the way from Haozhou, saying that Third Son has obtained an office." When old Mr. Bao heard this, he started to curse them: "It's one scare after another here in this house! The last time you cheated me out of three hundred strings of cash, and now you come again! Of my three sons, two studied the books, but they never got an office, and the third one is a simpleton who did not come home for many years. Now today people are telling me that with some other guy he is cutting wheat at the southern farm. How could there be an official in this house? It must be the Bao family in the village down the road, because they study the books." When these people heard this, they promptly left to go to the Bao family in the village down the road.

On the highway they saw two people cutting wheat, and the runners asked them: "Brother, if you take us to the Bao family in the village down the road, we will give you some wine and money." The Top-of-the-List replied: "I don't have the time to come with you. My boss wants me to cut this wheat. I can only go with you once that is done." The runners said: "Can you take us there if we will cut all the wheat for you?" The Top-of-the-List said: "Of course. I can take you there if you cut all the wheat for me." When the runners heard this, they all together cut the wheat. The Top-of-the-List then said: "We'll go there tomorrow morning." The runners said: "How do you dare fool us? You told us to cut all the wheat of this farm, and now you refuse to go!" And they set out to give the Top-of-the-List a beating. The little servant then cursed: "How can you show such disrespect towards your magistrate!" But the Top-of-the-List immediately said: "Don't let the secret out! Take them to the house!"

Sing:

The little servant took the runners to the main gate in front,
While the Top-of-the-List entered through the garden door.
He then straightaway went to the room of his sister-in-law,
Where he put on his green gown, and took his ivory tablet.

Speak:

While he was dressing up as an official in the room of his sister-in-law,
these forty-two runners once again announced their arrival outside the
gate by their shouts. Old Mr. Bao called for his daughter-in-law: "All
things come in threes — there is once again a nasty crowd!" He then
went to the door of her room to call her, but when he peeped into the
room there was a dog, and he screamed: "A ghost!" When his daughter-
in-law asked what kind of ghost, he said: "It has stolen your green skirt to
cover its body!"

Sing:

Then the eldest son's wife entered her room to have a look,
To see for herself what kind of person was hiding in her room.
   Her little brother-in-law was seated in her room, all dressed up,
A green gown covered his body while he held his ivory tablet.
The Top-of-the-List took his seat in the main hall of the house,
To receive those forty-two runners who had come from afar.
   They loudly shouted three times and bowed with lowered heads.
Four times two, eight times they bowed before their magistrate.
When afterwards they rose to their feet and looked at the man,
He closely resembled the guy they earlier saw cutting wheat!
   The Top-of-the-List lit a candle of incense from Guangnan;
Facing the Eastern Capital, he thanked the emperor for his grace.
He thanked the Humane Ancestor, the ruler embodying the Way,
And he next thanked his parents for the favor of giving him life.
   His father there in the hall said to him at the top of his voice:
"Please don't remember those earlier years, don't carry a grudge!"
The Top-of-the-List stepped forward with folded arms, saying:
"My dear father and my dear mother, please listen to my words!
   How would I ever be able to pay back the favors of my parents,
My mother's sufferings of the three years of nursing and feeding?"

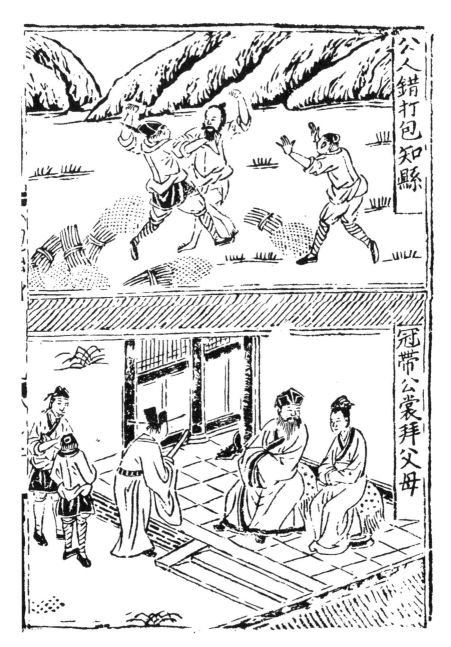

Fig. 1.2
Upper picture: The runners beat up Magistrate Bao by mistake.
Lower picture: Magistrate Bao bowing to his parents in full official dress.

As soon as he had finished bowing to his two elder brothers,
He bowed eight times in front of his sister-in-law, his benefactor:
"You were the one who supported and raised me, here back at home
And in the Eastern Capital there was the woman surnamed Zhang."

Speak:

From the hall he asked: "How long was the journey for you, who came to
welcome me here?" "Your Honor, that was one thousand three hundred
miles!" He also asked: "Who are the runners for recording the
documents?" The reply was: "That's us, Dong Chao and Xue Ba." The
magistrate then asked: "Do you recognize the man who cut wheat? If you
can recognize him, I will spare you!"

[*Sing:*]

Dong Chao and Xue Ba stepped forward and bowed down deeply,
And said: "Your Honor, please still your rage and halt your anger.
In our memory the man cutting wheat at the southern farm
Looked exactly the same in all respects as Your Honor yourself!"
　　When the district magistrate heard this, he was filled with rage,
And he shouted: "You had the nerve to beat up your magistrate!"
Dong Chao and Xue Ba were stripped of their headscarves and belts,
To receive the punishment of thirty blows with the heavy cudgel.
　　When his eldest brother's wife heard this, she lowered her head,
She laughed sarcastically a few times, and said: "Dear little brother,
Before you even assume your post and become an official,
You already have two innocent people beaten and bastinadoed!"
　　The little brother-in-law repeatedly asked his elder sister-in-law:
"How do I have two innocent people beaten and bastinadoed?"

Speak:

His eldest brother's wife said: "You show no understanding at all! How
can you give them a beating after they cut all the wheat on the farm
for you?"

Sing:

The little brother-in-law took the advice of his elder sister-in-law,
So did not administer a beating to the runners who welcomed him.

Only after three days of festive banqueting came the day of parting,
When he was to leave for Haozhou to become a district magistrate.
  He said goodbye to his father and mother and elder sister-in-law;
Relatives and neighbors brought wine to see him off on his journey.
After he had been on the road, traveling on, for a number of days,
He eventually arrived at the capital city of Haozhou prefecture.
  He paid his respects to the prefectural governor, Prefect Wang,
And then served as magistrate in his district for a full three years.
  Cases submitted in the morning were judged that same morning;
Cases submitted in the evening were clarified by lamplight.
The thirty-three strokes of the cudgel were administered sparingly,
And no case was referred to the prefecture, no person sent up.[21]
  The prefect of Haozhou thereupon was overcome by rage, and
He reported him to Commissioner of Transportation Zhang.
When the commissioner saw this, he also was overcome by rage,
And in his report to the Humane Ancestor he cursed Judge Bao!

Speak:

Commissioner of Transportation Zhang came to Dingyuan for the transfer inspection. The magistrate welcomed him in the hall, where the commissioner of transportation promptly said: "You are the district magistrate. You have failed to handle your cases timely."

Sing:

The district magistrate folded his hands, stepped forward and said:
"Commissioner of Transportation, please be so kind as to listen!
I pronounce honest judgments, based on the three thousand rules,
I govern the people on the basis of the regulations and the law."
  Hearing this, the commissioner of transportation became enraged,
In front of his sedan chair the district magistrate was forced to walk.

---

[21] In this way robbing his superior of a chance to extract squeeze. The sixteenth-century *Baijia gong'an*, a one-hundred chapter compilation of Judge Bao's cases, narrates in Chapters 79 and 80 that while serving as magistrate of Dingyuan Judge Bao executed the notorious criminal Li Ji without requesting permission from higher authorities as he should have done. Judge Bao also administered a beating to an arrogant prefectural runner, thus causing the ire of the prefect.

And when the district magistrate had walked for three or five miles,
He was allowed to go back by the commissioner of transportation.
　　When the district magistrate returned to his office, he was angry;
He promptly invited Prefect Wang and the assistant-prefect, saying:
"I have been humiliated by the commissioner of transportation,
That man is a person who lusts for riches and covets treasure.
　　The three hundred people who were following him in his train,
Were only concerned about precious goods, treasure and pearls."
When the runners in the yamen were inspected, they all had been
Robbed of their loads — thus he reported to the Eastern Capital.
　　Reading the report the Humane Ancestor was filled with rage,
And fired Commissioner of Transportation Zhang from his post.[22]

Our lord and king in his palace transmitted an edict and order:
"My dear ministers, please listen to what We will have to say.
Which person is capable of governing the prefecture of Kaifeng,
Of managing the mountains and rivers, establishing Great Peace?"
　　His Excellency Black Wang stepped forward and spoke:
"May Your Majesty be so kind as to listen to this humble servant!
The only suitable man is the governor of Chenzhou, Judge Bao,
He will be capable of presiding over the prefecture of Kaifeng!"
　　Our King immediately accepted the advice of this minister, and
A golden plaque was sent to summon the man surnamed Bao.
The officials in Chenzhou all came together in the prefecture
To receive the Grace of His Imperial Majesty, the Sagely Ruler.
　　Having thanked His Grace, they discussed the imperial edict,
But Bao did not dare procrastinate and go against the imperial will.
When the common people of Chenzhou heard about the matter,
They wanted to keep Judge Bao, that incorruptible upright man!

---

[22] According to the account in Chapters 81 and 82 of *Baijia gong'an* Judge Bao's behavior greatly impressed the Humane Ancestor, who had him called to court and appointed as censor. The ballad-story, however, abruptly moves forward to Judge Bao's appointment as prefect of Kaifeng following his administration of Chenzhou. This switch is so abrupt that one wonders whether perhaps some part of the original text is missing. One would at least expect to have seen a reunion of Judge Bao and the fortuneteller, and some kind of reunion of Judge Bao and Top Courtesan Zhang.

Lord Bao at that time promulgated an order in which he informed
The common people of all the streets and wards in the city
That he would only leave temporarily to see the Son of Heaven,
And then would come back here to govern the common people.

When none of the common people succeeded in detaining him,
All of them shed many tears, and shed tears in great profusion.
His Excellency left, seated in a "free and easy" sedan chair, and
A refreshing parasol, carried aloft, covered him with its shade.

After he had been on the road, traveling on, for a number of days,
He eventually arrived outside the gate of the city of Kaifeng.

He presented himself to his guarantor, Chancellor Black Wang,
Who explained to him the situation once they had finished their tea.
"The imperial brush of the Humane Ancestor has summoned you
And promoted you to the office of prefect of Kaifeng Prefecture."

Speak:

Lord Bao stepped forward and informed the Grand Tutor: "If I am going
to be the metropolitan prefect of Kaifeng Prefecture, I want eight officials
as guarantors." The Grand Tutor asked: "Which people?"

Sing:

"The first is you, now in the Secretariat serving as the chancellor;
Then General Fan, who controls the River and builds fortifications.[23]
Working for the state, protecting the dynasty — Prime Minister Shen;
Firming up the dynasty, pacifying the nation — Generalissimo Di.

Inside the city the man holding the rank of King Li's crown prince; (?)
The grandson and heir of the former kings of East- and West-Zhe.[24]
On top of these the imperial son-in-law Chai to the east of the city,
And in the southern yamen, the Sixth King, the emperor's uncle."

These eight high officials, all together serving as his guarantors,
Vouched for the suitability of Judge Bao as prefect of Kaifeng.

---

[23] This General Fan is most likely Fan Zhongyan (989–1052), whose distinguished career included active duty in the wars against the Xixia.

[24] This is Qian Hui or Qian Xuan, sons of Qian Weiyan (d. 1033) and grandsons of Qian Chu (929–988), the last king of Wu-Yue, who in 978 had submitted to the Song. Qian Hui was favored by Emperor Renzong.

Once His Excellency took up his position as prefect of Kaifeng,
The empire's mountains and rivers all were as level as could be.
Year after year the foreign countries came and offered up tribute,
Year in year out these exotic nations offered up the biggest pearls.
    Listen as I sing to you all the full story of Dragon-Design Bao —
May it circulate as an admonition for the people of this world!

*The Tale of the Early Career of Rescriptor Bao, Newly Printed, Completely
Illustrated, in Prose and in Verse.*

Zhu Yixuan (ed.) (1999). *Ming Chenghua shuocang cihua congkan*, Zhengzhou: Zhongzhou
guji chubanshe, pp. 113–125.

Judge Bao Selling Rice in Chenzhou

Newly Printed, Completely Illustrated, in Prose and in Verse

The Great Progenitor and Great Ancestor ruled by the Way,
The True Ancestor, the third emperor, started Common Peace.[1]
The fourth emperor, the Humane Ancestor, ascended the throne:
He was an arhat, protected by buddhas and dispatched by devas.

The Humane Ancestor was a true arhat of the seven jewels,
His civil officials and military officers were stars from above.
The civil officials protected the country like a golden screen,
The military officers rivers and mountains like a marble gate.

Each third day a breeze blew and rain fell each fifth day,
The rains fell at night, so during the day the skies were clear.
The fishermen presented treasures from the Eastern Ocean;
Hunters presented a unicorn that was caught in the mountains.

Happily he enjoyed Great Peace without a day of warfare,
Winds and rains came in their proper times — order reigned.
His Majesty the Humane Ancestor proclaimed an edict,
Awarding three cups of wine to all officials and officers.

The officials below the hall wished him a myriad of years:
Great Peace without warfare had ended all smoke and dust!
The Humane Ancestor showed his pleasure on his face,
But then a courier from the gate reported: "Your Majesty,

---

[1] These two lines enumerate the first three emperors of the Song as known by their posthumous titles — Taizu (the Great Progenitor; reg. 960–975), Taizong (the Great Ancestor; reg. 976–997), and Zhenzong (the True Ancestor; reg. 998–1022), whose posthumous title reflects his Daoist proclivities.

A terrible disaster has suddenly come about: there is a riot
At the Eastern Floriate Dragon and Phoenix palace gate!
Well over a hundred elderly men and notables of high age
Insist on coming inside to be received by Your Majesty!"
    His Majesty the Humane Ancestor proclaimed an edict:
"Summon them to come inside, and We will see them!"
But one censor stepped forward, and addressed the Throne;
Wishing his lord a myriad of years, he spoke to the King.

Speak:

One of the grand masters of remonstrance addressed the Son of Heaven,
[saying]: "To whom should one listen if one summons all these one
hundred and more elders to enter the court? One should only summon
one leader inside for questioning." The emperor [replied]: "We will follow
your proposal."

Sing:

Having received the emperor's order, he summoned the elders,
But he summoned only one of them to enter the court.
The more than one hundred elders all ceded the first place
To allow their leader to be received by the enlightened lord.
    The white hair on his temples was like that of Peng Zu,[2]
The full beard below his chin resembled Liang's silver.[3]
While his hand fingered the one hundred and eight pearls,
His mouth constantly recited the *Prajna-paramita sutra*.
    Three couriers led him inside the Golden Phoenix Hall,
Where, wishing his lord a myriad of years, he bowed down.
His Majesty the Humane Ancestor proclaimed an edict,
Questioning that elder, so advanced in years, as follows:
    "Are you from the Eastern Capital or the Western Capital?
Are you from the Southern Capital or the Northern Capital?
What cause for complaint do you have, which injustice,
That you create such a disturbance at our palace gate?"
    Crossing his arms before his chest and stepping forward,
The elder spoke: "Your Majesty, please listen to me,

---

[2] Peng Zu is said to have lived for over 800 years.
[3] Zhuge Liang (181–234), the principal adviser of Liu Bei, is usually portrayed as sporting a full white beard.

I live in Pacification Office in Chenzhou prefecture,[4]
We are from Xihua, Shangshui, and Wanqiu county.
   The three counties of Chenzhou suffer from a drought,
And two-thirds of the population has died of hunger.
All our bags are empty, so there is no rice left to sell;
Since many years ago dust is rising from the deepest wells.
   The early rice is scorched at the top and forms no ears,
The late rice is robbed of its heart and sets no seed.
All families, rich or poor, suffer the same disaster, and
Pressured by hunger they equally harbor evil thoughts.
   The bride simmers the flesh of her mother-in-law,
The groom cooks his own father-in-law in his wok.
The nuns in their convent steal the oil to drink, and
The monks in their monastery slaughter the corpses.[5]
   Nobody dares to walk on the street for even a minute,
This is why we have come today to inform the Throne.
Prostrating ourselves we hope You will show compassion:
Replace those in charge of the granaries and selling rice."

Speak:

The Humane Ancestor said: "We dispatched our imperial relatives with a
hundred thousand bags of army rice, for distribution to the starving
population in the three counties of Chenzhou. How could there be any
people dying from starvation? This old geezer deserves the death penalty!"

Sing:

Hearing this, the elder stepped forward and spoke as follows:
"May Your Majesty live a myriad years — please listen to me!
   The four who distribute rice are golden branches and leaves,[6]
They are imperial kin or the emperor's relatives by marriage.
For one peck of rice they demand thirty strings of cash,
And even so, two-thirds will be spoiled rice, chaff and husks.
   The one in charge of granaries and selling rice is Hou Wenyi,
The one checking bushels and pecks is Imperial Relative Zhao.

---

[4] The local gazetteers are puzzled by the place name Zhaonafu (Pacification Office), said to
be located outside the east gate of Chenzhou.
[5] Coffins were often temporarily stored at local monasteries.
[6] "Golden branches and jade leaves" is a common metaphor for imperial relatives.

The one who seals the storehouse is accountant Ma, and
The one who is in charge of security is surnamed Yang.
    They control the three counties of Chenzhou Prefecture,
And these people are all golden branches and jade leaves.
Prostrating ourselves, we hope You will show compassion:
Replace those in charge of the granaries and selling rice!"
    When the emperor, the Humane Ancestor, heard this,
He leaned to one side on his dragon couch and kept silent.
[Eventually he said:] "We relied on Our imperial relatives,
Now my own people create problems for my own people!"
    He then ordered the Treasury to pay out gold and treasure
As an imperial gift to the elder and to the other old people.
"Each and every one of you should go back to your home,
We'll replace those in charge of the granary and selling rice!"
    The elder expressed his gratitude, bowing before the hall,
Took his leave of the emperor, and left the palace grounds.
I will not sing of the elder, how he departed from the court;
Let me sing of the emperor, how he addressed his officials.
    "Who is there among all of the many civil officials, or
Who is the person among the many military officers —
Who of the many officials at court is so highly capable
He can be put in charge of the granaries and selling rice?"
    None of the civil and military officials dared to answer,
None of the many officials at court dared to raise his voice.
They knew how tough these four imperial relatives were,
And even none of the capable court officials dared to go.
    The civil officials suddenly seemed to be molded of clay,
The military officers all seemed to be carved from wood.
The mouths of the civil officials were carved from wood,
And the lips of the military officers were stuck with glue.
    The emperor, the Humane Ancestor, was sorely vexed,
And cursed all officials and officers present at the court:
"In times of Great Peace you just sit on your silver chairs,
But in years of revolt and rebellion you don't care at all!"
    As soon as the emperor, the Humane Ancestor, said this,
One man stepped forward from the rank of civil officials.
A purple gown, an ivory tablet, a belt made of gold —
Wishing his lord a myriad of years, he said: "Your Majesty,

Here in front of the golden steps I recommend a person,
A person to be put in charge of the granaries and selling rice.
Those four imperial relatives in Chenzhou are tough — none
Of the civil officials or military officers at court dares to go!
 If some other person must be found to sell rice in Chenzhou,
The only person who is fit for the job is that Bao Wenzheng!"
When the emperor, the Humane Ancestor, lifted his head,
He found the speaker was Chancellor Wang from Qingzhou.

Speak:

The Humane Ancestor said: "Do you recommend and guarantee Bao
Wenzheng?" Chancellor Wang replied: "Yes, the man from Little Bao
Village near Phoenix Bridge in Hefei county in Luzhou. When he served as
magistrate of Dingyuan county in Haozhou, he solved the criminal case of
"the double nail inquiry" within three months on the job.[7] When later he
had been promoted to be prefect of Haozhou, evil people did not report
[his achievements] to the court, so he abandoned his function and stepped
down from his job.[8] Too ashamed to return to his hometown, he now
practices self-cultivation at the Universal Light Monastery in the Eastern
Capital. This is the only person suitable to be in charge of the granaries and
selling rice in Chenzhou." Chancellor Wang further said: "This person has
the firmness to stabilize the state, and he has the courage to bring these

---

[7] The "double nail inquiry" refers to one of the best-known cases of Judge Bao. When the wife
of a coroner suggests to her husband that a murder victim on whom no wounds can be found
may have died of nails driven into his skull, this turns out to be the case. Judge Bao thereupon
asks the coroner whether he married a widow. When the answer is affirmative, Judge Bao
establishes that she murdered her first husband in the same way. For a discussion of the many
adaptations of this tale, see Sun Kaidi, "*Baogong an* yu *Baogong an* gushi," pp. 82–94.

[8] Yang Xurong, *Baijia gong'an yanjiu*, p. 63 suggests that this refers to Judge Bao's failure to
require authorization for the execution of the notorious criminal Li Ji while magistrate of
Dingyuan. However, it is more likely that "Haozhou" here is a mistake for Dingzhou.
According to Chapter 82 of the *Baijia gong'an*, following his service in Dingyuan, for a number
of years Judge Bao served as a censor at court. But when his own son, who had been appointed
as magistrate of Tianchang, at the end of his term of office returned with more money than he
could have saved from his salary, Judge Bao accused him of corruption, and also demanded a
demotion for himself. He was thereupon appointed as prefect of Dingzhou, but because of a
conflict with court officials his stellar achievements in local administration were not reported to
the throne. When he became the object of slander and was called back to court for an inquiry,
he abandoned his job and went into hiding in the capital by joining a monastery.

imperial relatives to justice!" The Humane Ancestor said: "Transmit him Our edict, ordering him to enter the court!" Chancellor Wang said: "This man has a fierce and stubborn character, so it is better that I go in person to invite him. But this person will only be willing to go and make every effort to save the people if Your Majesty promotes him to high office!"

Sing:

The emperor, the Humane Ancestor, agreed with his proposal,
And Chancellor Wang from Qingzhou went out through the gate.
Accompanied by his full cortege he set out on his trip, and soon
He had arrived at the gate of the Universal Light Monastery.
    One of the monks hastily reported to the monastery's abbot
That Chancellor Wang from Qingzhou had arrived at the gate.
Hearing this, the abbot made haste to welcome the chancellor,
And to invite His Excellency Wang from Qingzhou inside.
    He invited him to the abbot's room and to take a seat, and
The official visitor then sat down on a stringed folding chair.
After they had had their tea and the cups had been removed,
Chancellor Wang from Qingzhou told him the reason and cause:
    "A Bao Wenzheng from Luzhou has joined your monastery,
And currently practices self-cultivation here in this monastery.
An imperial edict of today summons him to come to court,
I have come here in person to invite that man surnamed Bao!"
    Hearing this, the monastery's abbot hastily replied as follows:
"I have no idea where that Bao Wenzheng is to be found!"
    But one of the acolytes at his side stepped forward and said:
"You must mean that man who goes by the name of idiot Bao!
Everybody here call that guy lazybones acolyte Bao, because
Every morning he sleeps until the sun reaches its highest point!"

Speak:

Chancellor Wang said: "Dear abbot, why do you not know him?" The abbot replied: "There are just too many monks and acolytes in this monastery!" The abbot said: "Tell the acolytes to come here!" When the acolytes arrived, the abbot asked: "Who is that acolyte Bao?" The acolytes said: "We will immediately go and ask him to come to the abbot's room." [They returned with idiot Bao.] When Lord Bao had greeted the abbot, he recognized [the visitor] as Chancellor Wang from Qingzhou. After they had formally greeted each other, the chancellor said: "Sir, the court summons you for an appointment. I have come here in person to bring the imperial edict and invite you." Bao Zheng replied: "How could I accept an official appointment now that I have taken monastic vows?" The chancellor said: "I am your guarantor and I recommended you because we had nobody to go to Chenzhou and take charge of the granaries and selling of rice. When you come to court, you will be appointed to high office. But you should only thank the emperor for his grace when you see me shake my hat. As long as I do not shake my hat, you should not yet thank the emperor for his grace."

Sing:

Having been told this, Lord Bao's heart was filled with joy,
He took his leave of the abbot, the man who had taken vows.
All the monks in the monastery came together as a crowd
And saw him off beyond the gate with incense and flowers.
    The two officials mounted proud and spirited horses, and
Accompanied by a full cortege they returned to the court.
After a while they arrived outside the gate of the palace,
At the Eastern Floriate Dragon and Phoenix Gate.
    They dismounted from their horses and entered the court,
And the commissioner of the gates announced their arrival.
The emperor, the Humane Ancestor, was filled with joy,
He summoned them to enter the gate and come and see him.
    Three ushers led them to the Golden Phoenix Hall —
The loyal official was gifted a purple gown and gold belt.
After Bao Zheng has dressed himself in formal court dress,
He bowed before his lord, bowing down twenty-four times.
    The emperor, the Humane Ancestor, proclaimed his edict,
Which was only addressed to one person, Bao Wenzheng:
"We award you this purple gown and this golden belt,
You are put in charge of the granaries and the sale of rice."
    Having been told this, Lord Bao stepped forward and spoke:
"I wish Your Majesty a myriad of years — please listen to me.
How on earth would your servant dare go to Chenzhou?
Over there they are all golden branches and jade leaves!
    If Your Majesty dispatches your humble servant to that place,
I am bound to lose my life as soon as I arrive there in Chenzhou!

There is really no harm in Your Majesty speaking the word
To appoint me to a yet higher office so I will not be despised!"

Speak:

The emperor said: "We will appoint you to four commissionerships, and on twelve feet of yellow gauze write out in person with the imperial brush the following eight characters: 'Wherever this Imperial calligraphy arrives, it is as if We arrive in person!' We appoint you as the commissioner for the granaries, the military commissioner, the commissioner for the salt stores at Cangzhou, and the commissioner for the supervision of the rice-distribution in Chenzhou."

Sing:

When the emperor had made these appointments,
He only looked at that one person, Bao Wenzheng,
But Lord Bao only looked at Chancellor Wang,
Whose hat did not shake for the tiniest little bit!
    So Lord Bao did not thank the emperor for his grace,
He followed His Excellency Wang from Qingzhou.
The emperor immediately proclaimed an edict,
Appointing Lord Bao to even more and higher offices.

Speak:

The imperial edict read: "As these offices are still too light, We appoint you to four more commissionerships: transportation commissioner-in-chief for the capital granaries, transportation commissioner for the eighty-one prefectures of Jiangnan, chief military commissioner for the fifty-four prefectures of Sichuan, and supervisory commissioner for the court officials of the Palace Treasury."

Sing:

The emperor, the Humane Ancestor, made these appointments;
These appointments concerned that one person, Bao Wenzheng.
Upon hearing this, Lord Bao's heart was filled with joy, but he
Did not dare thank the emperor for his grace on his own initiative.
    From the corner of his eyes he looked at Chancellor Wang, but
The latter's hat did not shake for the tiniest little bit. All the while

The emperor, the Humane Ancestor, felt depressed in his heart —
"How come Lord Bao does not thank Us for the imperial grace?"
    Chancellor Wang from Qingzhou stepped forward and said:
"May Your Majesty be so kind as to listen to me, your servant.
The offices to which you appointed Lord Bao are too small,
He still does not dare express his thanks for the Imperial grace."
    So His Majesty the emperor said to His Excellency Wang:
"In that case We will appoint Lord Bao to even higher office."

Speak:

The emperor said: "You will be appointed to four more commissionerships:
grand councilor and commissioner for the provisioners of the Five
Garrisons, superintendent and commissioner for the Fifteen Garrisons,
commissioner for the Twelve Bureaus of Appointment of Kaifeng, and
commissioner for the Three Departments and the Bureau for Military
Affairs of the Eastern Section. Upon your return from your mission to
Chenzhou for distributing rice, you will upon first recommendation ascend
the hall, and — all civil officials and military officers at the time changed
color — allowed to behead those who transgress the law without first
reporting the matter to the Throne, you will formally be appointed as
prefect of the capital prefecture of Kaifeng."

Sing:

Upon hearing this, Lord Bao was filled with joy as he thought:
"This is already eighty or ninety percent of my secret scheme!"
From the corner of his eyes he looked at Chancellor Wang, but
The latter's hat did not shake for even the tiniest bit.
    Lord Bao did not dare step forward to express gratitude and bow,
He still did not dare express his thanks in front of the golden steps.
The emperor, the Humane Ancestor, felt depressed in his heart,
And addressed the following question to that Bao Wenzheng:
    "We have appointed you to the most distinguished offices,
So why do you still not express your thanks for Our grace?"
    The prime minister, Chancellor Wang, stepped forward, saying:
"May Your Majesty live a myriad of years — please listen to me.
When Lord Bao is to go to Chenzhou, it is absolutely necessary
That he has the following eight magical weapons at his disposal:
    A big cangue made of pinewood and also a pinewood cudgel,
In case he has to sentence common people who commit injustice;

A big cangue of black lacquer and also a black-lacquered cudgel,
In case he has to sentence high officials and prime ministers;
    A big cangue made of yellowwood and also a yellowwood cudgel,
In case he has to sentence imperial kin and dynastic relatives;
And a big cangue of peach wood and also a peach wood cudgel,
In case he has to sentence gods and ghosts at night by lamplight.
    Moreover, he also needs an imperial battle-flag, and a sword,
With which to decapitate imperial kin and dynastic relatives.
Ten officials here at court will serve as his guarantors, and
Your Majesty will also sign that document with his thumb.
    In case one of the imperial relatives will kill Bao Wenzheng,
We will report to Your Majesty but act on our own initiative."
The emperor, the Humane Ancestor, accepted this proposal —
"Who are the ten officials then who will be his guarantors?"
    The prime minister, Chancellor Wang, stepped forward, saying:
"Your humble servant is willing to be one of the guarantors."
So the first guarantor was His Excellency Chancellor Wang,
The second guarantor was Commander-in-Chief General Fan.
    The third was Commandant-Escort Han of Headquarters, and
The fourth guarantor was His Excellency Chancellor You.
Prince Li of the Central Garrison was the fifth guarantor, while
Prince Qian of Eastern and Western Zhe was the sixth guarantor.
    The seventh was Commandant-Escort Chai of Dongjing, and
The eighth guarantor was the vice-premier surnamed Tian;
The ninth guarantor was His Excellency the Chancellor Tao,
And the tenth guarantor was the Grand Palace Eunuch Miao.
    These ten guarantors all put their thumbs on the document,
And His Majesty the emperor also added his thumb to it.
This document they presented to the pure official Bao Zheng,
So he could take charge of the granaries and the sale of rice.
    When Lord Bao looked at His Excellency Chancellor Wang,
His hat only now did shake, instructing him to make his bows.
With his bows he thanked the emperor, the Humane Ancestor,
Who offered his beloved servant three cups of imperial wine.
    "My dear minister, depart as soon as possible from the court,
The people of Chenzhou's three counties are starving to death!"
    Making his bows, Lord Bao took leave of the Son of Heaven,
Walking backwards for a hundred steps, he went out of the gate.
In front of the Five-Phoenix Loft he hastily mounted his horse,
And accompanied by a full cortege he went back once again.

He used the facilities of Kaifeng Prefecture's Southern Yamen,
And there His Excellency Chancellor Bao rested for a while.
All court officials, high and low, offered their congratulations,
Congratulating him in Kaifeng Prefecture on his appointment.
  Let's not sing about the banquet that was spread over there,
But let me now tell about His Majesty, the Humane Ancestor.
As His Majesty was sitting on the dragon couch, he saw
The grand commissioner of the Six-Palaces, who reported
  That Empress Zhang of the Western Palace now wanted[9]
To ascend the golden steps and speak with the emperor.
The emperor, the Humane Ancestor, proclaimed an edict:
"For what reason does she want to come here and see Us?"

Speak:

Empress Zhang said: "When in my palace I was not feeling well, and
looking up to the sky I made a vow to burn incense to the Eastern
Marchmount [if I would be cured]. So now I want to go and repay my
vow, and I hope you will grant me your permission.

Sing:

While I was in my palace I have made a vow, promising
To burn incense in the temple of the Eastern Marchmount.
  Prostrating myself I hope that My King will show compassion,
And on my behalf make a request to Empress Cao, as I
Would like to borrow the empress' six major ritual objects —
I'll be back when I have burned incense, repaid my vow."
  The emperor, the Humane Ancestor, agreed to her proposal,
And the great commissioner for the Six-Palaces went back.
The Main Palace reported this request to Empress Cao, and
She loaned these six major ritual objects to Empress Zhang.
  That very night all preparations were made in the palace;
At break of dawn she went out through the gate, in full dress.
  On her head she wore the jade chaplet with sun and moon,
She wore the Eight-Trigrams, Nine-Palaces pair of trousers,[10]

---

[9] This character is based on Precious Consort Zhang, Renzong's favorite concubine.
[10] The eight trigrams may be combined to make the 64 hexagrams of the *Book of Changes* and
signify the totality of experience. When they are arranged in a circle and the center is added,
they are referred to as the Nine Palaces.

Was dressed in the red silk jacket with the Five Marchmounts,[11]
And wore the skirt showing mountains and rivers of the realm.
　　To her left side was carried the seal of the Main Palace empress,
To her right side was carried the insignia stating "Main Palace."
The key and the seal to all of the thirty-six palaces —
These twenty-four objects she all carried with her!
　　Her Majesty was seated in a wheeled chair pushed by two,
Below gold-speckled parasols walked the ladies-in-waiting.
Those holding fans covered Empress Zhang from behind,
While she was protected on both sides by palace women.
　　When the cortege had left the Eternal Morning Hall,
The streets were cleared of people walking on both sides.
As Her Majesty is on her way to burn incense in the temple,
Let's tell again about Lord Bao in the Southern Yamen.

Speak:

Lord Bao ordered the servants on duty to saddle his horse so he could go and take leave of the court in order to depart for Chenzhou early the next day.

Sing:

The servants on duty transmitted the order of their master,
And the stable boys saddled the horse in front of the hall.
Accompanied by his cortege Lord Bao went on his way
To go to the court and take his leave of the Sagely Ruler.
　　When he arrived at the crossing with the Imperial Road,[12]
He ran into the cortege of Her Majesty the empress.
Lord Bao immediately dismounted from his black horse,
In order to make way for the consort of His Majesty.
　　When the empress in her wheeled chair had passed by,
He called over two of his trusted personal servants.

Speak:

He asked his servants: "Which empress was in that cortege? And where is she going?" Zhang Long and Zhao Hu replied: "This is the side-palace concubine Empress Zhang, but she has borrowed the cortege of the Main Palace in order to offer incense in the various temples." Lord Bao

---

[11] The Five Marchmounts refer to the holy mountains of the four directions and the center.
[12] The Imperial Road is the wide road leading south from the main gate of the imperial palace.

exclaimed: "What a lack of propriety! A side-palace concubine who uses the cortege of the Main Palace! This means that the state norms are all awry! I will have to first take care of this problem. Grab three of the ritual objects to serve as evidence!"

Sing:

When his underlings had received their master's order,
They ran and caught up with the cortege of the empress.
　They robbed their yellow-gauze gold-speckled parasols,
And scattered the frightened ladies-in-waiting and maids.
Her Majesty immediately returned to the imperial palace,
Wishing the emperor a myriad of years, she reported to him:
　"As soon as you have appointed that Bao to high office,
He starts to bully and abuse people out on the streets.
He robbed me of my yellow-gauze gold-speckled parasols,
And scattered the frightened ladies-in-waiting and maids."
　The emperor, the Humane Ancestor, was very annoyed:
"That Bao Wenzheng is really an unsupportable person!
He does not go off to Chenzhou to supervise the sale of rice,
But bullies my ladies from the inner apartments of the palace!
　You, my darling, go back to your own palace, and
We will summon that Lord Bao and ask him for his reasons!"
　When the emperor, the Humane Ancesor, heard her story,
He summoned Bao to the hall to submit him to questioning.
And when Lord Bao arrived in front of the golden steps, he
Reported by wishing his enlightened ruler a myriad of years.
　The emperor, the Humane Ancestor, was very annoyed,
And loudly started to curse that one man Bao Wenzheng:
"Bullying and abusing Empress Zhang of the side-palace
Is just like bullying and abusing Us, your lord and master!"

Speak:

The emperor said: "The empress went out to burn incense, so why did you rob her of her gold-speckled parasols and scatter the imperial concubines? You deserve the death penalty!" Lord Bao replied: "I may deserve to die, but allow me to ask a question. What day was it today that she went out to burn incense?" His Majesty answered: "Because the empress had not been feeling well, she had promised to burn incense." Lord Bao then asked: "And what was the position of this empress?" The Humane Ancestor replied: "She was a side-palace concubine." Lord Bao asked: "Why did she have the cortege of the Main Palace if she is only a concubine of a side-palace?" The Humane Ancestor replied: "Her elder sister ceded to her, and loaned her the six major ritual objects!" Lord Bao then said: "Your Majesty, if a side-palace can borrow the regalia of the Main Palace, can Our King also loan this golden hall to the Sixth Great Prince to sit on the Throne?" His Majesty said: "That would be an act of lèse-majesté!" Lord Bao said: "If that is an act of lèse-majesté, then Empress Zhang has also committed an act of lèse-majesté. No wonder there are so many floods and droughts and the whole country is in disarray. If your humble servant cannot set this matter straight, I cannot go to Chenzhou to supervise the distribution of rice. Our King does not maintain proper order in his family. As Empress Zhang improperly acted above her status, she should be fined one thousand ounces of yellow gold, and as Empress Cao did not properly guard her high status, she should be fined one hundred ounces of yellow gold." The emperor could only agree to his proposal.

Sing:

Hearing this, Lord Bao, stepping forward, addressed the Throne,
Wishing his lord a myriad of years, he thanked the emperor:
"Your servant does not care for the yellow gold of the fine,
But I will take it with me to Chenzhou and award the troops."
　　The civil officials and military officers were filled with joy,
This Bao Wenzheng had not been appointed to office in vain!
The emperor, the Humane Ancestor, ordered wine to be poured,
And offered it as a reward to His Excellency Bao Wenzheng.
　　In front of the Five-Phoenix Loft the latter mounted his horse,
And returned for the night to the yamen of Kaifeng Prefecture.
Lord Bao immediately saw to all the necessary preparations —
He was to be accompanied by fifty yamen runners as personnel.
　　The eight magical weapons were always at his disposal,
And the four large cangues were carried close behind him.
Above him a triple parasol was carried, and the officials,
Who came to see him off, were arranged on both sides.
　　At a distance of thirty miles from the Eastern Capital,
He arrived, traveling on, at the Forest of a Myriad of Pines.
After Lord Bao had brought his high-spirited horse to a halt,
He spoke as follows to the yamen runners there with him.

Speak:

Lord Bao said: "You runners should all go back, and come and find me in Chenzhou in ten days' time. I will go to the tea houses and wine houses, the monasteries and temples, and listen to the people's complaints. My servant, from now on you can only call me 'Sir,' and on no account can you let people know that I am Bao Wenzheng!"

Sing:

A hat like a bucket with two bands hanging down the back:
Those two broad bands signified the profession of letters.
He was wearing an unlined gown that was tattered and torn,
Held together around his waist by a piece of black rope.
    Lord Bao had costumed himself as a student of writing,
And the black boots on his feet did not even have heels.
The official runners confirmed their assent three times,
And he left the cortege that had accompanied him so far.
    Lord Bao took off, while riding a donkey, only followed
By his elderly personal servant, old master Tang, and
After they had walked a mile, they looked forward to the next;
After they had gone one stretch, there was yet another stretch.
    When Lord Bao lifted his head and looked all around,
They were quickly approaching the gate of some village.
A number of herding boys followed the road back home,
But two of them ran to willow-village,[13] leading their oxen.
    Lord Bao immediately called to master Tang, saying:
"Let's take a rest by the side of this carriage shed."

Speak:

Lord Bao said: "Master Tang, let's not try to find the house of some commoner to rest for the night. We have our own dried grains, and we can rest for the night in this carriage shed." He allowed his donkey to go grazing, and he said to master Tang: "To relieve my spirits I will write a poem on the theme of these herding boys!"
    The poem reads:

> *Bange Boy raises his hand and calls out to Wang Liu —*
> *Each day they take their buffaloes to abandoned fields.*

---

[13] "Willow-village" here probably refers to a temporary encampment of cattle-rustlers.

Fig. 2.1
Upper picture: Eldest Son Zhao mistakenly strings up Judge Bao.
Lower picture: Minister Bao fetches the daughter for the old man.

Oh slow so slow they wind the rope around the horns,
Oh short so short their linen shirts — till autumn's end!
With a stick they beat down pears, which are oh so sweet;
With their whips they get at dates, which are oh so sour.
East of the village there's a patch of melons, just now ripe:
"While you're on the lookout for people, I'll steal them!"

Sing:

After His Excellency had composed the above poem,
He went to sleep for the night under the carriage shed.
He slept until deep into the night, until before dawn —
But now I must tell of the man in charge of the yard.
　　This was Zhao Sheng, also known as the Eldest Son,
Who, together with some hired hands of his father,
Holding in his hands a cudgel made of mulberry wood,
Was making the rounds of the village to guard the gate.
　　Of course he eventually came to the carriage shed, and
Found the two students who were still soundly asleep.
Zhao Sheng, the Eldest Son, was extremely annoyed,
And loudly cursed them: "There by the cart — who are you?"
　　The old servant master Tang immediately replied:
"My master travels to the capital for the examinations!
My master is, as is plain to see, a student of writing,
And I am the servant who is serving him on his trip."

Speak:

Zhao Sheng, the Eldest Son, said: "Two water buffaloes are missing from the village and are nowhere to be found. The two of you must have stolen them!" He told the laborers to get a rope and string them up by their hands. "Tomorrow we will take them to the magistrate for questioning!"

Sing:

When Zhao Sheng, the Eldest Son, returned to the farm,
Once back home, he informed his father, old Mr. Zhao:
"I found two travelers on the cart in the carriage shed,
And I have strung them up by their hands in some tree."

When old Mr. Zhao heard this, he replied as follows:
"Make sure you do not beat up the wrong person here!"
When old Mr. Zhao went to have a look for himself,
He immediately recognized that student of writing.
    He shouted to his son: "Zhao Sheng, you foolish boy,
Untie these hemp ropes and set these people free!
My son really has earned the death penalty, as
He may have eyes, but does not recognize a good man!
    This is His Excellency Bao, selling rice in Chenzhou,
Who has secretly arrived in our village in disguise.
I hope Your Excellency will not blame my son for this,
Foolishly he was too blind to recognize Your Honor.
    Your Excellency, please come inside, into our manor,
Please allow me to host Your Excellency Bao Wenzheng!"
"When I'll have arrived in Chenzhou and assumed my job,
Only then, dear sir, will I be able to express my thanks!"
    Lord Bao mounted his donkey and continued his journey,
While his old servant, master Tang, followed behind him.
After they had passed the city of Zhengzhou, they went on
To find a place where they might stay for the night.
    When he saw Taikang County capital in the distance,
Lord Bao spoke as follows to his servant, master Tang.

Speak:

When they approached the capital of Taikang County, Lord Bao said to master Tang: "Let's first take a rest under these weeping willows, and then enter the city." When the two of them were taking a rest under the trees, they saw a few men on horseback with lances and swords and bows and arrows, with sleek dogs pursuing a river deer and coming in their direction. Farmers by their side called out: "Student, make way, so you will avoid them. This is Magistrate Qin of Taikang on a hunt, pursuing a deer. If you are in his way, you are dead!" The student said: "Is he that mean?" The farmers said: "He does not pay back with his life when he kills a person." Lord Bao then said: "Master Tang, get your luggage carrying pole and take up position by the road. Allow that deer to pass, but beat down a dog with one stroke."

Sing:

Hit by the pole the sleek dog fell down on the road,
And the terrified farmers dispersed in all directions.
   When the young master on horseback looked up,
He saw the student of writing, that bookish type.
"Why did you have to kill my dog with silver feet?
Trying to make a fool of me, son of Magistrate Qin?"
   He ordered the servant with him and other underlings
To arrest those two bookish students of writing.
They gave them a beating with cudgels and fists,
Then tied their hands behind their backs with a rope.
   "We'll take the two of them to Taikang County city,
Where we will throw those two into the city jail.
Wait till I will have returned from my hunting,
Then I will subject the two of you to questioning!"
   How pitiable! The two of them had without reason
Run into the demon of death and mourning guests.
The old servant master Tang loudly lamented his fate,
And tears flowed down from his eyes in profusion.
   "You are not lucky enough to be a salaried official,
And now you have even turned into a criminal in jail.
You may be aiming for fame and profit by this suffering,
But I, the old servant master Tang, also have to suffer!"
   Let's not sing of the way they progressed on the road —
As they traveled on, they reached the gate of the city.
When they arrived at the yamen of Taikang County,
The two of them were taken down to the city jail.
   They were handed over to the prison guards,
Who gave the two of them a vicious beating, and then
Strung the student up, hanging him high on the wall,
And also strung up the old servant, that master Tang.
   With their pliable hemp ropes and with solid cudgels
They gave them a beating as they questioned them:
"Who told you to offend the son of Magistrate Qin?
Now you are bound to die here today in this prison!"
   The servant, master Tang, cried as loud as he could:
"Dear brother prison warden, please listen to the truth!
This poor student of books has not a penny to spend,
Why are you beating us up without any good reason?"

Speak:

The prison guard Zhang said: "Student, those who serve the gods get their food from the gods, and those who serve the Buddha get their food from the Buddha. The only reason we beat you up is that we want some money for wine." Master Tang said: "Sir, please promise them some money, my arms are killing me!" The student said: "I have some money, but it is hidden in my belt, and I cannot take it out. If you let me down, I will get it for you." But the prison guard said: "I will get it for you."

Sing:

The prison guard was immediately ready to take it,
To take all treasures and jewels from his belt. But
When he pulled apart the cloth to have a good look,
He saw then the golden plaque, brilliant like the sun.[14]
    When the prison guard saw this, he was dumb-struck,
As fast as he could he hastily untied the hemp ropes.
Then he invited His Excellency to sit down in a chair,
And with lowered head he bowed eight times, saying:
    "Your Excellency Bao comes to Chenzhou to sell rice,
And traveling incognito has secretly arrived at this place.
    Alas that the son of Magistrate Qin may have had eyes,
But lacked the pupils to know the true worth of a man.
In his delusion he even had Your Excellency arrested,
And today had him locked up in this rotten jail of ours!
    Prostrating ourselves we hope You will show mercy,
And spare our miserable lives, preserve us from death!"

Speak:

The student said: "Prison guard, please let nobody know. Don't tell it to Magistrate Qin and his son. You get me with my donkey and luggage and master Tang out of this town, and I will forgive your crime."

Sing:

The prison guard Zhang Qing immediately did as asked,
He did exactly as His Excellency Bao had asked him to do.

---

[14] The golden plaque denotes the high rank and power of Judge Bao.

He brought him his donkey, he brought him his luggage,
And he guided His Excellency Bao to the gate outside.
　　When he had taken him out of Taikang County capital,
His Excellency explained the situation to him, saying:
"Prison guard, you have to go back and return to the city,
You're not to blame in this matter for even the tiniest bit.
　　When I have gone to Chenzhou and taken up my post,
I will send for the magistrate, both the father and his son."
If a story divides into two, it becomes hard to follow, so
We will limit ourselves to the tale of His Excellency Bao.
　　When the two of them had left the capital of Taikang,
They slowly went on their way, going farther and farther.
When they were at a place fifteen miles from Taikang,
They arrived, as they traveled on, at the gate of a farm.
　　There they saw an elderly man, quite advanced in years,
Who supported himself with a long bamboo staff, and
When this elderly man saw them, his tears gushed down,
As soon as he saw the student of books and his servant.
　　The student immediately addressed him as follows:
"Granddad, what is the cause of your crying and weeping?"

Speak:

The student said: "Granddad, why are you weeping?" The old man replied:
"I have been wronged but I can complain to no one. While hunting the
[son of the] magistrate of Taikang came to my farm, and when he saw that
I had a daughter, he kidnapped her, despite my protests. I have no other
child, and my wife and I rely on her." The student said: "So why don't you
lodge a complaint with the authorities?" The old man said: "His father is the
magistrate, so with whom should I lodge a complaint?" The student said:
"I will write a little note, and you take that and get your daughter back." The
old man said: "Only if you this very instant would turn into His Excellency
Bao!" The student said: "Don't ask any questions!" He asked him for a slip of
paper and then wrote: "This student instructs the magistrate: If you return his
daughter to him, all is fine and well. It is up to you not to give her back, but
then you will be in a tight spot when you later have to appear before Lord
Bao!" When he had written this out, he gave it to the old man. Lord Bao also
said: "You cannot walk that distance, I will loan you my donkey to ride. If he
has any questions, you just say: 'There was a student passing on the road,
who told me to come, and he said: "I am waiting here for you."'"

Sing:

When the old man heard him say this, he promptly left,
With large strides he walked out of the gate of the farm.
Having borrowed the donkey, he mounted the animal,
And on the winding road, he went as fast as he could.
    When he had arrived in the capital of Taikang County,
He immediately went on to the yamen of that county.
There the old man then promptly entered the high hall,
He entered the hall, while holding the note in his hands.
    The clerk on duty in the hall took the note from him,
And transmitted it to His Excellency, the magistrate.
When the magistrate had looked at it for some time,
He beat his table and started to loudly curse his son:
    "This child of mine is really bereft of all decency,
And now this has come to the knowledge of Lord Bao!
That prison guard Zhang Qing earlier told me his story,
So it turns out that that man truly was Lord Bao!"
    He ordered two of the underlings under his command
To get a sedan chair and bring it in front of the hall.
Then he invited the girl to come from her room, and
Returned her to her father, this man advanced in years.
    He gave her all the clothes she was wearing as a present,
And he also let the beauty have all the jewels in her hair.
On top of that, he gave her thirty ounces of yellow gold,
Hoping in this way that the old man would keep silent.
    The sedan-chair carriers carried the young girl, and
Walked out of the gate of the yamen with big strides.
Riding the donkey, the old man followed the carriers,
Going as swift on the road as a wind-blown cloud.
    Straightaway they arrived at the Gao family farm,
Where he greeted the student, who studies writing.
He told his daughter to thank him with a deep bow;
In the farm he expressed his gratitude to the student.

Speak:

The old man said: "Student, please don't blame me for being so blind that
I did not immediately recognize you as Your Excellency Dragon-Design
Bao! Today we have benefited from Your Excellency's grace — how will we
ever be able to pay you back?" He also said: "The magistrate informs Your

Excellency that Lord Qin will shortly arrive to ask forgiveness for his crimes in person!" The student said: "I am not going to wait for him. I will write a little note for him, which you can give to the magistrate." The little note read: "This student informs the magistrate that he is too busy to wait and will invite him for a meeting once he has arrived in Chenzhou."

Sing:

I will not sing about the way the old man feasted him,
Our student immediately left to continue his journey.
Master Tang followed behind him, carrying his luggage,
And the old man saw them off at the gate of the farm.
  He told the old man not to disclose to anybody that
He was the man who came to distribute rice in Chenzhou.
We will not talk about what happened there at the farm,
While His Excellency pursued his journey, traveling on.
  Resting at night, departing at dawn — no need for telling,
Traveling on, they stayed for the night where they arrived.
And when they arrived at the ferry across the Cai River,
They saw there the gate of a teahouse, of a winehouse.

Speak:

The student asked: "Where is the ferry boat? Let's go and have a cup of tea in that teahouse while we wait for the boat." He paid two hundred cash for the tea. The teahouse server said: "You stupid student, when you drink two cups of tea, it is five hundred cash, so why do you only pay me two hundred cash?" Master Tang said: "Because it is one hundred cash for one cup!" The server glared at master Tang, and then started to beat him up. He got a beating, "Because I want my five hundred cash!"
  When the student boarded the ferry boat, the man in charge of the ferry came collecting the money, and said: "For the two of you it is five hundred cash, and the donkey is two hundred cash, so together that makes seven hundred cash." Master Tang said: "Including the donkey it should be five hundred cash, so why do you want an extra two hundred cash?" The man punting the boat glared at them, and then started to beat up master Tang. As master Tang got such a terrible beating, he paid him his seven hundred cash. Once they had crossed the river, the student asked the man who was punting: "What is the name of the person in charge of the ferry?" The man who did the punting said: "He is Uncle Huang the Second Son, and the man who is running the teahouse is Uncle Huang the Eldest Son."

Sing:

Having been told this, our student was deeply annoyed:
"These people of Chenzhou's counties are unbearable!
Floods and droughts have brought turmoil and disaster,
But in business and buying and selling they are not fair. —
    The donkey's hooves, ink stones of brick: two brushes —
I'll write down their names in a ledger to keep a record.
When I have arrived in Chenzhou and assumed my job,
I will not forget to send an invitation to these two men."
    He refused to travel the highway for official travel, but
Secretly following the little lanes, he reached the city.
And when he eventually reached the city of Chenzhou,
The gates were closed so tightly no breeze could pass.
    A crowd at the Pavilion for Welcoming Officials
Was waiting to welcome His Excellency Lord Bao,
So when the student arrived outside a gate of the city,
Those in charge of the gate refused him entrance:
    "We are waiting to welcome His Excellency Bao,
So no students are allowed to enter the city at will."

Speak:

So the student thought: "What to do now?" Then he saw a courtesan who
was saying: "My feet are hurting so much and I want to go into the city."
The student said: "Young lady, where are you going?" The courtesan said:
"I was going to welcome His Excellency Bao, but because of all this
walking my feet are hurting too much!" The student then said: "I will loan
you my donkey, so you can ride, but you have to take me with you into the
city." The student took off his hat and led the donkey, while master Tang
followed behind.

Sing:

This way the three of them entered the city gate,
And nobody at the gate questioned the pretty girl.
When they had entered through the gate of the city,
They moved as fast as a cloud through the streets.
    After they had taken the courtesan back to her house,
The two of them rented a room at an inn for travelers.

The servant master Tang could not suppress his smile
As he said to His Excellency Dragon-Design Bao:
  "Purple gown and golden belt you thought too low,
But now you've risen to be the groom of a whore."
I will not tell how they slept together that night,
But let me sing what happened the next morning.
  The hat like a bucket with its two hanging ears,
The two broad bands signified the profession of letters.
He was dressed in a white and unlined gown, tied
Tightly together at his waist with a black belt.
  Dressed like this he left the inn for travelers,
To listen in the market to what people were saying.
Incognito he went to the government granaries,
Checking on those in charge of the rice distribution.
  The people buying the rice heaved many sighs,
One-third of it was spoiled rice, husks and chaff.

Speak:

When the student took a look at the rice, it was indeed bad, and he asked:
"How much do you have to pay for this rice?" The people who were buying
rice said: "Earlier this rice was sold for thirty ounces of silver for one *hu*,[15]
but recently, because it is said that His Excellency Bao is coming, it has been
reduced to twenty ounces of silver for one *hu*." The student said: "Just wait
a moment, and I will make sure that you get a *hu* of good rice." The student
immediately went up to the hall. After he had greeted the granary official, he
took a handful of rice and showed it to him, while asking: "For how much
do you sell this rice?" The granary official said: "For twenty ounces of silver."
The student said: "Even if it is all husks and chaff and spoiled rice?" Without
waiting for a reply, Lord Bao opened his hands and blew it all in the face of
the granary official, blinding the granary official with the chaff and the dust.

Sing:

The husks and the chaff blinded the granary official,
Angering the man in charge of the granary, selling rice.
"You intolerable student, you lack all common sense,
Thinking today that you can bully Imperial Relative Zhao!"

---

[15] One *hu* equals ten pecks.

He ordered his official underlings and his servants
To capture and arrest that student without any delay.
But the granary official had barely finished speaking,
When Tian Sanshu entered upon the scene.

He was one of Chenzhou's most powerful men,
And earlier had donated rice to the starving people.
When Tian Sanshu recognized His Excellency Bao,
He said to the man in charge of granaries and selling rice:

"Indeed, this student lacked all common sense, and so
He has offended Your Excellency, but I sincerely hope
That Your Excellency will show some compassion,
Because this student belongs to my establishment."

The granary official was willing to listen to Tian Sanshu,
And thereupon released this student of written texts.
Tian Sanshu took Lord Bao with him, and took him
With him outside through the gate of the granary depot.

"You had better settle down for a while at my place!"
Hearing this, the student promptly agreed and followed.
So he immediately went along with Tian Sanshu,
Who took him along to the hall of the Tian mansion.

After this student of writing had been allowed to rest,
His host prepared a banquet with many new dishes.

Speak:

The student then asked the elderly gentleman: "How did you recognize me?" Sanshu replied: "I had come to know Your Excellency when you served as prefect of Haozhou." Lord Bao said: "Lord Tian, let nobody know I am here! I will go out and buy some wine in a wineshop."

Sing:

Having taken his leave from the millionaire Tian Sanshu,
He went out of the house, walked around on the streets.
There is no need to sing of the main streets and alleys —
Walking on, he eventually arrived at a wineshop.

There was a steady stream of people buying wine,
And our student questioned them about its quality.
He asked them how much money they paid for a jug,
A five-headed bottle of one liter of water-clear wine. (?)

The student then promptly bought a bottle of wine,
Buying the wine, he closely looked at it for its proof.
"How come the wine other people bought is so clear?
How come the wine that I bought is so very muddy?"
    He then cursed the official in charge of the wineshop:
"How come you cheat and bully people from outside?"
The official selling the wine promptly ordered him beaten:
"You intolerable student, you lousy student of books!"
    Upon hearing this, our student was filled with rage,
And he pulled the bottle of wine from his hands.
Thereupon the yamen runners all attacked him, and
They arrested this student, this student of writing.
    They promptly locked the student in a cangue,
And the police officers escorted him to the jail.
Let's not tell about the sufferings he experienced —
Couriers on horseback arrived in the city like comets.
    The officials in the city all went out for the welcome:
Three cups of wine in the Pavilion for Welcoming Officials.
They welcomed the fifty yamen attendants, but
They did not see His Excellency Dragon-Design Bao.
    At the pavilion the officials thereupon asked:
"Where may His Excellency now be found?"
Zhang Long and Zhao Hu answered them as follows:
"His Excellency left Bianzhou way ahead of us.[16]
    He departed from the capital half a month ago,
And we, his yamen runners, have arrived only now."
They searched for Lord Bao on all streets and alleys,
They went to the granaries and depots to find him.
    When they could not find him on any of the streets,
Zhang Long and Zhao Hu went into the prisons.
And when they had a look in the Eastern Prison,
The pure official Bao Zheng was wearing a cangue!
    Zhang Long and Zhao Hu wanted to release him,
But Lord Bao ordered the two of them not to do so.
He told them to tell all the officials to come and see,
To see the man surnamed Bao locked up in prison!

---

[16] Bianzhou is an alternative name for Kaifeng.

Once the cangue had been opened, the chains removed,
His Excellency walked out through the prison gate.
The down-and-out student now walked in front, and
The four imperial relatives followed behind him.
    When they arrived at the Chenzhou prefectural office,
Lord Bao took his seat on the precious folding chair.
His Excellency immediately took his seat in the hall,
While yamen runners and clerks formed two rows.
    The whole city wanted to see this deity of flesh and blood,
And the prefectural yamen was filled with a noisy crowd.

Speak:

When Lord Bao had ascended the hall and taken his seat, he ordered his
personal retainers: "Bring out the imperial inscription on yellow silk, the
golden plaque, and the sword given to me by the emperor and display
them here in the hall, and place the pinewood cangue and cudgel, the
black-lacquered cangue and cudgel, the yellowwood cangue and cudgel,
and the peach wood cangue and cudgel, these eight magical instruments,
in front of the steps for all to see!"

Sing:

The personal retainers immediately executed his orders,
And arranged them in proper order before the steps.
Twenty-four sturdy fellows who would show no mercy
Were arranged in two rows on the steps of the hall.
    The four officials sent by the court all bowed down,
Bowing before His Excellency Dragon-Design Bao.
They begged His Excellency: "Please do not blame us
For having eyes but not the pupils to know a good man."
    His Excellency gave his orders there in that hall, and
Told his personal retainers and men under his command
Promptly to close the gate of the prefectural offices
And to arrest these four relatives of the emperor.
    The imperial relatives were stripped of their gowns,
And promptly subjected to a detailed questioning.
"Who was in charge of the granaries and the sale of rice?
Who had His Excellency Dragon-Design Bao strung up?

Who was in charge of the sale of wine in the shop?
Who ordered me put in the cangue there in that prison?"
The imperial relatives were given no time to confess —
The yellowwood cangue and cudgel stood before them!
    With an iron hammer the "swallow tails" were opened,
So the "monk's heads" were opened on both sides, and
In between the "merciless boards" were inserted, in order
To lock the four imperial relatives each in a cangue.[17]
    He then ordered that they should be taken to prison,
So he could later question the four imperial relatives.

His Excellency then wrote the documents and passes
For two police officers to take as fast as possible,
As fast as possible to Zhao Family Village, where
They were to arrest both the father and also his son.
    "Without reason they beat up His Excellency Bao,
Because they wrongly took me for a cattle-thief!"
    One more document and pass set out on the road,
As a couple of police officers departed from the city:
They went to Taikang County, inviting Magistrate Qin,
Who was told to bring along his son, the Young Master.
    Another document and pass set out on the road
As two police officers departed from the prefecture:
They went to the ferry across the Cai River, in order
To arrest the elder brother and the younger brother.
    Uncle Huang, the Eldest Son, and the Second Son
Would be the first to arrive in the city of Chenzhou.
When these three sets of documents all had gone,
He had Imperial Relative Zhao taken from prison.
    The four imperial relatives had no defense at all,
And in front of the hall they confessed to the facts.
They begged His Excellency: "Don't have us beaten,
We never should have transgressed the regulations."
    When their full confessions had been taken down,
A suitable day and good hour was set for decapitation.

---

[17] I assume that "swallow tails", "monk's heads" and "merciless boards" are technical terms referring to parts of the cangue, but I have failed to locate literature on the cangue that provides sufficient detail on its construction.

The execution grounds were swept, the swords whetted
For the execution of these four imperial relatives!

The gatekeeper entered the hall and announced
That the police officers had arrested their suspects.
They had brought from his village this Zhao Sheng,
Who was completely stripped bare before the steps.
  With pieces of vine and short cudgels he was beaten,
Beaten for being a rustic clown and an evil person.
"You wrongly took me to be a thief in your village,
You strung up an innocent man, hearing no excuse!
  For what kind of private grudge did you string me up
In order to hand me over to the court for punishment?
Today I am the one who questions you in this hall,
So you had better confess to the facts of your crime!"
  When his full confession had been taken down,
He was locked in a heavy cangue and put in prison.
  Uncle Huang, the Eldest Son, and the Second Son,
Were led before the hall and subjected to questioning:
"Your tea house server beat up my old master Tang,
The ferryman asked a high fee and also beat him up!"
  When their full confessions had been taken down,
They were locked in heavy cangues and put in prison.
  Magistrate Qin of Taikang County was also brought in,
Both father and son knelt down in front of the steps.
Each question was accompanied by one cudgel stroke,
"You abused your official position to bully the people!
  You kidnapped a villager's beautiful virgin daughter,
Innocent people were arrested and thrown into jail!
The crimes of both father and son are unequaled —
How could you be so arrogant to His Excellency Bao?"
  When their full confessions had been taken down,
The heavy cangues were placed before them. And
After the two of them had been taken to the prison,
A good hour was selected for their decapitation.

He also went to the granary to distribute the rice,
Lord Bao came to the rescue of Chenzhou's people.
At each of the four gates a written poster was hung,
And also throughout the villages of the three counties.

For one ounce of copper cash one got one *hu* of rice,
This applied equally to city people and country folk.
First the old rice in the granaries would be dispensed,
To succor the population of Chenzhou's three counties.
    Families with many mouths should ask for one *shi*,[18]
Those who came all by themselves for five liters.
His Excellency Bao, distributing rice in Chenzhou,
Enacted the Way on behalf of Heaven, protecting the people.
    When he had made arrangements for selling the rice,
He appointed local officials to succor the people.
"When I will have finished these criminal cases,
I will as before come back and succor the people."

Speak:

His Excellency Bao said: "I have temporarily appointed local officials to
continue the distribution of rice, and they cannot make any mistake. I will
go and pronounce sentence in these criminal cases." Lord Bao ordered the
runners and guards in the hall to bring in all the criminals, and line them
up in front of the steps. His Excellency said: "First bring the four imperial
relatives over!" He questioned them, saying: "You are imperial relatives,
and the court dispatched you to succor and aid the starving population,
hoping that you would make an effort on behalf of the state and share the
common people's worries. You must have heard the Humane Emperor's
Imperial Rescript, stating: 'Your salary and your honorarium/ Are the fat
of the people, the marrow of the people./ The lowly people may easily be
abused/ But High Heaven cannot be deceived!' But today you have
harmed the common people and deceived the court, by offending against
the regulations and breaking the law. You will be taken to the execution
ground for decapitation. Young Master Qin abused his father's official
position to abuse the common people by raping and kidnapping a virgin
daughter. His crimes demand that he be taken to the execution ground for
decapitation. Magistrate Qin will receive eighty cudgel strokes on the back,
and he will be removed from his office and dismissed from the ranks.
Zhao Sheng wrongly took an innocent man for a robber and privately
operated a prison. He will receive eighty cudgel strokes on the back, and
he will be tattooed in the face to be a soldier. Huang the Eldest Son and
Huang the Second Son demanded an overly high ferry fee, and bullied and

---

[18] One *shi* equals ten pecks.

Fig. 2.2
Upper picture: Judge Bao lowers the price and sells the government grain.
Lower picture: Executing the people who transgressed the regulations and broke the law.

beat innocent people. They will receive eighty cudgel strokes on the back, and will be tattooed on their faces to be soldiers. One-half of the family property of each of these persons will be confiscated and used for relief."

Sing:

As soon as Judge Bao had given his official orders,
The criminals were pushed to the execution grounds.
When they arrived at the execution grounds, they saw,
As before, the runners and soldiers arranged in rows.

The black banner was carried through the streets,
All people on the roads were scared out of their wits.
When this group of criminals had been taken there,
They were arranged in a row on the execution grounds.

The executioner for decapitations dressed himself,
And hastily put on a full set of different clothes.
While his body was wrapped in a black-gauze shirt,
His hand raised a sword of fish-belly white steel.

The executioner held his magic sword in his hands,
While soul-scaring prison guards stood by his side.
He called to the imperial relatives: "Don't blame me,
I follow official orders, I am not my own master.

Early tonight you will visit the Eastern Marchmount,
Tomorrow in the world of shade you will see the Prince.[19]
Today the world of shade will add some new ghost,
Tomorrow the court will produce a stalwart hero!"

Having decapitated the four imperial relatives,
He then also killed off the son of Magistrate Qin.
The people who committed crimes were sentenced,
Those tattooed on the face were forced to be soldiers.

Their property was confiscated, the figures recorded,
To succor and aid the people of Chenzhou's counties.
Because of his judgment in the Chenzhou cases, Bao
[Greatly pleased] all people who had suffered injustice.

But let's not tell about the relief and these verdicts —
Lord Bao composed a report to submit to the court.
After he had written this document and report,
He called in his servants Zhang Long and Zhao Hu.

---

[19] Cui fujun, one of the underworld judges.

"Now go the Eastern Capital and submit this report,
Submit it to the fourth emperor, the Humane Ancestor."
These two police officers, promptly set out to go and
Took their leave of that pure official Bao Wenzheng.

Once they had left the Chenzhou prefectural city,
They continued their journey on its winding way.
Ten miles, and they passed Peach Blossom Hamlet;
Twenty miles, and they passed Apricot Blossom Village.

The two police officers traveled as fast as they could,
And soon they saw the Imperial Capital in the distance.
Eventually they arrived in Kaifeng Prefecture, and went
Straight to the Eastern Floriate Dragon and Phoenix Gate.

When the two of them arrived outside the palace gate,
The soldiers of the guard questioned them closely.
Zhang Long and Zhao Hu immediately replied:
"We are Lord Bao's servants, here to submit a report.

His Excellency Bao, distributing rice in Chenzhou,
On purpose sends this report to inform the emperor."
The soldiers reported this to His Excellency Wang,
Chancellor Wang from Qingzhou was very pleased.

He promptly entered the court, greeted the emperor,
And then, as chancellor, addressed the Imperial Ruler:
"At present Bao Wenzheng in Chenzhou sends men
Submitting a report — they wait at the palace gate."

Hearing this, the emperor, the Humane Ancestor,
Ordered the text of the report be submitted to him.
Having read the report, he then heaved a heavy sigh:
"Relying on imperial relatives We harmed the people!"

The two rows of civil officials and military officers
All praised His Excellency Bao for his signal efforts.

"Traveling incognito he experienced much suffering,
He experienced a thousand, ten thousand sufferings!

Because the people of Chenzhou suffered hardship,
He is the man in charge of granaries and selling rice."
When the emperor had seen it, he was filled with joy:
"Now the people of Chenzhou are fortunately at ease!"

Having received the edict, they left the golden palace,
They continued their distant journey on its winding way.

Five miles — a single plaque: as easy as twisting fingers;
Ten miles — a double plaque: several lines of geese.(?)
    Let's not sing about the stretches of their journey
As soon they arrived in Chenzhou's prefectural city,
Lord Bao and the other officials welcomed them,
And invited them inside the prefectural offices.
    In the hall, the imperial edict was opened and read:
Lord Bao was summoned to return to the court.
When Lord Bao now received the imperial grace,
He bowed facing the palace to express his thanks.
    Let's not talk about the banquet of the officials —
Early the next morning he left for the Eastern Capital.
When the elders and the common people heard this,
They wanted to retain His Excellency Lord Bao.
    The common people of the whole city saw him off,
Officials, high and low, offered him parting drinks.
Actors and performers all gathered to see him off,
The music of drums resounded booming to heaven.
    Every family sacrificed incense, flowers and candles,
Every house made sure only the best incense was lit.
They venerated Lord Bao, wishing him a long life;
They burned good incense to thank for the royal grace.
    Lord Bao then left them the following instruction:
"I urge you, officials and all you common people,
    In buying and selling adhere to the current prices;
In cases of wrongs and injustices seek a fair deal;
Never offend against the royal laws and their rules,
As every transgression will be severely punished."
    The officials accepted this order of Lord Bao, and
Saw him off at the border of Chenzhou Prefecture.
The officials raised their cups to wish him farewell,
And the villagers and elders also poured him a cup.

When Lord Bao was summoned back to the capital,
All people on the roads praised this Great Peace.
Buying and selling in the counties was always fair,
Every family and every house was filled with joy.
    In the Eastern Capital he was called "The Balance,"
In Chenzhou they called him the People's Protector:

A lantern above the river, shining down to the bottom,
By which all dark affairs in Chenzhou were cleared!
    I have sung to its end this tale of exceptional virtue,
Which has been left in this world as a clear mirror.
I urge you all never to commit anything evil —
Above there are the gods, on earth punishments!
    Even though your heart may be as hard as iron,
The official law like an oven will turn it to ashes.
So I urge you all to turn to the Way of goodness,
May everyone's heart be fair and level like water.
    Today this newly transmitted ballad-story
Urges you all to be honest and not cheat others.
The people of Chenzhou sighed for admiration:
Without Lord Bao they'd never had Great Peace!

Judge Bao Selling Rice in Chenzhou, Newly Printed, Completely Illustrated, in Prose and in Verse, The End.

Zhu Yixuan (ed.) (1997). *Ming Chenghua shuochang cihua congkan*, Zhengzhou: Zhongzhou guji chubanshe, pp. 126–141.

The Tale of the Humane Ancestor Recognizing his Mother

Newly Printed, Completely Illustrated, A Complete Version in Prose and in Verse

The Great Progenitor, the Great Ancestor, and the True Ancestor,
And then the Son of Heaven the Humane Ancestor ruled the world.
When at the tender age of twelve he ascended the Golden Hall,
The myriad people enjoyed their life under this enlightened ruler.
    For forty-two years wind and rain arrived at their proper time,
Once every three years he sacrificed to Heaven in the suburbs.
Ten times he offered sacrifice in the suburbs — for thirty years;
Four times he sacrificed in the Bright Hall — for twelve springs.
    Lions were hiding themselves under the flowers of peonies,
And below the leaves of banana trees unicorns were resting.

Listen to me as I tell you of the civil official Chancellor Bao:
With a pure reputation he dealt with all cases strictly and rightly.
Because he went to Chenzhou and supervised the sale of rice,
He did away in that city with four evil relatives of the emperor.
    The common people, farmers and soldiers, were greatly pleased
And filled with gratitude towards that pure official Judge Bao!
Prince Zhao called him a man with a face as impassive as iron,[1]
The officials at court called him a man without any partiality.
    During daytime he judged the cases of injustice in this world,
And at night he lit a candle and judged the orphaned souls.

---

[1] Prince Zhao here refers to Emperor Renzong, whose surname was Zhao.

Three times he served as prefect of the prefecture of Kaifeng,
And during two terms he displayed his loyal service at court.
    The mountain beast arrived as soon as it had been summoned,
He solved the case of the ugly black pot from the ancient kiln.
Out on the street he saved the life of Lin Zhaode,[2] but he also
Beheaded the Imperial Relative Zeng on the execution ground.
    In Mingzhou he sentenced the Assistant Prefect Chen;[3]
The old crow lodged an accusation which spelled out the facts.[4]
In Zhushan he sentenced the ghost in the Sun family temple,
And he also once sentenced a crazy whirlwind, all for show.[5]
    He sentenced Seventh Sister Lang who proved deceitful,[6]
Thrice he nabbed the soft-shelled turtle, which was a spirit.[7]
He once sentenced the emperor's main wife, Empress Cao,
In a single jail he had sentenced two members of her family.
    Because of his sentence Cui Hu was reunited with his wife,
And he also once sentenced Sun Jiao, that person all alone.[8]
The thirteen strokes of the eight cudgels — all according to law:
Never was a guiltless person beaten without good cause.

Let's not sing of Chancellor Bao at this point in our story,
Let's return to the subject of His Majesty, the Zhao ruler.
    "If We do not see that Bao Wenzheng here before the hall,
We promptly feel Ourselves bereft of all spirit and energy.
So tell the civil officials and military officers before the hall
To summon that man surnamed Bao back from Chenzhou!"
    The high officials and officers transmitted the imperial order,
An edict was drafted before the hall, and the messenger left.
The daily stretches on his road: like snapping one's fingers;
He crossed hills and passed districts as quickly as a cloud.

---

[2] See *Baijia gong'an*, Ch. 78.

[3] See *Baijia gong'an*, Ch. 70.

[4] See *Baijia gong'an*, Ch. 35.

[5] See *Baijia gong'an*, Ch. 69. In many stories Judge Bao summons a whirlwind.

[6] See *Baijia gong'an*, Ch. 26.

[7] See *Baijia gong'an*, Ch. 60.

[8] Some of the court cases of Judge Bao on this list are treated in other ballad-stories, and some others may be identified in *Baojia gong'an*, but some have defied attempts at identification so far. See Xu Zhongming (2002). *Baogong gushi: Yige kaocha Zhongguo falü wenhua de shijiao*, Beijing: Zhongguo zhengfa daxue chubanshe, pp. 204–206.

Let's not sing of all the stretches he traveled on his road:
Eventually he reached the prefectural capital of Chenzhou.
As soon as Judge Bao saw an edict had arrived, he expressed
His gratitude for the imperial grace by burning fine incense.

   When the edict had been read out, no moment was wasted:
The guards were lined up for a return to the Eastern Capital.
The elders of the local community all submitted a petition,
Proposing to detain the chancellor, the man surnamed Bao.

   Monks and nuns, clerics and laypeople all shed tears,
Who could let go of this pure official, of such a governor?
Thousands and myriads of blue- and white-colored flags
Completely covered the prefectural capital of Chenzhou.

   The elders of the local community all came to see him off:
Children separated from their mother, without their father.

Don't ask about the stretches they traveled on the road —
The place they approached now was Big Mulberry Forest.

   The red disk was sinking in the west, it turned to evening;
The jade hare was rising in the east, brighter and brighter.[9]
Judge Bao at this moment spoke in the following manner,
Calling for his servants Zhang Long and Zhao Hu.

   He also called for his servants Dong Chao and Xue Ba:
"Come forward all of you and listen to what I will say!
Right here and now the sky is already turning to evening,
So I am wondering, where will we rest for the night?"

   Dong Chao, stepping forward with folded hands, reported:
"Your Excellency, please listen to what I will tell you.
The village ahead of us is the town of Mulberry Forest,
It lacks powerful families or people who are well-to-do."

Speak:

Judge Bao said: "It is absolutely not allowed to bother the common
people. Let's rest for the night at an inn or a temple!"

Sing:

Dong Chao and Xue Ba left without wasting a moment,
They went ahead to inspect the situation in Mulberry Forest.

---

[9] The moon, which is white like jade, is said to be inhabited by a toad and a hare.

When Dong Chao lifted his head to have a look, all around,
The buildings of one temple turned out to be all brand new.
     It was a temple sporting three halls, a temporary palace,[10]
So when Dong Chao had seen this, he promptly returned.
Straightaway he went to the tent and announced his presence:
"Your Excellency, please allow me to report my findings.
     Ahead of us there is a temple of the Eastern Marchmount,
There all our horses and men can rest for the night."
Judge Bao that very moment hastily and promptly set out,
His only desire to race to the gate of the temple compound.
     When His Excellency lifted his eyes to have a look, all around,
The building indeed was exceptional, and really very new!
The plaque above the gate was in red, carved into green lacquer,
Ghosts and gods had been painted in colors to both of its sides.
     When you entered the temple compound, once inside the gate,
Incense smoke rose up in front of the Sagely Emperor's pedestal.
Thick mists rose up from below the True Lord's throne, and
Auspicious clouds originated from the desk of the Mighty Duke.[11]
     Row upon row, the halls had been covered with bronze tiles,
One after another the brackets were all decorated with gold.
Civil officials and military officers were adorned with agate —
All inlaid with glass, the temple had become a crystal palace.
     When Judge Bao ascended the Hall that is Equal to Heaven,[12]
The Sagely and Enlightened Lord was covered by a banner.
His Excellency lifted the screen made out of yellow gauze,
And he fixed his eyes so as to observe the statue in all detail.
     Pure gold was used to weave the patterns in his dragon robe,
His ladies-in-waiting were adorned with kingfisher feathers.
Observing this, His Excellency was very pleased in his heart,
And prayed to the Sagely Lord and Ruler Equal to Heaven.

---

[10] As the main abode of the Great Thearch of the Eastern Marchmount is Mt. Tai in Shandong, all his temples are only palaces he inhabits temporarily while touring the world.
[11] Sagely Emperor here is one of the titles of the Great Thearch of the Eastern Marchmount; the True Lord and Mighty Duke are two of the gods in his elaborate divine bureaucracy.
[12] The full title of the Great Thearch of the Eastern Marchmount includes the epithet "Equal to Heaven."

Speak:

His Excellency said: "I will borrow the eastern gallery to temporarily judge the people's cases for three days, and also borrow the western gallery to dispatch the three kinds of documents.[13] If you grant me your permission, give me the best of the best outcome when I throw the oracle blocks. If you don't grant me your permission, give me the worst of the worst outcome."

Sing:

As soon as His Excellency had finished saying his prayer,
He threw, in front of the hall, the blocks to see the outcome.
The oracle blocks do not determine misfortune and fortune:
The first throw he threw ascended the gate of the temple.[14]
    On seeing this, His Excellency was very pleased in his heart,
And he thanked the Sagely Emperor who is Equal to Heaven.
He promptly called for his servants Zhang Long and Zhao Hu:
"Come forward now both of you and listen to what I will say.
    I now dispatch the two of you on no other business but
To go together and follow and catch all people who are bad.
All those people engaged in a quarrel or having a fist fight —
Report them all to me in this temple, this temporary palace."
    Dong Chao and Xue Ba then wasted no moment and went,
And together they shouted their orders, clear for all to hear,
But there was no one engaged in a quarrel or having a fight —
No person there suffered any injustice or carried a grudge.
    They shouted from south of the town to north of the town,
From east of the town to west of the town — for all to hear!

Speak:

Dong Chao shouted: "All those who carry a grudge or suffer an injustice, who have a quarrel or were in a fight, all come and report the crime committed against you to His Excellency Bao, who temporarily for three days will judge the people's cases in the Equal to Heaven Temple. If you let this opportunity to appeal to Judge Bao slip by, it may be impossible to meet with him at some later time. Come quickly, make haste!"

---

[13] I am not clear what kinds of documents are intended.

[14] I am unclear about the meaning of these two lines.

Sing:

When he had shouted his way to the eastern side of the town,
He eventually came, still shouting, to broken-down kilns.
Out of one of those kilns came a woman, a poor old granny,
Her body so scented by smoke that she did not look human.
    A bag of bones, the hair on her head was one disorderly mess;
The lice on her head looked just like the scales of a fish.
In her hair she wore a single comb, one without any teeth,
Her bun was fastened by a single pin of sharpened bamboo.
    Her forehead looked exactly like the bottom of a wok,
The dirt and grime on her breast came in layer upon layer.
Her single threadbare skirt had been patched so often
That on the balance it had come to weigh eighteen pounds.
    The many lice on her head performed their somersaults,
The fleas that landed on her head were erect dragon-flies.
With her upper arm she pressed a bamboo staff to her ribs,
And in her hands she was holding an earthenware jug.
    She promptly asked: "Officer, what may be the reason?
For what cause have you come to this kiln of mine?
Because of His Excellency Bao of the Eastern Capital?
You must be some underling of that old geezer Bao!"

Speak:

Dong Chao said: "Old woman, who told you to call him 'old geezer
Bao'? What punishment do you deserve? For what reason are you asking
about His Excellency Bao?" The old woman said: "I want to lodge an
accusation with Chancellor Bao." Xue Ba said: "Old woman, who do you
want to accuse and of what?" Dong Chao said: "If she wants to make an
accusation, let her lodge her accusation!" The old woman asked the officers:
"Where is His Excellency staying?" Dong Chao replied: "His Excellency is
staying in the eastern corridor of the Temporary Palace Temple."

Sing:

Hearing this, the poor woman was very pleased at heart,
And she hurried along to the Temporary Palace Temple.
Let's not sing of the stretches she traveled on the road —
She soon approached the gate building of the temple hall.

When Zhang Long lifted his head to have a good look,
The smell she gave off overwhelmed him totally, so he
Promptly blocked the poor woman from going inside:
"How can you dare go inside, into the hall of the temple?"

Speak:

Zhang Long and Zhao Hu said: "Woman, you can visit the three halls of the Temporary Palace any time you like, but at present Chancellor Bao is staying in this temple, so it is just like the prefectural office of Kaifeng — no one is allowed to enter!"

Sing:

The woman thereupon was overcome by frustration,
And the skin of her cheeks was all flushed with red.
She threw her earthen jug to the ground with force,
And with such force it broke into pieces beyond repair.
    Clutching Zhang Long with her hands, she fell down,
Loudly shouting "Injustice!" without ever stopping.

Speak:

Zhang Long and Zhao Hu were so scared they were covered in cold sweat. As fast as his legs could carry him [Zhang Long] ran to His Excellency, and panicking, told him: "There's a woman in front of the temple who wants to lodge an accusation, but Zhao Hu didn't dare admit her, as he was afraid that she might insult Your Excellency!" Judge Bao promptly ordered her to be admitted inside.

Sing:

Zhang Long and Zhao Hu hurriedly went back again,
In front of the gate they helped the old woman to her feet.
"Old woman, let me tell you, please rest your anger,
We will take you now to the hall to see His Excellency."
    Hearing this, the old woman was very pleased at heart,
Flowers appeared on her cheeks, her face was all smiles.
When she entered the temple hall, once inside the gate,
His Excellency saw her coming in, this aged woman.
    But when she saw His Excellency, she refused to bow;
In front of the steps she observed the man surnamed Bao.

李后跌倒在地

包相問婆子

Fig. 3.1
Upper picture: Empress Li collapses and falls to the ground.
Lower picture: Minister Bao questions the old woman.

Speak:

Judge Bao promptly asked her: "Where are you from? Tell me the truth!

Sing:

What is your surname? What is your name? Where do you live?
What is the township in which you were born to begin with?"
When the old woman heard herself addressed in this manner,
She just lowered her head and did not say even a single word.
 "Take your time to tell me the truth but make no mistake,
And Judge Bao today will redress any injustice you suffered!"

Speak:

Judge Bao said: "Woman, who are you really?" The old woman said: "Let me be your mother!" Judge Bao said: "What crime do you deserve by cursing an official like me?" The old woman said: "If I cannot be your mother, I will be your ancestor seven generations back." Judge Bao said: "Woman, who are you really? What kind of wrong have you suffered? Tell me truthfully!" The old woman said: "But I do not know whether you are the true Chancellor Bao or a fake Chancellor Bao." His Excellency said: "What makes for the true Chancellor Bao and what for a fake Chancellor Bao?" "I may be so old that I can't see clearly anymore, but I've heard it said that the one who served as the capital prefect of Kaifeng, the Eastern Capital, is Chancellor Bao, and that the one who rode his donkey backwards in Chenzhou is Chancellor Bao!" His Excellency said: "Then I am the true Chancellor Bao!" The old woman said: "If you are the true Chancellor Bao, you must have a wart[15] behind your ear." His Excellency said: "I have one." The old woman said: "If you have one, you must let me feel it with my own hands, and then I will tell you my injustice which is as huge as heaven and as deep as the ocean!"

Sing:

When Judge Bao heard her speak to him in this manner,
He was extremely annoyed by the words of this old crone.
"If I decide to allow this old woman to feel my wart,
I will be the laughing stock of all officers and officials.

---

[15] Literally, "a pole for tying up a horse." The *Baijia gong'an* account of this incident refers to "a lump of flesh."

If the emperor, the Humane Ancestor, hears about it,
How will I ever be able to show my face in court again?
But if I do not allow that old woman to feel my wart,
I'll never get to know the details of this case of injustice."
    His Excellency then stepped down from his silver chair,
And he hastily handed it over to the aged woman.
He allowed the old woman to feel his wart this way,
And she indeed felt his head till she touched his wart.
    Grasping him with her left hand, she held on to him,
And hastily she stretched out her right hand full flat.
In quick succession she slapped him seven, eight times,
Till His Excellency's face was all flushed with red.
    Each day three hundred people lodged an accusation,
But no one ever gave him such an atrocious beating!

Speak:

His Excellency said: "Woman, you deserve the death penalty! First of all
you call yourself my mother, and then you strike a high official. It's not
some minor crime you have committed!"

Sing:

That old woman then and there started to curse him,
She cursed him, saying: "Old geezer Bao, you're no man!
You cunning scholar who fashioned a world out of snow,
You cunning craftsman who produced the whole cosmos!
    The world of the house of Zhao is awry and out of order,
But they say that old geezer Bao restored it all to balance.
People may all call you the pure official Chancellor Bao,
But you are just as muddleheaded as a bowl of noodles!"

Speak:

The old woman said: "If you want me to speak, there can only be one
person present, no second person is allowed to know about it. If three
people would know of this, the great secret would leak out. Only if the
gods will not know of it, the ghosts will not learn of it, all birds will have
been netted and all swallows will have been killed, and only if you dismiss
all your underlings and officers, will I speak."

Sing:

When His Excellency heard these words, he said "Fine!"
And he ordered all his underlings to retire from the room.
The five hundred soldiers on duty were all told to disperse,
And the one man surnamed Bao was the only one to remain.
    His Excellency then once again questioned her as follows:
"Woman, from which township are you in the beginning?"
The old woman then finally spoke in the following manner:
"Your Excellency, please listen to what I will have to say!
    The disaster that I've suffered is as huge as high heaven,
The injustice that happened to me is as deep as the ocean!"

Speak:

His Excellency said: "Woman, who are you really? Tell me what is
bothering you." The old woman said: "Your Excellency, if I tell you the
injustice I have suffered, even two or three Judge Baos will not be able to
provide me justice!" His Excellency said: "Only tell me the truth, and
I will make sure that justice is done!"

Sing:

Awash in tears the old woman [spoke in the following way]:
"Your Excellency please be so kind as to listen to my story.
If I am going to tell you the facts of my family background,
The story is painful to me even where it is not painful.
    My natal family lived in Bo River District of Bo Prefecture,
I was born and bred locally, as a woman of Bo Prefecture.
My father was Military Governor Li of the same Bo Prefecture,
He was in charge of both the military and civil administration.
    Because my family was destined to be without posterity,[16]
My parents had neither son nor daughter, nor a single grandson.
From early till late they burned incense, praying for an heir,
And eventually I was born in response as their only daughter.
    The oracles they consulted predicted an early death for me,
So I was given as a Daoist nun to the Palace of Grand Purity.

---

[16] The final three characters of this line do not make sense to me, and the translation is
tentative.

When after some years I had reached the age of thirteen,
The four prefectures and eight districts all praised me highly.
     Of Daoist nuns with crowns of gold I was the number one,
Even the True Ancestor visited the Palace of Grand Purity.
As soon as the Son of Heaven saw how beautiful I was,
He took me home to his palace and made me a concubine.
     The True Ancestor cut off my career as a Daoist nun;
Housing me in the Western Palace, he made me a consort.
The Southern Palace housed Elder Sister Concubine Liu,
The Western Palace was reserved for me, Concubine Li.
     But then the northern barbarians raised a mighty army,
Shattering the peace when they invaded the Great Song.
The emperor appointed Sixth Son Yang as commander,
Who attacked and defeated the troops of the barbarians.[17]
     He made the barbarian Empress-Dowager Xiao his captive,
And the True Ancestor changed the spring to "Great Peace."[18]
On the third day of the Third Month of that "Great Peace"
A little crown prince descended to the Western Palace.
     But Elder Sister Concubine Liu of the Southern Palace,
Overcome by jealousy, thereupon hatched a cunning plot.

Speak:

Our story goes that the great commissioner of the Six-Palaces was named
Guo Huai. He conspired with her in her evil designs, and he took the baby
daughter of Concubine Liu to my Western Palace, where he exchanged her
for my little crown prince. Concubine Liu thereupon became empress of
the Main Palace. Holding the baby girl in my arms I collapsed with rage in
the Main Palace.

Sing:

That I collapsed and fell down was only a minor matter,
But accidentally I kicked and killed the little baby girl.

---

[17] For a summary description of the development of the saga of the wars between the Song
and their northern neighbors, the Khitan Liao dynasty, see Wilt L. Idema, "Something Rotten
in the State of Song: The Frustrated Loyalty of the Generals of the Yang Family," *Journal of
Song-Yuan Studies* 36 (2006), 57–77.
[18] There is no reign period "Great Peace" during the reign of Zhenzong, but the first reign
period of Emperor Taizong was Taiping xingguo ("Great Peace and National Resurgence").

I was therefore arrested and locked up in the Cold Palace,[19]
And I suffered bitter exertions day after day without end.

The food I got was spoiled rice, stored for too many years;
The soup I got was bitter herbs from the Southern Garden.
Altogether I stayed in the palace prison for thirteen years,
And my darling son gradually grew into an adult man.

Once, on the Third Month Festival of Clear and Bright,
The palace women were enjoying the hundred new flowers.
Let me tell you about a gardener Zhang of the Inner Palace,
He brought me in his arms the little crown prince, my son.

'On the third day of his life separated from his mother —
Yet later he will grow into the man who will revenge you!'
When the great commissioner of the Six-Palaces heard this,
He secretly told this to Empress Liu and to no one else.

Gardener Zhang was strangulated with a piece of white silk,
And his whole family was executed to the last man.
Altogether eighteen people were murdered, and horses
Trampled the corpses into mud, turning them into dust.

Judge Bao folded his hands and stepped forward, asking:
"Empress-dowager, please be so kind as to enlighten me —
Your Majesty had been condemned to the Cold Palace,
So how did you end up here in this old kiln?"

Her Majesty, awash in tears, replied in the following way:
"Your Excellency, please be so kind as to listen to my words.
When I had been in the palace prison for a full thirteen years,
My darling son had gradually grown into an adult man.

When the Son of Heaven the True Ancestor left this world,
My darling son ascended the throne, and became a fine ruler.
Three thousand palace women were set free and sent home,
Eight hundred charming beauties dismissed from the palace.

Condemned criminals in their prisons were all pardoned,
And I too was set free from the Cold Palace by that pardon.
But because I am poor and have no one to take care of me,
I survive here in Mulberry Forest by begging for food.

Now today I have been able to meet with you face to face,
I hope Your Excellency will be the man to revenge me.

---

[19] The Cold Palace refers to that section of the Inner Palace where women who had lost the emperor's favor were housed.

Report this case to my darling son, the Humane Emperor,
And he'll promote you, my Clear Sky Mighty Lord Bao!"

Speak:

Judge Bao said: "Your Majesty, what distinctive signs did the crown prince
display when you gave birth to him?" Her Majesty replied: "When I gave
birth to him, he refused to open his hands, so I told two concubines to pry
open his hands. His left hand showed the two characters 'mountains and
streams,' and his right hand showed the two characters 'land and millet' clear
for all to see!"

Sing:

His Excellency was so scared that he was dumbfounded,
His three souls had fled through the crown of his head.[20]
He helped Her Majesty to sit down on his folding chair,
With lowered head he bowed down before the empress:
    "I hope Your Majesty will forgive me for my crimes!"
Only then the empress-dowager started to feel at ease.
He provided scented hot water so she could take a bath,
And her whole body was changed into silks and satins.
    Her Majesty was helped into her gold-gilded carriage,
And the empress was hidden from view by yellow gauze.
In front and behind young maids crowded around her,
And her guard with yellow hammers was a novel sight.
    His Excellency then and there did not waste any moment,
But made all haste to hurry to the Eastern Capital city.
Let's not sing of the stretches he traveled on the road —
Let's not discourse on boring tales and idle words!
    When he arrived at the walls of the Eastern Capital,
Officials came out and welcomed the man surnamed Bao.
His Excellency then proceeded to the Southern Office,[21]
Here Her Majesty the empress-dowager stepped down.
    When Her Majesty had taken her seat in the high hall,
He called for his wife Lady Li from the room in the back.

---

[20] According to traditional Chinese physiology, every person has three souls and seven spirits.
[21] The Southern Office refers to the yamen (government building) of the prefectural
administration, which included the living quarters for the prefect. It was called the Southern
Office, in contrast to the imperial palace in the northern part of the city.

Arriving in front of the hall, she promptly bowed down:
"Your Majesty, what bitter hardship you went through!"

His Excellency then addressed her in the following way:
"Empress-dowager, please be so kind as to listen to me.
Please spend a few days in this office building of mine,
Even though it is too poor and simple for your stay!"[22]

She also asked the Lady for her surname and her name,
And in the office building they became tied as relatives.[23]
Scented water was carried in and mouth-washing water,
And a banquet was laid out there in the office building.

The banquet lasted from the first watch till the third,
The banquet of the third watch was done in the fourth.
The banquet came to the third point of the fifth watch —
Let's talk of the Son of Heaven, the Sage surnamed Zhao.

At the third point of the fifth watch he ascended the hall,
At the fourth point of the fifth watch he saw his officials —
The civil officials all lined up before the vermillion steps,
The military officers standing next to the Xiechai Pond.[24]

Prime Minister Wang atop the bureaus of the Three Offices;
The Five Ministers before the terrace of the Five Garrisons.[25]
The high dignitaries before the steps shouted "A myriad years!"
The senior officials filling the hall were engaged in discussion.

The summoning secretary stepped forward and reported:
"May your Sagely Majesty please listen to my words.
Chancellor Bao, who sold government rice in Chenzhou,
Returned yesterday and arrived in the Eastern Capital.

At present he has entered the Eastern Floriate Gate, and
Changed his clothes at the Assembled Immortals Pavilion.
But unless he receives the summoning edict of Our King,
He does not dare enter the court and greet the Sagely Ruler."

When the emperor heard this report, he was very pleased,
And promptly ordered Bao summoned to enter the court.

---

[22] Two or four lines in which Judge Bao's wife greets Concubine Li appear to have been dropped from the text.

[23] Judge Bao's wife Lady Li and Concubine Li share the same surname.

[24] The Xiechai is a mythical goat-like animal that will butt any wrongdoer.

[25] The first line of this couplet refers to the civil officials headed by Chancellor Wang, and I take it that the second line refers to the military officers attending the audience.

Three ushers led him inside, to the bottom of the steps,
And four assistants invited him to bow before the Sage.
    Highly lifting his dragon sleeves he beckoned the chancellor,
And invited him with his own hands to sit down next to him.
He ordered that a cup of imperial sealed wine be poured,
And offered that filled golden cup to Judge Bao to drink.

Speak:

Judge Bao said: "Your Majesty, I cannot drink this wine." The emperor
said: "Sir, you are the only one of the four hundred civil officials and
military officers in front of the hall who is allowed to drink a few cups. So
why do you refuse to drink today?" Judge Bao said: "Your Majesty, I am
suffering from the disease of indecisiveness, so I cannot drink wine." The
emperor said: "Sir, now what disease are you suffering from?" Judge Bao
said: "What I am suffering from is the disease of anger." The emperor said:
"Sir, you are the most powerful of all four hundred civil officials and
military officers. Who would dare abuse you?" Then the emperor said:
"I will have a medical official in gold and purple diagnose you." Judge Bao
said: "Even divine skill and miraculous herbs will not be able to save me."
The emperor said: "When a man becomes mean, even his diseases become
mean. Sir, please tell me whatever is on your mind — it won't matter!"
Judge Bao said: "My King, please forgive me so I will not be punished!"
The emperor said: "Sir, ever since We dispatched you to Chenzhou to sell
government rice, wind and frost have come timely. Report whatever you
have on your mind!" Judge Bao replied: "When I was in Chenzhou, I saw
a Daoist priest who had barred his window and wept for three days and
three nights on end. Because I could not bear to see this, I called him over
to question him, and he said: 'Mountains and streams, land and millet will
collapse!'" The emperor said: "Sir, on Our orders Yang Wenguang has
conquered the Nine Rivers and the Eighteen Grottoes[26] — our mountains
and streams are as firmly secured as an iron bucket!" Judge Bao said: "My
King, I also heard that Daoist priest say that they will collapse very fast!"
The emperor said: "Sir, and why will they collapse so fast?" Judge Bao
replied: "That Daoist priest said: 'When there is no truly appointed Son of

---

[26] This may be intended as a reference to the participation of Yang Wenguang in the campaign
against Nong Zhigao in Guangxi, but it also may refer to the separate story cycle of Yang
Wenguang's pacification of Fujian.

Heaven, there is not a single minister whose behavior is virtuous.'"
The emperor said: "We are the truly appointed Son of Heaven, and you are
a minister whose behavior is virtuous." Judge Bao continued: "That man
of the Way said: 'The truly appointed Son of Heaven displays in his left
hand the two characters 'mountains and streams,' and in his right hand the
two characters 'land and millet.'" The emperor said: "We do!" Judge Bao
said: "My King, if Your Majesty does, please allow me to have a look."

Sing:

The Son of Heaven then rose and left his dragon-throne
And he hastily showed his hands to the man surnamed Bao.
    From his imperial robe he stretched out his dragon hands,
And Judge Bao lifted his head to have a good look. Indeed,
The left hand showed the characters "mountains and streams,"
The right hand "land and millet" in characters clear and bright!

Speak:

"This fine 'truly appointed Son of Heaven' has become a bandit king!"
The emperor said: "Sir, for four generations we have been enlightened
rulers, so have the three preceding generations also been bandit kings?"
Judge Bao said: "Only Your Majesty has become a bandit king. How could
you not know the mother who gave birth to you unless you had become a
bandit king?" The emperor said: "Sir, how come all of a sudden you don't
know anymore that Empress Liu of the Bright Yang Hall is the mother
who gave birth to Us?" Judge Bao said: "My King, you are mistaken.
You truly do not know the mother who gave birth to you." The emperor
said: "So where is my own mother if she is not the mother who gave birth
to Us?"

[Sing:]

"Your own mother goes around begging in the streets,
She survives by begging for food from door to door.
In her hair she wears a single comb, one without any teeth,
Her bun is fastened by a single pin of sharpened bamboo.
    Her whole body is emaciated, she's become a bag of bones,
She is smelling so offensively she doesn't look human."
The emperor was so scared that he was dumbfounded,
For a long time he was lost in thought and said not a word.

Judge Bao addressed him again in the following words:
"Your Majesty, please be so kind as to listen to me.
If you do not believe the tale that I have told you,
Please question the two kinds of officials before the hall."

The emperor then asked the civil and military officials:
"Civil officials and military officers, please listen to Us.
Who of you witnessed my birth and my early youth?
Which empress is the mother who gave birth to me?"

None of the civil officials or military officers replied,
None of all of those in front of the hall spoke a word.
The civil officials looked as if sculpted from clay,
The military officers seemed to be carved from wood.

Eventually one man stepped forward from the ranks,
Holding his ivory tablet before his breast he reported.
It's said this was Chancellor Wang from Qingzhou,
[Who said:] "Your Majesty, please listen to my words,

My King, if you want to identify your birth mother,
You must question elderly people in the Rear Palace."

Speak:

Minister Wang said: "Your Majesty Our King, the civil officials and military officers in front of the hall are all people of recent years. If you want to know the truth of the matter, you will have to question elderly people in the Rear Palace. Only then will you discover all details." The emperor said: "In the Rear Palace there's the grand commissioner of the Six-Palaces Guo Huai. It's said that he witnessed my birth and early youth. So why don't We summon him with all speed and question him closely?"

Sing:

The emperor thereupon followed the minister's advice
And he summoned Grand Commissioner Guo Huai.
When Guo Huai, thus summoned, arrived before the hall,
He greeted the enlightened ruler with twenty-four bows.

The emperor then addressed him in the following words:
"I have some urgent business that depends on you alone.
You have witnessed both my birth and my early youth:
So which empress is the mother who gave birth to Us?"

Guo Huai reported to the enlightened Son of Heaven:
"Her Majesty Empress Liu is Your Majesty's mother!"

When the emperor heard him speak in this manner,
He lowered his head for some time, not saying a word.
 "That damned old geezer Bao, without rhyme or reason,
Has to stir up trouble with his foolish words, that rascal!"
He promptly ordered Chancellor Bao to be taken outside,
To be taken outside, straight to the execution grounds!

Speak:

Judge Bao said: "I will lodge an accusation for wrongful death!" The emperor said: "We represent the highest authority throughout the world, so to whom will you appeal?" Judge Bao said: "I will write a statement and report to the Jade Emperor, that High Lord!" The emperor said: "And of what will you accuse me?" Judge Bao said: "I will accuse you of a crime against Nature!

Sing:

Once the Son of Heaven commits a crime against Nature,
How can the world produce people practicing filial piety?
 I will write my statement on three feet of yellow gauze,
And then burn it in order to report to the Jade Emperor.
I will also report to the Three Purities in the high skies[27]
To arrest this Zhao emperor in his Golden Bells Hall."
 When the emperor heard this, he was really dumbfounded,
His three souls had fled through the crown of his head.
He then ordered old man Bao not to write his statement:
"Dear Sir, We've been too irascible with regards to you."
 Again the emperor questioned the officials and officers:
"Civil officials and military officers, I do want to know
Who it was who witnessed my birth and my early youth,
And which of the empresses is truly my mother by birth?"
 Before he had even finished speaking these words,
Minister Wang from Qingzhou stepped up to him.

---

[27] The Jade Emperor is the highest heavenly deity in the traditional popular pantheon. The Three Purities are the highest divinities in the Daoist spiritual realm.

Speak:

Minister Wang said: "Your Majesty my King, if you want to know all details, have Guo Huai handed over to the chief investigative censor for questioning under torture, and you will promptly know the truth of the matter."

Sing:

The emperor thereupon followed the minister's advice,
And promptly ordered the arrest of that man Guo Huai.
Guo Huai was stripped of all the clothes on his body,
Stripped of all his clothes, he was as naked as could be.
    Let's not sing of the long streets and short lanes —
He was taken to the chief investigative censor's office.

Speak:

The chief investigative censor said: "Guo Huai, in ordinary times you were the grand commissioner of the Six-Palaces and I would have to bow to you. Don't blame me today if I question you according to the statutes of the law at the order of the Son of Heaven!"

Sing:

The chief investigative censor addressed him as follows,
Addressed and questioned Guo Huai in the following way:
"You have witnessed the emperor's birth and early youth.
Who of the empresses is the mother who gave him birth?
    Today it is absolutely necessary for you to speak the truth
If you want to avoid suffering torture here in this prison."
Guo Huai stepped forward with folded hands, and replied:
"Chief investigative censor, please listen to my words.
    I have witnessed the emperor's birth and his early youth:
Her Majesty Empress Liu is the emperor's own mother."
The chief investigative censor was annoyed in his heart,
And immediately applied torture in questioning Guo Huai.
    A brightly lacquered huge cangue was placed to the side,
Guo Huai had only to see it to lose all spirit and energy!
No moment was wasted to open this "merciless wood"
And Guo Huai was that very moment locked in a cangue.

In the middle was inserted that one merciless board;
The two sides were nailed together, in no light manner.
The soft ones the hemp ropes, the stiff ones the cudgels:
How could the grand commissioner bear their pain?

Speak:

But our story goes that Guo Huai always had been the trusted conspirator
of Empress Liu, but now he had been handed over to the chief
investigative censor for questioning. When Empress Liu had learned that
the Front Palace had handed Guo Huai over to the chief investigative
censor for questioning, [she thought:] "If he were eventually to confess to
that crime, I too will be in danger." She thereupon disclosed her worries to
her trusted servant Palace Intendant Xu. The latter said: "That chief
investigative censor is no Chancellor Bao. You should give him gold and
treasure to make sure that Guo Huai will not be condemned." Empress
Liu said: "Who could go?" Palace Intendant Xu said: "I can handle it if
I go myself." Empress Liu immediately collected gold and treasure for
Palace Intendant Xu to take with him.

Sing:

Her Majesty the empress then wasted no moment
And collected treasure and pearls from the palace:
   Three bushels and three pints and a half of pearls,
And also ten ounces of gold and ten ounces of silver;
On top of that fifteen hair pins of gold and silver,
And she repeatedly impressed on Palace Intendant Xu:
   "Keep this secret from Chancellor Bao in the Southern Office,
Keep this secret from the Sagely Ruler in the Golden Bells Hall.
Palace Intendant, please spare no effort on my behalf,
And on your return I will give you a horseshoe in gold."
   Upon receiving this hoard of gold, the palace intendant
Took his leave of Her Majesty, and set out on the road.
Let's not sing at all of the long streets and short lanes —
He soon arrived at the chief investigative censor's gate.

Speak:

Just as the chief investigative censor was questioning Guo Huai under
torture, he saw that Palace Intendant Xu had arrived. After the censor had

greeted the palace intendant, he had Guo Huai escorted back to the Western Prison, and invited the palace intendant to enter the hall and sit down. After they had had a cup of tea, the palace intendant rose from his seat and addressed the censor with folded hands as follows: "Empress Liu ordered me to tell you that she is sending you some small trifles with which to buy wine or tea, hoping that you will take good care of Guo Huai in the Western Prison.

Sing:

When through your care this business will be finished,
She'll weigh out yellow gold as if it were melon seeds!"
As soon as the censor saw these pearls and this treasure,
It was just as if he saw his own mother and grandfather.
　　The chief investigative censor wasted not a moment,
And he had Sir Guo released from the Western Prison.
His long cangue and iron shackles were all removed,
And he was invited to enter the hall and have a drink.
　　Palace Intendant Xu was seated on the western side,
And Sir Guo was now seated on the eastern side.
The chief investigative censor was seated in the middle;
While drinking wine the three of them discussed the case.

Speak:

The censor said: "Sir Guo, when I earlier questioned you, I never had you really beaten. I was too afraid that you would name that stupid Concubine Li! When I will be questioning you in this manner again, you cannot mention her under any circumstances, just say it is Empress Liu!"

Sing:

Guo Huai stepped forward with folded hands, and then said:
"Your Excellency, you are like my own father and mother!
When through your good care this business will be finished,
I will weigh out yellow gold just as if it were melon seeds."
　　But just as they were sitting in the hall and having a drink,
They suddenly saw a young man who walked up to them.

Speak:

The chief investigative censor thought: "How can the gatekeeper have allowed that man to come inside?" So he asked the young man: "Where are you from?" The young man said: "I am the commander-in-chief of the two rows of civil officials and military officers in front of the hall, of the thirty-six palaces and of the forty-eight courtyards. Today at New Year I am asking for some New Year's money. All the other civil officials and military officers have already given me some, but I have not yet received anything from Your Excellency." The censor said: "Pay him ten strings of cash from the treasury!" When the young man had received his money, he also said: "I'm also thirsty and hungry." The censor said: "There's plenty of wine and food, so let the young man eat his fill." After the latter had eaten two bowls and also drunk one cup, he collapsed in front of the steps, crying foul: "That the Son of Heaven does not recognize his own mother is a great injustice, and coveting money and taking bribes is a small injustice!" The censor shouted to the young man: "What is it to you if he does not recognize his mother? Have him strung up!"

Sing:

His underlings and followers all took action together,
Who of them dared procrastinate or stay behind forever?
A hundred brown eagles swept down on a single hare,
And ten sparrow hawks swept down on a single quail!
    But as soon as they had strung up this young man,
The gatekeeper loudly called out, again and again.
He appeared in front of the hall, reported his presence,
Saying: "Your Excellency, please be so kind as to listen.
    His Excellency Chancellor Bao of the Southern Office
Has arrived in person outside the gate of this office."
When the censor heard this, he wasted no moment,
But hastily ordered Sir Guo to go back to his prison:
    "Go back to the Western Prison and hide inside there,
So as to escape for a while from your star of disaster!"
Guo Huai ran as fast as he could back to his prison,
Where hemp ropes and iron shackles secured his person.
    The censor hastily dressed himself in his formal gown,
In order to welcome the man surnamed Bao at the gate.
But in front of the gate he did not see Chancellor Bao,
He only saw five hundred men of fully armed troops.

Speak:

The chief investigative censor said: "Dong Chao, where is your commanding official?" The officer said: "My commanding official and Minister Wang from Qingzhou are discussing some matter in a teahouse, but he has ordered me to go ahead and tell you something. Let's go inside to talk, because there are too many people outside, so it is not safe." The censor led Dong Chao and Xue Ba inside to talk. When these two saw Chancellor Bao, who had been strung up on a tree in front of the hall, Dong Chao said: "Your Excellency, here you have my commanding official strung up on a tree, and yet you ask me for him!"

Sing:

The censor was in such a panic that he could not untie him,
With lowered head he bowed before the man surnamed Bao.
　　Only then he had Chancellor Bao untied and let down,
And His Excellency then was filled with a towering rage.
He condemned Chief Investigating Censor Wang
As a man who lusted after money and loved treasure.
　　The chief investigating censor addressed him as follows:
"Where are these silver and gold, these riches and treasures?"
This enraged that pure official, Chancellor Bao,
And he had the treasure and pearls taken from the office.
　　Three bushels and three pints and a half of true pearls,
Ten ounces of gold together with ten ounces of silver.
On top of that fifteen hair pins of gold and silver —
All these precious goods were clear for all to see.
　　Judge Bao shouted the order to have him beheaded,
And none dared procrastinate or stay behind forever.
He was stripped of all his outer and undergarments,
Stripped of all his clothes, he was as naked as could be.
　　Thereupon a large black flag was raised on a pole,
And the tablet ordering execution was displayed.
Judge Bao at that time was filled with great rage,
He ordered him beheaded, refusing to spare him.
　　Once the chief investigating censor had been killed,
His Excellency mounted his horse, set out on the road.
At that time he did not go off to the Kaifeng Office,
But he went single-mindedly to the Zhengyang Gate.

Upon entering the nine-bay Chaoyang Palace Hall,
He reported to his ruler in front of the white jade steps.
After he had made his twenty-four bows, [he said:]
"Your Sagely Majesty, please listen to my words.

    That damned Chief Investigative Censor Wang
Was a man who coveted money and loved treasure.
Three bushels and three pints and a half of true pearls,
Ten ounces of gold together with ten ounces of silver.

    On top of that fifteen hair pins of silver and of gold —
Because of all this, he neglected to question Sir Guo!
Each day he invited him to his hall to have a drink,
Judge and suspect passed the days drinking together!"

Speak:

Judge Bao said: "My King, these were pearls and precious goods of
Empress Liu. She urged the chief investigative censor not to question Guo
Huai. Every day they were drinking together, so I had him killed." The
emperor said: "You [indeed have the authority to] execute first and report
later." Judge Bao showed the gold and treasure to the Son of Heaven, and
the Son of Heaven was greatly angered at the sight.

Sing:

As soon as the Son of Heaven saw this, he was annoyed,
Overcome by depression, he had lost all spirit and energy.

    Judge Bao then addressed him with the following words:
"My King, please consider this carefully for yourself now!
If she really is the true mother who gave birth to you,
Why would she have to bribe that man surnamed Wang?

    Your Majesty, if you want to know the truth of the matter,
Allow me to take Sir Guo away from the Western Prison.
I will take him with me to the Southern Prefectural Office,
And gradually, after a while, we will just find the root."

    Before he had even been able to finish these words,
The emperor's wife, Empress Cao, entered the hall:
"If indeed Her Majesty would have committed this crime,
She also would not necessarily be my true mother-in-law!"

    After Judge Bao had taken his leave of the Son of Heaven,
He mounted his horse to return and set out on his road.

After a short while he had arrived at the censor's office,
And there he sat down, the pure official Chancellor Bao.
    He promptly called for Dong Chao and also Xue Ba,
And also for the couple Zhang Long and Zhao Hu.
These together with Zhang Qing and also Ma [Wan],
And the two soldiers Jin Chun and also Ruan Ding.
    When they had arrived in front of the steps of the hall,
His Excellency instructed them all in the following way:
"Escort that Guo Huai who is now in the Western Prison
To the Southern Office for questioning under torture."
    Guo Huai's hair was tied to the sides of his cangue,
He was beaten by sticks on the heels behind his feet.
Let's not sing about the long streets and short lanes —
He arrived at the Kaifeng Office, was locked up inside.
    Judge Bao in the hall questioned him in a loud voice,
In a loud voice he questioned him: "Listen, Sir Guo!
You witnessed the emperor's birth and his early youth,
Which of the empresses was the one who gave him birth?"
    Guo Huai in the hall replied to the question as follows:
"Your Excellency, please be so kind as to listen to me.
I have witnessed the emperor's birth and his early youth,
Her Majesty Empress Liu is the emperor's true mother!"
    This enraged that pure official, our Chancellor Bao:
"He was sent to the Western Prison to suffer torture.
The soft ones the hemp ropes, the stiff ones the cudgels —
How could he bear the judicial torture of the officers?"
    His Excellency in the hall was annoyed in his heart,
So he called for Dong Chao [and Xue Ba] to approach.
"He refuses to talk despite all beatings and questioning,
We will need some trick in order to make him confess."
    Gnashing his teeth, filled with hatred: Chancellor Bao;
High eyebrows, eyes bulging with rage: his two soldiers.

Speak:

Judge Bao said: "Those who succeed in extracting a confession from Guo
Huai will receive ten ounces of gold and a jug of fine wine, and I will
report them to the emperor for an appointment as an official." Dong Chao
said: "Your Excellency, don't worry. The two of us have our own way of
extracting a confession. Please give us your permission."

Sing:

Hearing this, Judge Bao was pleased in his heart:
"These are truly two soldiers who are hard to find!"
 Dong Chao and Xue Ba wasted not a single moment,
And they went off to the Western Prison straightaway.
There they removed Guo Huai's ropes and shackles,
And softly spoke to Sir Guo in a whispering voice.

Speak:

Dong Chao said: "Guo Huai, Empress Liu instructs you not to confess under any circumstances!" Xue Ba said: "Keep your voice down, otherwise people will find out!" Dong Chao said: "Xue Ba has brought three jugs of wine from the eastern gallery, so the three of us can have a drink."

Sing:

Dong Chao and Xue Ba did not waste a single moment,
And they quickly produced a jug of imperial sealed wine.
Guo Huai then addressed them in the following manner:
"How will I ever be able to repay you two for this favor!"
 Guo Huai went on drinking till he was drunk as a skunk;
And whispering in a low voice he said to the two soldiers:
"When through your good offices this business is finished,
I will weigh out yellow gold as if it were melon seeds!"
 Dong Chao addressed him, speaking in the following way:
"Within three days you'll be out of jail, that's a promise!"
Hearing this Guo Huai was overcome by joy in his heart,
And his cheeks were flushed with flowers, doubly red.

Speak:

Guo Huai said: "Brothers, when I leave this prison through your good offices, I will never forget your favors in life or death!" Dong Chao said: "Guo Huai, never confess under any circumstances, just say it is Empress Liu. As the proverb says: 'In being a man you have to be one till the very end; when killing a man, you have to continue till you see blood!' Dong Chao then said: "This place is no good. I'm afraid that someone might overhear us. Inside, no human being or ghost will be able to find out." So they pushed Guo Huai into the Western Prison, and once inside, they locked the gate.

Sing:

The two of them gave that Guo Huai such a mighty push
They pushed him into the darkness of the deep dungeon!
They nailed his whole body down so he could not turn,
They nailed him down from head to toe, from left to right.
    Dong Chao immediately started to hastily curse him,
Raising his voice, he promptly started to curse Sir Guo.
"If you still refuse to confess to your crimes today,
You'll be tortured according to law and suffer disaster!"
    Guo Huai now found it impossible to support the pain,
And this time around he could only tell the full story.
"It is all because I was improperly filled with jealousy
When the Western Palace gave birth to a crown prince.
    I, Guo Huai, then carried the true Son of Heaven away,
And Concubine Li was locked up inside the Cold Palace.
I am the one person who is to blame for this disaster,
I'm the one who wrongfully ruined the life of others!"
    As he told them one fact, they questioned him further,
Each word he confessed was written down as confession.
Eventually his confession filled one full sheet of paper,
And Dong Chao shouted an order for Sir Guo to shut up.

Speak:

Dong Chao said: "You damned Guo Huai, now sign this statement of your confession!"

[Sing:]

Guo Huai took the brush and wrote down his own name,
He personally wrote down his name on his confession.
After writing his name, he affixed the print of his thumb —
Dong Chao took the confession and set out on the road.
    He went straight up to the hall and reported his presence,
In the prefecture he delivered the confession to Judge Bao.
Once Judge Bao had seen it, he was pleased in his heart,
And he put on his court robes to go and see the emperor.
    When he had performed his twenty-four bows, [he said:]
"May Your Majesty be so kind as to listen to my words.

This damned Guo Huai, without any rhyme or reason,
Has ruined these other people because of his jealousy!
  At present in prison he has confessed to his crimes,
And I'm here to present his confession to Your Majesty."
Once the Son of Heaven had received the confession,
He beat on the dragon throne, overcome by great rage.
  He then had Guo Huai summoned back to the palace,
To be escorted before the golden steps to see his King.
Dong Chao and Xue Ba wasted not a single moment,
But went and fetched Sir Guo from the Western Prison.
  Let's not sing about the long streets and short lanes —
Guo Huai was escorted through the Zhengyang Gate.
The ushers summoned him and then led him inside,
Straight up to the golden steps, to see His Majesty.
  The emperor immediately addressed him as follows:
"You have committed grave crimes in the palace!
You have ruined the mother who gave birth to Us:
You'll be cooked in a vat of oil for that mortal sin!"
  Guo Huai then answered in the following manner:
"Your Majesty, please be so kind as to listen to me.
I could not bear the many thousand kinds of suffering,
As they bitterly tortured me to extract a confession.
  Don't read that false confession extracted from me —
That is all stupid nonsense, and nothing in it is true.
I could only confess to whatever they wanted,
In order to save myself from suffering in prison."
  The emperor thereupon was filled with frustration:
How was he going to handle this case, in what way?
Once again he had recanted his confession here in court,
It seemed that this contested confession wasn't true.
  In front of the hall Judge Bao spoke as follows:
"Your Majesty, be so kind as to listen to my words.
String Guo Huai up in the house of gardener Zhang,
And by tomorrow you will know false from true."
  The emperor acted according to his minister's advice,
And Guo Huai was led away from the golden steps.
Let's not sing about how they traveled on the road —
They soon arrived at the house of gardener Zhang.

When Dong Chao lifted his head to have a good look,
The bare pear trees offered him a desolate spectacle.
The buildings, courtyards, and walls had collapsed,
So they had to sit down below a withered pine tree.

Dong Chao's eyes were filled with tears on thinking
How the whole Zhang family had wrongly been killed.
The trees were still there, growing as in earlier days,
But the man who had planted the trees now was gone.

The hemp rope was fastened to the withered pine,
And Guo Huai was strung up by the side of the tree.

The red disk was sinking in the west, it turned to evening;
The jade hare was rising in the east, brighter and brighter.
All around, from all directions a deep darkness descended,
While the nine-curved Yellow River displayed its stars.[28]

The three thousand bright maidens returned to the palace,
The eight hundred pampered beauties all lit their lamps.
The four hundred military garrisons fastened the locks,
And the over seventy districts all closed their city gates.

When the five points of the first watch had been sounded,
The drums continued to beat throughout the second watch.
When the drums were beating the third watch at midnight,
The stars turned their signs during the double hour of *zi*.[29]

Judge Bao thereupon prayed to both Heaven and Earth,
He prayed to the gods of heaven and those of the earth:
"Allow me to borrow a whirlwind and lend me its force,
To help the emperor to recognize his own true mother."

As soon as Judge Bao had finished reciting his prayer,
All gods in heaven and on earth were suddenly startled.

A weird whirlwind shook even rocks with its force;
The dragon kings of the oceans brought black clouds.
The clouds covered the stars and moon in the sky,
It was impossible to see a man right before your eyes.

It lifted all the tiles of the roofs of people's houses,
And in the streams it created thousands of layers of waves.

---

[28] The Yellow River was believed to continue in the far west as the Heavenly River (the Milky Way).

[29] *Zi* refers to the double hour of midnight, from roughly 11 pm to roughly 1 am.

In big trees the branches were broken by the wind,
Little trees were ripped from the earth with their roots.

If we return to the subject of that person Guo Huai,
That twister for all its force did not blow him away.
And as soon as he saw that the whirlwind had passed,
He heard voices below the steps reporting their presence.
    On both sides, lanterns spread their light all around;
A single bright moon dazzled with the light of the sun.
Ghostly soldiers carried sabers like flashing lightning,
Divine troops wielded sharp swords shining as silver.
    Buffalo-headed and horse-faced demons announced
The arrival of His Imperial Majesty King Yama![30]
Once yakshas[31] had pitched a tent made of yellow gauze,
His Majesty King Yama descended from his mount.

Speak:

King Yama said: "Associate judge, were all eighteen members of the Zhang family fated to die?" The associate judge reported to King Yama: "Yes, they were fated to die." Then he asked: "Is Guo Huai fated to die?" The associate judge reported to King Yama: "He is not fated to die. He still has six years of great prosperity."

Sing:

Truly, as soon as the Son of Heaven started to speak,
King Yama brought up the issue of the fate of Sir Guo.
But when Guo heard the words of the associate judge,
He repeatedly exclaimed: "That's too good to be true!
    If I can live on for another six years in this world,
This place will be a completely different universe.
No need to fear Chancellor Bao of the Southern Office!
He isn't worth the dust below the soles of my shoes!"

Speak:

King Yama said: "I smell the stench of a living human being." A yaksha replied: "King Yama, there's someone strung up on that tree." The Great King said: "Yaksha, take him down."

---

[30] King Yama is the god of the underworld and the chief judge of the ten underworld courts.
[31] Yakshas are ferocious demons.

Sing:

The yaksha thereupon walked up to the withered tree,
And he let Sir Guo down from the tree to the ground.
He took him to the tent, and there Guo bowed down.
Upon seeing him, the Great King asked these questions:
    "In which district and which place do you live, and
For what cause have you been strung up in this tree?"
Guo Huai told him the whole story, from the beginning:
"Your Majesty, please be so kind as to listen to my words.
    My name is Guo Huai and I live in the Eastern Capital,
I'm the famous grand commissioner of the Six-Palaces.
It is all because of the business of Empress Liu that I
Have been strung up in this withered tree and suffer."

Speak:

The Great King said: "Guo Huai, you still have six years of great prosperity."
Guo Huai prayed to the Great King, saying: "May Your Majesty clear this
wrong and resolve this issue. When this business is over, I will tell Empress
Liu to perform limitless services as an expression of gratitude." The Great
King questioned Guo Huai: "Now tell me everything as it has happened."
Questioned like this, Guo Huai replied: "It was Empress Liu! She became
jealous, and I made the mistake of joining her in her evil scheme. In the
Western Palace I took away the crown prince of that stupid Concubine Li,
and then I made the mistake of accusing her to the True Ancestor. The
latter then condemned that stupid Concubine Li to the Cold Palace. It was
all my mistake if day in and day out she suffered all those many bitter
hardships."

Sing:

As he told them one fact, they wrote down that fact,
Each word he confessed was written down as confession.
Eventually his confession filled one full sheet of paper,
And then Guo Huai was loudly ordered to shut up.
    Now King Yama was actually the true Son of Heaven,
And the associate judge was the man surnamed Bao.
The green-faced yakshas and the white-faced ghosts
Were people under the command of old geezer Bao.
    The Son of Heaven went back and returned to the palace,
Judge Bao and his men returned to the Kaifeng Office.

Fig. 3.2

Upper picture: Questioning Guo Huai in the disguise of King Yama.

Lower picture: Rescriptor Bao introduces the emperor to his mother.

At the fifth watch's third point the King ascended the hall,
At the fifth watch's fourth point the ministers assembled.
The civil and military officials came to see the emperor,
Arranged before the golden steps, they stood motionless.

   They were joined by that pure official, Chancellor Bao,
Who with twenty-four bows greeted his gracious ruler.
When the Son of Heaven hastily lifted his head to look,
[He said:] "Minister Bao, please be so kind as to listen.

   Empress Liu is not the mother who gave birth to Us —
So where is my own true mother staying at present?"
Judge Bao stepped forward and once again reported:
"Your Majesty My King, please be so kind as to listen.

   One only sees a son who goes out to look for his mother,
One never sees a mother who goes out to meet her son."
The emperor fully adhered to the advice of his minister,
And his carriage was readied to go to the Kaifeng Office.

   Three cracks of the whip, and the carriage departed;
Riding his carriage the lord and king left the palace.
To his left and right the civil and military officials;
Surrounded by his crowding guards he left the Inside.[32]

The chancellor to the left
   And the chancellor to the right
      Closely followed the imperial carriage;
The nine ministers
   And the ten governors
      Walked behind their enlightened ruler.
Gowns with a hundred flowers,
   Belts studded with jade:
      The commanders in front of the hall;
Wearing high helmets,
   Clad in armor of gold:
      The troops in the front and in the rear.
Melon-staffs of gold,
   Melon-staffs of silver:
      Branch-like stretched, cudgel-like planted;

---

[32] The Inside refers to the Inner Palace, which is reserved for the emperor and his women.

Groups of golden lances,
    Groups of silver lances:
        The common troops of the imperial guard.
Now a larger group,
    Then a smaller group:
        On both sides preceding the carriage;
Officers in front of the hall,
    Officers behind the hall:
        Following the carriage all along the way.
The commissioners for tents
    And the commissioners for food:
        First clearing the road for His Majesty;
The assisting officials in front
    And the assisting officials in the rear
        Guiding and leading the many dignitaries.
Above his head was held
    One large umbrella
        Of pure yellow gauze, encrusted with pearls;
Seated in a gilded
    Carriage of white jade
        The enlightened ruler went on an excursion.

Under an umbrella of yellow gauze the Humane Ancestor,
Under an umbrella of purple gauze the queen of the nation:
In a little while they quickly arrived at the Kaifeng Office,
Where His Excellency welcomed the enlightened emperor.
    As the son arrived to greet and bow in front of his mother,
Flowers bloomed on the withered tree, experiencing spring.
Her Majesty the empress-dowager wept most copiously,
And His Majesty the emperor was also weeping hot tears.
    "While I was the Son of Heaven in the Golden Bells Hall,
I didn't know that you, my mother, suffered such hardship!
May I ask you, my mother, to step into this easy carriage —
An umbrella of pearls will cover you, the nation's mother!"
    Three hundred officials, walking in the front and in the rear,
Closely surrounded Her Majesty as she set out on her trip.
The emperor at this time asked his officials for advice:
"Civil officials and military officers, please listen to Us.

That damned Empress Liu acted without any principle —
Should she be expelled from the palace for her crime?"
Judge Bao stepped forward at that time and spoke thusly:
"Your Majesty My King, please be so kind as to listen."

Speak:

Judge Bao said: "My King, the law does not know of a sword with which
to behead a Son of Heaven or a vat of oil in which to boil an empress. If
one drop of their hot blood falls on the earth, a great drought of three
years will follow! Show consideration for the common people — My King
will be in danger too! If Your Majesty wants to do away with that person,
have her strangulated with a piece of white silk of one rod and two feet in
length, and send her to the flower garden in the rear, so her hot blood will
not fall on the earth. Guo Huai deserves to be boiled alive in a vat of oil."

Sing:

The emperor then acted on the advice of his ministers,
Ordering that Guo Huai be boiled alive in a vat of oil.
When the chief investigative censor received that order,
He didn't dare procrastinate or stay behind forever.
  Guo Huai was brought back to the imperial prison,
To be boiled in hot oil till he had turned into pulp.
The executioner, wielding his sword, addressed him,
Addressed him loudly in the following way: "Sir Guo,
  It's not because the emperor wants to boil you alive,
It's because you made the wrong decisions long ago.
You deemed the office of grand commissioner too small,
Even though it was gold when walking, gold when sitting.
  Having received the King's orders, I urge you once more:
Do not make any accusations down in the world of shades!"

The emperor summoned a eunuch, not wasting a moment,
And he explained the circumstances of the imperial edict:
"Go to the Rear Palace and summon for us Empress Liu,
She'll be ordered to die by strangulation without reprieve."
  His own mother immediately addressed him as follows:
"My lord and King, please be so kind as to listen to me.

After I had given birth to you here inside the palace,
I was separated from you, my son, after only three days.
Each and every day you drank three times at her breast,
For three years you received her favors as she fed you.

Out of consideration for your own mother I beg you
To pardon the person surnamed Liu in the Rear Palace.
My only wish is that you, my son, may rule for ever —
The divinities can testify to the sincerity of my feelings."

When the emperor saw his mother speak in this way,
He lowered his head for quite a while, not saying a word.
"If We would not act according to the advice of my mother,
We would upset Our dear mother, and be an unfilial son.

And even if it would be permissible to upset Our mother,
We would still cause Our officials to hate and despise Us."
He thereupon issued an edict pardoning a single person,
Pardoning the person surnamed Liu in the Rear Palace.

He asked the pure official Chancellor Bao to approach,
And appointed him by his own brush as prime minister.
He appointed him as the military governor of the world,
And he also promoted him to the rank of palace grandee.[33]

"We will hold your hand, we'll sit next to each other:
You will also be Grandee Bao who supports heaven!"
His Excellency bowed down in front of the golden steps,
Thanking the emperor for his grace — twenty-four bows.

Taking leave of his King, Judge Bao returned to his office,
So let's return to Her Majesty the empress-dowager.
Her Majesty the empress returned to the Rear Palace,
To the Rear Palace, to see the person surnamed Liu.

When Empress Liu greeted Empress-dowager Li,
She walked up to her and bowed down without end.
Elder sister and younger sister met each other again:
After twenty years of separation they were reunited.

They shared their food and drink, sitting together;
They slept together, sharing a bed, just like a couple.
In earlier days their enmity was as heavy as a mountain,
But it turned into a loving friendship as deep as the sea.

---

[33] Palace grandee is a lame translation for "the person who lifts the curtain in front of the palace," which I take to refer to the person who at the behest of the emperor announces the formal beginning of a court audience by lifting the curtain in front of the throne.

If you harm someone else, you will harm yourself —
His evil heart caused the ruin of that eunuch Guo Huai.
By treating Empress-dowager Li as her benefactor,
She repaid with this love the enlightened ruler Zhao.
 Pure and enlightened, proper and straight: Judge Bao;
Coveting money and taking bribes: the man called Wang.

I urge you, gentlemen, never to commit any injustice,
Never employ evil schemes in order to ruin other people.
If you secretly harm others, people may fail to see it,
But there are always divinities who witness your deeds.
 Three feet from the earth, they observe you from the air:
Fool other people as you may, but the gods are there.
The three luminaries of heaven and earth shine on you:
The sun, the moon, and the stars that witness your deeds.
 People in this world should do good deeds in secret,
Never employ evil schemes to secretly harm other people.
A talented poet composed this fine ballad narrative;
Intelligent gentlemen, make sure to listen to this tale.
 Those with a traitorous heart will rein in their heart,
Those who rein in their heart learn from Empress Li.
As soon as the heart generates a single good thought,
You immediately become the Thus-Come Buddha![34]
 No need to keep the fasts at all and accept the precepts:
Please consider your own thoughts very carefully.
This good tale of the emperor recognizing his mother
Will never deceive you, not in the slightest detail!

> *Clear Heaven, transparent and blue, cannot be deceived:*
> *It knows your thoughts before you have formed them.*
> *Good and evil in the end will all have their retribution,*
> *The only difference is whether it comes early or late.*

Newly Printed, Completely Illustrated, in Prose and in Verse: The Tale of the Humane Ancestor Recognizing his Mother, The End.

---

[34] Thus-Come is an ancient epithet for the Buddha.

Zhu Yixuan (ed.) (1997). *Ming Chenghu shuochang cihua congkan*, Zhengzhou: Zhongzhou guji chubanshe, pp. 142–158.

Dragon-Design Bao Sentences the White Weretiger

Newly Composed in Verse and in Prose

From the time when Pangu opened up heaven and earth,[1]
There have been many emperors and also many ministers.
Many Sons of Heaven were in possession of the Way,
But there were also many rulers who had lost the Way.
  The Great Progenitor, the Great Ancestor, the True Ancestor —
The fourth emperor, Humane Ancestor, abided by the Way.
For forty-two years a lord in possession of the Mandate;
Assisted by buddhas, dispatched by devas, ruling the people.
  When a king abides by the Way, the ministers have virtue,
To this very day his court produces many men who are wise:
Among civil officials, we only mention His Excellency Bao,
Among military officers, we mention those surnamed Yang.
  His Imperial Majesty pure and righteous, the ministers wise:
In all eight directions there is no war — no more bloody battles.
The small states in foreign lands enter court to offer tribute,
The whole wide world has no worry and enjoys Great Peace.
  Fishermen present treasures found in the Eastern Ocean,
And hunters present a unicorn caught in the mountains.

Dragon-Design Bao is as righteous and clear as autumn floods,
During daytime, a judge in this world, at night, in the other.
When people commit a crime and end up in Bao's hands,
He pulls out the tree with its branches to get at the roots.

---

[1] According to an ancient myth, the world was created out of the body of the deceased giant Pangu.

Thirty-six criminal cases that offered no clue or lead
All were correctly solved and sentenced by Judge Bao.
Let's not talk of the righteous purity of Dragon-Design Bao,
Let's change the topic and first tell about someone else.

There lived a very rich man by the name of Millionaire Shen,
The family was wealthy and noble, rich in gold and silver.
His offspring were only one son and one daughter —
He had only been blessed with a single son and heir!

The name chosen for him was Yuanhua; he was smart,
So they sent him to school where he studied the books.
And when later on he had grown to the age of sixteen,
He fully grasped the Nine Classics and the *Three Tactics*.[2]

After First Night and the New Year Festival had passed,[3]
He went, in the Second Month, out for a springtime walk.

When he arrived in the city and saw all sights and scenes,
Crowds were thronging the six streets and three markets.
When he had made his way through that bustling crowd,
He saw a conspicuous yellow poster he could not miss.

On that poster no other announcement was made but
That of the Humane Ancestor, ruling in possession of the Way,
On the third of the Third Month would hold examinations,
And summoned all students of books throughout the world!

When Yuanhua saw this, his heart was filled with joy, as he
Wanted to jump across the Dragon Gate by use of his brush.
"If I obtain only a single office or even half an appointment,
I will be able to change our status to that of a noble house!"

When his father and mother heard this, they were annoyed:
"My dear son, please do not leave in search of some office!
Our offspring are only one son and one daughter, so
On whom are we to rely now that we have reached old age?"

But Yuanhua was fully determined that he wanted to go,
So he stepped forward and addressed his parents as follows:
"At the most, it will take one year; if shorter, only six months,
So please do not worry too much and think of me always."

His parents, despite all attempts, could not make him stay,
And they allowed their son to trek to the Eastern Capital.

---

[2] *Three Tactics* is the title of a military treatise.
[3] First Night is the first night of a full moon, on the fifteenth of the First Month. It was
celebrated with the Lantern Festival and marked the end of the New Year festivities.

Once Yuanhua had obtained this permission of his father,
He dressed himself for his journey and was ready to leave.
    In front of the hall he bowed to say goodbye to his parents;
And his father and mother shed tears in great profusion.
His parents repeatedly warned him with great urgency
That he had to be very careful on mountain-road stretches.
    "To retire early and depart at dawn — that is number one,
And don't be one of those who desire flowers and love sex.[4]
When you have obtained one post or half an appointment,
Come back home and we'll bring in a bride as your wife."
    When Yuanhua heard these words of advice from his father,
He carefully memorized each and every one of them, and
Then he turned around, and once again took his leave, as
His heart and mind were all set to depart on his journey.

When he had been on the road for quite a number of days,
Gradually, he came closer to a densely wooded mountain.
When he saw how high this mountain was, he concluded:
"The mountain forest must be the perfect place for robbers!"
    The name of this mountain was Precious Cloud Mountain,
The mountain's peak tore the clouds apart on its sides.
Yuanhua was secretly overcome by fear in his heart, but
Ahead of him there was no inn, and behind him no village!
    The very moment our student was vexed by these worries,
He lifted his head and espied the gate of a temple building.
Above the gate an inscription, written in gold, proclaimed:
"His Majesty the Great King who Subjugates Tigers."
    When Yuanhua walked over and entered the temple,
The Great King's awesome might truly terrified him.
But our student nevertheless decided to rest here a while,
He would spend the night here and wait for break of dawn.
    In his mind Yuanhua was secretly filled with apprehension:
A gust of a freak whirlwind suddenly entered the temple.
And when the wind had passed, it promptly started to rain,
And, following that, he noticed a beautiful young maiden.
    One moment she wept and one moment she laughed —
She had clearly deliberately come to meet with our student.

---

[4] "Wild flowers" are a conventional metaphor for prostitutes and courtesans.

The student thereupon addressed her in the following way:
"Dear young lady, of what family may you be a daughter?"
  The girl greeted him in a very soft voice, and she said:
Dear sir, please listen to what I will have to tell you.
I've lived all my life here on Precious Cloud Mountain,
And I was born and raised in the house of the Bai family.[5]
  But alas, my own mother died long ago, at an early age;
My father brought a second wife home as my stepmother.
I have now reached the tender age of sixteen years, but
My stepmother does nothing but beat me and curse me.
  I wanted to go to the house of my mother's mother, but
It is now quite late and the dusk is turning to darkness.
So I would like to rest here in this temple for the night,
And then tomorrow morning I will go to my grandmother."
  She then also asked: "Dear sir, and where do you live?
And do you already have a wife who keeps you company?"
Our student then answered her in the following manner:
"Dear girl, now listen to what I am going to tell you.
  I am in fact, if you want to know, a son of the Shen family,
My family is wealthy and noble, rich in gold and silver.
At present Our King is going to administer examinations,
So I want to jump across the Dragon Gate with my brush.
  I have reached the age of sixteen years this year and
We have not yet brought in a bride who will be my wife."
When the girl heard him tell this, she was filled with joy:
"This is eight- or nine-tenths of what I had hoped for!"
  "Dear sir, if you do not reject me as being too ugly,
I'd like to be the one who shares your bed and cushion!
Let's ask the Great King to be matchmaker and witness —
Dear sir, let me know what do you think of such an idea?"
  When our student heard this, his heart was filled with joy:
Such a beautiful young maiden was really exceptional!
He remembered the instructions of his father and mother,
Who had told him not to agree to a marriage in a temple.
  But because he saw how pretty this girl turned out to be,
Without any equal in this world, a face surpassing others,

---

[5] The Chinese surname Bai is written with the character for *bai* (white).

[He thought:] "If I let this opportunity slip by tonight,
I will never be able to meet this kind of woman again!"
    Our student then spoke to her, agreeing to her proposal,
And husband and wife spent one night together till dawn.
And when the girl had finished her hairdo and her toilette,
The student also got dressed for the trip and they set out.
    Husband and wife, the two of them, were filled with joy,
On the long and distant road this made for a pleasant trip.
But let's not sing of the daily stretches of their journey —
Eventually the two of them arrived at the Eastern Capital.

The student and the girl entered the gate of the city, and
Took lodging in a tea shop and slept till the next morning.
When the two of them woke up, they sat down in the shop
And had breakfast: one bowl of soup, three cups of wine.
    But let's not sing of the student and the girl sitting there —
Let's change the topic and sing of someone else: [a priest.]
When our student was invited by him, he hastily replied;
He hastily made a slight bow to greet the Daoist abbot.
    The abbot then addressed him in the following manner:
"Dear sir, please listen carefully to the words I will say.
If I invite you today, it is for no other purpose or reason,
But to come with me to my temple and have some tea."
    The student thereupon addressed the girl, and he said:
"I will go along with the abbot for a springtime walk."
The abbot walked in front, and the student followed —
"Please, let's go to the abbot's room and have some tea."
    The abbot then addressed him in the following manner:
"Dear sir, on what business did you come to the capital?"
The student thereupon answered in the following way:
"Dear abbot, please listen to what I will have to say.
    I am in fact, if you want to know, a son of the Shen family,
My parents are, since generations ago, rich in gold and silver.
I learned that Our King is going to administer examinations,
So I want to jump across the Dragon Gate with my brush."
    When the abbot had heard this, he said: "That's wonderful!
But, sir, now please listen to what I have to tell to you.
I see that you are looking great and have all the signs
To become at some later date a duke or high dignitary.

Now sir, if you are willing to listen to what I will say,
I'll save your life from a certain and imminent destruction.
Now be honest with me: what's your wife's natal home?
Please tell me the facts, in all detail, from the beginning!"
			Questioned like this, the student replied in these words:
"Dear abbot, please listen to what I will have to tell you.
I came to this place in the hope of winning an office,
And while on the road, I met with this beautiful creature."
			When the abbot saw he replied in an honest fashion,
He enlightened the student completely, as he told him:
"In your eyes, your wife looks like a very pretty woman,
But her body is actually that of a white tiger demon.
			High on the peaks of Precious Cloud Mountain, she has
Been killing men for thousands, ten thousands of years!"
When the student heard the abbot's words, he begged:
"Dear abbot, please save my life with your magical power!
			Indeed, when on my journey I had arrived at that place,
I lodged in the Temple of the King who Subjugates Tigers.
When I had slept in that temple till after dusk had fallen,
A freak whirlwind and violent rain woke me up again.
			The girl then also sought lodging there in the temple,
And attracted by passion and sex, my heart was moved.
Because of our mutual love, we became man and wife;
Without matchmaker or witness we became a couple."
			When the abbot heard him give this account, he said:
"Dear sir, you really acted in a very unintelligent way!
That tiger demon changes into the shape of a woman;
It transforms its original form in order to devour men.
			It is only waiting for you to obtain some office or rank,
And then it will secretly devour you, both life and soul.
Then it will borrow your body to assume your office,
And nobody will know that it's actually an evil demon."
			Hearing this, the student lowered his head and bowed,
So scared that his whole body was soaked by his sweat:
"Dear abbot, I pray you, please show some compassion,
And save my miserable life, both my life and my soul!
			If I later obtain some office or even half an appointment,
I will never forget your favor as long as I will live!"

The abbot then addressed him in the following way:
"Dear sir, please listen to the words I have to say.
    The white tiger demon has great supernatural powers,
Its numerous transformations are beyond description.
Because I want to save your life from great danger,
I will give you a numinous amulet that you must use.
    You have to take this amulet with you back to the inn,
But on no account should you let the monster know.
Wait till tonight when the demon has soundly fallen asleep,
Then burn the amulet and it will show its true shape.
    When you have seen that its original shape is a tiger,
I'll eradicate this danger first thing tomorrow morning."
The student expressed his gratitude to abbot Zhang,
And he hid the amulet he had received on his body.

The student took his leave and returned to the inn,
He hurried as fast as he could, and arrived back at the inn.
But alas, that tiger demon had great supernatural powers,
And, back at the teashop, already knew everything:
    "How intolerable that Daoist priest Zhang at his temple!
How dare he come and instruct my husband to kill me!
The love of husband and wife has not yet been satisfied,
But once that love is satisfied, I will definitely devour him!
    Devouring my husband, however, is just the beginning:
I will then transform myself into the shape of my man.
In that shape I will wait for an appointment by the court,
For an appointment somewhere, in charge of the people.
    And once I will have been appointed by the court,
I will in some distant prefecture devour the country folks.
But that priest Zhang in his Temple of Heavenly Blessing
Has to intervene with his babbling and wants to kill me!
    Man may indeed harbor no intention to harm the tiger,
But only in the case the tiger does not harm other people —
For today I will not devour my own dear darling husband,
But I will devour that abbot, that man surnamed Zhang!"
    When the girl secretly conceived this evil intention,
She saw her husband come in, back from his outing.

Fig. 4.1
Abbot Zhang and the white weretiger battle each other, riding the clouds.

She welcomed him with a smile, [and then she asked him:]
"Where did you go to that you come back now?
   When this morning that abbot of some temple invited you,
What kind of business did he want to discuss with you?"
The student then addressed her in the following manner:
"He asked me about policy issues at the imperial court."
   The girl actually already knew all about it in secret,
But she wasn't going to let anything out to her husband.
When they had been sitting together till dusk was falling,
The student still recited his books by the light of a lamp.
   The girl knew perfectly well what her husband was up to,
So she said to her husband: "Now please listen to me.
I will go to bed and try to get some sleep; once
I have had some sleep, I'll be even smarter in bed."
   But the girl never once closed her eyes for a minute,
Because she was secretly guarding against his designs.
Her husband was so sleepy he could no longer stay up,
And once he decided to sleep, he extinguished the lamp.
   When he had extinguished the lamp and gone to bed,
He saw no demon shape, could not thus learn the truth.
But when the girl saw her husband sleeping so soundly,
She slipped away and stepped down from their couch.
   "How intolerable that Daoist priest Zhang in his temple!
He wants to murder me with the amulet he has written!
Today I will refrain from hurting my lord and master,
And first devour that abbot, that man surnamed Zhang!"

The girl then employed her great supernatural powers,
And changing her shape she then rode on the clouds.
Riding the clouds to the Temple of Heavenly Blessing,
She looked for its abbot, that man surnamed Zhang.
   The abbot was seated in his room at that very moment,
Reciting the books of the Way in a booming voice.
When suddenly he heard a freak whirlwind rushing in,
The abbot's body was promptly covered in cold sweat.
   He thereupon immediately started to work his magic,
Pulling out his hat pins and holding them in his hands.
Spitting out a mouthful of holy water, he said: "Change,"
And his hand held a divine lance of one rod two feet!

Next he threw incense ashes all over on the ground,
And black clouds rose up that carried the abbot aloft.
When the tiger demon saw the temple abbot approaching,
She resumed her original shape in order to devour him.

The temple abbot promptly made use of his lance,
While the tiger demon tried her best to devour him.
Atop the clouds the two of them battled in magic, but
After three or four rounds no winner had been decided.

Even though the abbot's magical powers were great,
The supernatural powers of the tiger were far greater.
After they had fought for more than ten rounds,
The abbot's capacities turned out to be falling short.

The priest had no option but to turn around and flee;
As fast as he could, he returned to the abbot's room.
He entered the room in order to hide himself there,
But the tiger demon pursued him, showing no mercy.

As fast as she could, she followed him into the room,
And there grabbed the abbot, the man surnamed Zhang.
"The Top-of-the-List and I lived as husband and wife,
What matter is it of yours that you wanted to kill me?

This trouble arises only because you couldn't keep silent,
Your vexations all follow from your own interference.
If man has no intention to harm the tiger, so is the rule,
The tiger lacks the evil intent to eat innocent people.

So today I will not murder my husband and master,
For the time being I will only eat you as a little snack."
Holding his neck in her maws, she strongly shook him,
And all his ceremonial gowns fell off, slid to the floor.

She thereupon devoured the abbot's complete body,
Only leaving the head and the arms and legs behind.
The tiger demon ate so much that she was quite satisfied,
And when she had eaten her enemy, she slipped away.

Riding auspicious clouds she returned to her husband,
As on the drum tower the fourth watch was sounded.
When the girl saw her husband sleeping quite soundly,
She conceived of a trick as she spoke to her husband:

"Tonight I couldn't sleep all through the long night;
Five times I got up, I couldn't find any rest or peace.
I went out and devoured the raw flesh of the abbot,
So I'm afraid my man and master might be enraged.

When they find in the temple that Zhang is missing,
The court case is bound to create trouble for people.
I'll go and inform His Excellency Dragon-Design Bao,
Out of fear that you, my husband, will be implicated.

You had better as soon as possible have a good plan —
I'll ride on the clouds back to Precious Cloud Mountain.
As before I will run and return to the mountain rocks,
And safely hide in a grotto somewhere on the mountain."

Let's not talk about the girl, who returned to the mountain,
Let's change the topic — listen as I sing of the student.
When he had slept till the fifth watch, when the sun arose,
He didn't find the beautiful maiden anymore in his room.

When he got up and didn't find his darling wife anymore,
He had no idea at all where she might have gone off to.
He left his room and then spoke to the manager, saying:
"My darling wife has somehow disappeared last night.

Now dear Mr. Manager, I have something to tell you,
Dear Mr. Manager, please listen to the words I will say.
That priest Zhang of the Temple of Heavenly Blessing —
That man really possesses outstanding magical powers!

When painting a dragon or tiger, it's hard to do the bones;
When you know a person, you know his face, not his heart.
When a few days ago he passed in front of this shop,
He saw the exceptional beauty of my dear darling wife.

This man must have fallen in love with my darling wife,
And he must have snatched her away, without a trace.
But in his room at the temple he wrote an amulet for me,
And told me that my dear darling wife was a tiger demon.

He coveted my darling wife because she was so pretty —
It was that man who was led astray by his evil desires!
I'll draft an accusation to submit to His Excellency Bao,
I want to find out what happened to my darling wife!"

The inn's owner thereupon spoke to the student, saying:
"He is a proper and upright man who practices cultivation!
How would he be willing to cheat you out of your wife?
Dear sir, please wait a while, have a little more patience!"

Let's not sing for the time being about our student, but
Change the topic and sing about another group of people.
Listen as I sing about that Daoist Zhang who at his temple
Had died a cruel death without any cause or reason.

Each night in the fifth watch, as bell and drum resounded,
The temple's priests opened the gate and recited their books.
They all assembled in the dining hall of the temple, but
How come they did not see the abbot amongst them?

He must still be in his room, sunk in a deep sleep, so
His acolyte went over to invite the abbot to join them.
The abbot had an acolyte who had the surname of Lu,
And he went over to the abbot's room to invite him.

He called a number of times, but heard no answer at all,
But how horrible! Blood was flowing all over the ground!
When the acolyte stretched out his hand to feel around,
He found by feeling a head with which he held in his hands.

He carefully mulled this matter in his mind, thinking:
"How can one make sense of this terrible disaster?
Only the head and the limbs of my master are left,
And there is no sign of where his body may have gone!"

Upon careful consideration the acolyte at this time
Did not return to the dining hall and inform the others.
Because he was covered all over his body with blood,
He fled back to his own family to hide himself there.

Let's not talk about this acolyte, fleeing back home —
By and by the day had progressed to the hour of noon.
Because the other priests still did not see the abbot,
They went to his room to see what might be going on.

As soon as these priests had one look inside the room,
They were so scared that their souls left their bodies!
They saw that the room was all covered with blood,
But they had no clue at all who the murderer might be.

They only found the abbot's head, his arms and legs,
And they had no clue where his body might have gone.
When they looked for the acolyte, he had disappeared,
So who could it be who has killed our dear abbot?

It had to be the acolyte who had killed the abbot,
Who had stolen his money and made himself scarce!
When the priests had seen this, they were dumbstruck,
And decided they must go to court to report the crime.

When the assembled priests had written a statement,
They submitted it to His Honor Dragon-Design Bao.
In reporting the murder at the monastery, they stated
That their abbot had been killed by his own acolyte!

The acolyte had his domicile in Bamboo-Pole Alley;
Surnamed Lu, he had been with the abbot since youth.
"We hope that Your Honor will accept this statement,
As our abbot died a cruel death without any reason."

When Dragon-Design Bao received this case statement,
He promptly produced a warrant for the arrest of this guy.
He then dispatched Zhang Long and also Li Hu, saying:
"You are not allowed to tarry, you cannot procrastinate!

Go as fast as you can to that Bamboo-Pole Alley, and
Quickly arrest that acolyte who carries the surname Lu!"
When the two of them had arrested that acolyte Lu,
They took him to the prefecture to present to Judge Bao.

Dragon-Design Bao cursed him in the following words:
"In what manner and why did you kill your own abbot?
For how many years had you served your master? And
What was your reason for perpetrating this murder?"

The acolyte piteously wept as he made his statement:
"Your Honor, please still your rage and halt your anger!
I have been serving my revered teacher for ten years,
And I never conceived an intention to kill the abbot.

I have no clue at all who may have murdered the man —
May your bright mirror bring about a clear verdict!"
His Excellency was filled with rage at this point,
And promptly ordered Zhang Long and also Li Hu

To take him to prison for interrogation under torture:
"In this murder case I definitely need a confession!"
Zhang Long and Li Hu did as they were told,
And immediately took the acolyte with them to prison.

Let's not sing of the sufferings of the poor acolyte,
Let's change the topic and sing of someone else again.
Dragon-Design Bao had just taken his seat in the hall —
Listen as I sing of that student seeking out the judge.

The student had also drawn up an official accusation,
In which he named the abbot, the man surnamed Zhang:
"How horrible! This man, bereft of any human decency,
Employed his magic skills to snatch away my dear wife!

I thus humbly beseech Your Honor to issue a warrant,
To summon the abbot, and submit him to interrogation,
So as to free my dear darling wife and return her to me —
May your bright mirror bring about a clear verdict!"
     When Dragon-Design Bao heard this, he faintly smiled:
"There is something quite ridiculous about this case!
     Just a moment ago those priests submitted a statement:
Their abbot, this man surnamed Zhang, was murdered.
I have no clue which of these statements may be true,
So I must clearly establish the facts in this court case."
     Dragon-Design Bao thereupon promptly gave the order
To quickly draw up his escort, and leave by the left gate:
"Let's first investigate the Temple of Heavenly Blessing,
To find out what's true or false, to establish the facts!"
     When Dragon-Design Bao dismounted from his horse,
The priests of the temple came out to welcome him in.
But when Dragon-Design Bao saw the head of the victim,
He only saw the human head, he did not see any body.
     Dragon-Design Bao could only take the head along,
Promptly producing a warrant for the murderer's arrest:
"If it had been the acolyte who committed the murder,
He would have dumped the body, not leaving anything!"
     Dragon-Design Bao hastily returned to the yamen office,
And took his seat in the hall to conduct his interrogation:
"Dear sir, tell me the whole story from the very beginning,
To allow me to clearly establish the facts in this court case."
     The student thereupon stepped forward and spoke:
"Your Honor, please listen to what I have to tell you.
This humble student has reached the age of sixteen, and
My parents had not yet brought in a bride as my wife.
     I was on my way to the Eastern Capital, to seek an office,
And my mind was all set on completing my journey.
When I arrived on my trip at Precious Cloud Mountain,
It was already evening time and dusk was falling.
     The mountain so high, the road still long — I had no lodging,
But then I saw in front of the mountain a temple gate.
I promptly entered the temple to sleep there for the night,
And then I met with this woman who told me her story.

That very night she and I became husband and wife,
And so the two of us arrived here in the Eastern Capital.
All of a sudden I ran into this temple abbot Zhang,
Who told me that my wife was actually a tiger demon!
    He invited me to his temple where he told me this story,
And wrote out an amulet with which I could kill her.
I slept till the fifth watch, only to wake up late, and
At dawn discovered that my darling wife was gone!"
    Dragon-Design Bao said: "This doesn't look good!
But I will have to establish the facts of this court case."
With all due haste he then drafted a written warrant for
The arrest in the mountains of that white tiger demon.
    He then promptly ordered Zhang Long and also Li Hu
To go and make the arrest with due care and diligence:
"Do not endlessly tarry and procrastinate on the road,
But hurry up and depart, and then promptly come back!
    If you manage to make that arrest within three days,
I will reward you with ten ounces of snow-white silver.
But if you cannot make that arrest within three days,
You'll be condemned to serve as sailors in Qingzhou!"

When Zhang Long and Li Hu received this command,
They set out on the road, bringing the warrant with them.
But first they went off to a winehouse to drink some wine,
And the two of them drank till they were drunk as a skunk!
    They did not care whether it was an official or a commoner,
It was all the same: an imperial relative or a superior officer!
Once the two of them were drunk, they opened the warrant —
Not for the arrest of an ordinary commoner on main street!
    They were not to arrest an imperial relative or high officer,
They were to arrest a white tiger, a devilish beastly demon!
Having read this written warrant, the two of them wondered:
How were they going to handle this awkward assignment?
    At that very moment Zhang Long and Li Hu felt at a loss:
There was no road to flee up to heaven, no gate to enter earth!
"We always called His Excellency Bao the Pure and Right,
But it turns out the man is as muddled as a bowl of noodles!
    We have no clue where to find that white tiger, that big beast!
Dragon-Design Bao must be out to torture small people like us!"

The two yamen runners deliberated together in great detail
How on earth they might well arrest this white tiger demon.
    "The best we can do is to hand in again this written warrant —
Let him dispatch two other people to try and make this arrest!"
But when the duo appeared in court to make this request,
Dragon-Design Bao flew into a rage as soon as he saw them.
    "I will spare you this one time and not have you beaten,
Now make the arrest so I can proceed with the interrogation.
If you manage to make the arrest within three full days,
I will reward you for your service with the very best wine."

The two yamen runners were quite annoyed in their hearts,
As again they left the court, carrying the warrant with them.
They had no choice but to set out on their journey, in order
To check the situation out on Precious Cloud Mountain.
    Zhang Long thereupon told Li Hu that they had better
Buy in advance some paper prints and three kinds of meat.
When the two of them arrived at Precious Cloud Mountain,
They there indeed saw the gate leading to a temple hall.
    After burning some bright incense, they lit wax candles
And set out the three plates of meat as offerings to the god.
They also presented a fine jug of wine as a sacrificial gift,
And they begged the god: "Dear Deity, please listen to us!
    We come here with a written warrant of Dragon-Design Bao,
In order to arrest the white tiger, that devilish beastly demon!"
They displayed the written warrant on the altar table, and
The duo fervently prayed, bowing in front of the deity.
    "May Your Majesty display his great numinous power,
And chase that great beastly demon from its mountain lair!"
The two of them continued to bow with lowered heads, saying:
"Your Majesty, please be so kind as to save our lives!
    In case you do allow us to arrest this demon and monster,
We'll throw in our first attempt a sagely sign on the floor.
In case you'll not allow us to arrest this demonic monster,
We'll throw in our first attempt a Yang sign on the floor."
    When they had finished their prayer, they threw the blocks,
And the first throw resulted in a sagely sign on the floor.
When the two of them saw this, they were filled with joy,
And with lowered heads they bowed once again to the King.

When they were finished bowing, they burned the paper gifts,
And took away the plates of food and the jug filled with wine.
The two of them were filled with joy in their hearts, and,
Greatly relieved, they opened the jug and drank their cups.
    The two of them went on drinking till they were drunk;
Totally drunk they collapsed in the gate of the temple hall.
And as they were snoring away there in that temple hall,
The Great King appeared in a dream to the two of them:
    "You've come here at the order of Bao the Pure and Right
In order to arrest that great beastly monster of the mountain.
This great beast has extensive supernatural powers indeed,
Which allow it to transform itself into the shape of a woman.
    A beautiful maiden will soon show up, and when she comes,
You two will have to make sure to arrest her then and there!
But that tiger demon has great supernatural powers indeed —
Once you let her escape, it will be impossible to find her.
    But, now if you spray dog's blood all over her body,[6]
She will be unable to change, despite all her divine powers!"
When Zhang Long and Li Hu woke up with a start,
They still clearly remembered that dream in their heart.
    Li Hu thereupon went to the eastern side of the mountain,
And there he saw a granddad, a man advanced in years.
Li Hu thereupon promptly addressed that man, saying:
"Dear granddad, please listen to the words I will say.
    My colleague and I are from Kaifeng prefecture,
We have been dispatched here by Dragon-Design Bao.
We have come here carrying His Honor's written warrant
For the arrest of the white tiger, that great beastly monster.
    We stay at the Temple of the King who Subjugates Tigers,
But we have to be back in court within three days at most.
The Great King gave a sign that we will make the arrest,
But also said the demon has great supernatural powers.
    If we douse the animal with dog's blood, it cannot change,
Only then will we be able to arrest the monster effectively."
When the granddad heard this, his heart was filled with joy:
"This tiger demon has killed many people in this region.

---

[6] Pig's blood and dog's blood were widely believed to have the power to break magic.

This white tiger monster has many transformations, and
It has devoured thousands, even tens of thousands of people!
A hundred miles around this mountain one finds no trace
Of pig or goat, goose or duck, none is allowed to survive.
    But now, as His Excellency orders its arrest and capture,
The people in all directions will live quietly and in peace.
If you need some dog's blood, you'll get it here and now,
As I will kill my dog with one stroke and give it to you."
    That very moment he killed his dog on the spot,
And the dog's blood he gave to Li Hu to take with him.
Bowing he thanked the granddad, leaving for the temple;
Hastily he set out on the road and made his way back.

In one stretch he arrived on top of the high mountain,
And there he met again with his partner, Zhang Long.
    Li Hu at that time addressed Zhang Long, saying:
"How come that tiger demon has not shown up yet?
I've got the dog's blood right here now with me,
The only thing we can do is to wait and make the arrest!"
    After a while they were indeed visited by a woman,
And it turned out to be a very beautiful young maiden.
Zhang Long and Li Hu wasted no time to arrest her,
They placed that beautiful young maiden under arrest!
    When that woman had been arrested, she cursed them:
"I'm a daughter of the Bai family, east of the mountain.
You have ruined my beautiful make-up and appearance —
I will go to the Eastern Capital and lodge an accusation!"
    Zhang Long and Li Hu, feeling very much annoyed, [said:]
"How intolerable! You woman, you think you can escape?
We have Dragon-Design Bao's written warrant for your arrest;
He wants to interrogate you in his Kaifeng yamen!"
    Hearing this, the woman's heart was filled with rage;
She wanted to transform herself and devour these two men!
When the two of them saw this transformation underway,
Li Hu at this crucial moment kept his wits about him.
    He quickly beat the bamboo container to smithereens,
Dousing her through and through in fresh dog's blood.
When the woman found herself subdued by this blood,
She was incapable of turning herself into a fierce tiger!

With tears pouring from her eyes, she piteously wept:
"The blood has dyed my clothes and polluted my body!
I am a daughter of the Bai family here on the mountain,
So please allow me to go and leave this mountain forest."
    Zhang Long and Li Hu cursed her in the following words:
"You rotten slut! Do you think you could still escape?
How would you ever dare come to this mountain temple,
If you were not the beast that roams these mountains?
    I do not care whether you are young Miss Bai or not —
You will have to appear before His Excellency Judge Bao!"
Li Hu promptly tightly tied her up with a hemp rope,
While the beautiful maiden shed tears in great profusion.
    By the looks of it, he resembled an eagle catching a rabbit:
They left the mountain forest again as fast as they could.
And even though the beautiful maiden had bound feet,
They made haste like a cloud, carrying and pulling her.

The girl at this time conceived of a plan how she might
Escape from these two men, Zhang Long and Li Hu.
She begged them: "Dear Mr. Runners, please listen to me!
Now tell me, how could I be some big beastly monster?
    I'm a daughter of the Bai family here in the mountain,
And will be happy to let you use my jade-white body.
If you set me free here in the clouds on the mountain,
I will express my gratitude with lots of gold and treasure!"
    When the two runners heard her speak to them like this,
They smiled and they nodded, only too eager to comply.
Upon hearing this, the two of them were filled with joy,
And immediately came to a halt, filled with a mad desire.
    In their eyes this woman was extraordinarily beautiful;
She was also willing to let them have their way with her!
Circling mountains and crossing ridges with their warrant
They had suffered thousand, nay, ten thousand sufferings!
    Most likely she was not a devilish demonic monster, and
Dragon-Design Bao would set her free as soon as he saw her!
His Excellency, irascible as he was, would be quite annoyed
And the two of them were bound to be punished anyway.
    So better than wondering whether or not she was a tiger,
They might as well take their pleasure with the girl now!

"As long as your eyes do not see, no desire will be stirred;
When heart and mind are full of joy, the bones are weak."
    Now just as Li Hu was about to untie the hemp ropes,
Conceiving a clever scheme to trick the beautiful maiden,
But before he could finish the words he had begun to say,
A god suddenly manifested himself in the bright sky.
    His body was fully dressed in an armor of yellow gold;
He twirled the divine lance he was holding in his hands,
And he shouted: "You two, do not be deluded by desire,
Do not allow that sexy tiger demon to run off and escape!
    That woman is not a daughter of some common family,
She is no one else but the tiger demon of this mountain.
Once you have untied the ropes that bind her, she
Will work her supernatural powers and flee on a cloud.
    She was trying to bamboozle you with her clever words,
But where would you find her once she had run off?
His Majesty, fearing that she would not submit to you,
Dispatched me to escort you all down the mountain road."
    When Zhang Long had heard the words of this general,
He was so scared he was covered in a cold sweat all over.
"We believed her when she said she was of common stock —
Had she run off, it would have been a very serious crime!"
    When the beautiful girl saw this, she was very much vexed,
Big tears coursed down from her eyes in great profusion.
She might have a mouth, but found it impossible to reply;
Keeping silent she said not a word, made no sound at all!
    Zhang Long marched in front, and Li Hu followed behind;
Pulling and dragging her along, they ran on like a cloud.
Never stopping on the road they traveled for many days,
Escorting her as fast as they could to the Eastern Capital.

Arriving at the prefecture, they wanted to hand her over,
So she could appear before Dragon-Design Bao.
Girls and women all came out to have a look, saying:
"What kind of person might this beautiful girl be?
    These two runners have brought her to this place, so
She must be that monster that committed that crime.
But this woman is indeed quite a beautiful person —
She looks more like the pretty daughter of some family!"

The two runners brought her before the steps of the hall;
Bowing down, they reported to His Highness the Judge.
These two runners addressed him in the following way:
"We have succeeded in arresting that tiger demon!"

When His Excellency lifted his head to have a look,
He loudly cursed the two runners in the following way:
"Why did you fail to summon that big beast here?
What kind of person is that beautiful girl over there?"

"Having received a written warrant from Your Highness,
We arrested this demon at Precious Cloud Mountain.
The Great King who Subjugates Tigers in his great power
Ordered it to change itself into the shape of a woman."

His Excellency could only lean his head to one side,
As he was unsure whether she was the true tiger demon.
Wavering between belief and disbelief, Dragon-Design Bao
Was at that moment mulling the matter over in his mind.

If the white tiger, that big beast, had not been arrested,
He would, without any cause, kill an innocent person.
His Excellency thereupon interrogated them as follows:
"How come you arrested and brought me this maiden?

Bring this girl over here, so I can ask her some questions.
Devilish demon, how dare you devour a human being?
You devoured that Daoist priest Zhang there in his temple:
While you were at peace, you brought suffering to others!

The temple submitted a statement, accusing you, stating
That you had murdered the temple's teacher and abbot.
If you confess your crimes in court, [all is well],
But if you do not confess, you are bound to suffer greatly!"

The beauty was awash in tears and wept most piteously,
Tears coursed down from her eyes as she cried for justice.

And she said: "Your Excellency, you are pure and righteous,
Please listen as I tell you the crime of which I am a victim.
I am a daughter of the Bai family there in the mountain,
And I am not some white tiger demon from the mountain.

Because I was on my way to relatives west of the mountain,
I ran into these two yamen runners in front of the mountain.
Because the two of them noticed that I am quite beautiful,
They immediately were overcome by their wanton desires.

And precisely because there was no one around on that side,
These two violent scoundrels tried to abuse me, to rape me!

They grabbed me and were unwilling to set me free again —
I cried out to Heaven but all in vain, I had no way to flee!
    When I refused to comply, they harbored evil intentions, and
Conceived a fine plot to force me to bend to their wishes.
They said: 'You hussy, if you are not willing to comply,
We'll arrest you and take you to Dragon-Design Judge Bao!'
    That's why they arrested me and brought me to this place,
Where I cannot but defend myself and explain the situation!
Your Excellency, if you believe the story told by the runners,
You will wrongfully rob humble me of my life and my soul.
    I have no grudge or feud with that master of magic methods,
And I have no idea at all where to find his temple and gate.
If you here order me to pay for his life with my own,
The sky lacks its sun — you'll murder an innocent person!"
    His Excellency was overcome by a multitude of doubts:
"How do I arrive at a clear sentence in this murder case?
This woman has, on consideration, a quite convincing story;
It is hard to believe that such a beauty could be a tiger demon!"
    But then His Excellency suddenly hit upon a brilliant idea:
He shouted an order to bring in the student, her husband.
The student hurried to the court hall with all possible haste,
And there he was ordered to identify the beautiful maiden.
    As soon as the beautiful maiden saw the student approaching,
She transformed her appearance so she could not be identified.
His Excellency loudly interrogated the student, telling him:
"At present we have succeeded in locating your wedded wife."
    After the student had carefully scrutinized her, he stated:
"This beautiful maiden, however, is not my wedded wife at all!"
Hearing this, Dragon-Design Bao was very annoyed in his heart,
He beat his table, and loudly voiced his rage and his anger:
    "It is absolutely intolerable how that Zhang Long and Li Hu
Are trying to bamboozle me [by making such a false arrest].
They failed to summon and bring in that big beast from the hills,
But arrested this woman, causing an innocent person to suffer."
    When the woman heard this, her heart was filled with joy;
For a moment her heart was secretly filled with happy joy:
    "Now His Excellency is overcome by a multitude of doubts,
He is bound to set me free and allow me to return to the hills.
I will escape with my miserable life away from the maws of death,
On my mountain I will spend some more years in pleasure."

When His Excellency observed the face of the beautiful maiden,
He noticed the faint smile on the face of that beautiful maiden.
So His Excellency could only mull the matter over once more:
"Could it be that she was that devilish tiger demon after all?

Arrested and brought here to court she displays no vexation,
Because of her supernatural powers she will be able to escape.
It is not permissible yet to set her free and allow her to leave;
Today I must make sure not to allow this person to leave!"

He thereupon ordered the jail warden and prison guards
To shackle her feet and tie up her arms with hemp ropes.
"Disregarding for the moment who is right and who is wrong,
We'll have her locked up in prison as a common criminal!"

As large tears coursed down her cheeks, the woman [cried:]
"Your Excellency, you cause an innocent person to suffer!"
Zhang Long and Li Hu were also taken away by the guards;
All three were locked up together in the same prison cell.

Zhang Long and Li Hu started to curse His Honor Judge Bao:
"His Excellency is as muddleheaded as a bowl of noodles!"
Following that, the two of them started their cursing all over,
This time around they used their words to curse that woman:

"You devilish demon are really capable of cunning tricks,
Telling your fantastical story in a most charming tone of voice!
After a thousand, ten thousand troubles we had arrested you,
Still we were willing to show some mercy and set you free.

But that general clad in golden armor called from the sky,
And stated that you were the very demon that murdered men.
He told the two of us never to set you free and let you escape,
Because you were the white tiger demon there in the hills.

But today you had to come up with this fantastical narrative,
And as a result we are now implicated and have to suffer!"
The beautiful maiden bowed to them, begging as follows:
"Please do not blame me for causing you so much hardship!

My only hope was to escape and return to the mountain,
How could I know that today we would suffer such disaster?
Because I have been covered with dog's blood by you two,
I cannot use my supernatural powers to run away and escape.

But if you help me to be released so I can return to the hills,
I will show you my gratitude with lots of gold and treasure!"
While the three of them were having this prison conversation,
They had no idea someone outside was listening in on them!

When Lord Bao outside the prison had heard what they said,
[He concluded]: "So she is that devilish tiger demon after all!"
The following morning, when the sky had turned bright,
He called for the two runners, to appear in front of the hall:
    "I'm giving you a reward of two hundred strings of cash
And ten jugs of the finest wine, to divide between you.
I appoint you as corporals serving here in the court hall,
Because you managed to arrest and bring in that tiger demon."
    The two yamen runners immediately knelt down to bow,
And after thanking His Lordship with a bow they left the hall.

Dragon-Design Bao thereupon was wondering in his mind
How he might best sentence and execute this devilish demon,
Afraid it might show its supernatural powers when executed,
And through its powers of transformation harm the people.
    Hastily he wrote a report to be transmitted to the Throne,
Reporting to the emperor on the tiger demon to be beheaded.
Bringing his report, Dragon-Design Bao went to the palace, and,
With his ivory tablet before his breast, reported to the emperor.
    When His Majesty saw the report and opened it for reading,
Every character and every column wrote down the true facts:
"In recent days a white tiger from Precious Cloud Mountain
Devoured a local temple abbot, a man surnamed Zhang.
    Your servant had this tiger demon summoned and arrested,
And I beseech Your Majesty to behead this devilish monster.
At present it has transformed itself into the shape of a woman,
And she has been locked up in prison in order to suffer pain."
    His Majesty addressed Chancellor Bao, speaking thusly:
"How best to deal with that big beast with its evil intentions?
If we behead that big beast, it is capable of transformations,
And We fear that it may bring destruction to common folks!"
    His Majesty thought silently for a while, then had a strategy:
"Let's invite the Celestial Master to destroy this tiger demon!"[7]
An imperial edict was hastily sent to invite [the Daoist pope],
And the Celestial Master promptly arrived at the palace gate.

---

[7] The Celestial Masters of the Zhang family, headquartered at Mt. Longhu in Jiangxi, were
the hereditary heads of the Zhengyi Sect of Daoism. Widely renowned for their magical
powers, they enjoyed the patronage of the emperors of the Song and Ming dynasties. In view
of their eminent position in the Daoist church, they are often referred to as the Daoist pope
in earlier Sinological literature.

Fig. 4.2
The Heavenly Master and Dragon-Design Bao sentence the white weretiger.

He bowed down twenty-four times, wishing an eternal life,
Wishing the emperor a myriad of years, as his humble servant.
His Majesty the Humane Ancestor personally ordered him
To be seated on a brocade stool, and then told the situation:
    "The white tiger demon roaming Precious Cloud Mountain,
Has powers of transformation and threatens to harm the people.
It has devoured abbot Zhang in his temple [here in the capital],
But Judge Bao had the demon arrested and locked up in prison.
    If We did not yet dare behead this monster right away today,
It is because We fear that it may frighten the people in the city.
We invited you, Your Holiness, only for the single purpose of
Beheading this devilish demon with the power of your magic!"

The Celestial Master received a personal order of the emperor
To behead the demon in close cooperation with Judge Bao.
The latter invited the Celestial Master with him to his hall,
And after they had had a cup of tea, they discussed the situation.
    The Celestial Master addressed Dragon-Design Bao, saying:
"Where is this devilish demon at present? We will need
To bring in a karmascope, in which she will have to look,[8]
So she can be killed as soon as she changes her appearance."
    Dragon-Design Bao replied: "I have such a thing in the office,
So we will have her manifest her true nature in the karmascope."
He thereupon ordered Zhang Long and also Li Hu
To take the woman from her prison [to the execution ground].
    When she was taken to the execution ground to be beheaded,
The beautiful maiden shed tears, falling in great profusion.
The Master of Magic, the ruler of Heaven's Reed in his hand,[9]
Ordered her to change and assume the shape of a tiger demon.
    Shaking its head the tiger terrified the crowd into fear, and
Whipping its tail it was bound to devour the watching people.
When the yamen runners saw it, they were overcome by fear,
But fortunately there was His Excellency, Dragon-Design Bao!

---

[8] The karmascope, or "mirror of sins", shows the true nature and all sins of the person who looks into it. It is used in the underworld courts to identify and convict sinners.
[9] Heaven's Reed (Tianpeng) is the name of a fierce exorcistic deity. The cult of this deity can be traced from the Song dynasty onward.

He loudly ordered the yamen runners to attack all together,
And its head fell on the ground as soon as it was hit by a sword.
The tiger demon might have great supernatural powers, but
It was no match for the Celestial Master's magical powers!

   The Celestial Master immediately addressed him as follows:
"Let's take this head and present it at the gate of the palace!"
They reported to the court that they had cornered the monster,
And they offered up the tiger's head at the Zhengyang Gate.

   People from all directions flocked together to have a look,
And it has been preserved and transmitted to this very day.
When the emperor saw it, his heart was filled with joy,
And he ordered the Master rewarded in a magnanimous way.

   All civil and military officials at court came to see him off:
The Celestial Master, taking his leave, set out on the road.

Dragon-Design Bao at that time took his seat in the court hall,
And loudly ordered the release of the abbot's acolyte.

   Then he ordered the student brought in for his disposition:
"You have also been in transgression of the regulations!
In vain you studied the books in order to be a gentleman,
But lusting for flowers and sex you failed to be a man.

   You secretly tricked a tiger demon into marrying you,
So the crime you have committed today is quite serious.
Even if you are Top-of-the-List, you will lose your rank,
Degraded to the status of a commoner, forever banished.

   Even if you were an official and had passed the exam,
You would have to go back home for another few years.
Wait for another three years, for later examinations,
Then come back again to jump across the Dragon Gate."

The student, very annoyed, returned to his hometown,
He collected his luggage and went out of the city gate.

   Let's not sing of the stretches he traveled while on the road —
After one stretch he arrived at Shen Family Village.
When he arrived at the gate, he hurriedly walked inside;
He walked into the hall to bow in front of his parents.

   When his parents saw their son falling down from heaven,
[They asked:] "My son, how did you do on the exams?"

Yuanhua greeted his father and addressed him as follows:
"Despite my sufferings on the road, I did not succeed.
     When I arrived on the top of Precious Cloud Mountain,
I met there in the mountains with a white tiger demon.
It had changed itself into a woman and came to join me,
And I took her with me to the capital to take the exams.
     After she devoured abbot Zhang in his temple there,
The Heavenly Master cut off her head, not sparing her.
Judge Bao also reported that I had committed a crime,
And I was found to be a commoner, forever banished."
     When his parents heard this, they answered as follows:
"My dear son, please do not be worried by all of this!
Only what fate predestines you to have, you will have;
If it is not in your fate to have it, don't try and seek it.
     At home you have plenty of gold and silver and treasure,
Enough for you to spend your life in pleasure and ease.
Your father and mother will go and find you a wife,
We will find you a nice young person in this village."
     They brought in a bride as his wife who was smart:
Like a fish in the water, such was their mutual love.
A couple of husband and wife, in pleasure and ease —
That reputation spread through the world for all to know.

I urge you, all you wise and virtuous gentlemen,
Do not imitate those men who lust for flowers and sex!
Now I have sung this book to the very last line, as an
Offering to this esteemed audience to hear and enjoy!

> *Yuanhua, going to the examinations, traveled to the Eastern Capital,*
> *But on White Cloud Mountain he met with a bewitching demon.*
> *Once this demon devoured abbot Zhang*
> *Judge Bao had it summoned and cut off its head.*

Dragon-Design Bao Sentences the White Weretiger, Newly Composed in Verse and Prose, The End.

Zhu Yixuan (ed.) (1997). *Ming Chenghua shuochang cihua congkan*, Zhengzhou: Zhongzhou guji chubanshe, pp. 252–263.

Rescriptor Bao Decides the Case of the Weird Black Pot

Newly Composed, in Prose and in Verse: A Case of Dragon-Design Bao — *The Weird Black Pot*

From the time Pangu opened up heaven and earth,
There have been many emperors and many ministers.
Many Sons of Heaven were in possession of the Way,
But there were also many rulers who had lost the Way
    The Great Progenitor, the Great Ancestor, the True Ancestor —
The fourth emperor, the Humane Ancestor, abided by the Way.
For forty-two years a lord in possession of the Mandate,
Assisted by buddhas, dispatched by devas, ruling the people.
    When a king abides by the Way, the ministers have virtue,
To this very day his court produces many men who are wise:
Among civil officials we only mention His Excellency Bao,
Among military officers we only mention Generalissimo Di.
    His Imperial Majesty pure and righteous, the ministers wise:
No war disturbs the border regions, free of smoke and dust.
The small states in foreign lands enter court to offer tribute,
In all eight directions there is no war, law and order prevail.
    Fishermen present treasures found in the Eastern Ocean;
And hunters present a unicorn caught in the mountains.

Dragon-Design Bao is as righteous and clear as autumn floods,
During daytime a judge in this world, at night in the other.
When people commit a crime and end up in Bao's hands,
He pulls out the tree with its branches to get at the roots.

Thirty-six criminal cases that offered no clue or lead
All were correctly solved and sentenced by Judge Bao.
But let's not talk of the purity of Dragon-Design Bao,
Let's change the topic and first tell about someone else.

Listen to me as I sing of the city of Fuzhou, and there,
Thirty miles from the west gate, is White Goat Village.
In that village lived a powerful man, Millionaire Yang;
His family was noble and rich, having gold and silver.
    Millionaire Yang had only a single son,
Had only a single son, a little boy.
His parents cherished him like their hearts' treasure,
They loved their son no less than a pearl in one's hand.
    When the little boy had grown to be seven years of age,
He turned out to be intelligent and smart, quite capable.
When his father and mother saw how quick-witted he was,
They had their son go to school and study the books.
    First he recited *Primary Studies* for his enlightenment,
And later he recited essays for the examination sessions.
    The chosen name by which he was called was Yang Zongfu,
And he was well acquainted with the Classics and Histories.
Studying, he acquired the mind of Confucius and Mencius,
And he even surpassed by far the capabilities of Yan Hui.[1]
    Light and shade, fast as an arrow, urge people on to age,
Sun and moon, moving like a shuttle, go on day and night.
When Zongfu had grown up to be eighteen years of age,
His parents brought home as bride his predestined wife.
    They asked a good matchmaker to make arrangements,
And their son married a young girl of the Wang family.
Once their son had married that girl of the Wang family,
The couple of husband and wife was extremely devoted.
    And only two years after Zongfu had married his wife,
Both a son and a daughter were playing in their house.
The young couple had both one son and one daughter,
And the family loved them like a pearl in one's hand.

---

[1] Yan Hui was the favorite student of Confucius. Yan Hui lived in poverty and died at an early age.

One day when Zongfu was thinking of this and of that,
He decided he wanted to go to the city and have a look.
Zongfu thereupon immediately got properly dressed,
Went out there and walked through market and street.
　　When he eventually arrived at the city of Fuzhou,
He roamed everywhere to have a good look for himself.
Within the city of Fuzhou there are many fine sights:
The six streets and three markets were one noisy crowd!
　　The riches and glory of Fuzhou cannot be fully told —
In due course he arrived at the prefectural offices. When
He passed in front of the gate of the prefectural offices,
He saw an imperial placard which stated very clearly
　　That the Humane Ancestor opened the examination halls,
Summoning throughout his realm the students of books.
Seeing this placard, Zongfu's heart was filled with joy,
As it was his ambition to jump across the Dragon Gate!

He thereupon promptly turned around and went back;
He hurried back home to talk to his father and mother.
As soon as he arrived at the gate, he called: "I'm home!"
With folded hands he stepped forward to tell the reason.
　　"When your son went to Fuzhou to walk around for fun,
I saw the imperial placard which stated quite clearly
　　That the Humane Ancestor opens the examination halls,
Summoning throughout his realm the students of books.
Your son has a full understanding of literary composition,
I want to present writings and brush to our present ruler."
　　Hearing this, his father and mother were very annoyed:
"Our son, now please listen to what we have to say.
　　If you leave to compete for office, it is like a vacation,
But on whom are your aged and elderly parents to rely?
We have nobody here to manage our many possessions,
So it would be far better, our son, if you would not go."
　　As soon as Zongfu heard his parents speaking like this,
[He said:] "My dear parents, please listen to my reasons.
　　For ten years I studied by the window and nobody cared,
But once I pass the exams, the whole world will know me!
When I obtain a single office or even half a function,
I will be a man of high rank and change our family's status!"

When his father and mother heard him talk in this way,
[They said:] "Darling son, please listen to our words.
If you still want to leave in order to seek an office,
Please go to her room and ask your wife for her opinion."

Zongfu thereupon promptly went to the room of his wife,
And said to her: "My dear wife, please listen obediently.
    When I went to Fuzhou and walked around there for fun,
I saw an imperial poster which clearly stated that on
The third of the Third [Month] the examination halls will be opened
And that students are summoned throughout the realm.
    For ten years I studied by the window, suffering greatly:
I'll jump across the Dragon Gate, using writing and brush!
When I informed my father and mother before the hall,
They told me to set out as soon as possible on my journey."
    When his dear wife had heard this, she was very annoyed:
"My dear husband, please listen to what I have to say.
If you leave to compete for office, it is like a vacation,
But to whom do you want me to look when I lift my eyes?
    My parents-in-law in the hall are advanced in years, and
Our darling son and darling daughter need constant care.
There is no one to take care of my aged parents-in-law,
And who is there to take care of the money in the vault?
    We have no limit of gold and silver and precious goods,
And then we have silk and gauze of all kinds of colors.
There is more than enough for us all throughout our life,
So it would be far better, my man, if you would not go."
    When Zongfu heard her speaking in this manner and way,
[He said:] "My dear wife, now please listen to my reasons.
    For ten years I studied by the window and nobody cared,
But once I pass the exams, the whole world will know me!
When I obtain a single office or even half of a function,
I will be a man of high rank and change our family's status."

When his wife again and again could not make him stay,
He went to the hall, and informed his father and mother.
And when his parents heard him speak in this manner,
[They said:] "Our son, please listen to what we will say.

If you leave to compete for an office, it is like a vacation,
But on whom are we who stay here at home then to rely?
And then there is your wife, the Wang family's daughter,
And on whom should your little son and daughter rely?
   You will not rise to high rank until good fortune arrives,
So you had better stay here at home for another few years."
When Zongfu heard them speak in this manner and way,
[He said:] "Dear parents, please listen to my arguments.
   How will I ever obtain high office and be a great man,
If I do not go and compete for office in the examinations?"
Zongfu realized that it would be impossible for him to go,
So tears gushed down from his eyes in great profusion.
   As soon as Millionaire Yang saw this, he spoke as follows:
"My dear son, please listen to what I have to say.
   When you leave to compete for office, it's like a vacation,
But we will be thinking of all your sufferings on the road.
Once you have left to compete for office, we will have no news;
When will you come back home and greet your parents?"
   Zongfu immediately replied in the following manner:
"My dear parents, please listen to what I have to say.
   When I succeed in obtaining an office or a function,
I will come back home and inform my father and mother.
If it takes long, it will take three years, but if shorter, two,
And if still shorter, I may come back home in one year."
   When his parents heard this, they both shed tears, saying:
"Our darling son, please listen to what we will say.
As you have made up your mind and really want to go,
You must go to the capital with sufficient travel funds."
   When Zongfu saw this, his heart was filled with joy,
He beamed with a smile, and his face was all flowers.
His father and mother produced gold and treasures,
To provide their son with sufficient funds for his trip.

Speak:

This son of Millionaire Yang wanted to go and compete for office. When
Millionaire Yang and his wife could not stop him from going, they
involuntarily started to cry. Millionaire Yang then said: "My son, I am
unable to make you stay, so please go to the Eastern Capital." He promptly

brought out gold and silver, silk and gauze, and other textiles, and then
and there told Zongfu: "You should make sure to take these traveling
funds now that you leave to take the examinations and establish your
name." Zongfu thereupon hurried to ready his luggage, went to the hall to
take leave of his parents and wife, and then set out on the journey.

***Sing*:**

Listen as I tell how Zongfu set out on his journey,
Took leave of both his parents and then set out.
His wife saw him off, and followed him to the gate,
And she urged her husband in the following words:
    "Come back home as soon as you have obtained an office,
Don't be one who clings to his office, loves his function!
    Make sure to guard against robbers while on the road,
Make sure you are not attacked because you are too bold.
Find an inn early and set out at dawn, that is the basics;
Make sure you are not one who loses the way out of greed.
    My dear husband, you will be constantly in my thoughts;
My parents-in-law are quite old and they rely on you.
Your little son and little daughter have no guardian now,
To whom do you want me to look when I raise my eyes?
    It is me, your wife, who is urging you in this manner,
So, dear husband, please listen carefully to what I say.
While on the road you have to make sure to be careful,
And come back home as soon as you have an office."
    When she had finished admonishing her husband,
Tears streamed down her cheeks in great profusion.
"Your father and mother always think of you, their son,
Think of all the hardship you will suffer on the road."
    When lady Wang could no longer see her husband,
She went back inside, loudly wailing and weeping.
Let us not sing of the sufferings of his parents and wife —
Our student was pursuing his journey in greatest haste.

When he had walked a mile, he wanted to walk the next,
When he had gone for one stretch, he went on to the next.
As he was making his way it was the Third Month of Spring,
So the weather was mild and pleasant, good for walking.

Fig. 5.1
Zongfu takes leave of his parents to go and seek an office.

Whenever he ran into a road, he would cross that road,
Whenever he came to a village, he passed that village.
On the road there were flowers, there was also wine,
But he just traveled on, not caring for flowers or wine.

Mile after mile he traveled on — let's not sing about that,
Let us not waste words on his passing through counties.
Nor let us speak of the stretches he traveled by boat —
Eventually he saw the city of Yuezhou in the distance.[2]

When he entered the city of Yuezhou, he found that
Streets and markets were teeming with a noisy crowd.
But he had no desire to look at the main street or alleys,
Our student hurried to leave the city through the gate.

Once out of the city he hastily walked on once again,
He soon arrived at the ferry across the Qiantang River.
He expressed his relief and hastily traveled on, and so
He had arrived at the walls of the city of Hangzhou.

Before him he saw the prefectural capital Hangzhou,
So he promptly entered the gate of Hangzhou city.
Inside the city of Hangzhou was Black Sand Town,
With six streets and three markets he went to see.

The Eastern Market continued as the Western Market,
People selling flowers called to people buying flowers.
North and south the singsong houses trading in love,
And winehouses welcoming guests from everywhere.

There were three hundred sixty Buddhist monasteries,
The Buddha images in each of them were a miracle!
The flower streets and willow lanes offered romance:
How many dashing gentlemen, how many young girls!

Our student at this moment sighed with admiration,
"I left to compete for office, and I came to this place!"
The fine scenes in the city cannot all be described,
Let's not discuss the lofty glory of streets and wards.

Our student did not want to waste time by sightseeing,
So he promptly departed again from Hangzhou city.
He left through the north gate, on the government dike,[3]
And only when evening fell he would rest for the night.

---

[2] Yuezhou refers to the modern city of Shaoxing.
[3] Along the Grand Canal.

Once on the government dike, he quickly walked on,
And once past Chongning, he arrived at Jiaxing.
He had no desire to go and have a look at Jiaxing;
By way of Pingwang and Bali, he came to Wujiang.
    Of Wujiang I will only mention the Long Bridge,
The fine scenes of its West Lake resemble heaven!
Once he had passed Wujiang, he came to Suzhou,
So thereupon he passed through the city of Suzhou.
    Once past Suzhou he followed the government dike,
So let's not talk of Wangting and also not of Xushi.
Eventually he passed the county capital of Wuxi,
Entering by the south gate, leaving by the north gate.
    Leaving by the north gate, it was overgrown land,
His straw sandals were worn through — how saddening!
He had walked so much his two legs were hurting a lot,
He realized he would not make his stretch for the day.
    To go forward was frost, but to shirk back was snow,
So he could only hang in there and travel on forward.
After he had passed through Henglin and also Luoshe,
He eventually arrived at the city of Changzhou.
    I will not sing of any of the fine sights of Changzhou —
The passed-through four counties all have no name!
Changzhou's markets offer all kinds of wares for sale,
And then they also have sundry goods and novelties.
    Inside the walls the sights are even more exceptional,
The city of Changzhou truly has no equal in the world.
But he had no desire to enjoy the sights of Changzhou,
As his heart was set on hurrying to the Eastern Capital.
    On the road of bitter suffering he hurriedly walked on,
Where another would use two steps, he would take one.
The thousands and myriads of sufferings caused remorse,
But now he had no option left but to travel on forward.
    Let's not talk at all about these sufferings of the road —
He passed through Benniu and also through Lücheng.
He had no desire to have a look at the city of Danyang,
Our student was anxious to hurry on and travel forward.
    Alone and lonesome he traveled without any companion,
All by himself, with only his shadow following behind.
I will not sing at all of the road through Zhenjiang —
He went to the bank of the river to see for himself.

When he stood on the bank of the river, he had a look
At the stormy white-capped billows and was terrified!
But there were also other travelers who wanted to cross;
When the oarsmen lowered their oars, the boat took off.
    In the distance he saw the lofty buildings on Jinshan;
He saw the deep green of the mountains and streams.
But arriving in the middle of the river, he was frightened
By the terrifying white-capped billows that rose to heaven!
    When he had crossed the river, he sighed with relief,
He hurried to get off the boat and to pursue his journey.
Let's not sing of the way in which he traveled on and on,
Let's not discuss all the prefectures and all the counties.
    Eventually the sun was sinking behind the western hills,
And the jade hare was rising in the east, getting brighter.
Our student at this time started to look for an inn to stay,
But ahead of him there was no inn, behind him no village.
    The fishermen on the river had all stopped their angling,
The weaving girls, done with the loom, had gone to bed.
The woodcutters, descending the hills, had gone home,
But he still traveled on, like a cloud blown by the wind.
    The pretty girl lit the lamp, retiring within the bed curtains,
Other girls, the heart filled with love, waited for their lovers.
The red disk sank in the west, and evening was falling,
Eventually the day turned to evening, dusk turned to night.
    Our student now felt as if his guts were tied in a knot:
"How will I be able to find a place to rest for this night?"
And as our student was overcome by his many vexations,
He felt lonely and lost, depressed, and sick with worry.

Speak:

When this student had come to the region of Tianchang and Liuhe,
there was neither a house nor an inn to be seen. Eventually the day
turned to evening and dusk set in. He traveled without any companion,
and as he considered that his baskets were filled with gold and silver and
precious goods, our student was truly desolate. He took a few steps
more, but then he suddenly saw a small house in some village. The
student was filled with joy, just as if the clouds had been shattered to
display the moon, and also as if an antique mirror had been polished
again. He sighed with relief now that he had accidentally discovered this

house. The student put down his baskets, and promptly entered the house. There he saw an old woman. Her hair was as white as silk, and she recited the name of the Buddha while her hands held a rosary. The student stepped forward and said: "Many blessings, dear lady! I am on my way to the Eastern Capital to seek office. I am tired out from traveling, and evening has already fallen. So I hope that you, my dear lady, will allow me to stay here for the night — tomorrow I will be on my way at the crack of dawn!"

When the old lady heard this, [she thought to herself:] "He must be a student of books, so he must have plenty of gold and silver and precious goods in his baskets, so if my two sons see him, they will definitely be filled with evil greed, so how could this be?" So she thereupon said to the student: "We cannot put you up." The student then asked: "My dear lady, why can't you provide me hospitality? The ancients said: 'When a man comes, he seeks refuge with other men; when birds come, they seek refuge in a grove.' After a thousand towns and a myriad of miles I have come to this place. Please put me up for the night, and tomorrow I will pay you for board and lodging." The old woman said: "Dear sir, my two sons are evil. By day they are potters, but at night they are thieves. They are always dressed in armor and carry a long lance in their hands. Throughout the region of Tianchang and Liuhe they will grab their opportunity when they are in the majority, robbing the travelers who pass through. They will kill the men and kidnap the wives and daughters. In case my two sons would come home and see that you have so much gold and silver and precious goods in your baskets, they will be overcome by evil greed and kill you, so it is not safe here for you." When the student heard this, cold sweat soaked his body, and with tears streaming down, he said goodbye to the old woman and continued his journey.

Sing:

When the student heard this, suffering filled his heart,
Cold sweat soaked his body, and tears streamed down.
Immediately he secretly thought to himself: "I have to
Get out of this house as fast and as quickly as I possibly can!"
    After thanking the old woman, he continued his journey,
His heart was set on hurrying on and traveling forward.
But his legs were hurting him so he could hardly walk,
And tears were falling in great profusion from his eyes.

Gradually the evening was falling and the sky turned dark;
Our student suffered intensely and was deeply grieved.
He now also feared that robbers might block his way,
And rob him of his precious goods and gold and silver.
    "If I had only known earlier I would suffer like this,
I would never have set out on this journey back then.
But if I wanted to reconsider and go back home again,
I would have suffered these thousands of pains in vain!"

So he could do nothing else but pursue his journey,
His only desire was to hurry and reach his day's goal.
But just as he had walked for one mile, he encountered
Two men who came towards him from the other direction,
    Both dressed in such a way that they looked menacing.
Our student was so terrified that sweat soaked his body.
He promptly put down his baskets and everything else,
And with lowered head bowed in front of these bandits.
    "I humbly beg you, Generalissimo and Grand Guardian,
To allow me to buy my way to the Eastern Capital."
The two men promptly replied in the following way:
"Dear student, now please listen to our explanation.
The way ahead of you is the road to the city of Haozhou,
But the distance would be more than forty-five miles.
    Dear student, please listen to us as we tell you the truth:
We will tell you exactly who we are, without any deceit.
We are no generalissimo and also no grand guardian,
The two of us are village headmen of the countryside.
    Prefect Bao, the current official of this prefecture here,
Has charged us to make our rounds and catch any thieves.
His Excellency has charged us all to make the rounds
And to catch and arrest all bandits and thieving robbers.
    Because when officials and merchants pass through here
They are often robbed of their jewels and also their pearls."
    The student then addressed them in the following words:
"Gentlemen, may I ask you to be so kind as to listen to me —
Is there in that direction a house where I might lodge?
I would like to rest for the night and not travel on."
    The two men thereupon told the student the following:
"Just come closer and listen to what we can tell you.

In that direction all you will find is abandoned fields,
There is no inn where you can lodge, and no village.
    The best thing for you would be to come to our house,
And you can pursue your journey tomorrow at dawn."
When the student heard this, he was filled with joy,
And he accepted the advice of these two bandits.
    He thereupon accompanied them back to their house,
And walked into the web of heaven, the net of earth!
And this filled with joy Geng One and Geng Two,
The two of them were filled with joy as they schemed.
    As their eyes observed the student and his baskets,
The hearts of these two men were filled with great evil.
"These baskets must be filled with gold and treasure,
But today he is bound to give it all to the two of us."
    After they had invited the student back to their house,
They set out a meal of rice and wine to feast their guest.

Speak:

These two robbers invited the student to come back with them to their
house to rest for the night. The student then did not say anything, but
he thought to himself: "A moment ago that old woman said that her two
sons were both bandits. Could it be these two guys?" After the student had
had this thought, he said to the two men: "I am on my way to the Eastern
Capital to seek office. I only want to go on ahead, I don't want to turn
back." These two men then said to the student: "The forty-five miles
ahead of you are all abandoned and overgrown fields, with lots of snakes,
wolves, tigers and panthers. It's much better to come with us to our house
and take a rest — wouldn't that be the best thing to do?" The student at
that time could only do as they suggested and follow them. At this time
Geng One said: "Sir, you must have quite some treasure in your baskets!"
But the student answered him, saying: "Grand Guardian, there is nothing
of great value in these baskets, except some clothes for the summer and for
the winter, and ink and brushes for writing." When Geng One heard this,
he was very much enraged in his heart: "That such a rotten student has the
guts to tell such a lie!" Together, the three of them walked back.

Sing:

The student secretly felt deeply annoyed in his belly,
He could only follow them and walk back with them.

But as he was walking, his heart kept thinking:
"If I secretly think about it, I've to fear for my life."
    Geng One then addressed him in the following words:
"Sir, please listen now to what I have to say to you.
Come to think of it, you must have suffered quite a lot,
Traveling this distance must have taken all your energy.
    On top of that, you also want to carry your own luggage,
That must have given you thousands and myriads of pains.
Why don't you give us those baskets to carry for you, and
Then you walk along with us, as we travel this stretch."
    The student could only agree to what he suggested,
And he allowed the two men to carry his carrying pole.
Geng Two shouldered his carrying pole to carry his stuff,
And the student followed behind, walking like a cloud.

Eventually they drew near to the house of these two,
And the student observed it carefully to be fully sure:
This was the place where he earlier had sought lodging,
Now again he entered the gate of the Geng family home.
    The student at this time greatly suffered in his heart,
And tears coursed down his cheeks in great profusion.
"This time around I will be killed at the hands of these two,
Remorse is now of no use — how do I escape with my life?
    If only I would have listened to the words of their mother,
I would have been able to flee from this gate of disaster."
In his mind he considered the matter a thousand times,
As he debated his sorry situation secretly with himself.
    Zongfu thereupon prayed to Heaven and also to Earth,
Calling on the Dragon Kings he had passed[4] as witnesses:
"If I succeed in making this trip to the Eastern Capital,
I will repay Heaven's favor as soon as I have an office.
    But if I now lose my life here in the house of these two,
May Heaven and Earth and all the gods be my witnesses,
Also because my father and mother are advanced in years,
And at home they have no one to manage their wealth."
    The student was secretly suffering from acute anxiety,
But he had no option but to enter the gate of the house.

---

[4] Each body of water, whether river or lake, has its own divine dragon.

But let's not sing of all the sufferings of this student,
Let's first narrate about this Geng One and Geng Two.

Speak:

These two men took the student along with them to their house. Their
hearts were filled with joy, and they called out to their mother: "Today we
have a student who will stay with us for the night. He must be tired out
from walking, so let's make a late night meal for him." When their mother
heard this and came out to have a look, it turned out to be the student
who earlier had sought lodging with her. "I told him to go back! But he
must have run into these two sons of mine, these bandits, so he is bound
to lose his life!"

Sing:

This old woman, we must tell, was devoted to goodness,
She recited the name of the Buddha and read the sutras.
So when the student asked her for lodging for the night,
She had told him to go and find some other place to sleep.
    "I told him how evil they are — so why didn't he listen?
How come he walks right into this man-catching trap?
Now today this man has run into these two sons of mine,
He will in the end have no way to escape with his life.
    Today that student will definitely die at their hands,
And the precious goods in his baskets will go to others.
When my eyes see this student, my heart suffers for him,
And on top of all of this, he is such a smart young man!"
    The old woman did not dare say this to him in his face,
She secretly muttered to herself, and secretly commented.
But she had no alternative but to go and heat up the stove,
And to make some nighttime snacks for the three of them.

Speak:

This Geng One shouted: "Mother, quickly cook some rice for this student.
This student is starved! And also hurry and kill that big rooster behind the
house, so we can offer the student three cups!" When the student heard
this, he bowed and said: "Grand Guardian, I should not be causing you so
much trouble! My gratitude has no bounds. Tomorrow I will get a large

piece of silk from my baskets to express my thanks." When the two men
heard this, they coldly smiled, as they thought to themselves: "Don't say
you will give us one piece of silk. Even if you have a thousand pieces, you
will have no share of them!" At that time the old woman had cooked the
rice, she had also prepared the rooster, and when she had laid out the
table, the three men drank wine. The student soon had drunk so much
that he was totally drunk, and then Geng One and Geng Two prepared the
back room for him so he could sleep there.

   Alas! The student might be totally drunk but he still was smart, and
he thought: "I have quite some gold and silver, so I cannot sleep too
soundly." He then attached an iron chain to the top of the baskets.
"If they open the baskets, the iron chain will make some noise." He also
attached a hemp rope to his own body, and only then he went to sleep.
Geng One and Geng Two waited until midnight, and when they heard
the student snoring away like thunder, they hurriedly got up and
strangled the student with a handkerchief. The student wanted to shout
but could not utter a sound, and eventually he died, his fate going off to
the Yellow Springs.[5]

Sing:

The student was strangled and eventually he died,
As tears coursed down his cheeks in great profusion.
He opened his mouth to shout, but uttered not a sound,
And eventually he died to go off to the Lord of Shade.
   His three souls slowly returned to the roads of darkness,
His seven spirits in darkness entered the gate of death.
But let's not sing of the way in which the student died,
Let's change the topic and sing again of those two men.
   Geng Two called his brother and said the following:
"Dear brother, please listen to what I have to say.
   Now this student has passed away, let's open his baskets
And have a good look to find out what's really in there."
Geng One thereupon quickly hurried to open the baskets,
And, indeed, when he looked, he found gold and silver!
   The two brothers were filled with joy in their hearts —
"Why go out of the house when riches come to your door!

---

[5] The Yellow Springs is one of the common designations of the abode of the dead.

He came and brought this gold and silver to the two of us,
We'll be rich for the rest of our lives — an eternal spring!"

The elder and younger brother now hastily set to work,
They stripped the student's whole body of all its clothes.
When they also saw the student's silk and gauze textiles,
The elder and younger brother were truly filled with joy,
   When they had stripped him of the clothes on his body,
All his limbs were as stark naked as the day he was born.
   Geng Two once again called out to his brother, saying:
"Dear brother, please listen to me and give your opinion.
Now we have stripped this student of all of his clothes,
Where are we going, tell me, to dispose of his corpse?"
   Geng One thereupon replied in the following manner:
"Dear little brother, there is absolutely no need to panic.
It's just one student who disappears without a trace.
It's not as if we had killed a dozen traveling merchants!
   Now do me a favor and wrap up the corpse, and then
We will carry it between us to the gate of the kiln.
Then we will carry him right into the heart of the kiln,
And we will cover that corpse with piled-up black pots.
   Then we will have to wait until the evening tomorrow,
When we will carry plenty of charcoal into the kiln.
If we burn the kiln for one extra day and night too,
We will have burned that corpse without leaving a trace."
   When the two brothers had decided upon this plan,
They carried the corpse in between them into the kiln.
But let's not sing of the great evil of the two of them,
Let's sing of the old woman, the mother of these two.

When the old woman saw this, her tears gushed forth.
"How sad that they have wronged this fine student!
His gold and silver have fallen into the hands of my sons,
And moreover his soul has left for the Lord of Shade.
   If he only would have taken my advice straightaway,
He might have been spared from dying here today.
But now he has been done in by those vicious two —
That bitter pain wounds my feelings — it is unbearable!

How sad that such a man stuffed with fine writing
Has become a character in a Southern Branch dream!"[6]
    As her hands fingered her rosary, she cried and wailed,
And as she recited the name of the Buddha, tears fell.

But let's not sing of the old woman's mental torment —
Let's sing once again of the son of the Yang family!
The body had been burned in the kiln for seven days,
And the bones were all burned — not a shard was left!
    His murderers forgot that Heaven and Earth do exist,
That sun, moon, and stars were witness to their crime!
The two of them only thought that they now were safe,
Little did they know he had changed into a black pot.
    Eventually, when after a day the kiln had cooled off,
The elder and younger brother entered the kiln.
When they opened the kiln to take out their black pots,
They found there, with the others, one ugly black pot.
    Geng One thereupon addressed his brother as follows:
"My brother, please listen to what I now have to say.
For many years we've been firing pots in this kiln,
But how did we ever produce an ugly pot like this?"
    Geng Two replied to him in the following manner:
"My brother, please listen now to my explanation.
This pot is deprived of any skill and craftsmanship,
I'm afraid it must have been made by our father.
    Because it was not a good pot, he left it in the back,
So it wouldn't be out in front, for all to see and rage.
Now the next time yamen runners come here again,
We can give it to them as a gift — let's give it away!"

Let's not sing of these two, these criminal elements,
Let's change the topic — I'll sing of somebody else.
This man lived in the prefectural capital of Haozhou,
And for three generations his family had sold pots.

---

[6] In a famous tale from the Tang dynasty a man experiences a brilliant career, only to wake up from his dream and realize that he had been an ant in the anthill of the southern branch of the huge acacia tree in his garden.

So let's tell about this Sun Xiao'er from Haozhou,
Who one day came to the kiln to buy his black pots.
With ten strings of copper cash, these green bats,[7]
He came to the kiln of the Gengs to buy black pots.
    When he arrived at the kiln, he was filled with joy,
And said to Geng Two: "Now, please listen to me!
    My family has been a steady customer buying pots,
We buy our pots, as you know, only from your family.
When buying pots elsewhere, we never come to a deal,
We only come here to your family to buy black pots."

Speak:

When this Sun Xiao'er had arrived at the kiln of the Gengs, he put down his baskets, and chatted for a while with Geng One. After he had bought a number of pots for ten strings of cash, he loaded them onto his carrying pole, and said: "Brother Geng One, all these many years you have never given me an extra pot in the bargain, so how about giving me today an extra pot to pay for my travel expenses?" When Geng One heard this, he told Geng Two: "Get that ugly black pot at the back of the kiln and give it to Xiao'er for his travel expenses." Geng Two hurried to give the pot to Sun Xiao'er without any further ado. When Sun Xiao'er received this free pot, he was filled with joy, and with his carrying pole on his shoulder, he hurried to say goodbye and made the trip back home.

Sing:

Carrying his pots, Sun Xiao'er set out on the road,
And ran as fast as he could to the city of Haozhou.
Once he had arrived there back in Haozhou city,
He promptly set out to offer his black pots for sale.
    He offered his pots for sale on crossroads and streets,
And sold them to the city people who wanted to buy.
He managed to sell all the black pots in his baskets, but
Then there was one, and only one, lonely pot still left.
    He cried out his wares from the east to the west, and
He cried out his wares both in the south and the north.

---

[7] The traditional Chinese copper coins (round with a square hole) were referred to as "green bats."

But each and every one said that his pot was too ugly,
And nobody wanted to buy this one ugly black pot.
    Sun Xiao'er at this time grew extremely annoyed,
Because of these vexations in his mind he became enraged!
But let's not sing of Sun Xiao'er trying to sell this pot,
Let's change the subject and sing of the man surnamed Bao!

Everybody called him Bao the Pure and Righteous —
During daytime a judge in this world, at night in the other.
One day he returned from a visit to the Southern Temple;
His attendants, clearing the road, shouted like thunder.
    His three-tiered parasol resembled floating clouds, and
His folding chair and silver basin gleamed in the sunlight.
But when he passed by the baskets of the man selling pots,
Suddenly a freak whirlwind blew people to the ground.
    The top of His Excellency's sedan chair was blown off,
And each and every one was blinded by this freak wind.
His Excellency the prefect was extremely annoyed, and
Immediately hurried to order his official underlings:
    "This freak whirlwind shows no respect or decency at all!
Arrest the King of the Winds and bring him before me!"
He had his folding chair put down and sat down on it,
And promptly transmitted this order to his underlings.
    The assembled yamen runners came and bent down,
Each and every one filled with fear for His Excellency.
"Who of you all is the person who is on duty today?
Let him quickly come forward and listen to my words!"
    When Pan Cheng heard this, he quickly answered, saying:
"Your Excellency, inform me of the business at hand.
Today I should be the one yamen runner who is on duty.
Please inform me of the matter at hand and your order."

Speak:

His Excellency the prefect sat down on his folding chair, and called on the
yamen runners under his command. When in this way Pan Cheng had
reported for duty, His Excellency said: "Take this warrant and summon
His Majesty the God of the Winds, so he may be questioned in detail."
When Pan Cheng heard this, he thought: "This must be the most stupid
prefect in the whole world! We use warrants to summon common people

in the countryside, but from Pangu to the present, I have never heard of a case of summoning the God of the Winds!" Pan Cheng thereupon addressed His Excellency, saying: "The Divine King of the Winds is a divinity up in the skies, how could we people in the world of light ever see him?" When His Excellency heard this, he grew very annoyed, and striking the table he loudly cursed Pan Cheng: "If you succeed in summoning the God of the Winds, I will award you with ten strings of cash and two bottles of good wine. But if you can't summon him, it's thirty strokes of the heavy bamboo for you!" When Pan Cheng had his warrant, His Excellency returned to his office.

Sing:

Pan Cheng could not get out of taking on this warrant,
He was terribly angry, and his anger turned to rage.
"What a disaster! This prefect is truly a stupid fool!
Now he cleverly cooked up a scheme for a warrant!"
　　Having taken receipt of the warrant, he was not happy,
And mumbling and grumbling he went on his way.
"It must be my bad luck to run into this stupid fool,
He really is a fool acting without any proper thought!
　　These warrants are only used for summoning people,
I have never heard about people who summoned gods!"
At this time Pan Cheng could only go back to his house;
Filled with vexation and sorrow he greeted his mother.
　　Pan Cheng thereupon addressed his mother as follows:
"Dear mother, now please listen to what I will tell you.
Today I ran into the most foolish prefect in the world:
He hands me a warrant and wants the God of the Winds!
　　He sets me a term of three days to bring him to court,
And then he will award me with a few bottles of fine wine.
But if I cannot bring him to court within these three days,
It's thirty strokes of the heavy bamboo — without mercy!
　　Speak of bad luck — today my bad luck is beyond words.
Where should I go to find and arrest a God of the Winds?"

Speak:

When his mother heard this, she said: "My son, don't worry. If His Excellency gave you this order, how could you dare not comply? Tomorrow you will only have to go to the crossroads and streets, shouting loudly: 'Your Majesty the God of the Winds, I have a warrant here from His Excellency Bao, so I have come here to summon you! Quickly report!'"

Sing:

Pan Cheng complied with the suggestion of his mother,
And so he had to wait for early morning the next day.
I will not sing of all his vexations throughout the night —
As soon as the sky had turned bright, he left the house.

　　He walked over the crossroads and through the streets,
Calling: "God of the Winds in the sky, now please listen!
This warrant of His Excellency Bao summons you, so
Appear with all possible speed at the prefectural office!

　　By your improper actions you angered Prefect Bao,
So hurry up to appear at the yamen and listen to him!"
On the main streets, in little alleys, he called out loudly,
Everywhere, on each street, he shouted again and again.

　　Each and every one said that he was struck by madness,
That, acting this way, he must surely have lost his mind.
He was definitely a madman, a lunatic, and a silly fool,
Because how could one summon this God of the Winds?

　　As he was screaming on the crossroads and the streets,
He suddenly ran into two other runners of the prefecture.
He ran into his colleagues Dong Chao and Xue Ba, and
The three of them struck up a conversation, got talking.

Speak:

This Pan Cheng said: "I've run into a prefect who is a fool! He has issued this warrant, ordering me to summon the God of the Winds to report to him. Now the God of the Winds is a divinity in the skies, so how could I ever summon him?" When Dong Chao and Xue Ba heard this, they replied: "Please show us the warrant, so we can have a look at what it says." Pan Cheng immediately got it out and showed it to them, but then a freak whirlwind blew this warrant off into the sky — so what to do now?

Sing:

The warrant had been blown away by the wind, and
Gradually it floated halfway up to the blue clouds!

Pan Cheng was now even more filled with vexations:
"What can I do about this crime of mine of today?"
  Looking up, he prayed to Heaven, but no response;
Looking down, he saw no gate by which to enter earth.
Dong Chao and Xue Ba were both dumbfounded, and,
As they looked at each other, neither now said a word.
  Pan Cheng lifted his head and looked into the skies,
Following his warrant on its flight with anxious eyes.
But after a while it was eventually blown to the ground,
At a distance of half a mile and even some more!
  Pan Cheng ran as fast as he could to catch the warrant,
And he found that it had fallen down on the ground.

Speak:

As soon as this Pan Cheng saw that the warrant had fallen down, he
hurried to catch it, and it turned out to have landed in the black pot in a
basket in front of the house of the seller of black pots, Sun Xiao'er.
When Pan Cheng then saw this, his heart was filled with joy, and he
quickly retrieved it. When Pan Cheng saw this black pot, he then thought:
"Let me buy it for my mother to pee in!" So he said to the guy who was
selling these pots: "How much do you ask for this black pot?" Sun Xiao'er
said: "To others I sell it for thirty pennies, but I will let you have it for
twenty if you are interested." When Pan Cheng heard this, [he said:] "I am
not looking for a soft deal, I will give you thirty." When Xiao'er heard this,
he was filled with joy. Once Pan Cheng had bought the pot, he took it in
his hands, caressing it warmly! When he came home with it, he gave it to
his mother to use as a chamber pot.

Sing:

After Pan Cheng had bought this pot, he went home,
He hurried back home to give it as a gift to his mother.
He had no desire to stay standing in the streets, calling out,
So, carrying his black pot, he ran like a moving cloud!
  He intended the pot he had bought for their use at home,
Little did he know it was the soul of someone who died.
When he came back home, it was about the time of dusk,
So he planned to have a late meal and then go to bed.
  When his mother saw her son coming back home, she
Promptly started to ask him how things had been going.

"Did you succeed today in summoning the God of the Winds?
Tell me the truth: do you still have to succeed to do so?"
    Pan Cheng thereupon addressed her in the following way:
"My dear mother, please listen to what I have to tell you.
I never succeeded in summoning the God of the Winds, but
Without any cause or reason I was struck by disaster.
    As I was walking across the crossroads and the streets,
I ran into my colleagues Dong Chao and Xue Ba, and
When I took out the warrant to let them have a look,
A gust of a sudden freak whirlwind blew us all over!
    This freak whirlwind also blew this warrant off and away,
It blew it up into the skies, way beyond the highest clouds!
It only fell down after it had floated on for quite a stretch,
And only then it fell down once again on the ground.
    When this warrant had fallen down, I could retrieve it,
And also managed to buy then this one black pot.
This black pot I bought there is truly extremely ugly,
So you can only use it, my dear mother, as a chamber pot."
    When his mother heard this, she was filled with joy:
"How filial this son of mine is to his dear mother!"
Here the story divides into two parts, remember it well:
Each of them went off to a separate room to sleep.
    Later that night, when she had slept till midnight,
Pan Cheng's mother reached for the black pot to use it.
That very moment the black pot then started to speak,
Scaring her so much her body was soaked in cold sweat.

Speak:

When the old woman had slept to the hour of midnight, she got up to
urinate. When she held the pot in both her hands to pee, the black pot
suddenly started to speak to her: "Old woman, you have no decency at all!
I am a good person, and I was on my way to the Eastern Capital to seek
office when I ran into Geng One and Geng Two. As they wanted to steal
my gold and silver, gauze and silk and other textiles, they killed me. They
then carried my corpse into the kiln to burn it, causing me to die unjustly."
When the old woman heard this, she was so scared that her body was
soaked in cold sweat, and she called to her son: "There's an apparition here
tonight in my room! That black pot has started to speak! Get up and have
a look!"

***Sing*:**

Pan Cheng's old mother started to scream loudly:
"My son, please come and listen to what I have to say!
A ghost has appeared here tonight, here in my room,
Inside that black pot there is some kind of monster!"
  When Pan Cheng heard his mother screaming like this,
He hurriedly got out of his bed to ask her what happened.
He promptly asked her: "Dear mother, what is the reason,
How come you are screaming so loudly again and again?"
  Pan Cheng's old mother then addressed him as follows:
"My dear son, now please listen to what I have to tell!
That black pot, believe it or not, started to speak to me,
It called out to me, saying that he was a good person!"

***Speak*:**

When Pan Cheng heard this, he then promptly asked the black pot:
"What kind of person are you? And why did you decide to appear? Tell me quickly so I may know, and then I will take you with me the next morning so you can lay your complaint before His Excellency the prefect, so he can judge your case."

***Sing*:**

Questioned like this, the black pot then told the whole story:
"Dear Mr. Police Officer, please listen to what I will say!
My family lives in Fuzhou, outside the city's western gate,
We live in White Goat Village, outside the walls of the city.
  My father is a rich man by the name of Millionaire Yang,
Over generations the family accumulated gold and silver.
I am the only son to be born to that Millionaire Yang,
And I am at present just a little above thirty years of age.
  I married a daughter of the Wang family to be my wife,
And we only have two children, a son and a daughter.
When I heard that His Majesty announced examinations,
I wanted to jump across the Dragon Gate, using my brush.
  When I passed through the area of White Hair Village,
I ran into two criminals on the road outside the village.
There I met with the brothers Geng One and Geng Two;
Both of them were people with hearts as black as coal.

They invited me to their house to spend the night,
And there they plied me with drinks, round upon round.
When they had filled me with wine till I was dead drunk,
They strangled me with a handkerchief and I lost my life.
    They carried my corpse between them into their kiln,
And they fired the kiln for seven days and seven nights.
They thought that my body would never be found,
But I was transformed into the shape of a black pot.
    They schemed to get my gold and silver and treasure,
The thousand strings of cash and also the gauze and silk.
But now, thanks to that seller of black pots Sun Xiao'er,
I was carried here to Haozhou as he wanted to sell me.
    When I saw His Excellency passing by Sun's baskets,
I wanted so much to lay my complaint before His Excellency!
So it wasn't the God of the Winds who blew off the top,
And you shouldn't try to summon him with your warrant.
    I beg you, Mr. Police Officer, to show me some mercy,
To take me with you, so I may appear before His Excellency."
    When Pan Cheng had heard this long story, he replied:
"Mr. Black Pot, now please listen to what I will say.
Let's wait till tomorrow, and at the first crack of dawn
I will take you with me into the gate of the court!"

Speak:

When Pan Cheng had heard what the black pot had to say, he sat waiting
for early dawn the next day to present himself to His Excellency. So he
took out a sheet of paper, got his ink and brush, and wrote out a deposition
to present the next day to His Excellency.

> "The police officer Pan Cheng of Kaifeng Prefecture, the Eastern
> Capital, submits the following deposition to the local prefect for
> his perusal. Following your orders, I went out to summon and
> arrest the King of the Winds. When I came to the crossroads and
> streets, I met with Dong Chao and Xue Ba, to whom I showed
> the warrant, which was then by a gust of a freak whirlwind blown
> high into the sky, to fall down before the door of a seller of black
> pots, and end up in one of the pots. I immediately retrieved the
> warrant, but also bought the pot, which I took with me back
> home, where I gave it to my mother as a chamber pot. At midnight,

the black pot suddenly started to speak, and I promptly questioned it in detail. It said that he hailed from White Goat Village to the west of Fuzhou, and was the son of Millionaire Yang. He was on his way to the Eastern Capital to participate in the examinations, when he arrived at White Hair Village, where he met with the bandits Geng One and Geng Two. Scheming to rob his gold and silver, gauze, silk and other textiles, they strangled him with a handkerchief, and carried his corpse into a kiln. After they had fired the kiln for seven days and seven nights, he turned into a black pot. After Sun Xiao'er had carried it to Haozhou to sell, Your Excellency yesterday passed him by. The black pot then raised the wind that blew off the top of your sedan chair. This had nothing to do with the King of the Winds, it was just that the black pot wanted to appear before Your Excellency. Questioning revealed this to be the facts, and it is therefore fitting that the pot be submitted together with the deposition. Taken down according to statement."

Sing:

When Pan Cheng had finished writing this deposition,
He took the black pot with him as he left the house.
Without interruption he arrived at Kaifeng Prefecture,
To present himself, with the pot, to His Excellency.
  Right then, Judge Bao ascended the hall and sat down,
So Pan Cheng immediately entered the prefectural court.
Arriving before the hall, he hastily knelt down, saying:
"Your Excellency, please listen to what I have to say.
  Yesterday Your Excellency issued a warrant, wanting
Me to arrest the King of the Winds, that vicious trickster.
But it was not the King of the Winds who played a trick,
It was a black pot that wanted to appear here in court.
  I hope that Your Excellency will have this investigated,
And that you will judge this case like a bright mirror!"

Speak:

When Pan Cheng arrived at the office building, he hastily submitted the accusation. When His Excellency had received it, he read it carefully. So Pan Cheng thought only that the black pot had made its case clear to

His Excellency, but then the latter said to Pan Cheng: "Bring that pot over here. I will question it in detail myself." His Excellency then questioned the pot: "In which town of which county of which prefecture do you live? What is your surname and personal name? Tell me quickly, so I can find a life to pay for yours." He questioned him a number of times, but he got no answer at all. His Excellency was greatly enraged and cursed Pan Cheng: "Ever since the time of Pangu no one has seen a black pot talk. I dispatched you to summon the King of the Winds, but instead of doing that, you bring me this black pot, making a fool of your superior official. Take that pot out! I will spare you for now, but go and summon the King of the Winds and bring him here. If this time around you fail to summon him, it's thirty strokes of the heavy bamboo without any mercy. That will teach you to make a fool of your superior official!" When Pan Cheng heard this, he felt very annoyed: "That rotten black pot has no decency at all! Back in my house it talks, but when it appears before His Excellency, it doesn't say a word!" But he could do nothing but take his leave from the judge and the hall.

Sing:

Pan Cheng was filled with annoyance in his belly, and,
Taking his leave of the prefect with a bow, he went out.
When he eventually had gone out through the gate, he
Immediately started to curse that ugly black pot, saying:
    "Because His Excellency today in his rage cursed me out,
It will now be my turn to beat you into tiny little pieces!"
The black pot called out, saying: "Please, don't break me,
Please listen now to me, I will give you an explanation.
    That Geng One and Geng Two had no decency at all,
They stripped me of all of my clothes — not a shred was left.
They stripped off my outer clothes and undergarments,
And then placed me stark naked in the fire to be burned.
    They fired me in the kiln for seven days and seven nights,
That is why I am now transformed into the shape of a pot.
It is not that I had lost the power to speak, but I could not
Appear in front of His Excellency without any clothes.
    So please be so kind as to do me this favor, I implore you,
To buy me a set of clothes in which I can dress myself.
If you buy me a set of clothes and then give them to me,
I will definitely make sure to answer all his questions."

When Pan Cheng heard this, he said: "Now this is great!
Mr. Black Pot, now please listen to what I have to say.
You want me to buy clothes, but I have never seen you,
So I do not know whether you prefer linen or silk.
    I do not know what color you, sir, may prefer,
What kind of color you prefer for the clothes you wear."
The black pot thereupon addressed him as follows:
"Dear Mr. Police Officer, please let me tell you the truth.
    I would like to have a long-sleeved gown and short jacket,
And below that a set of underwear and also a linen skirt.
And I would also need leather boots and a handkerchief,
I have to be fully and properly dressed from head to toe.
    If you buy these clothes for me and then burn them for me,
I will surely speak even without questioning to His Excellency."
Pan Cheng heard it speak to him in this manner, and
Went back to his house and there greeted his mother.

When he came home, he called out to his mother, saying:
"Dear mother, please listen now to what I have to tell.
    When I took this black pot with me into the court hall,
Little did I know that it would refuse to tell its story!
So His Excellency in his rage started to curse me,
And shouted to me: 'Get out, you and your black pot!'
    Once I had left the court hall, the pot spoke again,
Telling me it couldn't appear all naked before people.
So it ordered me to buy it some clothes to wear,
Then it would answer the questions of the judge."
    When his mother heard him tell this story, [she said:]
"My dear son, now please listen to what I will say.
As poor Mr. Black Pot has no clothes at all to wear,
You had better buy a full set of clothes for the pot."

Speak:

So Pan Cheng took ten strings of cash and went out to buy a set of
clothes according to the specifications of the black pot. When he
returned home, he burned some good incense, and announced to the
pot: "I will burn these clothes for you. But if you still don't say a word
the next time you appear before the hall, I will have spent these ten
strings of cash in vain, and I will be punished!" The black pot then spoke
and informed the police officer: "You must take these clothes to the

Temple of the City God and burn them there for me. When I have claimed a life [to pay for mine], I will of course pay you back." When Pan Cheng heard this, his heart was filled with joy, and when the next day had come, he took the clothes to the temple and burned them on behalf of the black pot.

Sing:

Pan Cheng at this time was filled with joy in his heart,
And he waited for the sky to brighten the next morning.
There is no story to sing at all for that one long night —
Earlier than expected the Golden Cock announced dawn.
    In the east it called forth the sun from the Fusang-tree,
So the people on earth did not have to walk in darkness.
As soon as Pan Cheng noticed the sky had brightened,
He made haste and got down from his sleeping couch.
    And when he had combed his hair and washed his face,
And had also eaten his breakfast, he left the house.
And after he had hurried to the Temple of the City God,
He lit incense, bowed down, and burned the clothes.
    Pan Cheng communicated his intentions in great detail:
"Mr. Black Pot, please come and inhabit these clothes!"
As he burned the clothes, he communicated his intentions,
Explaining them in detail in his prayer to the City God.
    Once he had burned the clothes, he returned to his home,
And when he came home, he informed his dear mother:
"Now I have burned and transformed his clothes today,
I will take the pot with me to see the Living King Yama!"
    He then took the pot with him and left the house, and
Hurried to the office building of Kaifeng Prefecture.
When His Excellency saw Pan Cheng show up again,
He did not say a word, but mulled the case over in his mind.
    When Pan Cheng arrived before the steps of the hall,
[He said:] "Your Excellency, please listen to the facts!
Mr. Black Pot has told me he is truly intelligent, and
Today he will come and enter into the hall of this court."

Speak:

Pan Cheng informed his superior official: "That black pot can speak in a truly intelligent way! He said that he was stripped of his clothes by Geng One and

Geng Two, and was carried stark naked into the kiln where he was burned and then turned into a black pot. Because of this, he had no clothes on his body and didn't dare appear before Your Excellency. So yesterday I bought a set of clothes, which I took to the Temple of the City God to transform by burning, so the clothes might be conveyed to the lonely soul of Mr. Black Pot. Today I have brought him along to appear before Your Excellency, and I am sure he will speak!" When His Excellency heard him talk like this, [he said:] "Bring him here, and I will question him in detail once again!" His Excellency thereupon called out to the black pot: "From which township in which county in which prefecture do you hail? What is your surname and given name? Tell me in detail so this official can demand a life on your behalf!" He put the same question a number of times, but he got no response at all.

Sing:

His Excellency the prefect was greatly enraged in his heart,
He beat on his table and shouted enraged at the top of his voice:
"How intolerable! Pan Cheng, you have no decency at all —
Making a fool of an official is not some minor misdemeanor!"
    He then asked who were the people on duty that day, and
Ordered them to arrest that Pan Cheng in front of his court!
"That intolerable Pan Cheng is trying to make a fool of me!"
And he ordered: "Give him a thorough beating with the rod!"
    Pan Cheng, suffering a beating, felt very annoyed in his heart,
And he thought to himself: "How intolerable is this black pot!
The best thing is that this time I get off with a beating,
I can only fear that he will get even more angry the next time!"
    As soon as Pan Cheng had suffered his beating to the end,
He came forward, expressing his thanks to His Excellency.
    His Excellency called out to him, this single person, and said:
"Take that black pot there in front of the hall with you, and,
As before, go and serve that warrant on my behalf, and quickly
Arrest the King of the Winds. Make him appear here before me!"

Pan Cheng had no other option but to take the warrant, and
Leave the court after expressing his thanks to His Excellency.
As soon as he walked out through the gate of the court hall,
Pan Cheng wanted to beat that black pot to smithereens!
    The black pot addressed him again, speaking as follows:
"I beg you, Mr. Police Officer, please listen to what I will say!"

When Pan Cheng heard this he was very annoyed in his heart:
"Mr. Black Pot, you are indeed truly and utterly incompetent!
    When I want you to appear before the prefect, you don't.
But as soon as we are outside, you start talking to me again!
I wasted ten full strings of cash, of those green bats, in order
To buy a set of clothes for you, so you could cover your body!
    I had hoped that this time in front of the hall you would speak,
But you kept silent, said not a word, didn't make any sound!
This angered His Excellency so much that his gall ran over,
And he ordered me beaten — and all for what reason?"
    The black pot thereupon addressed him as follows, saying:
"Dear Mr. Police Officer, please listen to what I will say!
At present I have become a lonely soul far from my home,
And I have not a single relative who can guide and lead me.
    At this moment I am greatly, indeed greatly, indebted to you,
But the god of the soil of this office does not let me in.
Because I have not a single relative, I cannot enter the gate,
And so I cannot enter the court and ascend the court hall.
    I hope, Mr. Police Officer, that you will show compassion,
And buy some paper gold and silver to burn before the gate.
Burn that for the gods of the gate and the god of the soil,
And only then will I be able to ascend the hall of the court.
    If I ascend the court hall that time, I will definitely speak,
And I will explain each and every detail to His Excellency!"
When Pan Cheng heard him provide this full explanation,
He took the black pot with him and went out through the gate.

He promptly went off to buy some paper money and prints,
And thereupon promptly prayed to the gods of the gate.
After praying to the gods of the gate and the god of the soil,
He entered the gate of the prefecture, carrying the black pot.
    When His Excellency saw Pan Cheng enter one more time,
He did not say a word, but mulled the matter over in his mind:
"Just a moment ago that Pan Cheng did suffer a beating,
So what can be the reason that he now comes back again?"
    Pan Cheng stepped forward and hastily knelt down, saying:
"I pray you, Your Excellency, please listen to my words.
Your humble servant does not want to make a fool of you,
But this black pot wants to make a statement of its case.

If this time around the black pot still does not speak up,
You may condemn me to death and I will not complain!"
    When the prefect heard this, his heart was filled with joy,
And he then promptly started questioning the black pot.
The prefect questioned him in great detail, in these words:
"Black pot, tell me the cause of your coming in detail!"
    The black pot immediately in a loud voice called out:
"I am the victim of a crime, and that's why I am a pot!"
When His Excellency heard that the black pot could speak,
He promptly took some fine incense and lit it reverentially.

    He burned one candle of incense from Guangnan, and
Questioned him from the beginning and in great detail.
"If you have a statement to make, start from the beginning,
And don't try to scare this official with nonsense talk!"
    When the black pot was questioned, he piteously wept,
And weeping piteously he addressed His Excellency:
    "Sun and moon may be high, but they are easily seen,
But it was hard for this person to see Your Excellency.
Now today I am allowed to see Your Excellency's face,
It is as if an old mirror has become bright once again!

    My home is outside the western gate of Fuzhou city,
In White Goat Village, thirty miles from that city.
My father is Millionaire Yang, a very wealthy man,
My mother is addressed before the hall as 'My lady.'
    The wife I married is a daughter of the Wang family,
And we have one son and one daughter in our house.
My father does not have any other sons except me,
It is I who is his one and only son and heir.

    From my earliest youth I've devoted myself to study,
And I am acquainted with the Classics and Histories.
When I heard that His Majesty is holding examinations,
I wanted to present my writings skills to Our Ruler.
    Carrying my travel provisions I set out on the road,
And walking my way, I experienced much suffering.
When I eventually passed by White Hair Village,
I had the bad luck to meet with bandits, two of them.
    I ran into the two bandits Geng One and Geng Two,
And each of them had a heart that was black like coal.

They blocked my way and had me stay at their house,
And then they urged and insisted that I should drink.
They did not accept any excuses but had me drink;
They forced me to drink so much I ended up drunk.
And when it was about the hour of midnight, they
Strangled me with a handkerchief, and so I died.
They burned my corpse in a kiln seven days on end,
That's how I turned into the black pot I am now.
They schemed for my thousand strings of green bats,
For my ten ounces of gold and ten ounces of silver.
I also had ten pieces of red-bordered gauze,
Course and fine white textiles and silk materials.
They thought that I was gone without leaving a trace —
Today I've come to appear before Your Excellency.
Some days ago Your Excellency passed my basket,
And I wanted to appear before Your Excellency, so
It wasn't the King of the Winds who played a trick,
It was I who committed that crime — a major offense!
Now I beg Your Excellency to investigate this case,
To lift your bright mirror, I ask, and pass judgment.
If Your Excellency can demand a life on my behalf,
I will never forget your grace as I rest in my grave."
The prefect heard how he told the story of his woes,
Which he told in such a sad way it broke one's heart,
So His Excellency pondered in his heart how he might
Arrive at a verdict in this case of the ugly black pot.

Speak:

When His Excellency heard how pitiable the story was of the black pot, he ordered Pan Cheng to clearly write down the words of the black pot, and he placed the black pot behind the screen [behind his seat]. His Excellency said: "Pan Cheng, when this case is concluded, you will be handsomely rewarded." Pan Cheng expressed his gratitude to His Excellency, and left the hall.

Sing:

Let's not sing about Pan Cheng as he left the yamen,
Listen as I sing of that upright man Dragon-Design Bao.

He summoned the yamen runners to the front of the hall,
And thereupon addressed the yamen runners as follows:
"How many kiln-firing potters are there in this prefecture?
How many potters are there in the countryside villages?"
When the runners heard the prefect ask this question,
They immediately answered His Excellency as follows:
"Inside and outside the city there are thirty such families,
Please let us know what Your Honor's orders may be."
When His Excellency heard them reply in that manner,
He pondered the case in his mind, and mulled over the matter.
He then asked: "Who are the ones who are now on duty?
Quickly take some warrants and summon these people!
These thirty potters all have to appear in front of me,
And each and every one should bring his best black pot."
As soon as His Excellency had given his official orders,
The warrants were written — they left to arrest these men.

Speak:

His Excellency had come up with a clever scheme. When the warrants had been written, he dispatched Liu Wang the yamen runner on duty for that day to arrest with all possible speed the thirty potters of the city, and each had to appear in person, bringing a black pot. "They should understand," he claimed, "that they are presenting the pot to me, to plant the flowering osmanthus trees that have been offered in tribute by the Northern Barbarians." Liu Wang set out on his mission as he had been ordered, and within two days he had summoned them all, and they came to the hall to present their pots. Judge Bao immediately ordered Pan Cheng to replace one good pot with the weird pot, and then he ordered the potters: "You people, take your own pot, and come and present your pots tomorrow." When these potters heard this, they also checked for their mark, and when twenty-nine potters had left with their own pot, only one elderly guy was left. He was mumbling, gesticulating and refusing to leave. Judge Bao then asked him: "Why don't you leave?" Old Mr. Geng said: "Your Excellency, my pot was a fine pot, but someone, I don't know who, must have exchanged it and taken mine." When His Excellency heard this, he promptly asked old Mr. Geng: "Is this pot your handiwork or not?" Old Mr. Geng replied: "This is the handiwork of my sons." When His Excellency heard this, he ordered Pan Cheng to produce the good pot, and he again asked old Mr. Geng: "Is this indeed the handiwork of your sons?" His Excellency promptly ordered his underlings: "Arrest this old thief, and don't let him escape!"

Sing:

His Excellency at that time was filled with rage in his heart,
And he quickly ordered the underlings on both his sides:
"Arrest this old man Geng and subject him to interrogation,
Subject Mr. Geng to interrogation here in front of the hall."
  Old Mr. Geng at that time suffered quite a fright, and he was
So scared and terrified that his three souls fled from his body.
The clothes on his body were all stripped off, and, arrested,
He was subjected to interrogation there in front of the hall.
  Without intermission fifty strokes of the yellow-thorn cudgel:
He was beaten till his skin broke and blood soaked his body.
Then they took the long cangue and fastened it on his neck,
And they took him to the Western Prison for further torture.
  Once the investigating officer had taken him to the prison,
He questioned him under torture, asking him for the facts.
The ends of the cangue had been tied to a high rafter, and
To his waist had been attached stones of a hundred pounds.
  "With your heart black as coal you schemed to kill Yang,
We'll beat you and torture you till you confess to the truth.
Now take your time to make sure you remember all the facts,
How you schemed to get hold of his gold and treasure.
  The corpse you carried into the kiln, as it was your hope
That the fierce fire would burn it without leaving a trace.
You only thought at that time that no one had seen you —
Little did you know that the sky is filled with divinities!
  Your victim there in the kiln was miraculously transformed,
The lonely soul was transformed into that ugly black pot!
Today that black pot has come here to accuse you of murder,
So make haste to confess as you are now already in prison."
  When old Mr. Geng heard them speak in this manner,
He kept silent and said not a word, not uttering a syllable!
He wanted to confess to the facts, yet he could not confess,
But it was impossible to endure the sufferings of torture.
  So in the end he could not but confess the facts of the case,
In order to avoid enduring these horrible sufferings in jail.

Mr. Geng provided a full and detailed confession, saying:
"Mr. Investigating Officer, please listen to what I will say.

It was my sons who schemed to kill that rich merchant Yang,
They wanted to get hold of his yellow gold and white silver.
It was they who carried his corpse into the kiln, in the hope
That they could burn it in such a way not a trace was left.

It is not the case that I personally committed the murder,
It was my two sons who are living with me in my house.
It was my two sons, that Geng One and also that Geng Two,
Because these two both have hearts that are black like coal."

When the investigating officer heard this, he was very happy,
And he appeared in front of the hall to report to the judge.

Speak:

When the investigating officer had extracted a confession from old
Mr. Geng, he submitted it to His Excellency. When the latter had seen it,
he wrote a letter, and ordered Pan Cheng to go and invite Geng One
and Geng Two. The letter only said: "The quality of your handiwork is
excellent, and the black pots you produce are beautiful. So I have kept
your father at the yamen to feast him on a banquet, and I invite the two
of you over so I may give you a reward." [Judge Bao said to Pan
Cheng:] "Now go in all haste!" Pan Cheng set out on this assignment as
he had been ordered, and within a day he arrived at the village of the
Geng family. He promptly said to Geng One and Geng Two: "Prefect
Bao sends you a letter of invitation, saying that the quality of your
handiwork is excellent, and that he has detained your father at the yamen
to treat him to wine." When Geng One heard this, he accepted the
letter, and when he hastily opened it, its contents were indeed as he had
been told. His heart was filled with joy, and he quickly got out some
good wine to entertain Pan Cheng. They would all leave together early
the next morning.

Sing:

When Pan Cheng thereupon walked into this house,
He felt his heart booming and booming in his chest.
He was all alone here by himself without any companion,
He was filled with fear they might harbor evil intentions.

"Come to think of it, I'll have to stay tonight in this house,
But I am so afraid that they will end up killing me too.
Because they have seen the judge mentioning the black pot,
They must be constantly filled with worry, fearing all others.

　　If they would kill me off, it would only be a minor matter,
But on whom are the old and young in my family then to rely?
I would prefer not to have to stay here in their house, but
There is no other place where I can sleep or seek lodging."

　　In his heart he hesitated a hundred times, a thousand times:
"Come to think of it, this night here will worry me sick!
I can only rely now on the protection of Heaven and Earth,
Which must ensure that these two harbor no evil intentions.

　　If tomorrow morning I am still in one piece and alive,
I will thank the gods with paper, candles, and five dishes."

Let's not tell how Pan Cheng was frightened and fearful,
But let's rather tell about Geng One and Geng Two.
Geng One called his brother and spoke to him, saying:
"Dear younger brother, please listen to what I will say.

　　His Excellency highly praises the quality of our handiwork,
And a letter has come in which he invites the two of us.
It is quite an honor that His Excellency has invited us,
So we should entertain that man surnamed Pan quite well."

　　Behind the house they caught a goose and then killed it,
They even killed the fattest goose to prepare a fine meal.
They caught a fish from the pond which they had cooked,
And they further filled the plates with a variety of fruits.

　　The wine was an old cooked wine of some years back,
The wine cups and food plates were all sparkling new.
"Tonight we will treat him to a banquet and fine wine,
We will treat that man surnamed Pan really very well!"

　　Before one cup had been emptied, another cup came,
Before one bowl was downed, another bowl was filled.
Pan Cheng had drunk so much he was drunk as a skunk,
And in his belly he considered the matter, mulled it over.

　　"That guy Yang some time ago was also dead drunk,
And so he was strangled by them, thereby losing his life.
I have no clue with what intentions they treat me so well,
Please, let them not have the evil intention to kill me!

Even though I do not carry any gold or treasure on me,
I am still afraid that they may decide to finish me off.
So it would be far better if I would drink a few cups less,
In that way I will stay sharp and alert till break of dawn."
  Pan Cheng thereupon hastened to excuse himself, and
He thanked them for their hospitality and lavish meal.
"But from birth I've been unable to drink much wine,
So let me have my evening meal before I go off to bed."
  Pan Cheng thereupon promptly got his evening meal,
They treated Pan Cheng to fish soup and to fine food.
They also killed the fat chicken to serve as a side dish,
Perfectly prepared, it smelled so good people fell over!
  When Pan Cheng had eaten his fill, he was very happy,
And went to sleep in the room at the back of the hall.
Even though Pan Cheng was lying on his bed, he was
Obsessed in his belly by his fear of these two men.
  "I'm afraid these two men are guys without goodness,
I am afraid that they may kill me, both body and soul!
But I am the famous police officer Pan, who all his life
Has had as an article of faith to do favors to other people!"
  All through the night he never once closed his eyes,
He constantly continued to cough till break of dawn.
Throughout the night he sat fully clothed on his bed,
Waiting and waiting for the sky to brighten in the east.
  And as soon as the sky started to brighten in the east,
He made sure he got out of his bed as fast as he could.
And when he had combed his hair and washed his face,
He raised his hands high and thanked the dragon god!

But let's not sing of Pan Cheng at the back of the hall,
Let's change the topic and sing again of those bandits.
They called out to their mother: "Please listen to us,
Make us some breakfast so we can set out on this trip.
  Today we will be going to the city of Haozhou, where
We'll be received by His Excellency Dragon-Design Bao."
When they had finished their breakfast, they got dressed
To set out on the trip in the company of Pan Cheng.
  The two of them wore gowns that were white as snow—
In their new boots and pairs of pants quite dashing fellows!

Their gold-speckled lotus-pouches were the latest fashion,
And the leather boots on their feet were the newest color.
　Their heads were covered by tapering head-scarves, and
The rings hanging down on their necks gleamed in the sun.
When the two men had finished dressing themselves up,
They promptly set out on their journey to Haozhou.

Together the three of them went off to Haozhou, and
In the prefecture they appeared before His Excellency.
At that time His Excellency was seated in the hall, and
Pan Cheng announced their arrival, deeply bowing down.
　"Yesterday Your Excellency wrote an invitation letter,
Inviting these two people to come here from their village."
Geng One and Geng Two hastened to make a deep bow,
Lowering their heads they bowed before His Excellency.
　His Excellency Bao widely opened his three-cornered eyes,
And as he looked at them, a deadly rage rose in his breast!
When he had seen these two people he said: "Intolerable!
They're truly the type that breaks all regulations and laws!"
　So he ordered his underlings to set to work immediately,
To submit these two fellows to questioning then and there!
These two men were totally surprised at that time, but
They had already been arrested and had no way to flee.
　The runners grasped leather whips and strong cudgels,
On both sides they applied yellow thorns to their thighs.
Each of them got fifty strokes of the cudgel on his thighs,
Then were taken to the Eastern Prison for further torture.
　There the two of them were also locked in the long cangue,
And these two fellows were really suffering bitter pain.
Once Geng One and Geng Two were in the Eastern Prison,
Old Mr. Geng was brought out from the Western Prison.

When old Mr. Geng had been led out of the compound,
He appeared in front of the hall before His Excellency.
He begged His Excellency, saying: "Please spare my life,
Please spare the miserable life of mine, this old man!"
　His Excellency loudly questioned old Mr. Geng, saying:
"Where did you hide the gold and silver that you stole?"
Old Mr. Geng, now questioned like this, wept piteously,
And begged the prefect: "Your Excellency, please listen.

This gold and silver is not something that's in my hands,
So I have not the slightest clue where it may be stored.
These two good-for-nothing criminals in my family
Never discussed anything about this robbery with me!"
    His Excellency at that moment was very much annoyed,
And he said: "Old guy, now you really must listen to me.
If you refuse to confess to the crime and its circumstances,
You'll be taken to the Western Prison for further torture!"
    Old Mr. Geng at that time wept most piteously, saying:
"How can I confess to that crime and tell all about it?"
So at that time he was once again taken to the prison,
Where he would suffer bitter pain as he had done before.

His Excellency mulled this matter over in his belly, concluding:
"We'll have to interrogate those two fellows under torture."
So he ordered the runners to apply all possible pressure
When interrogating these two men in the Eastern Prison.
    So the two of them were strung up high by their cangue,
Their cangue was strung up high — it was truly distressing!
The Number One Tiger General applied the cudgel, and
Once beaten with this cudgel you are bound to confess!
    They were continuously beaten from head to toe, and
Every trace of the cudgel soaked their bodies with blood.
    Following this beating, the investigating officer asked them:
"Why did you two scheme to kill that man surnamed Yang?
Were you scheming for his gold and silver, silk and gauze?
What was the reason that you robbed that man of his life?"
    Now be smart and confess to the crime here in this prison,
So you'll be spared this beating, this torture and bitter pain.
But if you refuse to confess to the crime you committed, you'll
Be beaten till your skin is broken, your bodies soaked in blood."
    The two men, as they were beaten, wept piteously, saying:
"Mr. Investigating Officer, please listen to what we tell you.
We never schemed to get at his gold, at his silver and silk,
We never schemed to kill any man who is surnamed Yang."
    When the investigating officer heard this, he was annoyed,
And he decided to interrogate them through another torture.
The ends of their hair were tied to the ends of their cangue,
And stones of a hundred pounds hung from their waists.

Loudly shouting he questioned Geng One and Geng Two:
"I want the two of you to confess to premeditated murder!"
Questioned like this, the two of them answered as follows:
"Mr. Investigating Officer, please, you must listen to us!

His Excellency praised the quality of our work as potters,
For generations our family does not cede to any other.
Our old mother at home recites the name of the Buddha,
So how could we be so amoral as to murder a traveler?

We beg you, Mr. Investigating Officer, to show mercy,
Not to wrongly administer a beating to common folks!"
Hearing this, the investigating officer grew very annoyed,
And he decided to interrogate them through another torture.

His disciples called this the "chicken-scratching torture,"
Once you are tortured this way, you are bound to confess!
Long needles are stuck under the nails of your ten fingers,
And long nails are also nailed into the heels of your feet.

The investigating officer asked following this torture:
"Why did the two of you turn into this kind of criminal?
You schemed to get at Yang's gold and silver and silks,
Now confess to your crime, and tell me all the details!

If you are willing to confess to the crime in all detail,
You will be spared this bitter suffering here in this prison."
The two of them at that time addressed him as follows:
"Mr. Investigating Officer, please listen to our words.

We never schemed to rob him of his gold, silver and silks,
We never schemed to kill any man who is surnamed Yang.
We implore you, Mr. Investigating Officer, to show mercy,
And not to unjustly administer a beating to common folks.

His Excellency wrote us a letter, in which he invited us,
We never expected to enter this gate of disaster and trouble."

The investigating officer then secretly conceived of a plan:
"Let me inform His Excellency of the situation so far."
He hurried over to present himself in front of the hall,
And explained the situation in full detail, as he stated:

"Yesterday I received the high order of Your Excellency
To interrogate these two men under torture in the prison.
I submitted Geng One and Geng Two to three tortures,
But they stubbornly refused to confess to their crime.

In a single day I have tortured them three or five times,
I have tortured them in prison, but they do not confess."
When Judge Bao heard him give a report in these words,
He considered the matter in his mind and a plan was born.

He promptly called for Pan Cheng to appear before him:
"You must listen to what I will tell you here today!"
Yesterday you summoned those people to come here,
They are truly men with skin of bronze, bones of iron!

In one day they have been tortured three times in prison,
But they stubbornly refused to confess to their crime.
We'll wait till tonight for the hour of midnight, then you will
Impersonate the ghost of the victim and interrogate them!"

Speak:

His Excellency ordered Pan Cheng: "Wait till midnight, and impersonate
the ghost of the victim. Use a ladder to climb up to the roof, and then
shout into the inner courtyard: "I am Yang Zongfu! Geng One and Geng
Two, return me my life!" Pan Cheng did as His Excellency had ordered
him. When it became night, he went to the roof of the Eastern Prison, and
called to Geng One: "So the two of you are now here! I am Yang Zongfu.
Now quickly give me back my life!" When Geng One heard this, he did
not react in any way. But Pan Cheng again loudly shouted his demand
three times. Geng One and his brother then said: "Mr. Yang, we never
touched your gold and silver, silk and gauze, it is all at our place. We never
should have killed you. Please don't demand from us the return of your
life! If we manage to get out of this court case, we will use all your gold
and silver, silk and gauze to burn incense and have rituals performed to
make sure you will be reborn on a higher plane, in heaven." At this time
he also loudly called to Geng One: "Where have you hidden my gold and
silver, silk and gauze?" Geng One shouted; "Mr. Yang, please don't
mention my name! Your gold and silver were buried in the small kiln thirty
passes to the south of the main kiln. Your silk and gauze and copper cash
are all hidden under the bed of our mother. You don't have to worry. Wait
till we are released, and then we will have many masses read, so you will be
quickly reborn in the realm of heaven." The moment Pan Cheng had
learned all these details, he left.

Sing:

Inside the hall the prefect was waiting for the results,
By the light of a painted candle waiting for Pan Cheng.

When Pan Cheng got precise answers to his questions,
He appeared before the hall to report to His Excellency.
　　He told him all the true facts from the very beginning,
He clearly explained everything to His Excellency.
　　"The gold and silver are all hidden in the southern kiln,
Inside that small kiln it has been hidden under cover.
The copper cash is hidden under the bed of their mother,
The gauze and the silk are lying there in the middle."
　　When His Excellency heard this, he was filled with joy,
And he stayed there, sitting idly, waiting for the dawn.
　　When eventually the skies brightened, lighting the east,
And travelers started walking, setting out on the road,
His Excellency Bao gave an order to the effect that
Old Mr. Geng be brought to him from the Western Jail.

When old Mr. Geng was brought from the jail to the hall,
His cangue was removed, his chains were unshackled.
When old Mr. Geng was released, he was filled with joy,
And with lowered head he bowed to thank Judge Bao.
　　The latter thereupon dispatched thirty yamen runners,
Together with the head of the watch and Pan Cheng.
The neighborhood chief and village head were summoned,
To retrieve the gold and silver in White Hair Village.
　　They also took old Mr. Geng along with them, and then
They shouted their "Yes, Sir" and set out on the trip.
　　Let's not sing about their journey out on the road —
In due time they arrived there in White Hair Village.
When they entered the house of old Mr. Geng,
Grandma Geng was so scared she lost her three souls.
　　Thereupon they all went to the site of the kiln, where
They dug up the earth to find out the truth of the facts.
Indeed they discovered that the gold and the silver
Had been placed in the smaller kiln to be hidden.
　　They also took all the gold and silver in the house,
And when everything had been collected, they left.
They still took old Mr. Geng back with them, and,
Once in the prefecture, they reported to Judge Bao.
　　When all the runners had assembled before the hall,
Pan Cheng formally reported to His Excellency:
"In conformity with the command of Your Excellency
We retrieved the gold and silver from Geng Village.

We found the gold and silver, and the silk and gauze,
And then we also found the thousand strings of cash.
Today in the hall we hand over the full amount, and
Not the slightest item from the list here is missing."
    Judge Bao thereupon issued the following order:
"It is not fitting at all that old Mr. Geng be released.
Not strictly controlling his family, he committed a crime,
As he allowed his sons to kill officials and commoners.

    You will not be put in the cangue because you are old,
But you will be taken to prison as a convicted criminal."
When old Mr. Geng heard this, he was filled with sorrow,
As he was going back to prison where he would suffer.

Let's not sing of old Mr. Geng and his added sufferings,
But listen as I tell of the prefect with the surname Bao.
    At that time he called for Pan Cheng and ordered him:
"Now come forward and listen to what I will say.
I will dispatch five runners of proven capacities
To travel with you together to the city of Fuzhou.

    You will visit the Yang family to the west of the city,
And you will tell his old father to come to this place."
The assembled runners made all possible haste, and,
Having taken their leave of the prefect, they took off.

    Coming to prefectures and counties, they slept there,
Passing through townships and villages they moved on.
On the road, as they traveled on, they wanted to hurry —
Just like wind-blown clouds by the side of the moon.

    They did not ask about high mountains, curving rivers;
They did not discuss dark mountains or blue streams.
After passing nine prefectures and fourteen counties,
They eventually arrived outside the city of Fuzhou.

    They promptly entered the gates of the city of Fuzhou,
The city was densely populated and full of fine sights.
They had no desire to admire the streets and markets,
But asked at the west gate for persons surnamed Yang.

    Thirty miles outside the city of Fuzhou they came to
Fine villages amidst green fields and blue streams.
When asking people outside for the house of the Yangs,
They found White Goat Village just ahead of them.

Green willows in front of the gate welcomed visitors,
Red apricots and blooming peaches shaded the gate.
Seen from afar the gate building was one rod high,
On all its sides it was surrounded by the freshest flowers.
In front of the house there was a bridge of flowers, and
Below that bridge there was an ever-flowing stream.
When this party arrived outside the gate building,
They gave three shouts, resounding like thunder.

When old Mr. Yang came to the gate to have a look,
He saw five yamen runners standing before his gate.
Old Mr. Yang then asked them the following question:
"What kind of business brings you here to this place?"
The yamen runners thereupon addressed him as follows:
"Please listen to what we have to say to you today.
The son of this family left to compete for an office,
And we are here on purpose to bring you his news."

Speak:

When Pan Cheng and his party of five yamen runners had arrived in White
Goat Village, they found the house of the Yang family. When he had
greeted old Mr. Yang, he thought to himself: "I will not yet tell him the
truth, because I am afraid it might be too much of a shock to the old
man." So Pan Cheng then told old Mr. Yang: "We are runners who have
come to report the results!" When Mr. Yang heard this, his heart was filled
with joy, and he promptly invited the runners to come inside to the hall.
When they had had a cup of tea, he treated them to three cups of wine.
Only after they had finished their meal did Pan Cheng step forward and
say: "Dear sir, we are no runners reporting the results of the examinations.
Your son left to compete for office, but when passing by White Hair
Village in the area of Tianchang and Liuhe, he ran into Geng One and
Geng Two, who schemed to rob him of all his gold and silver and other
treasures. His ghost then transformed into a black pot, which recently in
Haozhou lodged a complaint with the prefect. His Excellency has
dispatched us to come here and report this to you.

Sing:

He dispatched us, these runners, to inform you of this,
His Excellency ordered us to come here and visit you."

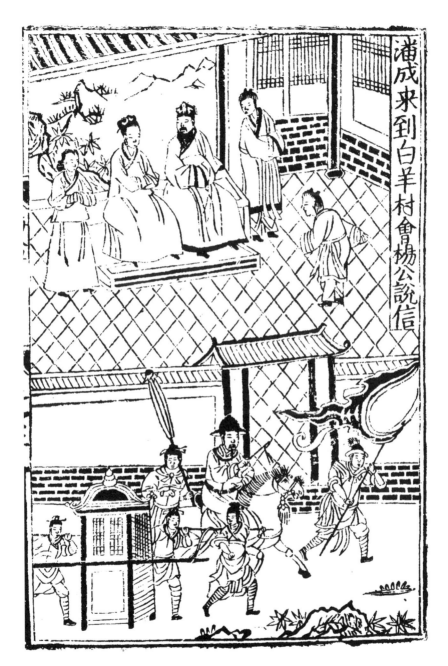

潘成來到白羊村會楊公說信

Fig. 5.2
Pan Cheng arrives at White Goat Village and informs Mr. Yang.

When old Mr. Yang heard this, he fainted from shock,
He collapsed in front of the hall, not uttering a word.
    Two of the runners came up and helped him to his feet,
And old lady Yang in her room also learned about it.
She ran into the hall to ask them what had happened,
Why old Mr. Yang had collapsed at the gate of the hall.
    She hurried to fetch some water to help his recovery,
And eventually he came back to life, regained his senses.
"One raises a son as an insurance against later old age,
Little did we know that today we would be separated!"
    She also told the news to his wife in her chamber, saying:
"Dear daughter-in-law, please listen to what I have to say.
Your husband has passed away, he has been murdered,
And he has left us to meet with the lord of darkness."
    When his wife heard this, her breath stuck in her throat,
And she fainted that very moment, losing life and soul.
She regained her senses only after more than an hour.
And in her own chamber she suffered a thousand pains.
    "Back then I hoped we would live together till old age,
Little did I know that the two of us would be separated!"
The whole family, old and young, wept most piteously,
How could it not break your heart, all these sad people?
    With tears in his eyes old Mr. Yang thereupon said:
"Dear officers, I will order all of you properly rewarded.
Each will receive as reward a string of three hundred cash
For all your trouble," he said altogether a number of times.
    Pan Cheng stepped forward and hastily offered his thanks,
And he said: "Dear Mr. Yang, let's set out on the journey.
His Excellency the prefect is waiting for you right now,
Please be so kind as to quickly set out on the journey."
    When old Mr. Yang now heard him speak in this manner,
He said to his daughter-in-law: "Please listen to me.
    Get together money for the expenses to make this trip,
We all must make this journey to the Eastern Capital.
We will have to go to Haozhou to see the prefect,
And only then will we learn all the details of this case."
    Old lady Yang was mulling the matter over in her heart,
And she concluded that she never again would see her son.
But let's not sing of the sufferings in the old lady's heart —
They got the money together needed to make the journey.

The party of yamen runners set out to make the journey,
The orphaned son and daughter also joined the group.
After they had taken their leave of their grandmother,
They set out on the road, weeping as they were walking.
    After passing a number of mountains, a number of ridges,
They crossed the Qiantang River by taking the ferry.
Once they had crossed the Qiantang River at the ford,
They entered the gates of the city of Hangzhou.
    They had no desire to look at the fine sights in the city,
Their desire was only to hurry on and get on ahead.
They had no desire to admire green hills or blue streams,
They passed through prefectures and counties — that is all.
    Having gone for a mile, they longed for the next one,
Having walked for a stretch, they hoped for the next one.
After they had been on the road for many long days,
They arrived at Guazhou, where one crosses the river.
    They then crossed the Big River without any incident,
And in this way they came to the city of Haozhou.
The whole party entered the city of Haozhou,
As their urgent desire was to arrive at the yamen.

Pan Cheng promptly entered and went to the hall,
He gave three loud shouts, resounding like thunder.
With his hands crossed before his breast, he reported:
"Your Excellency, please listen to what I will say.
    You dispatched this humble servant to go to Fuzhou,
To inform all members of the Yang family, and today
The members of the Yang family have all arrived here,
They've arrived at this yamen to learn all the details."
    When His Excellency heard this, he gave his orders,
Calling for all members of the Yang family to enter.
The members of the Yang family came before the hall,
With lowered heads they deeply bowed before Judge Bao.
    Lady Wang made a deep, deep bow before the steps,
And both her son and her daughter were awash in tears.

Speak:

Old Mr. Yang came together with his daughter-in-law, grandson and
granddaughter to the yamen, where they presented themselves to the

prefect. With lowered heads they deeply bowed, as tears streamed down their cheeks. As soon as Judge Bao saw them, he said to Mr. Yang: "Please, don't be so saddened." Old Mr. Yang thereupon reported to His Excellency: "I only had this one son. His name was Zongfu. At the age of thirty he married lady Wang as his wife, who bore him one boy and one girl. They are now here with me. My son — how painful the memory — wanted to compete for an office, and his father and mother and wife could not keep him at home. So upon whom am I now to rely?" His Excellency then said to old Mr. Yang: "When your son came to White Hair Village he ran into Geng One and Geng Two who killed him because of his gold and silver, gauze and silk. These two murderers have been arrested by me and have been locked up in jail. I will exact revenge for you!"

Sing:

Old Mr. Yang's heart at that time was filled with suffering,
Because of his pain and suffering his tears were heart-rending.
The prefect addressed old Mr. Yang in the following manner:
"Please now come forward and listen to what I will say.
    The money and goods, the gold and silver will be returned,
Will all be returned to you to take home for use in old age.
Now today please go back to the inn where you're staying,
Set your mind at rest, and wait for what's going to happen."
    Let's not say more about the instructions of His Excellency —
A weeping lady Wang thereupon addressed His Excellency,
Loudly weeping in a piteous manner she spoke as follows:
"Your Excellency, be so kind as to listen to me, a mere woman.
    Please allow me now to have a look at that ugly black pot,
So I may have at least one good look at that ugly black pot."
When the prefect saw how much she suffered in her heart,
He ordered one of his men to bring out that ugly black pot.
    He had it placed by him on the steps in front of the hall,
And at the same time also had the finest incense burned.
And when they had lit a candle of incense from Guangnan,
His Excellency spoke to the ugly black pot in these words:
    "Today your father has made the long journey to this place,
Your wife and your son and your daughter are all present."
When the lonely soul heard this call from His Excellency,
He spoke from below the table carrying the incense burner.

The black pot then promptly spoke at the top of its voice:
"My dear father, please listen to what I now have to say.
Little did I know that after leaving my father and mother,
I would run into this couple of inveterate criminals here.

They had their eyes on my gold and silver, silk and gauze,
So they strangled me with a handkerchief, taking my life.
They then carried my corpse into the middle of their kiln,
And burned by the fire I was turned into an ugly black pot.

Now I have died I will not be able to return home,
And I have betrayed my parents' favors in raising me.
I had hoped that returning home after winning an office,
I would then have been able to repay your parental care.

We will only have this one opportunity to be together,
Later I will not be able to go back to our house and home.
Please tell my dear mother not to be saddened too much,
Don't let her hope that her son will miraculously return.

[You, my dear wife,] take good care of family affairs,
Give all your energy to the care of our darling children."
When Mr. Yang heard this, he was overcome by pain,
And tears streamed down from his eyes in great profusion.

"People in this world should die when in their old age,
But you, my son, have died in a way that is not proper.
I had hoped that you would accompany me in my old age —
One plants a tree in wintertime to have shade in summer.

Back then you did not follow the advice of your parents,
And now you cause your father bitter pain in his heart.
I am now old and aged, and have no one to look to,
Looking around me, I nowhere find the slightest comfort.

Now today my son has died and departed forever,
It causes me such bitter pain that it wounds the heart.
Only today, now His Excellency serves as the witness,
Do I believe the dire news because I have seen my son."

The wife then stepped forward, weeping most piteously.
"My dear husband, please now listen to what I will say.
I hoped to share a hundred years with you till old age —
Little did I know that this day we would be separated!

If back then you only would have listened to my advice,
We could have spent a few more springs together at home.
On whom are my old and aged parents-in-law to rely
Now you have died and will never return back home?

It's a minor matter for me to keep to a cold chamber,
But on whom are your son and your daughter to rely?
You now have died and will never return back home —
When will I ever be able to see my dear husband's body?"

The lonely soul once again spoke up in clear words,
As he said: "My dear wife, now please listen to me.
I had hoped that once I obtained an office and returned,
I would back home be able to take good care of my wife.

Little did I know that I would run into these criminals,
Who would kill me because of my gold and my silver.
I now lost my life before my allotted span had run out,
Betraying the united love between husband and wife.

Please remember the days we spent together at home,
And do not give your body in marriage to another man.
Still, if you would remarry, that is only a minor matter,
But it would be too hard on our son and our daughter.

Once back home please respect your aged parents-in-law,
Heaven and Earth and all the gods will duly take note.
Back at home please don't scold our son and our daughter,
Make every effort to raise them, and so spend your years.

We only will have this opportunity to meet each other —
My wife, don't hope to see your dear husband's body."
The lonely soul then once more spoke up in clear words:
"My dear child, my darling daughter, please listen to me.
Today, alas, your daddy has died, you'll have no father
To take good care of you, my little child, from now on.

When later you will have grown up into a young lady,
You're bound to be married and joined to another man.
Please make sure to properly respect your parents-in-law,
Filially obey your parents-in-law, the elder generation.

Be diligent in your study of using needle and thread,
Let it not be said you're lazy and lax, not a full person!
Learn to make the thousand different patterns of clothes,
Stick to your mother's guidance while still at home."

Instructing his son and his daughter, he piteously wept,
"Today we are separated only halfway on the road!"
He then called out to his son, "Yang Zhibao, my child!
My dear son, please listen to what I will have to say.

Now your father has died, you have none to rely on,
Please, be diligent in your studies and recite the books.

When later you will have grown up into a young man,
Make sure to respect your grandfather and grandmother.
     Make sure to respect your own dear mother in her room,
On no account should you ever allow any rift to develop.
Maintain good relations with the neighbors, high and low,
Don't get into squabbles that make people get mad at you."
     After he had left these instructions, they fell to weeping —
His Excellency too was moved to tears by this sight.
The yamen runners present there all shed tears, and
People who chanced to be around were deeply affected.
     Judge Bao then had the pot taken back inside again,
His Excellency carefully mulled the matter over in his mind.
He thereupon called for old Mr. Yang below the steps:
"You, sir, please come forward and listen to my words.
     The gold and silver, silk and gauze are returned to you,
So take them home with you for use in your old age.
Take the copper cash and the checks also back home,
And have masses said for the rebirth of your son's soul.
     Now please leave this hall and find an inn to stay;
And once back home, try to get by as best as you can.
Wait till this judicial case is fully concluded, and then
I will dispatch runners to accompany you back home."
     Old Mr. Yang thereupon bowed with lowered head,
Expressed his thanks to the prefect and then left the hall.

Let's not sing how Mr. Yang went out to find an inn —
His Excellency gave the following order to Pan Cheng:
"Now go to the prison, and torture those two criminals
Until you will have extracted confessions out of those two!"
     Pan Cheng thereupon went over and entered the prison,
To question them under torture to learn the true facts.
Pan Cheng addressed the investigating officer, saying:
"His Excellency orders to subject those two to torture."
     When the investigating officer received this order,
He set out, there in the prison, to torture these criminals.
The first torture is called the torture of oppressive walls,
This is a torture that is bound to result in confessions!
     A bottomless vat is buried in the ground in such a way
That it only leaves your head and face still sticking out.

A wall of charcoal on all four sides is burning red-hot,
And the heat of the fire once it burns is really oppressive!
   The investigating officer addressed them as follows:
"Why did you plan to murder that man surnamed Yang?
You wanted to get at his gold and silver, silk and gauze,
And carried his corpse into the kiln to be burned by fire.
   If you make a full confession from the very beginning,
You will not be subjected to this bitter suffering in jail.
I will tell His Excellency to be mild in his sentence, and
Spare your lives so you may even go back to your home.
   But if you refuse to confess to the crime and the facts,
We'll subject you to bitter suffering, day in and day out.
We'll torture you till your skin breaks, bones pulverize —
The yellow thorn will beat your body from head to toe."
   These two piteously begged the investigating officer:
"Mr. Investigating Officer, please listen to what we say!
For generations we have been high-quality potters, and
We never raised a hand to kill another living person!"
   Hearing this, the investigating officer said: "Damn it,
These two truly have skin of bronze and bones of iron!
But if these two criminals will not sign their confession,
We will try out another torture to torture these two!"
   This second torture is called the torture of sharp nails,
This is a torture that is bound to result in confessions!
Sharp nails are nailed into the upper side of a board,
And the sharp nails are sticking out as white as silver.
   They ordered the two of them to walk across the nails,
To walk until the bottoms of their feet were fully shredded.
Their fresh blood was streaming all over the nail-board —
They subjected them to the most bitter pain and suffering.
   The investigating officer called out to Geng One, saying:
"Now hurry up and confess to the crimes you committed!
If today you still refuse to confess to the facts of the crime,
We still have other tortures in store to torture you with!"
   Geng Two shouted to the investigating officer, saying:
"We never schemed to murder that man surnamed Yang!"
Hearing this, the investigating officer grew very annoyed,
"Damn it, these two scoundrels now really piss me off!"

He thereupon heated one pan of sesame oil, meaning
To use this third kind of torture to torture these two men.
He then put hemp and leather in this pot of heated oil,
And after taking the hemp and leather out, hung it on them.
    Skin and flesh all over their bodies were wounded this way,[8]
And the investigating officer cursed them as follows:
"Now you two scheming murderers, you listen to me!
Hurry up and confess to the crime, to the facts of the case,
So you won't have to suffer this bitter pain here in prison."
    The two of them addressed him in the following words:
"Mr. Investigating Officer, please listen to what we say!
We never schemed to murder that man surnamed Yang,
We never schemed to rob him of his treasure and pearls."
    Hearing this, the investigating officer said: "Damn you!
These are men with skin of bronze and bones of iron!
If these people refuse to confess to the facts of the crime,
I have to report in front of the hall to His Excellency!"

He reported to His Excellency, saying: "Please listen,
Your Excellency ordered me to subject them to torture.
I subjected them to torture three times in a single day —
They have not confessed to their crime in the slightest."
    When the prefect heard this, he said: "How intolerable!"
He considered the case in his heart and a plan was born.
    He thereupon ordered Pan Cheng to go once again and
Impersonate the victim's soul on the roof of the prison.
"When this judicial case is finally finished and done,
I will reward you handsomely, not in a niggardly way!"
    When Pan Cheng at that moment received this order,
He impersonated once again, as before, the lonely soul.
He waited for the third watch, for the hour of midnight,
To impersonate, as before, on the roof, the victim's soul.

Speak:

When the hour of midnight had arrived, Pan Cheng got a long ladder and
climbed onto the roof. When he got to the inner courtyard, he cried: "Geng
One and Geng Two, give me back my life! Return all the gold and silver,
gauze and silk to me!" He called this three times in a row, but there was no

---

[8] One line of verse appears to be missing in the original following this line.

reaction at all. The lonely soul then called out again, and when Geng One was named, he said: "Mr. Yang, please don't come here and demand a life! We may be in prison now, but we will never confess, even if it means our death. If we manage to get out of here, we will sell all of your belongings and have the rituals performed for your rebirth in heaven." The investigating officer then said to Geng One and Geng Two: "You said that you did not murder Mr. Yang, so how come he now comes here to claim a life?"

Sing:

Before Geng One had been able to finish his sentence,
The investigating officer asked him what this was all about.
The investigating officer addressed him in the following way:
"You scheming murderers, now make sure to listen to me!
    You said that you did not kill that traveler Mr. Yang, and
You stubbornly refused to confess to the facts of the crime.
But who is it now who has come to demand a life in return?
And what are you promising to do on behalf of that man?"
    The two of them didn't know how to answer those questions,
They kept silent, said not a word, and did not utter a sound.
"When we torture you early tomorrow, we will not spare you,
So confess to the facts of the crime from the very beginning."
    Now finally the two of them hastened to speak, saying:
"Mr. Investigating Officer, please listen to what we will say.
It is indeed the case that back then we acted too rashly,
We now will tell you all the details, so make sure to listen.
    In a momentary impulse we killed that traveler Mr. Yang,
We wanted to get at his yellow gold and his white silver.
He also had silk and gauze and a thousand strings of cash —
The corpse we carried into the kiln to be burned by the fire."
    Hearing this, the investigating officer was filled with joy,
They confessed to the facts of the crime, from the beginning.
So he got out paper and brush and he wrote it all down:
That light touch of the brush weighed a thousand pounds!
    They confessed to the crime and he wrote it all down,
They placed their fingerprints and wrote out their names.
Seeing them confess, the investigating officer was happy,
At break of dawn he would report to His Excellency!
    Soon it was the fifth watch and the skies became bright,
And the investigating officer walked out of the prison.

He hurried to present himself in front of the court hall,
And he narrated what had happened from the beginning.
"Your Excellency, please be so kind as to listen to me.
Tonight they have given a full and complete confession.
The confession states the truth of the facts of the crime,
It has been written up according to form, and here it is!"
    When the prefect saw it, his heart was filled with joy,
And he burned some fine incense in the incense burner.
Judge Bao, seated in the hall, gave the following order:
"Now bring me old Mr. Geng from the Western Prison."
    Mr. Geng was brought from prison and came to the hall,
His Excellency thereupon explained to him his reasons:
"When annihilating weeds, one always pulls out the roots —
But in my compassion I take your age into consideration.
A filial and obedient family produces filial sons, but
A disobedient and rebellious one produces evil sons.
    You did not control your sons, did not rein them in,
And allowed them from early on to have evil designs.
You did not control your family, so you are punished,
You are sentenced to distant banishment as a soldier."
    When old Mr. Geng heard this, his tears flowed down,
His tears coursed down his cheeks in great profusion.
"I raised these sons as insurance against later old age —
Little did I know they would involve me in their crime!"

His Excellency then called for Pan Cheng, saying:
"Now today you must go and summon old lady Geng!"
When Pan Cheng heard this, he immediately set out,
Carrying the warrant with him, he set out on the road.
    While on the road, he tried to travel as fast as he could,
And soon he had arrived at the gate of the Geng family.
When he had arrived at the house of old Mr. Geng,
He immediately addressed old lady Geng, saying:
    "I have a warrant of His Excellency, summoning you!
So hurry up and get ready to set out on the journey!"
When grandma Geng heard this, she was in a panic,
But she had no option but to set out on the journey.
    When Pan Cheng had summoned this grandma Geng,
He hurried as fast as he could back to the yamen gate.

When Pan Cheng and grandma Geng had arrived,
Pan Cheng in the hall narrated what had happened.
"As per your orders I left from here with the warrant,
And today I report I have arrested that old lady Geng."
Hearing this, His Excellency promptly called for her,
Ordering her to come forward so she could hear him.
Old lady Geng ascended the hall and fell on her knees:
"Dear Mr. Prefect, be so kind here as to listen to me.
When I saw that student coming in, asking for lodging,
I immediately told that student he should be on his way.
Little did I know he would run into these scoundrels,
Who murdered him to get at his gold and his silver.
They carried his corpse into the middle of the kiln,
Where they burned it with fire so as to leave no trace.
Each and every day I would argue with the two of them,
But they never listened to my advice and only grew angry.
At home I spend my days reciting the name of the Buddha,
The rosary with its numbered pearls never leaves my side.
Each and every day I fast, only eating vegetarian food —
I never suspected to give birth to such utterly evil people!"
His Excellency the prefect thereupon gave his orders,
And pronounced his verdict concerning old Mrs. Geng:
"In principle the complete family shares the punishment,
But I will spare you because of your Buddhist piety."

His Excellency thereupon once again gave his orders,
Loudly commanding the decapitation of those two men.
They selected a favorable hour and also a lucky day
To behead these two criminals on the execution grounds.
The prison warden thereupon promptly left in a hurry,
To bring these two men from the prison that held them.
He brought out not only Geng One but also Geng Two,
And he brought them before the hall for interrogation.
His Excellency thereupon personally examined them,
He concluded that they had clearly confessed the crime.
They had placed their fingerprints, written their names:
Soon they would be taken to the execution grounds!
White rice and fine wine were set out before them:
A sacrificial meal that allowed them to eat their fill.

This rice is called the rice of the eternal rest, and
This wine is called the cup of separation forever.
    The officials and officers of the five halls all went
To the execution grounds for the double beheading.
When they eventually arrived at the execution grounds,
The executioner lifted his sword, as white as silver.
    He ordered the two criminals: "Make sure to listen:
Don't go to the world of shade and try to accuse me!"
Their heads fell to the ground with a single sound —
Elder and younger brother off to the world of shade!

Let's not sing of how those two men lost their lives —
The officials and their runners made the trip back.
When they all had returned, [Judge Bao] took his seat,
In the hall His Excellency not only called for Pan Cheng,
    But he also called for old Mr. Yang and his relatives —
"Let them all come here and listen to what I will say!"
Old Mr. Yang thereupon lowered his head and bowed,
With lowered head he bowed down before His Excellency.
    Judge Bao at that time gave the following orders, saying:
"Take the black pot with you and then go back home.
Make haste to go home and have the rituals performed
That will ensure the higher rebirth of this lonely soul."
    Judge Bao gave Pan Cheng a thousand strings of cash,
To reward him for all his recent exertions in travel.
Old Mr. Yang expressed his thanks, bowing deeply, and
Lady Wang fell on her knees in front of His Excellency.
    "We are grateful to Your Excellency for exacting justice,
Once back home we'll never forget Your Honor's grace.
The gauze and silk, gold and silver we do not need at all,
Please award it to the runners as an expression of thanks."
    His Excellency then addressed old Mr. Yang as follows:
"Take this with you back home to use in your old age."
Old Mr. Yang didn't dare make arguments for too long,
So he said: "Allow me to thank Your Excellency again.
    Allow me also to thank Pan Cheng for all his efforts,
And to give to him these ten string of cash, of green bats.
I express these feelings here on behalf of my young son —
Burning our own flesh as incense would not be enough!"

Pan Cheng thereupon hurried to make a light bow, as
An expression of his thanks to the man surnamed Yang.
Pan Cheng thereupon addressed him as follows, saying:
"Allow me to thank you, Mr. Yang, for your generosity!
　　You will now be making the long journey back home,
Make sure to take good care of yourselves till you are home!"
Old Mr. Yang thereupon bowed with lowered head, and
Lady Wang fell on her knees to thank His Excellency.
　　When they had taken their leave, they all left the hall,
They all took leave of each other as they passed the gate.
Judge Bao further dispatched a number of runners
To escort old Mr. Yang on his long journey back home.

Old Mr. Yang took, of course, the black pot with him,
The gold and silver, silk and gauze all followed behind.
Bitterly weeping, old Mr. Yang set out on the journey,
And the party of runners then also set out on the road.
　　While on the road they hurried on, making great haste,
Their feet were hurting, their waists were wrecked by pain.
When they walked for a mile, they longed for the next,
When they had gone a stretch, they hastened on again.
　　Passing through prefectures and counties, they suffered,
"We suffer this bitter pain here today because of my son!"
Let's not sing of the bitter sufferings of old Mr. Yang —
Listen as I tell of the prefect, the man surnamed Bao!

He hastily composed a report to be sent to the Throne,
To be sent to His Imperial Majesty, the Humane Ancestor.
He dispatched a messenger to run as fast as he could, and
Hurry to the capital Chang'an, a city of flowery brocade.[9]
　　The messenger hurried and ran while he was on the road,
Flower streets and willow alleys he passed in great haste.
After he had spent a number of days on the road, running,
He arrived at Chang'an, the capital city of the empire!
　　He quickly delivered the report to the Office of Tribute,
And the secretary for submissions presented the report.

---

[9] Chang'an had been the capital of the Western Han (206 BCE-8CE) and the Tang (617–906). Here it refers to the capital Kaifeng.

At the third notch of the fifth watch the audience starts:
Then he presented the report to the enlightened ruler.
He placed it on the table covered by imperial silk, and
When His Majesty lifted his eyes, he read the contents.
The document told him that Prefect Bao of Haozhou
Reported to His Majesty an important criminal case.
An ugly black pot had lodged an accusation of murder,
And once justice had been done this report was sent.
The report also suggested that soldiers be dispatched
To White Hair Village and make the place into a pass.
If soldiers would be dispatched to garrison this place,
There would be no more evil elements to kill people.
Upon reading this report, the emperor was very happy:
"That Lord Bao knows his job! He's really a good man!
He could handle the murder case of the ugly black pot!
He's truly a pure official, this upright man Bao Zheng!"
His Imperial Majesty thereupon pronounced an edict:
Haozhou's sprout taxes were lessened by three-tenths;
All private debts were remitted according to the rules,
And official state taxes were lessened by fifty percent.
One hundred regular troops were promptly dispatched
To establish their camp in the Tianchang-Liuhe area.
The imperial edict was to be sent to Haozhou Prefecture
To instruct Dragon-Design Bao, that upright minister!
When the prefect received the sagely edict of his king,
He set out an incense altar to thank for the royal grace.
Having thanked for the grace, he opened the edict, and
Learned what the words it contained had to tell him.
The three decisions on taxes followed old precedents,
But troops were also dispatched to set out on the road.
Soldiers had been sent, a full hundred troops, and they
Would establish a garrisoned pass at White Hair Village.

Let's not sing about the events at White Hair Village,
Let's change the topic, sing of the man surnamed Yang.
After old Mr. Yang had been traveling for many days,
He eventually arrived at the city of Fuzhou prefecture.
He went out of the west gate and went on ahead, and
After one stretch of road he arrived in his home village.

When grandma Yang heard this, she welcomed him home,
Coming out of the gate to welcome her husband back home.
Once she had welcomed her husband below the gate, she
Asked him about his experiences from the very beginning.

Her daughter-in-law stepped forward and made a bow:
"Dear mother-in-law, I hope you have been doing well.
Please do not ask all these questions outside at the gate,
But let's go inside and we will tell you the story there."

When old Mr. Yang arrived in the hall and sat down,
He promptly called for wine to treat the yamen runners.
When wine had been brought, he also called for rice,
And when the runners had eaten, they got up to leave.

Old Mr. Yang took out three hundred strings of cash,
Which he gave as a reward to this party of yamen runners.
The yamen runners, once rewarded, were filled with joy;
They took their leave of Mr. Yang and set out on the road.

When the yamen runners had left for their journey home,
Mr. Yang in the hall of his house fell to loud weeping.
The whole family wept painfully, pained in their hearts —
Who would not be hurt in his heart by their bitter pain?

Their relatives and their neighbors all came together,
They wept most piteously, and all were awash in tears.
When old Mr. Yang had finished weeping, he said:
"We should create some good karma for my dear son."

He went out to invite some monks and some laborers
For a ritual of seven days and nights to benefit his son.
Old Mr. Yang at this time was suffering in his heart,
And he then promptly had the mourning hall erected.

He invited the monks and he invited the local elders,
And when the masses were read, they all listened.
Incense and flowers: a ritual of seven days and nights,
At which ten eminent monks were reading the sutras.

Inviting gods and devas: they had miraculous power,
Performing the service for the deceased they kept busy.
The Liang Emperor's Repentance Form was read out,
The *Ksitigarbha* and *Diamond Sutras* were recited.

The vegetarian feast was very well organized indeed,
The relatives were treated to a hundred kinds of dishes.

They only dispersed after seven days and seven nights,
Only then all the relatives returned to their own homes.
　　When they all had dispersed after seven days of ritual,
Old Mr. Yang was secretly wounded by pain in his heart.
"One raises a son as insurance against later old age, but
Little did I know that today we both would be separated.
　　A thousand deaths, a myriad of deaths — we all must die,
But why did he have to die so, without any reason or cause?
Fortunately His Excellency Bao acted there as our witness,
And he succeeded in claiming a life and a soul for our son."

I have now sung to the end this heart-rending tale, and
I urge all you later people to practice goodness of heart.
　　You only have to look at the cruel death of Yang Zongfu,
He lost his life at the hands of these two violent criminals.
I urge you all to please never commit such shameful deeds:
Such will be witnessed by the sun, the moon, and the stars.
　　People who are filial and obedient are aided by Heaven;
Rebellious, disobedient people enrage even the Buddha.
They kill someone in secret, hidden to all human beings,
But they forget that up in the sky there are the divinities.
　　If you don't believe it, look at the case of Yang Zongfu:
His corpse and soul were transformed into a black pot.
But thanks to Dragon-Design Rescriptor-in-Waiting Bao
Justice was enacted and his life was paid back with a life.
　　Do goodness — encounter goodness: it's your own effort;
Commit evil and the Lord of Heaven will not favor you.
The retribution of August Heaven is without any mistake,
It never, never makes even the tiniest, slightest mistake.
　　Goodness has its own reward, which comes in the end,
Evil has its evil rewards as disasters will seek you out.
Never say there are no divinities up in the empty sky:
The roaring clap of the thunder is heard everywhere!
　　I have finished writing this history of the black pot:
May it be transmitted to later times for people to hear!

> *Transparently clear Heaven cannot be deceived:*
> *Before you conceive of an idea it already knows.*
> *I urge you all never to commit shameful deeds:*
> *Who in past or present has ever been spared?*

Printed by the Yongshuntang Bookshop in the final month of fall of the *renchen* year of the Chenghua reign period (1472).

Rescriptor Bao Decides the Case of the Weird Black Pot, Newly Composed, Fully Illustrated, in Prose and in Verse, The End.

Zhu Yixuan (ed.) (1997). *Ming Chenghua shuochang cihua congkan*, Zhengzhou: Zhongzhou guji chubanshe, pp. 159–187.

The Tale of the Case of Dragon-Design Bao Sentencing the Emperor's Brothers-in-law Cao

Newly Printed, in Prose and in Verse

From the time when Pangu opened up heaven and earth,
There have been many civil officials and military men.
But where are the Three Rulers and Five Thearchs now?
At present one does not see the men of the past anymore!

For painting a dragon one needs a true dragon-painter,
For drawing a phoenix one needs a true phoenix-master.
The painted dragons and phoenixes may survive the years,
But the masters who made the paintings have disappeared.

Spring goes and summer comes, then later fall arrives,
And once winter has come to an end, spring comes again.
Light and shade resemble an arrow, urging people to age;
Sun and moon are like a shuttle as far as they never stop.

The Great Progenitor, the Great Ancestor, the True Ancestor;
The fourth, the Humane Ancestor, in possession of the Way:
The Humane Ancestor was a true arhat of the seven jewels,
His officials and officers were all stars from the world above.

He ascended the throne when he was only twelve,
And completely relied on the officials and officers at court:
For the civil officials we only mention His Excellency Bao;
As for military officers there was that great General Di.

Because the civil and military officials were all so great,
They helped the Humane Ancestor in establishing Great Peace.
Every third day the wind blew, every fifth day rain fell down;
Two showers each ten days blessed the soldiers and farmers.

When a wind blew, it only moved the grasses in the garden,
When a rain fell, it always sprinkled the pines before the palace.
The winds and rains were timely, the people stuck to their job;
The five grains gave good harvests — all enjoyed Great Peace!

Let's end this idle talk, and let's not sing of it anymore —
Hear me sing of the Humane Ancestor, who possessed the Way.
The third quarter of the fifth watch: the king ascends the hall,
The fourth quarter of the fifth watch: the ministers all assemble.
    The civil officials all are standing on the left side, whereas
The military officers are all arranged on the right-hand side.
Twenty-four bows: they wish him longevity like a mountain,
They wish him a myriad of years, call themselves "servants."
    Their lord and king on his throne opens his golden mouth, saying,
"Civil officials and military officers, please listen to my words.
If there is any business, may one of you ministers report to Us,
If there is no business, you ministers exit through the inner gate."
    Before the king had even finished speaking these few words,
One high minister rushed forward from his place in the ranks.
A purple gown, an ivory tablet, a golden belt around his waist:
Holding his tablet before his breast, he addressed the emperor.
    When his lord and king lifted his head to have a good look,
The man turned out to be Prime Minister Wang from Qingzhou.
Prostrating himself on the golden steps, he addressed his lord,
"Your Majesty on your throne, please listen to what I will say.
    You will remember that the Southern Barbarians started a war,
That Di Qing and Yang Wenguang went to that border region.
They subdued the barbarians after nine years and six months,
And now the mountains and rivers have achieved Great Peace.
    But ever since these generals victoriously returned to the court,
Horses and soldiers have been left in garrison at the borders.
Di Qing and Yang Wenguang may have returned to the court,
But we have not yet properly rewarded these common soldiers.
    Your Majesty here at court may live in peace and happiness,
But we neglect the horses and soldiers serving at the border.
I therefore beseech Your Majesty to display some compassion
And to properly reward the horses and soldiers at the border."
    His lord and king agreed to his proposal in all details, saying,
"Thank you very much, Our dear minister, for reporting to Us!

We agree in each and every detail with your proposal to Us,
And We are grateful, Our dear minister, for your report to Us!

We are the ruler of the whole country's mountains and rivers,
But the wide world relies on the contribution of you ministers."
The emperor on his throne hastened to issue an edict, ordering
The preparation of clothes and grain for distribution to the troops.

"Who of the officials at court can journey to the border region
And there deliver these million-worth of clothes and grain?"
Chancellor Wang thereupon addressed the emperor as follows:
"Please allow me to recommend and guarantee one official.

He serves in the Southern Office as the prefect of Kaifeng;
Pure and fair, proper and straight, he sticks to laws and rules.
Dispatch him to take responsibility for these clothes and grain,
And to distribute these goods to the troops in the border region."

Hearing this, the emperor was filled with joy in his heart,
And he then summoned this man surnamed Bao to his court.
As soon as His Excellency was summoned by his lord and king,
He greeted the emperor by bowing down at the golden steps.

His Majesty the Humane Ancestor addressed him as follows:
"Dear Minister Bao, please listen to what We have to say.
We want you to take a million-worth of clothes and grain
To the border region, and so impose a bitter burden on you.

Distribute these goods to the soldiers and horses of the army,
And set out on your trip on a good hour and lucky day."
When His Excellency Bao received this imperial edict,
[He replied:] "I will happily make this trip to the border."

His Majesty the Humane Ancestor was filled with joy,
And added yet another office to the one he already had:
As inspector-general of the Nine Regions of the empire,
His authority extended to the army and common people.

The officials and officers at court acted as his guarantors;
Judge Bao expressed his gratitude and left the court gate.
And as soon as he had left the Grand Audience Hall,
The treasury provided him with treasures and precious goods.

He loaded a hundred government ships with this cargo,
And the helmsmen and deckhands were very numerous.
The banners and flags were as bright as the sun and moon,
And sounded gongs and beaten drums steered the fleet.

At court Judge Bao bade adieu to the Humane Ancestor,
And the civil officials and military officers all saw him off.

But let's not sing in our tale of His Excellency Bao —
Let's talk about the emperor, the ruler surnamed Zhao.
The emperor late at night returned to the Rear Palace,
And in the palace he went to the Right Yang Apartment.
     The first watch was sounded — there is nothing to tell;
The second watch was sounded, and all was very clear.
The third watch was sounded at the time of midnight:
Stars were turning around the pole at the hour of *zi*.
     As the emperor was sleeping inside the yellow curtains,
He saw a teacher who was completely clad in black.
That man was followed behind by thousands of others,
Who all threw stones and bricks at the palace gate.
     His Majesty the Humane Ancestor was terrified,
And he was drenched from head to toe in cold sweat.
He woke up with a start and thought about the dream,
Not knowing whether it predicted good fortune or bad.
     He waited for the fifth watch, until dawn in the sky,
When he could question the military and civil officials.
     The third quarter of the fifth watch: the court horses moved
And the civil and military officials entered the inner gate.
Twenty-four bows: they wished longevity like a mountain,
And at the golden steps they greeted their Sagely Lord.
     His Majesty the Humane Ancestor addressed them thus,
"You civil officials and military officers, please listen.
This last night We saw a dream, and We do not know
Whether that dream predicts good fortune or misfortune."

[*Speak:*]

Our story goes that as soon as His Majesty the Humane Ancestor had spoken, Chancellor Wang stepped forward from his place in the ranks, and said: "Your Majesty, there are many kinds of dreams. In the first watch one sees dreams of longing; in the second watch one sees dreams of imagination; in the third watch one sees responsive dreams; in the fourth watch one sees empty dreams; and in the fifth watch one sees terrifying dreams. May we know what Your Majesty has seen in his dream?" The emperor said: "We saw a teacher dressed in black, leading thousands of students who broke into the palace, throwing bricks and stones. What could this mean?"

***Sing*:**

His Excellency Wang thereupon immediately replied,
"This dream does not predict any good fortune or bad.
　　The teacher who appeared in the dream was no one else
But the King of Instruction, that sagely master Kong![1]
Every three years national examinations are to be held,
Widely summoning the students throughout the empire.
　　But ever since Your Majesty has ascended the throne,
You have yet to open the gates of the examination grounds.
This way you have ruined all fine scholars of the empire;
You have suffocated all students throughout the world.
　　And so the Master, leading his three thousand disciples,
Has on purpose appeared in your dream inside the palace.
Your Majesty, please kindly accept my proposal, and
Grandly open the gates of the examination grounds!"
　　His Majesty the Humane Ancestor accepted the proposal;
A yellow poster at the court gate publicized his edict:
The first third day of the Third Month had been selected
For students throughout the empire to take the exams.
　　All prefectures and districts thereupon put up posters,
Widely summoning the students from all over the empire.

Let's not tell how the emperor called for examinations,
But let's talk now in our story about a certain student.
　　This man hailed from Chaoshui District in Chaozhou,
From the village of Iron Hill in Filial and Fair Township.
His surname was Yuan and his name Yuan Wenzheng;
The wife he had married carried the surname Zhang.
　　When this "flourishing talent" happened to go into town,
He saw the yellow poster, which spelled it out clearly.
So he went home and promptly told his wife, saying,
"Today's happy event is not some minor matter indeed!
　　Fortunately the emperor is holding an examination,
Widely summoning the students all through the empire.
I cannot stay at home, and bury my talent and study,
I'll make the journey alone to sit for the examination!"

---

[1] The sagely master Kong is Confucius.

When his wife heard this, she answered as follows,
"My dear husband, please listen to what I will say.
We get by here at home without any trouble at all,
So why don't you wait here for a few more years?"

    The student promptly answered her in these words:
"My dear wife, please listen to what I have to say.
By the window I have studied the texts for ten years,
For nine years I've been reading by the light of a lamp.

    If I manage to obtain just one office or half a function,
The bitter study by lamplight won't have been in vain.
If I become famous by success in the examination,
I will glorify my family and make my ancestors proud.

    Passing the opportunity this year may be a minor matter,
But after another three years, my chances might be nil.
Students of letters are going, and those of martial arts —
I don't mind whether I pass in literary or martial arts!"

    His wife once more tried to talk him around, by saying:
"My dear husband, please listen to what I have to say.
I have no parents-in-law and I have no elder sisters,
We only have this little baby boy of three years old.

    If something untoward would happen to you, my husband,
How would I ever come to know of it, here back at home?
And if something untoward would happen here at home,
You, my dear husband, would be unable to learn about it."

    They considered the situation: she had no one to rely on,
So the three of them would go to the Eastern Capital.
They carefully selected a good hour and also a lucky day,
And then packed their luggage and set out on the road.

    They said goodbye to the neighbors living on both sides,
And all their distant relatives too came to see them off.
"Take good care of yourselves going to the Eastern Capital,
May you pass the exam at the first try and become famous!

    When husband and wife return home all clad in brocade,
You will glorify your family and be a man of high status!"
After they had said goodbye, they set out on the road:
Husband and wife and their baby traveled on ahead!

When they had walked a mile, they went on for a mile;
When they had gone one stretch, there followed another.

They left at dawn and rested at night — no need to explain;
They passed mountains, crossed ridges — all the old stories.
  When they had crossed quite some mountains and rivers,
When they had passed through many districts and towns,
When they had been on the road at least for some months,
They arrived outside the walls of the Eastern Capital.
  They gazed at the walls more than ten *zhang* in height,
Then entered the triple gates that were wrapped in iron.
The main streets and markets went on to the south,
This was a flowery road that was woven of brocade.
  The Eastern Market went on until the Western Market,
The Southern Street looked out on the Northern Street.
Shops selling linen faced shops selling all kinds of silk,
And the shops selling tea faced the shops selling wine.
  The shops selling herbs faced the shops for medicines,
And people buying flowers called those selling flowers.
Husband and wife feasted their eyes on the city's sights,
Without noticing that the sun was sinking in the west.
  As soon as the student saw that the sky became dark,
He asked around for an inn taking in traveling merchants.
They entered an inn to take a room there for the night,
And Mrs. Wang, the innkeeper, came out to greet them.
  They selected a fine room to settle there for the time,
And Mrs. Wang treated them in a most royal manner.
When they had finished their dinner, they settled down;
By the light of a lamp the student reviewed his books.
  All through the night he read his books without a rest,
He reviewed the text of the Histories and Five Classics.
On the first day of the Third Month they had arrived;
On the third day of the Third Month he'd take the exam.
  When they rose early next morning, they went for a walk,
Husband and wife and the baby, to see the capital's sights.
So once they had locked the door of their room, they also
Informed Mrs. Wang, the innkeeper, of their intention.

Speak:

The student said: "Mrs. Wang, the three of us will go for a walk to see the sights, and we will be back by evening." Mrs. Wang answered: "The first

Fig. 6.1

The younger imperial brother-in-law meets with Yuan Wenzheng and his wife out on the streets.

place is the area around the Forbidden City, where the Son of Heaven lives; the second is Kaifeng Prefecture; and the third is the mansion of the Cao family. They are evil and dangerous in a most terrifying way, so do not say anything foolish." The student replied: "I am a gentleman who reads the books and I am well conversant with the norms. I wouldn't dare talk foolishly."

Let's tell how the student
    Left the gate of the inn
        To observe in all its details,
To see the Eastern Capital,
    This flowery world,
        This cosmos made of brocade.
Big iron smithies
    And small silver workshops
        Resounded with hammering sounds;
At the riverside market
    The many boats there
        Were loaded with gold and silver.
In gold and silver shops,
    In silk and linen shops,
        People were crowding together,
While the courtesans,
    Each and every one,
        Were the most beautiful women.
The Central Secretariat,
    The Six Ministries,
        And the offices of the Censorate —
Look how the emperor's
    Grand Audience Hall
        Rises up right into the blue clouds!
Those who exit and enter
    The Eastern Floriate Gate
        Are civil officials and prime ministers;
Those who come and go through
    The Western Floriate Gate
        Are military officers and imperial kin.
In the Imperial Capital
    The shops for flowers and powder
        Are too numerous for anyone to know;

The brokers and merchants,
    Those engaged in buying and selling,
        Are many thousands of myriads of men!

Wasn't it because they went to see the sights of the capital
That they seduced knife upon knife to slice off their lips? (?)

Just as husband and wife were watching the city's sights,
A high official and his cortege appeared on the street.
Husband and wife hastily moved to the side of the road,
To the side of the road to evade this high civil official.
    When the official, riding on horseback, saw them,
He fixed his eyes on the features of the woman, and
Saw her features were those of a woman like a flower,
Seductively charming and more beautiful than Guanyin!
    This official was not some other servant of the Throne,
He was Her Majesty the Empress Cao's second brother.
    When this man saw how beautiful this woman was,
He immediately ordered a uniformed soldier in his guard
To go and invite the woman and the student together,
To invite them to his mansion for a few drinks of wine.
    When the student learned they had been invited there,
He and his wife and the baby set out on the journey.
Following the soldier they entered the Cao mansion,
Where a banquet was spread out to have some drinks.
    Fat lamb and pure wine were there in all variety,
And deer and boar and roe and hare filled the plates.
There were Fuzhou longans and Xuanzhou pears too,
The seafood and seasonal delicacies were all fresh.
    The empress' brother offered him three cups of wine,
He raised the cup and urged the student to drink.
As soon as one cup grew cold, another one was warmed;
One cup's warmth was enough to make one drunk.
    The student did not realize that this was all a trap,
So he went on drinking till he was drunk as a skunk.
When the empress' brother saw that he was drunk,
He immediately conceived a most devilish scheme.
    He ordered his soldiers and men to come into action,
And to arrest that student then and there in the hall.

With a three-foot-long hemp cord they strangled him,
That very moment they strangled the student to death.
  They also killed the couple's three-year-old baby,
Then dumped the corpses in the Qiong-flower well.

Lady Zhang witnessed all of this with her own eyes,
Her heart and liver seemed to be consumed by fire!
  "I'd like to die by bashing my head against the steps,
But then my husband's death will never become clear.
In my earlier lives I must have neglected to do good,
So I ran into this impetuous and vicious star of fire!"
  She did not dare voice her grief through loud wailing,
But from her eyes her tears coursed down in profusion.
  "How detestable is that imperial brother-in-law Cao!
With force he wants to make a married wife his lady!
That man has locked me up here in this hidden room,
Watched by soldiers in front and behind the gates."
  Living in this hidden room, she had no way to escape,
So tears continuously coursed down across her cheeks.
  "I once learned a fitting saying of the people of old,
Those two lines of verse are really telling the truth:
Since ancient times true gentlemen have been scarce;
Mean people worm their way into groups of good men."
  After she had been kept in that room for three months,
She had lost all idea of north and south, east and west.
She had heard about that pure judge, His Excellency Bao,
But when would she ever be able to lodge an accusation?

Let's not sing of this married woman surnamed Zhang,
Let's sing about the young gentleman of the Cao family.
When he obtained the office of governor of Zhengzhou,
He took the woman with him to the city of Zhengzhou.

Let's not sing of the married woman he took with him,
But let's sing about what happened in the Cao mansion.
  Ever since that student of books had been murdered,
Gods wailed and ghosts wept, leaving no one in peace.
The mill stones whirled around without being pushed,
And the rice mortars kept on stamping all by themselves.

Her Ladyship the mother of the empress was terrified,
And she decided to move away, to Black Chicken Lane.
A completely new mansion of halls and rooms was built,
The gate building so broad and high it reached the clouds.

Let's not sing in our ballad about the Cao family mansion,
Let's rather sing about the student who studied the books.
Father and son, dead and buried in the Qiong-flower well,
Would for a myriad of years never be able to turn around.
    Failed in his ambition to obtain an office or function, he
And his son had been deeply buried, and only if someday
The rumor would be blown into the ears of Judge Bao,
Would this Cao fellow by any chance die by the sword!

Let's not sing of the student who had died a cruel death,
I'll sing of the Humane Ancestor, who possessed the Way.
    The emperor ascended the Golden Hall for the audience,
And the civil and military officials entered the inner gate.
When the emperor saw them all arranged in their ranks,
He asked both the civil officials and the military officers,
    "If there is any business, may a high minister report to Us,
If there is no business, may you all leave by the inner gate."
Before the emperor had finished speaking these words,
The grand commissioner of the Main Gate addressed him.
    "At the present moment the pure judge, His Excellency Bao,
Having returned to the Eastern Capital, waits at the inner gate.
He is now at the Eastern Floriate Dragon and Phoenix Pavilion,
And doesn't dare return to the court and greet Your Majesty."
    His Majesty the Humane Ancestor was obviously pleased,
And quickly told him to summon that man surnamed Bao.
Three ushers led Judge Bao inside the Golden Phoenix Hall,
Where he greeted His Imperial Majesty, the emperor.
    He bowed before his king, executing twenty-four bows;
Wishing him a myriad of years, he called himself "servant."
His lord and king rose himself from the dragon-throne,
And with his own hand invited him to sit down on a stool.
    He then ordered imperially-sealed wine to be poured out,
And his lord and king offered him three rounds of wine.
His Majesty the Humane Ancestor then asked the question,
"How are our troops and horses doing in the border region?

Do the military colonists and common people live in peace?
Do the villagers think of Our person with feelings of love?
Has there come an end to the fighting on the four borders?
Or are there attacks by violent rebels and thievish robbers?"
    Judge Bao stepped forward and immediately reported:
"Your Majesty, please be so kind as to listen to my words.
    First of all thanks to Your Majesty's extensive good fortune,
And secondly thanks to the fine generals serving this court,
The eight directions are pacified and all fighting has stopped,
And the four borders are pacified, now enjoying Great Peace.
    The troops and horses in the border region are very happy;
There are no incursions by violent bandits or thievish robbers.
The lances and swords have been turned into resting staves;
Books of military strategy have been replaced by study texts.
    The high observation posts are now overgrown with weeds,
And there is hardly any criminal in the death row prisons.
The farmers can plow and sow their land in the proper seasons,
And trade and commerce are flourishing all over the place.
In each and every prefecture and district people are happy,
Filled with gratitude for Your Majesty's favors and grace."
    His Majesty the Humane Ancestor was filled with joy,
And showered His Excellency Bao, that one man, with gifts:
A hundred rolls of fine silk and a hundred jugs of wine,
And also one hundred fat sheep he gave to that one person.
    He also awarded him with a million strings of ready cash,
A hundred ounces of yellow gold and a hundred of silver.
Having received the money and the treasure His Excellency
Expressed his gratitude for this favor by twenty-four bows.

Upon his arrival at the Parade Grounds he took his seat,
And then called together the non-commissioned officers.
He awarded all the ready money and the precious gifts
To the non-commissioned officers and common soldiers.
    Receiving these rewards the army was filled with joy,
And they all praised His Excellency Bao as truly unique.
When he had distributed the rewards, he left to go home,
And rested when he arrived on the Prefectural Bridge.
    Suddenly a weird whirlwind rose up from the ground;
As soon as he saw this, he was filled with apprehension.

He halted his horse, and hastily shouted the question:
"You whirlwind, are you a ghost or are you a god?
If you are a man who was murdered, then turn to the left,
If you are the wronged soul of a woman, turn to the right!"
    When the whirlwind had heard the judge's questions,
It turned to the left three times without ever once stopping.
Following these three turns to the left, it went to the south,
And Judge Bao ordered his men to follow that whirlwind.
    Wang Liang and Li Wang hastily ran after the whirlwind,
And they pursued the whirlwind for quite some distance.
    Then the whirlwind disappeared into a fine high mansion,
And this truly scared these two police officers to death.
The gate with its two door panels was securely locked,
And on all sides not a single person was to be espied.
    On the brightly red gate large characters had been written,
Which spelled it out clearly, which said it out loud:
"If anyone but speaks of this gate and these buildings,
His tongue will be ripped out, not a shred to be left;
    If anyone but points at this gate and these buildings,
His hands and feet will be cut off, nothing to remain.
If anyone but looks at this gate and these buildings,
His eyes will be gouged out and he will lose his life!"
    Wang Liang and Li Wang were terrified in their hearts,
And these two police officers promptly turned around.
And when they arrived back at the Prefectural Bridge,
They reported their presence, told what had happened.

Speak:

His Excellency asked Wang Liang and Li Wang: "To where did you
follow this whirlwind?" The two men reported to His Excellency:
"We pursued it to Little Horse Lane, and there the whirlwind blew into
a high mansion. On its gate were written the following few lines:
'If anyone points inside the gate, his hands and feet will be removed;
if anyone talks about this mansion, his tongue will be ripped out; and if
anyone looks inside the gate, his eyes will be gouged out.' We don't
know the name or surname of that official, or his ranking among his
brothers." When His Excellency heard this, a rage rose up in his heart,
and hatred was born in his gall. He promptly ordered the officers under

his command to form a formal cortege to go and have a look at this high mansion.

Sing:

His Excellency applied the spurs to his high-headed horse,
And set out to see this high mansion, this official abode.
When the whole party arrived in front of this high mansion,
He dismounted from his horse to observe the situation.

The police officers then set out his silver folding chair,
And His Excellency sat down on his chair in the street.
Thousands and ten-thousands of people crowded together,
And so blocked all traffic of people going up and down.

His Excellency then immediately gave out his orders,
And promptly called for Zhang Long and also Zhao Hu.
"The two of you must go to the main street with its shops,
And there find me an elderly person, someone of years.

Then ask him to which imperial relative by birth or
To which relative by marriage this mansion may belong."
The two police officers did not linger for any moment,
But hastened to leave the high mansion, this great house.

When they arrived on the main street with its shops,
They saw an elderly person there, someone of years.
The police officers promptly called out to that person:
"You granddad, now listen to what we have to say!

The prefect of Kaifeng Prefecture, His Excellency Bao,
Down the street, would like to ask you some questions."
This elderly man fully prostrated himself in the street,
As he racked his brain, he said not a word for a while.

"Old as I am, I haven't committed any crime or offense,
So for what reason has your superior taken me in?
Police officers, please come with me to my house,
So I can question my children, all three of my sons!"

The police officers thereupon followed the old man
Straight to his home to question his sons and grandsons.
He promptly called his children, all three of his sons:
"A disaster has struck, which is as deep as the ocean!

Who of you committed some crime or offense, and so
Aroused the rage of the prefect of Kaifeng, Judge Bao?

Today his police officers have come to arrest me, so
Let the one who did the deed confess to the crime!"

   His three children hastened to answer him as follows:
"Father, please set your mind at rest, do not worry!
None of us committed any crime or offense, and that
Pure judge will never unjustly condemn a commoner."

   The two police officers did not allow further delays,
And wanted to leave, pulling the old man with them.
The old man was awash in tears, [as he exclaimed]:
"Today I am bound to die, and I soon will be dead!

   Now I have fallen into the claws of that Judge Bao,
I'll be a dandy for sure if I do not lose my life! (?)
If one way or another I die in Kaifeng Prefecture,
Be sure to summon my soul with one of my shirts."

   The whole family, old and young, wept piteously,
And the old man too wept as he walked on ahead.
When he then arrived at the market of the capital,
He ran there into His Excellency right on the street.

Speak:

When this old man arrived in front of the judge, he made four times
two, eight bows, and His Excellency rose to his feet to return the
greeting. The old man then knelt down, and His Excellency said:
"Please get up!" The old man thought to himself: "Those two police
officers came to arrest me in a most terrifying manner, but when I bow
to the judge, he returns my greeting. What is going on here?" His
Excellency asked him: "Granddad, you are an inhabitant of the Eastern
Capital. For how many generations has your family been living here?"
The old man replied: "We have been living here for three generations,
I was born here and I grew up in this locality." Hearing this, His
Excellency had him offered some wine.

[*Sing*:]

The officers under his command quickly poured him wine;
As he swallowed the first cup, two more were poured out.
And when the old man had drunk these three cups of wine,
He had no idea anymore of north and south, east and west.

His Excellency asked the old man the following question:
"How many officials are there here in the Eastern Capital?"
The old man then answered him in the following words:
"Your Excellency, please listen as I tell you the numbers."

Speak:

This old man said: "The capital has an inner wall and an outer wall, and a hundred and eight thousand soldiers. There's the Eastern Market Street, the Western Market Street, the Great Bridge, and the Small Bridge. Then there are the emperor's relatives by birth and the emperor's relatives by marriage, the officials at court and the prime ministers. Even a little child of three years old knows all of that!" His Excellency then said: "I won't ask you any questions about the emperor's relatives by birth and the emperor's relatives by marriage, the officials at court and the prime ministers. I only want to know to whom this mansion belongs." The old man said: "I know everything about all other places, but I don't know a thing about this mansion."

[Sing:]

When His Excellency heard this, he was filled with rage;
A brazier of burning coal could be gathered from his heart!
In his hand he raised his tablet with its golden flowers, and
He stepped forward as if he wanted to beat that old man.
    "Now be smart and tell me right now whatever you know,
And then everything will be fine — you'll be off the hook.
But if you refuse to tell me today the things you know,
You'll end up as a corpse, beaten to death by this tablet!"
    The old man stepped forward and answered as follows:
"Your Excellency, please still your rage and your anger!
If I do not tell you what I know, I am bound to die, but
As soon as I open my mouth, I'm bound to lose my life.
    If today I don't inform you about this mighty mansion,
I'll be beaten to death by the tablet of Your Excellency,
But once I have told you about this mighty mansion,
The Caos will not allow me to live as soon as they know.
    I will tell you everything in detail, from the beginning,
Hoping for Your Excellency's protection of my person,
Because if we talk of these imperial relatives by marriage,
They are not your ordinary kind of people or even less.

Their elder sister is Empress Cao, the emperor's wife, so
Their brother-in-law is that virtuous Humane Ancestor.
These great princes are the emperor's own brothers-in-law;
Their mother is Her Ladyship, the emperor's mother-in-law.
　　Of all the many imperial relatives by marriage in the city,
They're the foremost family linked that way to the emperor.
Not only are their offices and functions of the highest,
But they also kill thousands and ten-thousands of people.
　　If they kill a soldier, they do not pay with their life, but
They contribute three pounds of raw iron to the court.
If they kill a citizen, they do not pay with their life, but
They are not allowed to wrap their hair for three days.
　　If they kill by any chance a monk or a nun or a priest,
Their mouth is only stuffed with four pounds of pork.
And if they see someone's wife who is very beautiful,
They abduct her to their mansion and make her a lady.
　　Now if her husband refuses to accept that state of affairs,
He's cut in two with one stroke, which makes her a widow.
Numerous innocent people have been killed this way:
Ghosts from the world of shade then haunted the house.
　　The millstones whirled around without being pushed,
And the mortars rose into the sky without being worked.
In the kitchen the lids on the pots were like broken tiles,
And earthenware vats crumbled as they were standing.
　　The wooden spoons and gourd ladles all moved around,
All through the night this place is a true Gate of Ghosts.
This is their mansion but nobody lives there any more:
Gods wail and ghosts weep, robbing a man of his rest!
　　The family has currently moved to Little Chicken Lane,
Where a new and mighty mansion has been constructed.
I now have told you everything, from the very beginning,
And hope for Your Excellency's protection of my person."

When His Excellency heard this, he was very happy,
And he had the old man rewarded with a goat and wine.
　　"You can go safely back to your house without delay,
Sleep without a worry, and put your mind at rest.
If people come from the Cao mansion to arrest you,
You first come to me and inform me of the situation."

The old man thanked him and returned to his house;
His Excellency promptly ordered his uniformed soldiers
To pick up two big rocks which were laying in the street
And to break open the double-tongued lock on the gate.
　　When they had managed to open the doors of the gate,
His Excellency was the first to enter this fine mansion:
When opened, the gate sounded like the Golden Rooster;
When closed, the gate resembled the song of the Phoenix.
　　When His Excellency entered this mansion of the Caos,
The sights inside resembled those of a heavenly palace.
His Excellency sat down in the mansion's high hall;
His five hundred troops stood arranged on both sides.

Speak:

His Excellency then ordered the two police officers Wang Xing and Li Ji
to appear before him, and he asked them: "You two are very brave men,
so can you arrest anyone?" Wang Xing and Li Ji replied: "Your Excellency,
we cannot arrest the Jade Emperor in the world above, and we cannot
arrest King Yama in the world below; we cannot arrest the White Tiger in
the Western Mountains and we cannot arrest the Green Dragon in the
Eastern Ocean. But apart from these few, we can arrest each and every
one, whether they are imperial relatives by birth or imperial relatives by
marriage, court officials or prime ministers, soldiers or commoners,
monks, nuns, or priests."

Sing:

His Excellency in the hall was filled with joy, and he
Ordered wine to be poured out to reward these men.
When the two soldiers had drunk three cups of wine,
He also rewarded them with ten strings of ready cash.
　　Wang Xing and Li Ji were very much filled with joy,
And expressed their gratitude to His Excellency Bao.
Only when the two of them were drunk as a skunk,
Did His Excellency write out the order for an arrest.
　　When he had applied his seal to the official document,
He handed it over to the two officers there in the hall.

When the two of them had received this official paper,
They shouted: "Yes, Sir!" and left the office building.
Once they had gone outside and were out on the street,
They muttered under their breath, cursing all others.
    "Who of these guys dares drink the wine of Bao?
We have finished off two or three jugs of his stuff!
All you other guys are nothing else but a bag of pus,
All of you are people who hug pus and make blood!"
    Zhang Long and Zhao Hu were enraged in their hearts,
And went to the hall to complain about this couple.
"Your Excellency, please be so kind as to listen to us.
That Wang Xing and that Li Ji are truly intolerable!
    Now they have drunk your imperially-sealed wine,
They have lost all reason and curse all of us others.
'Who of these guys dares drink the wine of Bao?'
They loudly curse all the people serving under you!
    We are all, these two say, nothing but a bag of pus,
All of us are people who hug pus and make blood!"
Hearing this complaint, His Excellency grew angry,
And had Wang Xing and Li Ji appear before him.

Speak:

His Excellency angrily called Wang Xing and Li Ji before him, and said:
"You two are very brave indeed! I dispatched the two of you to summon
the whirlwind ghost who presented an accusation in front of my horse to
appear in court and submit his statement, but the two of you have to make
a drunken fool of yourselves on the street." When Wang Xing and Li Ji
heard what His Excellency told them, they looked more closely at the
order of arrest, and it was indeed for the summoning of that whirlwind
ghost! Wang Xing and Li Ji then said: "Your Excellency, if you dispatch us
to summon a man, we tie him up with a hempen cord and escort him to
the hall so he can appear before you, but now you dispatch us to arrest a
whirlwind, which has a visible shape but no physical form, and also cannot
speak, so how can we make an arrest?" His Excellency ordered Zhang
Long and Zhao Hu: "Grab that Wang Xing and that Li Ji, and give each
thirty strokes with the thick cudgel. You two will be banished to a distant
labor camp if you do not bring that whirlwind in by tomorrow!" When the
two of them had left the office, they discussed the matter: they had no clue

where the whirlwind might be, but they would be punished anyway, so they could only walk up and down the street summoning that whirlwind!

Sing:

The two of them, carrying the order of arrest with them,
Cried loudly on the southern and on the northern streets,
Crying: "Whirlwind, come and lodge your accusation,
His Excellency summons you to clearly settle the case.
    If you have suffered any injustice, report all the facts,
Don't cause trouble for the two of us by not showing up!"
They cried this way from the noon hour till the afternoon,
They cried this way from the afternoon till the evening.

Let's not sing of these policemen crying in the streets,
Listen as I sing of His Excellency Dragon-Design Bao.
    His Excellency all this time was seated in the hall, and
Instructed the soldiers and officers under his command:
"Tonight do not close the gate of this office building,
By the light of a single lamp I'll judge wronged ghosts."
    When he had finished speaking, the sky turned dark:
No people were ferried across anymore at the fords,
The fisherman on the river laid down his angling rod,
Weaving women halted their shuttle, closed the gate.
    Seven lamps were arrayed like the Northern Dipper,
And six wax candles shone as brightly as the day.
There was one bowl of pure water, and one sword,
As fine incense was burned in the golden brazier.
    His Excellency took his seat at the head of the hall;
His five hundred officers were arranged in two rows.

Speak:

In front of the gate this Wang Xing and this Li Ji once again loudly called out: "Whirlwind, His Excellency has taken his seat and waits for you to submit your statement!" But nothing happened at all. They shouted three times in a row: "His Excellency waits for you to submit your statement!" When they were done shouting, a black wind indeed rose up from the ground right before their eyes and turned into a whirlwind, and the sand and stones that flew about greatly terrified Wang Xing and Li Ji.

[**Sing:**]

When they had finished speaking, a whirlwind arose,
Which whirled into the gate of the Cao family mansion.
  The flying sand and stones scared them out of their wits,
The yellow sand blown into their faces bowled them over.
Above it crashed against heaven, below against earth,
And people's heads were covered with streams of blood.
  A wronged ghost complained of the injustice it suffered,
As weeping and wailing it entered the mansion's gate.
The soldiers were so terrified they were dumbfounded:
A weird whirlwind penetrated through the open gate.
  Bareheaded, the hair unbound, and the body all blood,
Around the neck the hempen cord still tightly wound —
In his arms he was carrying his own dear baby son,
Complaining without end of the injustice he suffered.
  His Excellency promptly questioned him in a loud voice,
Questioned him: "Orphaned soul, now listen to me.
In which prefecture did you live? In which district?
From which township do you hail in terms of origin?
  Zhang or Wang or Li or Zhao — please tell the facts,
Tell me everything in detail, from the very beginning.
If you tell me the facts, I will base myself on the facts;
If you tell me the truth, I will base myself on the truth.
  But if only one word of what you say is false or wrong,
You will be sent to the underworld to suffer as sinner!"
The soul told everything in detail, from the beginning:
"Your Excellency, listen precisely to what I will say!
  I lived in Chaoshui District of Chaozhou Prefecture,
I lived in Iron Hill Village of Filial and Fair Township.
My surname is Yuan, and my name is Yuan Wenzheng;
The wife I was married to carried the surname Zhang.
  Since my earliest youth I devoted myself to the letters;
I was conversant with the Histories and the Six Classics.
Now recently the court announced an examination, and
Widely summoned students throughout the empire.
  Because I wanted to participate for fame and profit,
I traveled with my wife and son to the Eastern Capital.
We arrived here on the first day of the Third Month,
And on the third of the Third Month I'd take the exam.

On the second day I got up early and went for a walk
With my wife and my son to see the Eastern Capital.
And only because I wanted to see the Eastern Capital,
I seduced knife upon knife to cut and slice off my lips. (?)
    When my wife and I were taking in the sights of the city,
A high official and his cortege appeared on that street.
My wife and I hastily moved to the side of the street,
To the side of the street to be out of that official's way.
    That official was the second imperial brother-in-law Cao,
And that man feasted his eyes on my dearly beloved wife.
When he saw how beautiful my wife's features were,
He invited us to his house to drink a few cups of wine.
    I didn't realize that this was only an underhanded trick,
And I kept on drinking till I was drunk as a skunk.
Then that damned second imperial brother-in-law Cao
Strangled me with a hempen cord, and I was a corpse.
    They also killed our little baby son of three years old,
And the bodies of us both were dumped into the well.
After he had robbed me of my wife, that darling woman,
He forced her to become his wife and made her his lady.
    I had died and had gone off to the Offices of Shade,
And had no opportunity to meet with Your Excellency.
When I saw Your Excellency passing through the street,
I presented my accusation on the Prefectural Bridge.
    I have been told Your Excellency is as pure as water,
You sentence imperial relatives and the emperor's kin.
I pray Your Excellency to show some compassion, and
Be the person who on my behalf will take revenge!
    If you sentence the second imperial brother-in-law Cao
I'll never forget your favor in existence upon existence."
    His Excellency then asked him the following question:
"What are at present the whereabouts of your wife?
Why didn't you have her lodge an accusation with me,
So I could pronounce a clear verdict right from the start?"
    The student informed His Excellency of the following:
"The criminal has taken my wife with him to Zhengzhou.
Three months ago he took her with him to Zhengzhou,
So it was impossible for my wife to see Your Excellency.

In front and in back she is surrounded by his soldiers,
So how could my wife escape and arrive here in Kaifeng?"
The student repeated his statement with greatest urgency:
"Your Excellency, please be the one who exacts revenge!"

His Excellency thereupon friendly instructed the ghost:
"My dear ghost, now please return for the time being!
Tomorrow morning I will devise a most devious plan
In order to bring that relative of the emperor to justice."

The ghost expressed his gratitude and returned to hell;
Weeping most piteously he became a whirlwind again.

Let's not sing of the student going to the Land of Shade;
Listen as I sing of His Excellency Dragon-Design Bao.
When in the fifth watch of that night the sky brightened,
He said to his five hundred soldiers: "Men, all listen!"

His Excellency addressed them in the following way,
He informed the soldiers under his command as follows:
"That whirlwind last night was not some sorry ghost,
It was not the soul of a man who had been murdered.

It was the divine lad who serves as guard of the well,
Who came last night to tell me something interesting.
He said that ten thousand ounces of gold have been
Buried here in the rear garden's Qiong-flower well.

Now who of you police officers can be brave enough
To go down into that well and retrieve me that gold?
And when you are really able to bring that gold to light,
The reward for each of you will be quite substantial!"

Hearing this, the police officers were filled with joy,
And the whole party soon arrived in the rear garden.
Two police officers hastened to descend into the well,
Let down by a hempen cord, they searched the well.

When the police officers carefully looked around,
They discovered the corpses at the bottom of the well.
The two police officers were overcome by fear, and
In a panic scrambled to get out of there immediately!

When they had greeted His Excellency, they reported:
"It's scary down there — two of our three souls are gone!
There is no gold or treasure at all down there in the well,
All we found down there was two murdered corpses!"

Prime Minister Lord Bao flew into a terrible rage, and
Loudly cursed the two officers in the following manner:
"Whether it is a corpse or gold and all kinds of treasure,
Bring it all out in the open so it can be fully inspected!"

The two police officers hastily descended into the well,
And with all speed carried the corpses up to the surface.
When His Excellency saw these, he was filled with joy,
And he heartily laughed loudly for a number of times.

"If I had not come up with this marvelous plan, who
Of you all would have been willing to go into that well?"
Then they removed one door leaf from its sockets, and
On it transported the corpses to the Southern Office.

The people of streets and wards all crowded together
To watch as this clueless case entered the prefecture.
They arrived without stopping at Kaifeng Prefecture,
Where the corpses were stored in the western corridor.

Let's not sing of His Excellency arriving at his office,
Listen as I sing in this ballad about his wife Lady Li.
When she heard her husband had returned to the court,
She made all due arrangements to welcome him back.

When she had welcomed His Excellency back home,
A banquet was spread out to drink a few cups of wine.
Fat lamb and pure wine were there in all variety,
And the fruits and seasonal delicacies were all fresh.

Deer and boar and roe and hare — dishes of all kinds,
They only lacked dragon liver and phoenix heart.
In front of the table flutes and reed-organs played;
Beautiful female singers sang their warbling tunes.

Lady Li offered him three cups of wine, and said:
"My dear husband, a trip to the border is not easy!
On the road you suffered from wind and frost, but
Today you have happily returned safe and sound!"

When she had said this, the banquet was over, and
Each and every one retired to his room for the night.

No need to sing of the five watches of the night —
One heard the Golden Rooster crow its wake-up call!
In the Eastern Ocean the sun rose up from Fusang,
So that people would not have to walk in darkness.

His Excellency rose early and ascended the hall;
The officers thunderously reported their presence.
Making their bows, they took their assigned places;
The five hundred officers were arranged on both sides.

Speak:

Judge Bao then asked, "Zhang Qian and Ma Wan, where did the imperial brothers-in-law Cao move to?" The police officers replied, "Earlier their old mansion was at the entrance of Little Horse Lane. But Her Ladyship their mother couldn't live there anymore, and now they have moved to Little Chicken Lane, and the move has already been completed." When His Excellency heard this, he was very pleased, and said, "Zhang Qian and Ma Wan, get me two sides of fat lamb and four caskets of wine from the prefecture, and I will pay Her Ladyship a visit to give her a housewarming present."

Sing:

When Zhang Qian and Ma Wan received this order,
They did not dare procrastinate or tarry for a while.
They promptly went to the inner section of the office,
And got out the lamb and wine to prepare for the trip.
    When the cortege was assembled outside the office,
This was reported to His Excellency so he would know.
"The fat lamb and pure wine have all been provided,
Your sedan chair and horse are ready for departure."
    His Excellency then immediately left the prefecture,
He took his seat in the bright wickerwork sedan chair.
He was preceded by the three cudgels and six swords,
Followed by folding chair, silver bowl, handkerchief.
    The police officers had both tattooed arms and legs,
They were all heroic fighters, men of great courage.
When they loudly shouted, "Judge Bao has arrived,"
Even the city god and god of the soil rose to their feet!
    When they arrived at Little Chicken Lane, they halted;
Judge Bao stepped down from the sedan chair for his visit.
Now this party of police officers had all arrived,
The gatekeeper went inside to report to Her Ladyship.
    "At present His Excellency Bao of Kaifeng Prefecture
Has arrived in person before the gate of this mansion."

When Her Ladyship heard the name of Minister Bao,
She did not pay the announcement any attention at all!

Speak:

When the gatekeeper saw that Her Ladyship did not pay any attention, he
promptly returned to the gate, and reported to His Excellency: "The two
imperial brothers-in-law are not at home, and Her Ladyship is advanced in
years, so she told me to come out and escort you." When Judge Bao heard
this, he walked inside, and when he saw Her Ladyship, he showed his
respect with four times two, eight bows. Her Ladyship did not return his
greeting, but asked Judge Bao: "Where have you been?" His Excellency
replied: "In conformity with the emperor's order I recently visited the
border region to reward the troops. When I came back, I did not realize
that Your Ladyship had moved to this location, so I had not yet paid you a
visit. Now I have brought a simple gift of lamb and wine for Your Ladyship
as a housewarming present." Her Ladyship replied: "I will have none of
your presents of lamb and wine. Take them back home with you, for your
wife and dependents." When Judge Bao heard these words, his heart was
filled with rage, and said: "Your Ladyship, why do you say such words
when I come and visit you with the best intentions to present these
housewarming gifts?"

Sing:

Her Ladyship thereupon ranted in a language most foul,
She immediately started to curse Judge Bao: "You beast!
　　Down in the countryside your father is a village chief,
And your mother weaves linen and picks mulberry leaves.
Your elder brother operates a pawn shop in the village,
Your second brother sells booze in the village to the west.
　　When you grew up you were the third son, imbecile Bao,
You recited the *Classic of Filial Piety* while herding cows.
On behalf of others you held the inkstone and rubbed ink;
You filled the inkstone with water in the service of others.
　　When you heard that the Humane Ancestor held an exam,
You jumped across the Dragon Gate with brush and paper.
Now you may out of the blue have obtained some office,
But you are less than the dust below the sole of my shoes!"

Cursed like this, Judge Bao did not know how to reply,
And flustered and flurried he fled from the Cao mansion.
Once outside the gate, he hastily mounted his sedan chair,
And filled with hatred he repeatedly gnashed his teeth.
    "If I do not sentence and cut off this Cao family mansion,
I am not worthy to be the prefect of Kaifeng Prefecture!"

His Excellency and his cortege went off toward the south;
On the street they met with the elder imperial brother-in-law.
Right there they ran into the elder imperial brother-in-law,
Who had come to the Eastern Capital to visit his mother.
    One shout of his guards terrified both Heaven and Earth;
The roaring rumble of the golden drums was quite scary.
He was preceded by two banners burnished with gold;
He was followed by twenty-four lances all made of gold.
    One pair of men with a bow, one pair with a crossbow;
A couple of men were facing another couple of men.
The cudgels with golden gourds were twenty-four pairs;
The folding chair and silver basin gave a brilliant light.
    The men of his guard had both tattooed arms and legs,
And behind them came men carrying eagles and falcons.
The flames of the red banners — a mountain-burning fire!
On embroidered flags was written: "The emperor's kin."
    Below a raised nine-layered parasol inlaid with gold,
The emperor's relative was seated on a red-mane horse.
Zhang Qian and Ma Wan were overcome by fear, and
Came forward to report the situation to His Excellency.
    His Excellency then dismounted from his sedan chair,
And stood in front of the steps in the lower position.
When the imperial brother-in-law noticed Judge Bao,
He hastily dismounted from his horse to make a bow.

Speak:

The imperial brother-in-law promptly asked: "Judge Bao, where have you
been?" Judge Bao replied: "In conformity with an edict of His Majesty,
I have recently visited the border regions to reward the troops, and
I didn't know that Her Ladyship had moved. Today I provided some lamb
and wine to take to Her Ladyship as housewarming gifts. She not only

refused these gifts, but also cursed my family in a hundred ways for being peasants, and I did not dare reply at all." The imperial brother-in-law answered: "Dear Judge, the ancients said, 'Listen on no account to the words of women!' If I had been at home, things would not have happened like this. I definitely hope, Your Excellency, that you will not carry any grudge." When their conversation was finished, each of them mounted his horse.

Sing:

The two of them each returned to their official abode,
And so they said a few words of greetings at parting.
Let's not tell in our story about His Excellency Bao,
But listen as I sing of the eldest of the Cao brothers.

On horseback, he pondered the matter a million ways,
His expression betrayed his worries, he said not a word.
Without stopping he arrived at Black Chicken Lane,
And the gatekeeper announced his arrival in the hall.

"A thousand felicitations, nay, a myriad of felicitations!
The eldest young master from Jiangnan is back home!"
Her Ladyship his mother was filled with joy in her heart,
And she raised herself to welcome "My darling son!"

When the imperial brother-in-law came into the hall,
The finest incense was burned in the golden braziers.
He bowed four times two, eight times to his mother,
And the whole household, old and young, was happy.

Her Ladyship ordered that a banquet be laid out, so
A banquet was provided so they might drink some wine.
When mother and son sat down to drink the wine,
The imperial brother-in-law did not drink a drop.

Her Ladyship his mother addressed him as follows:
"My dear son, please listen to what I will have to say.

What is the reason your brow is furrowed by sorrow,
What is the reason you are so depressed and down?
Has some official at court taken advantage of you?
What is the cause that you are not happy and merry?"

The imperial brother-in-law folded his hands, saying:
"My dear mother, please listen to what I will say.

That prefect of Kaifeng Prefecture, that Judge Bao,
Does not come to our mansion without some reason.

My dear mother, so why did you have to curse him
When he brought housewarming gifts, lamb and wine?

My younger brother has committed a capital crime,
And I am afraid that this Bao may have heard about it.
If indeed this Judge Bao comes to learn all the facts,
Second brother is bound to leave for the Lord of Shade.

My heart is overcome with fear of that iron-faced Bao,
I am filled with anxious thoughts, depressed and down."

When she heard this, Her Ladyship laughed heartily,
And she said with a smile: "My dear son, don't worry.
Your sister's husband is the current Son of Heaven,
Your elder sister is the empress, the emperor's wife!

You are the transport commissioner for Jiangnan;
Your younger brother is the governor of Zhengzhou.
I myself am the mother-in-law of our lord and king,
We are the highest-ranking relatives of His Majesty.

In my eyes that imbecile Bao is not even worth
The dust at the tip of my shoes or under my heels!
My dear son, if you speak fearful language like this,
You diminish the force of your own vital energy!"

The imperial brother-in-law then said to his mother:
"My dear mother, what you say lacks any scruple!
He is not to be compared to his predecessor Zhang —
This pure official really fills all men with great fear.

He is by all accounts a pillar that supports heaven —
Rivers and mountains have produced a good man.
Because of his visit to Chenzhou to distribute rice,
He beheaded four members of the imperial family.

You will remember that my sister the empress then
Allowed Concubine Zhang to borrow her carriage.
On her way back to court in that carriage the latter
On the street ran into that man surnamed Bao, and

With a single shout he shattered the palace maidens,
Whereupon he reported this matter to the emperor.
My elder sister was even fined three thousand strings,
And she had to hand over the money to this man Bao.

Once the fourth emperor, the Humane Ancestor, held
A banquet at Zhengyang Gate and had some drinks.

This too was found out by that man surnamed Bao,
Who chased him away with his shouts from the gate.[2]
    When he participated in the audience at break of dawn,
He fined his lord a hundred thousand in notes and gold.
His lord and king handed him the gold and the money,
And he distributed it as a reward to the army soldiers.
    At court he once sentenced the emperor's in-law Tao,
And in Zhengzhou he condemned Lord Lu to death.[3]
He summoned that tiger which had committed murder,
And he solved the case of the black pot from the kiln.
    He loves to sentence the emperor's kin and relatives,
This Judge Bao is truly bereft of all common sense.
The four hundred civil and military officials at court
And the emperor's kith and kin all fear this man Bao!
    Intelligent and incorruptible, without any partiality,
He sentences the living by day and the ghosts by night.
When the emperor saw how pure and upright he was,
Our lord and king bestowed on him a golden tablet.
    On that tablet the king wrote a column of characters:
'Irrespective of one's status as an imperial relative,
Empress, imperial concubine, or prime minister,
Whoever breaks the law, all will be treated equally.'"
    Upon hearing this, Her Ladyship was dumbfounded;
She pondered the matter for quite a while, then said:
"Your younger brother's problem of six months ago —
He strangled and killed that student devoted to study.
    He also killed the man's little boy, and thereupon
Dumped both these bodies in the Qiong-flower well.
This way he stole his wife, a girl in hairpins and skirt;
At present he has taken her with him to Zhengzhou.
    Could it be that the rumor of this shady business
Has been blown into Judge Bao's ears so he knows?
Could it be this Judge Bao had come to know of it,
And had come to our house to learn more about it?"

---

[2] The story summarized in these four lines is otherwise unknown.
[3] The case of the emperor's in-law Tao is otherwise unknown. The case of Lord Lu probably refers to the story adapted for the stage in the *zaju* play *Lu Zhailang*. Also see *Baijia gong'an*, Ch. 92.

Speak:

The woman cried out: "My eldest son, in all cases it would be best if your younger brother's wife lady Zhang would never be able to talk. What to do if she at some later date would want to seek revenge for her husband and we would fall into the claws of that Bao?" The eldest brother-in-law of the emperor said: "It's just because I was afraid of this that I was so annoyed, but after some thinking I now have come up with a plan. The best would be if I would write a letter to my younger brother, telling him to kill that lady Zhang, so there will be no witness at some later date who can cause trouble for him." When Her Ladyship heard this, she was greatly pleased.

Sing:

When Her Ladyship heard this, she said: "Perfect!
Get some paper and hurry to write him that letter!"
　　The imperial brother-in-law promptly started writing,
And the letter was written as clear as it could be.
He instructed his younger brother in Zhengzhou
To kill his wife, lady Zhang, as quickly as possible.
　　"And if you do not kill that woman surnamed Zhang,
Your mother will not tarry at all to kill you in person!
A few days ago Judge Bao came and visited mother,
He came to our house to learn about this business.
　　If you do not comply with the message in this letter,
You allow a lot of trouble to emerge at a later date.
I urge you on all accounts to obey your elder brother
And not to forget at any time your mother's grace!"
　　When he had finished writing and sealing this letter,
He promptly dispatched two very fast messengers.
And these two uniformed soldiers wasted no moment;
They did not dare procrastinate and tarry for a while.

They hurriedly got dressed and then left the mansion,
Exerting themselves to the utmost they went on ahead.
Once they had left the walls of the Eastern Capital,
They proceeded along the road as storm-driven clouds.
　　They got to the five-mile marker like flicking a finger,
And then the ten-mile marker appeared before their eyes!
Thirty-six miles — they came to Peach Blossom Lane;
Twenty-four miles — it was Apricot Blossom Village.

They rested at night, left at dawn — no need to tell;
Eventually they arrived at the city of Zhengzhou.
Once they had entered inside the city of Zhengzhou,
They ran like clouds through its streets and lanes.
    When they came to the imperial brother-in-law's office,
The gatekeeper hastened inside to report their arrival.
    Announcing their presence before the hall, he reported:
"Commander, please listen to what I have to say.
A letter has arrived from Her Ladyship your mother,
So you should go outside to receive it with respect."
    Hearing this, the governor hastily dressed himself,
And in full formal attire he reverenced his mother.
After lighting a candle of incense from Guangnan,
He received the letter from home, and opened it.
    When he had opened the letter and read it,
He read each word and each line for its message.
Reading this letter, the emperor's brother-in-law
Pondered the matter in his mind, and wondered:
    "A woman who has such beautiful features —
How could I give her up and have her killed?
But if I don't do as I'm told in my mother's letter,
This may later create trouble and cost me my life."
    In his heart he conceived a dragon-catching plan:
Ply her with drink till she is drunk, and then kill her!
He thereupon immediately entered the rear section
And told the servant girls to go and invite his lady.
    The two servant girls went to the lady's room,
And there addressed the lady in the following way:
"The imperial brother-in-law told us to invite you
To a banquet in the hall and to have some wine."
    When the lady heard that her husband invited her,
She kept silent but thought about what it meant.

Speak:

The woman was in the throes of anxious thoughts, and when on top of
that she was invited by the serving maids, she did not say a word, but
thought to herself: "For the last three days my skin is shivering and my
eyes are jumping, I am not at ease whether sitting or laying down, I am

shivering with cold all over my body, and my cheeks are bright red. Last night I dreamed that I was bound to die — this must all be because the crime in the Eastern Capital has come to light. I have heard that Judge Bao has returned to the capital, and I'm afraid he must have received a letter from home, telling this man to kill me. Now today he invites me to drink some wine, he will definitely kill me, and inescapably I will die by his vicious hands. Today he wants me to drink till I'm drunk, but it is better to die with a clear mind than with a darkened mind, so I will wear a double-lined jacket, pour the wine inside, and feign to be drunk, so I will be a clear-headed ghost when I die." She could not but dress herself in all her finery, and when she had done so, she prayed to Heaven and appeared from her room.

Sing:

When two serving maids brought the invitation,
She dressed in full attire before leaving her room.
Facing the mirror she applied rouge and powder,
Artfully drew her eyebrows, lightly dotted her lips.
  She combed her hair into a coiling-dragon chignon,
The twelve hairpins were placed following the hours.
On her head she wore a golden-phoenix pearl-chaplet;
The locks on her temples combed as black as clouds.
  She wore a jacket of Sichuan silk, smelling of musk,
And under that a skirt with the waves of the Xiang.
The curved shoes on her feet measured three inches,
And lightly moving her lotus steps she left her room.
  She looked like Chang'e when she leaves the moon,
Resembled an immortal who descends to this world.
Not too tall, not too short — all the right proportions;
Neither fat nor skinny — she surpassed all in features.
  Her cheeks were like red lotus flowers emerging from a pond;
Her mouth was like the one dot of red of a fully ripe cherry.
Her eyebrows resembled early willow leaves in spring;
Her eyes were autumn waves transparent all through.
  Her neck was like three inches of unblemished jade;
From the pearly earrings in her ears hung gold chains.
Her thirty-six teeth were as white as pieces of jade, and
The breath from her mouth had the fragrance of musk.

Watched from any corner this woman looked great,
Just like Weaving Maiden descending to this world.[4]
Tens of serving maids preceded her as she walked,
All carrying gold incense burners as they led the way.
  When the imperial brother-in-law saw her, [he thought:]
"I cannot let go of this woman, a beauty so unique!"
When he saw her, his eyes overflowed with tears;
Tears coursed down from his eyes in great profusion.
  He welcomed the lady to the hall, let her take her seat,
And he poured her some of the finest imperial wine.
The lady took the wine and made as to drink, but
Having taken the wine, she poured it into her jacket.
  When eventually they had drunk for quite some time,
The lady, feigning to be overcome by wine, collapsed.
When the imperial brother-in-law saw she was drunk,
He ordered the serving maids to help her to her feet.
  Serving girls both left and right helped her to her feet,
And supported her as she returned back to her room.
The lady, still drunk, collapsed inside the bed-curtains;
She collapsed on the ivory bed and did not get up.

She feigned to be overcome by wine but did not sleep —
Let's talk about the second master of the Cao family.
  As he held a sword in his hand with its shining blade,
He came into the room and intended to kill the lady.
But when he walked into her room and looked around,
He started thinking again as soon as he saw her face.
  A number of times he walked into the room and looked,
But how could he take action and kill that lovely person?
Pondering the matter from all sides, he saw no solution,
And lost in thought he was standing there in that room.
  As the imperial brother-in-law was lost in thought,
An elderly man walked in from the rear garden, and
When this old house servant Zhang got to that spot,
He addressed the young master in the following way:
  "My dear lord, what are you doing here with a sword?
You seem down and depressed — whom will you kill?"

---

[4] Weaving Maiden is an astral deity.

The imperial brother-in-law answered him as follows:
"Uncle, please listen to what I will have to tell you.

If I do not tell you, you do not know the background,
So I will tell you everything from the very beginning.
This lady is actually not my own dear darling wife —
Her husband was a student from outside the capital.

Now my mother and brother have written me a letter,
Informing me that Judge Bao has visited our mansion.
If he would come to know of the murder I committed,
The punishment I might get later would be substantial.

They want me to cut off the head of this woman, but
How could I do such a deed, kill such a lovely person?
Considering the matter in all detail, I see no solution,
As I do not know how on earth I could kill this person!"

The old man thereupon addressed him as follows:
"Your Royal Highness, you are acting most foolishly!

If you would cut off her head right here in this place,
Her soul would haunt this room and allow you no rest.
Allow me to come up with a dragon-catching scheme,
Which will ensure she'll never trouble Your Highness."

Speak:

This elderly man said: "Your Royal Highness, in the rear garden is an old
well, which is so deep it has no bottom! If I push the woman into that
well, she will die as soon as she hits the water. In that way her corpse will
be in one piece, and you will not be troubled by her wronged ghost." The
prince said: "I will give you ten ounces of top-grade silver if you rob this
woman of her life." And the imperial brother-in-law next asked: "Uncle,
what will be the sign?" The elderly man said: "Your Royal Highness, when
you hear the splash of the water, that will be the sign." The imperial
brother-in-law fully trusted his words.

Sing:

When the man had received his ten ounces of silver,
He then immediately entered the room of the lady.
Hurriedly he helped this beautiful woman to her feet,
And hauled her to the garden located behind the hall.

While he was walking he was also talking to himself,
This elderly man was loudly debating within himself:
"I would like to save this woman surnamed Zhang,
But she is totally drunk and not aware of the world!"
　　When the woman heard him speak like this, she said:
"Uncle, please save my life in one way or another!
If you, dear sir, will be able to save me from death,
I will not forget your favor till the day that I die!"
　　This elderly man then addressed the woman, saying:
"Dear lady, please do not worry, set your mind at rest."

Speak:

This Zhang Qing said: "All I wanted was to save you, but then I was afraid
that you were drunk and couldn't find your own way, so you would be
captured and that would be a risk. Please get on the railing of the well, and
walk three times around going left, and three times going right. If you do
not fall into the well, I will save your life."

Sing:

When she heard this, the lady was overcome with joy;
Three times she circled the well as easily as a cloud.
She never lost her footing, didn't make any misstep —
A large rock was dropped into the well with a splash!
　　When the imperial brother-in-law heard this splash,
Tears gushed from his eyes and fell down in profusion.
"Alas, that such a young woman as pretty as a flower,
Became a person in a dream of Southern Branch joy."

The elderly servant thereupon instructed her as follows:
"Let me give you these ten ounces of top-grade silver.
You and I now happen to share the same surname, so
Remember well it was Zhang Qing who saved your life."
　　He thereupon opened the gate of the rear garden, and
Hastily guided the woman to the outside of the garden.
"Now tonight I will help you to get out of this flower garden,
And you will flee to the Eastern Capital first thing tomorrow."
　　The elderly servant also gave her the following advice:
"Be careful, guard yourself against dangers on the road!

And if you succeed in getting to the Eastern Capital,
Make sure to lodge your accusation with Judge Bao!"
    The woman expressed her gratitude to the servant:
"I will never forget your favor, even in future lives!"
And when finally the fifth watch arrived and dawn,
She immediately sneaked out of the city of Zhengzhou.

    With her small feet in tight shoes it was hard to walk;
A storm blew in her face till her cheeks were all red.
And as the woman remembered her life back home,
She wailed and wailed and bitterly wept sometimes.

    "Looking up, I call on Heaven, who doesn't answer;
At what hour and day will I get to the Eastern Capital?"
And while she was walking, she was also talking,
Each and every word a complaint against her husband!

    "I told him not to go to the Eastern Capital, but he
Wanted to go there to participate in the examinations!
He never achieved any high office, and now today
I am here out on the road, fleeing for my dear life!"

    Because the woman was busying herself with weeping,
She startled the Star of Great White in the sky above.[5]
"This person is not a woman of the mortal world,
She was originally an immortal from Penglai Isle."[6]

    When the Metal Star of Great White had spotted her,
He turned himself into an aged fellow of this world.
He was pushing a wheelbarrow with a ram's head,
And by the side of the road he greeted the woman.

    This elderly man promptly addressed her as follows:
"Dear young lady, where are you planning to go?"

    When the woman was asked this question by him,
She replied to this elderly man in the following manner:

    "I was born on the western side of the Eastern Capital,
But my father and mother married me off to Zhengzhou.

---

[5] Great White is one of the names of the planet Venus (which corresponds to the element Metal). The astral deity of Great White may descend to this world in any guise in order to help out people in distress.

[6] Penglai is one of the three floating islands in the Eastern Ocean that are the abode of the immortals.

Because my husband has died and I have not one son,
My father- and mother-in-law have chased me away.
   I now want to go back to the village I come from,
But on small feet in curved shoes it is hard to walk.
Uncle, if you are willing to take me back to the village,
I will give you five ounces of silver as white as snow!"
   The woman climbed onto the wheelbarrow and sat down,
And she raised her pressed palms to above her crown.
The elderly man pushed the wheelbarrow and walked,
And the city gods and gods of the soil all helped out.
   King Mara made the beautiful woman fall asleep,[7]
And the wheelbarrow then floated through the air.
Riding on clouds and mists it sped like an arrow, and
Within an hour it arrived outside the Eastern Capital.
   The cloud put down this woman in hairpins and skirt;
The Metal Star of Great White made itself scarce.
So when the woman woke up and looked all around,
She did not see that dear uncle, that nice elderly man.
   From afar she saw the towering walls of the capital,
And she wondered where on earth she might be.
   When she considered the matter more carefully,
She realized he could not have been a common mortal.
"Fortunately the heavenly gods came to my rescue;
Divinities brought me here to the Eastern Capital!"
   When she had entered the triple gates of the city,
She walked quite a stretch on the main streets.
And when she lifted her head to have a good look,
She recognized the innkeeper, that woman Wang!

Speak:

When this woman arrived back in the Eastern Capital, she recognized the
inn of woman Wang. She walked inside to ask for a room, and she would
pay for the room the next day. Woman Wang said: "Missus, I have thirty-
six rooms, but these are all occupied. There is only one room. Half a year
ago a student with his wife and little son stayed at my inn, and the three of
them went out to see the flower streets, and I have never seen them come

---

[7] King Mara is the Buddhist divinity who rules the worlds of desire.

back. I don't know whether the student became an official or failed, and till today I haven't dared open that room." Lady Zhang said: "I am all alone and by myself and I haven't any luggage with me. I wouldn't dare touch their stuff."

Sing:

When the old woman heard her speak in this manner,
She promptly went off to open the door of the room.
When she had opened the door and cleaned the room,
She invited her guest to come in and enter the room.

When she arrived at the room and looked all around,
She recognized the belongings of her dear husband:
Garments and shoes and socks she had made herself.
In the room she wept bitterly; tears fell in profusion!

When the old lady heard her guest weep like this,
She came back and questioned her in great detail.
She asked the young lady the following questions:
"From which prefecture are you? From which district?
For what reason have you come to this place here?
And for what reason have you come to this very inn?"

Hearing this, the beauty stepped forward and said:
"Dear aunt, please listen to what I will have to say.
We live in Chaoshui District in Chaozhou Prefecture,
In Iron Hill Village of Filial and Fair Township.

I was born as a daughter of the Zhang family there,
And the husband and master I married was a Yuan.
Hearing that the Humane Ancestor was holding an exam,
The three of us came together to the Eastern Capital.

We rented a room right here in your inn, dear aunt;
The next day we went out to see the Eastern Capital.
As we were idly walking around on the streets,
We ran by coincidence into a man who was evil.

He was the younger imperial brother-in-law Cao,
Who invited us to his mansion to have some wine.
But when he saw how well I could hold my liquor,
He robbed me and locked me in a room as his lady.

He murdered my dear husband by strangling him,
And he also killed our little baby boy of only three.

Three months ago he took me with him to Zhengzhou,
And there he also ordered that I should be killed.
 The old servant Zhang Qing kindly saved my life,
And early at dawn I arrived in the Eastern Capital.
Now I came to your inn and rented a room here,
I recognized the belongings of my late husband.
 I beseech you, dear aunt, to show compassion,
And to teach me the way to appeal to Judge Bao.
If I can exact repayment for my husband's life,
I will never forget your favor till the day that I die."
 When the old woman heard her speak in this way,
She set out rice and wine to treat her guest well.
Having eaten her food, she then washed her feet,
And the beauty rested for the night in her room.

As soon as the fifth watch arrived and dawn came, she
Combed her hair, washed her face, and went outside.
And when she stood outside the gate of the inn,
Streets and markets were filled with busy crowds.
 All people in the streets were sweeping the ground,
And they said that Judge Bao would soon visit.
"Today he is offering incense in all the temples,
And then he will return to his Kaifeng Prefecture."
 Hearing this, lady Zhang was filled with joy —
The best would be to appeal to the man right here!
And just as she stood waiting in front of the steps,
An official and his cortege startled the crowds.
 In front came one banner all inlaid with gold,
There behind followed twenty-four golden lances.
One pair of cudgels and then one pair of swords;
One couple of men facing another couple of men.
 A red-silk umbrella was raised in front of the horse,
His folding chair and silver basin sparkled brightly.
Lady Zhang then stepped forward, bowed deeply,
And knelt in front of the horse to lodge her complaint.
 The official on horseback addressed her as follows:
"Woman, for what reason do you lodge an accusation?
What is your surname and name? Where do you live?
What is the injustice from which you are suffering?"

Lady Zhang immediately answered as follows:
"Your Excellency, please listen to what I will say.
I hail from Chaoshui District in Chaozhou Prefecture,
From Iron Hill Village in Filial and Fair Township.
The husband I was married to was Yuan Wenzheng,
He studied the books by the light of window and lamp.

When he heard the Humane Ancestor was holding an exam
And widely summoned students throughout the empire,
His mind was set on the pursuit of fame and riches,
And with my husband I came to the Eastern Capital.

But because we went to see the sights of the capital,
We ran into a man who was evil right on the street.
He was the younger imperial brother-in-law Cao —
And we had stepped aside to avoid that official!

When the imperial brother-in-law saw my looks,
He invited us to his mansion to drink some wine.
My husband did not realize that this was all a trick;
He kept on drinking till he was drunk as a skunk.

He strangled my dear husband with a hempen cord,
And he also killed my little baby boy of only three.
He locked me up in a room and he made me his lady,
And then took me with him to the city of Zhengzhou.

Later, when the imperial brother-in-law had received
A letter from home, he also gave the order to kill me.
I am deeply grateful to Zhang Qing, who saved me;
He set me free, allowing me to escape with my life.

That same night I fled from the flower garden, and
This morning I have arrived in the Eastern Capital.
I beseech you, Dragon-Design Bao, to take pity on me,
And to be the man who exacts revenge for my sake!"

Hearing this, the imperial brother-in-law exclaimed
Full of rage: "This is a nonsensical false accusation!"
He shouted to his guards and to his personal servants:
"Beat that woman to death with your iron whips!"

Before he had even finished speaking these words,
Some uniformed soldiers rushed out to lady Zhang.
They immediately grabbed and whipped the woman
Right in the middle of the street, leaving her for dead.

The high official and his cortege then went further —
The old woman the innkeeper was scared witless!
She walked into the street to look at lady Zhang,
And then called for two young maids to help her.

    Hastily they helped this lady Zhang to her feet,
And on her back she carried her back to the inn.
They poured a bowl of hot bouillon into her mouth,
And they also sprinkled her face with cold water.

    The old woman prayed to Heaven and to Earth,
She burned the finest incense in front of the gods.
Eventually, after quite some time, they saved her,
As lady Zhang came to and regained her senses.

    She was breathing heavily and felt hot all over;
Lady Zhang heaved heavy sighs a number of times.
When she saw the people around her, she cried;
Wailing and bitterly weeping she told her story.

    "Everybody talks about that pure official Bao,
But he turns out to be a muddleheaded fellow.
Before he had waited for me to tell him the facts,
He told them to kill me so I would lose my life!

    Dear aunt, if you had not come to my rescue,
My soul would have left to see the Lord of Shade!"

    The old woman then told lady Zhang the following:
"Now please listen to the explanation I will give.
You did not appeal at all to His Excellency Bao,
That was the eldest imperial brother-in-law Cao!

    When you want to appeal, you should ask me —
Once outside, you misidentified the central figure!
I had wanted to take you to Kaifeng Prefecture,
But then I was afraid the Caos would come to know.

    Because if the Caos would come to know of this,
None in my family, old or young, would survive!
Now you cannot stay here any longer, so go quickly
To the Southern Office and lodge your accusation."

    The old woman then addressed lady Zhang, saying:
"Now let me show you the way to Kaifeng Prefecture.

    When you leave this inn, you walk straight south,
And you go straight on till the Prefectural Bridge.
On the other side of the bridge you then go west,
To the great office which opens toward the south.

On the gate are written three lines of characters;
When you tell the truth, the verdict too will be true.
  [On his tablet] one reads an edict of the king,
'Irrespective of one's status as an imperial relative,
Empress, imperial concubine, or prime minister,
Whoever breaks the law will be treated equally.'
  In the western corridor the bronze gong resounds;
In the eastern corridor the grievance drum is clear.
A man lodging a complaint thrice beats the drum,
A woman lodging an accusation strikes the gong."

Lady Zhang thanked the old woman and departed,
And she went toward the south on the main street.
In one stretch she arrived at the Prefectural Bridge,
Where numerous people were coming and going.
  Across the bridge she went in a westerly direction,
And there indeed she found the prefectural office.
On its gate were written three lines of characters;
The bronze gong and grievance drum to the sides.
  Lady Zhang went to the western corridor, and she
Thrice, shaking Heaven, struck that bronze gong!
His Excellency in the hall heard the sound clearly;
He promptly ordered policemen to go and check.
  Zhao Hu and Zhang Long wasted not a minute,
But stepped forward and questioned her, saying:
"What kind of wrong or injustice did you suffer?
Judge Bao sends for you to question you closely!"
  When lady Zhang managed to arrive in the hall,
Tears flowed from her eyes as she made her appeal.
His Excellency thereupon addressed her as follows:
"What is your surname and name? Where do you live?
  Are you perhaps an inhabitant of the Eastern Capital?
Or do you perhaps rather live in the Western Capital?
Have you been cursed by the neighbors east or west?
Or were you in a fight with some girl or some uncle?
  Who gave you such a beating that your skin is torn?
Who gave you such a beating you're bloody all over?
Tell me everything in detail from the very beginning:
If you tell me the truth, the verdict too will be clear."

Tears flowed from the eyes of lady Zhang, who said:
"Your Excellency, please be so kind as to listen to me.
　I hail from Chaoshui District in Chaozhou Prefecture,
From Iron Hill Village in Filial and Fair Township.
The name of my own husband was Yuan Wenzheng,
And the family in which I was born was the Zhangs.
　My husband studied the letters from earliest youth;
By the side of a cold window he recited the books.
Then His Majesty the Humane Ancestor held an exam,
And widely summoned students throughout the empire.
　Because my man wanted to pursue fame and riches,
The three of us came together to the Eastern Capital.
We arrived here on the first day of the Third Month;
On the third day of that month he would take the exam.
　On the second we walked around throughout the day,
The three of us were taking in the sights of the capital.
And because we were taking in the sights of the city,
We brought about the gruesome situation of today.
　As my husband and I were taking in the city's sights,
We unexpectedly ran into a man whose heart is evil.
That was the second imperial brother-in-law Cao —
The cortege and guard of that man terrified us all!
　My husband and I moved to the side of the street,
But he nevertheless fixed his eyes on my figure.
When that man saw how well I was proportioned,
He invited us over to his mansion to have some drinks.
　My darling husband didn't realize that this was a trick,
So he kept on drinking till he was drunk as a skunk.
That man strangled my husband with a hempen cord,
And also killed my baby boy of only three years old.
　With brute violence he forced me to become his wife;
He also took me with him to the city of Zhengzhou.
But when the governor received a letter from home,
He also gave the order that I should now be killed.
　The old servant Zhang Qing managed to save me,
And yesterday I arrived here in the Eastern Capital.
And when I arrived here inside the Eastern Capital,
I rented a room in the inn of that old woman Wang.
　This morning I got up early and stood by the gate,
When a high official and his cortege entered the street.

People all said that Judge Bao was burning incense,
So in front of that horse I appealed to Judge Bao.
But it was the elder imperial brother-in-law Cao,
I made the mistake of appealing to my arch-enemy!
Without listening till I could have told my story,
He shouted to his soldiers and servants to beat me.
Their whipping with iron whips left me for dead,
And they also robbed me of my ten ounces of silver.
The innkeeper, that old woman, came to my rescue;
Pouring hot bouillon into my mouth she revived me.
She was so kind as to point out the way to me, so
I found Kaifeng Prefecture to lodge my accusation.
Now today I am able to see Your Excellency's face,
It's like an ancient mirror that is bright once again.
I beseech Your Excellency to show compassion,
To bring light to the capital with your bright mirror.
What is the punishment for killing without a cause?
And for the violent abduction of a good man's wife?
I very much hope Your Excellency will take pity,
And I hope that you will exact revenge for my sake.
If you sentence the two imperial brothers-in-law Cao,
I will not forget your favor till the day of my death!"

Hearing her accusation His Excellency was happy,
"I just wanted to bring clarity to this murder case!"
He then immediately ordered two police officers,
To escort her to the corpses for an identification.
When lady Zhang came to the western corridor,
She recognized the corpses of her husband and son.
When she saw her husband, she wailed and wept;
She wailed and wept bitterly, speaking as follows:
"I told you not to go in pursuit of fame and riches,
But you had to take the exams in the Eastern Capital!
And before you had obtained any office or function,
You were buried, you two, both father and son!"
His Excellency in the hall questioned her as follows:
"How do you recognize the body of your husband?"
Lady Zhang immediately answered him as follows:
"Now Your Excellency, please listen to what I say.

This is the man with whom I shared bed and cushion,
Of course I'm positive this corpse is my husband."

His Excellency in the hall then gave out an order,
He promptly dispatched two police officers, saying:
"This woman mentions the elder of the Cao brothers,
But I am afraid it is not necessarily this official.

There are plenty of imperial relatives in this city,
And all those many court officials and high ministers!
Go and summon that woman Wang for questioning —
Only then will we know the full truth of the matter."

Speak:

These two men reported: "Your Excellency, there are two inns in the
Eastern Capital which are operated by a woman Wang, so we don't know
which one it is." Lady Zhang said: "If you cross the bridge and go straight
north, there is an inn with thirty-six rooms, and that's the one." That very
moment old woman Wang in her inn was saying: "That lady who got such
a beating she was left for dead has not yet returned from lodging her
accusation." Right when she was saying this, she saw two police officers,
who said: "Judge Bao asks you to come as quick as fire!"

Sing:

The old woman went along with the police officers,
And they hurried to the prefecture's Southern Office.
When she had entered the triple gates, she greeted
His Excellency Dragon-Design Bao by bowing down.

His Excellency in the hall addressed her as follows,
He asked the old woman, the innkeeper, this question:
"This lady here who had rented a room at your inn —
To which official did she appeal out on the street?
He had this lady beaten and then left her for dead,
But you came to her rescue so she could revive.

Which relative of the emperor was this official?
Or which official at court or which high minister?
Tell me everything in detail according to the truth,
Because you, my auntie, are the witness in this case."

The old woman folded her hands and there said:
"Your Excellency, please listen to what I will say.

This lady wanted to lodge an accusation at dawn,
And on the street she appealed to a high official.
    This high official was nobody else, but happened
To be the elder of the imperial brothers-in-law Cao!
He had this lady beaten and then left her for dead,
And then I came to her rescue so she could survive."

    Hearing this, His Excellency was filled with joy:
"Dear auntie, now go safely back to your place!"

Let's not sing how the old woman went back home,
But let's sing of that pure official, Minister Bao.
"Now I've established the facts in the lady's case,
I'll devise a scheme to lay my hands on that man!"

Speak:

His Excellency called a family servant to him, [and said:] "Please lead this
lady to the rear apartment for some tea and conversation with my wife.
I will call for you when I have arrested the two imperial brothers-in-law."
Seated in the hall, His Excellency did not say a word as he thought to
himself, "Their father the grand teacher was a major elderly statesman,
their mother is a lady of the highest rank, and their elder sister is the
empress in the Main Palace. The elder imperial brother-in-law is transport
commissioner for Jiangnan and the younger imperial brother-in-law is the
governor of Zhengzhou, so who would dare take them in?" After he had
thought of a clever scheme, he called for Zhang Qian and Ma Wan, [and
told them:] "You will spread the rumor on the streets that His Excellency
suffers from wind in the bones and is unable to hold court. That way all
officials definitely will come and visit me. On that occasion I will first arrest
the elder imperial brother-in-law, and then later I will arrest the younger
imperial brother-in-law. This is the most marvelous scheme."

Sing:

His Excellency conceived of a most devious scheme:
I will have to feign an illness to get hold of that man.
He immediately disappeared into the rear apartment:
His face was a sallow yellow, he had lost all energy!
    When seven days — three audiences — had gone by,
He still did not come to the hall to hear criminal cases.

He washed his face with a hot lotus-leaf concoction;
It looked exactly like he was suffering from a disease.
  When seven days — three audiences — had gone by,
All officials came and visited the man surnamed Bao.
The prefect in the Southern Office, His Excellency Bao,
Was so ill he likely would soon join the Lord of Shade!
  Zhang Qian and Ma Wan hastily reported the message,
Reported this information to the rear apartment room,
  And they said: "Your Excellency, please kindly listen.
All officials have arrived at the gate of the prefecture.
What is the information which you want us to relay?
What should we tell to all these assembled officials?"
  When His Excellency heard them say "all officials,"
He said to Zhang Qian and Ma Wan: "Now listen.
Just tell them that I have been taking my medication,
And just now I have fallen asleep in a fitful slumber."
  They hastily went outside and said in front of the hall:
"Your Excellencies, please be informed that Judge Bao
Is seriously ill and has not yet woken up from his fever.
He hopes to meet with you all here tomorrow morning."

Speak:

His Excellency told Zhang Qian and Ma Wan: "You two stand outside the gate tomorrow morning, and if the officials come again to see me, you promptly tell them that I am seriously ill, have been seen by a doctor and am taking my medications, and cannot come out." The next day the officials indeed came to see him, and Zhang Qian and Ma Wan said what His Excellency had told them to say, so all these officials returned by themselves.

Sing:

Let's not sing of the feigned illness of Dragon-Design,
Listen as I sing of the assembled officials at court.
  They discussed that Judge Bao was stricken by illness,
And most likely would soon join the Lord of Shade.
When tomorrow they all came to the Golden Bells Hall,
They had to report this matter to their Sagely Emperor.
  When the fifth watch came and the court horses moved,
The emperor ascended the hall and received his officials.

When the whip was cracked thrice, the emperor entered;
When the large fans were removed, they saw his person.

His Majesty the Humane Ancestor ascended the hall,
Civil and military officials were arranged on both sides.
On his head the emperor wore a Level Heaven Crown;
Without-a-Worry's on his feet,[8] he sat on a brocade stool.

There in the hall their lord and king addressed them,
And asked the many civil officials and military officers:
"If there is business, may a high minister report to Us;
If there is no business, all leave through the inner gate."

Before this edict had been even fully promulgated,
The assembled officials bowed before the emperor,
And they reported that Rescriptor-in-waiting Bao
Was seriously ill and might join the Lord of Shade.

When he heard this, the Humane Ancestor shed tears,
And told the civil officials and the military officers:
"We may rule all-under-heaven, but We lack the luck:
Minister Bao soon will die and join the Lord of Shade.

If Rescriptor-in-waiting Bao indeed is going to die,
On whom will the altars of the state, this empire, rely?
If His Excellency Bao will be absent from this court,
It would be the same as losing half of Our officials!

Whoever will be able to restore Judge Bao to health
Will be granted a promotion, privileges for his sons:
Every male child at seven will be appointed to office,
Every female child at eight will enjoy the emperor's favor."

Even before this edict had been fully promulgated,
The elder imperial brother-in-law stepped forward.
With twenty-four bows — longevity like a mountain;
"Your Imperial Majesty, please set your mind at rest!

Upon leaving this court your humble servant will go
Today to the Southern Office to visit Minister Bao.
If he is indeed still suffering from a serious disease,
Let's ask the imperial physicians to visit his mansion."

Hearing this, the Humane Ancestor felt very happy,
And the imperial brother-in-law left the audience.

---

[8] The emperor's boots are called Without-a-Worry's, suggesting that the way he goes about his business will cause no disturbance.

The uniformed soldiers and servants formed a cortege,
And set out through the main streets and small lanes.
    One pair of cudgels confronted one pair of swords,
And one couple of men faced another couple of men.
Both arms and legs of all of them were fully tattooed,
They were all brave-hearted men without any scruples.
    As soon as they shouted but once: "Clear the way!"
Anyone on the road stopped in his tracks and looked.
In front of the wineshops the banner was taken down,
And inside the teahouses all visitors were terrified.
    At the shout: "The imperial brother-in-law is here!"
Each and every family lit its finest incense.
After a while they arrived at the Southern Office —
Zhang Qian and Ma Wan were shaking with fear.
    They hastily ran to the inner apartments to report
That the imperial brother-in-law had arrived outside.
Hearing this, His Excellency was filled with joy:
"That guy's fallen into my trap for ninety percent!"

Speak:

When Judge Bao learned that the elder imperial brother-in-law had come to visit him, his heart was filled with joy, and he ordered the police officers: "Now go and tell the imperial brother-in-law that His Excellency is seriously ill and cannot come outside to welcome him. Then invite the imperial brother-in-law to descend from his sedan chair and come inside on foot, to have some tea and conversation." When the imperial brother-in-law heard this account, his heart was filled with joy. He promptly descended from his sedan chair and walked into the mansion.

Sing:

The imperial brother-in-law did not know he was tricked;
He promptly descended from his sedan chair and entered.
His Excellency welcomed him in front of the stairs, and
Greeted the imperial brother-in-law, that eminent official.
    Three times he inclined his body to show his respect,
And in the hall they engaged in some trivial conversation.
Judge Bao folded his hands, stepped forward, and said:
"I am greatly honored by your visit to this lowly office."

When the imperial brother-in-law had greeted Judge Bao,
He scrutinized him: the skin of his cheeks was black again![9]
"Earlier it was said that he was stricken by some illness,
But today he is that old Judge Bao again, as sturdy as before."
    The imperial brother-in-law addressed him as follows:
"Your Excellency, to my joy I see you are fully recovered.
At the early audience this morning I promised our lord
That I would pay you a visit to see how you have been."
    Judge Bao inclined his body and hastened to thank him:
"Allow me to express my thanks for visiting me at home."
    He then ordered the servants on duty to lay out a banquet
To entertain the imperial brother-in-law, that high official.
His Excellency immediately started to pour him wine,
All kinds of seasonal dishes urged one to have a drink.
    Goose-egg pears from Zhengzhou, Xuanzhou chestnuts;
Then there were longans from Fuzhou and fresh lychees.
There were a hundred kinds of dishes to go with the wine,
And each of the precious fruits on the plates was fresh.
    During the first cup of wine not one word was said,
And during the second cup, no word was said either.
But as soon as they had downed their third cup of wine,
Judge Bao rose to his feet and explained the situation.

Speak:

Judge Bao said: "Imperial brother-in-law, I have a problem on which I
have not yet reached a decision and would like to hear your advice. There
is this woman who has a really good figure. Her husband has been
strangled by an official, who has also killed her three-year-old baby son and
taken her to be his wife. That official's elder brother wrote him a letter
ordering him to kill that woman. Zhang Qing saved her life, and that very
night she fled to the Eastern Capital, and wanted to appeal to me. But by
mistake she appealed to the elder brother, who had her beaten to death
with iron whips. But the woman was once again saved by an old woman,

---

[9] On the Peking Opera stage, Judge Bao indeed has a black face. But the term "black" also
has the meaning of sun-burned and one wonders whether originally Judge Bao was called
"black" (in the meaning of sun-burned) because of his lowly background.

an innkeeper. Now this woman has appealed to me but I don't know the name of that official." When the imperial brother-in-law heard this, his face looked like a leaf of cabbage!

Sing:

The very moment the judge had finished speaking,
Lady Zhang rushed forward in front of the hall.
Her face was black and swollen, her body all blood,
And so she knelt down in front of the hall and said:
    "Precisely this elder imperial brother-in-law Cao
Had me beaten on that street and left me for dead.
He also robbed me of my ten ounces of fine silver,
But aunt Wang came to my rescue and I recovered.
    I now beseech Your Excellency to show some pity,
And to exact revenge for this murder for my sake!"
    When the imperial brother-in-law heard these words,
He seemed to be hit by Heaven, scared by the thunder.
He shouted: "You woman, you are bereft of all reason,
How dare you curse a person like me in this hall?
    When did I give you a beating, leave you for dead?
When did I ever see that snow-white silver of yours?
Making an unfounded accusation is a major crime!
I'll take you back to my office, have you questioned!"
    His Excellency Prime Minister Bao flew into a rage,
Cursed him, shouting: "Elder imperial brother-in-law,
You presently committed a crime that breaks the law,
That innkeeper, old woman Wang, was the witness."
    He loudly ordered the police officers to take action,
And there in the hall they arrested the emperor's kin.
They stripped him of all his outer and undergarments,
Locked him in a large cangue and dragged him to prison.
    Then they closed the gate of the prefectural office,
And arrested the men under Lord Cao's command.

His Excellency Minister Bao now was very pleased,
And thought about how to capture the second brother.
The best would be to come up with a clever scheme —
A scheme that would assure one hundred percent success!

He got one sheet of letter paper with floral patterns,
And prepared a fragrant ink to write a private letter,
Which read: "Your mother has something to tell you,
My dear son, my darling boy, take heed of my words.

At present your mother is suffering from an illness,
Very soon, I fear, I will die to join the Lord of Shade.
One raises a son to provide against old age, they say;
One hoards grain to provide against famine, it's said.

Abandon Zhengzhou and all its troops and its horses,
And travel throughout the night to see your old mother.
If you postpone to come for only a little, little while,
You will arrive too late to see your dear mother alive.

These are a mother's instructions to her darling son,
So I will not repeat them again to urge you to come.
As soon as you will have received this single letter,
Please hurry here, traveling by day and also by night."

When Judge Bao had written this "letter from home,"
He entrusted it to a couple of his uniformed soldiers.
"I will give each of you one horse, which can run
More than five hundred miles within a single day.

When you see the younger imperial brother-in-law,
Make sure not to divulge anything of what happened.
If I can arrest that second imperial brother-in-law,
I will give you a handsome reward on your return!"

Having received their instructions they hastily left,
Disguised as personal servants of the Cao family.
Once they had left the Southern Office of Kaifeng,
They resembled storm-driven clouds in the skies.

No need to sing of their stretches on the road —
Eventually they arrived at the city of Zhengzhou.
And when they had entered the wall's triple gate,
They straightaway hastened to the lofty mansion.

They walked to the hall and made a deep bow,
And when the younger imperial brother-in-law
Asked them why they had come, they immediately
Handed him the letter wrapped in its envelope.

"The elder lord back home urgently informs you
That your mother is ill, and not likely to recover.

Very soon she may die and descend into darkness,
So Your Highness should travel in greatest haste.
    If you arrive early, you may still see your mother;
If you are late, you will not see your mother alive."
When the imperial brother-in-law read the letter,
Each word and each line told him the same story.
    Having read the letter, he was beset by worries,
And immediately ordered his horse to be saddled.
The imperial brother-in-law mounted his horse,
And rushed back home, traveling day and night.
    He whipped on his horse, which ran as if it were flying,
All he wanted was only to see his mother alive!
No need to tell about the stretches of the road —
Eventually he arrived at the great Eastern Capital.

Let's not sing about the imperial brother-in-law,
Let's sing of His Excellency Dragon-Design Bao.
    He had dispatched two police officers, and these
Waited outside the city gate for Lord Cao's arrival.
And when these saw that Lord Cao had come back,
They informed Judge Bao as fast as shooting stars.
    When His Excellency heard this, he was pleased,
And he hastily rode out to meet him on the street.
With a party of soldiers and his personal servants,
He welcomed the younger imperial brother-in-law.
    The two of them both dismounted from their horses,
While their servants and soldiers stood on both sides.
On the street he offered his greetings, bowing deeply,
And the imperial brother-in-law answered in kind.
    He also asked why he had come here this morning,
And His Excellency replied in the following manner:
    "Her Ladyship was stricken by a serious disease,
So this humble official came to visit Her Ladyship.
Fortunately your mother has now fully recovered,
And as I returned I met here with Your Highness."

Speak:

His Excellency then asked: "And Your Highness, why did you come back?"
The imperial brother-in-law replied: "Because my mother was gravely ill

and might die any moment, I received a letter from home which told me to return as soon as possible to see my mother." His Excellency then replied: "Your Highness, please accept my felicitations, because Her Ladyship your mother has fully recovered from her disease — she is now as hale and healthy as before. I am now just coming back from my visit." When the imperial brother-in-law heard this, he was overcome by joy and felt very relieved. His Excellency thereupon invited the imperial brother-in-law: "Please come to my humble abode, so I can offer you a few cups of wine." The imperial brother-in-law said: "That can't be done. Let me first go back home and see my mother, and then I will join you for a drink at some later day." Judge Bao invited him over and over again: "First we should celebrate that Her Ladyship has recovered, secondly we should celebrate the success of Your Highness' governorship, and thirdly we should celebrate your safe arrival from your trip — let me offer you a few cups." Hearing this, the imperial brother-in-law accepted the invitation and riding alongside His Excellency he entered the Southern Office.

Sing:

When the two of them arrived at Kaifeng Prefecture,
They dismounted from their horses and went inside.
The second imperial brother-in-law sat on the left,
And His Excellency took his seat on the right side.
     He ordered a banquet to be spread before the hall
To entertain the second master of the Cao family.
To their left and right musicians played their songs,
And serving girls urged them to drink their wine.
     When they had had their drinks and eaten their fill,
The two of them had become drunk as a skunk.
But His Excellency continued to ply him with drink,
Till a woman suddenly appeared in front of the hall.
     This was the aggrieved party, this was lady Zhang,
Who knelt down in front of the hall and then said:
     "This man is the second imperial brother-in-law Cao,
Who strangled my husband and also killed my son.
He violently forced me to become his darling wife,
But then in Zhengzhou he wanted to cut off my head.
     Fortunately, Zhang Qing intervened and saved me,
And I came to Kaifeng Prefecture to demand justice.

Your Excellency, for my sake produce a clear verdict
Now that today the imperial brother-in-law came here."

In a towering rage the imperial brother-in-law then
Loudly shouted: "You low-class slut without shame,
When did I ever kill your husband and your son?
When did I ever force you to become my lady?
Who are you that you dare in such a brazen way
Curse your betters right here in front of the hall?"

In a towering rage His Excellency Minister Bao
Loudly shouted: "Now listen, Second Master Cao,
Right now you committed acts that break the law
By strangling that student and then taking his wife.

The aggrieved party, the wife, lodges the accusation,
And the corpses are presently stored in the prefecture.
While the person who disclosed your crime is here,
You still insist on your innocence and curse her instead!"

He loudly ordered the police officers to take action
And right there arrest that imperial brother-in-law.
They fetched the large yellowwood cangue, and locked
The younger imperial brother-in-law in that cangue.

After they had escorted him to the Eastern Prison,
The two groups of guards were then ordered released.

When these two groups of guards had been set free,
They hurried in all haste to the Cao family mansion.
When they had greeted Her Ladyship, they told her
That a terrible disaster had occurred, deep as the sea.

"Their Highnesses committed acts that break the law,
And have fallen into the claws of that Prefect Bao!
In the Eastern Capital he arrested the elder master,
And in Zhengzhou he arrested the younger master.

They have both been taken to Kaifeng Prefecture,
Have been locked in a cangue and placed in prison.
We too were detained there in Kaifeng Prefecture,
But we were released today and returned to report."

When Her Ladyship heard this, she was very upset,
Pondering the matter in her heart, she saw no solution.
The whole household, old and young, was terrified —
What to do now they had run afoul of Prefect Bao?

Her Ladyship wasted no moment, and eight men
Carried her in her sedan chair to Kaifeng Prefecture.
Without stopping they arrived at Kaifeng Prefecture,
And officers announced this to His Excellency Bao.

His Excellency Minister Bao then ordered to fetch
The two imperial brothers-in-law from their prison.
From the Eastern Prison they fetched her second son;
From the Western Prison they fetched her eldest son.

With hempen cords they strung them up in the hall,
And they got fifty strokes to serve as an appetizer.
The two men were strung up in a heart-rending way,
And their tortured thighs were covered with blood.

His Excellency in the hall ordered them to be beaten,
Just as Her Ladyship came running into the court hall,
And exclaimed: "You are bereft of all human reason!
How dare you give a beating to the emperor's kin?"

In a towering rage His Excellency Minister Bao
Loudly cursed her: "Old low-class slut without shame!
If the emperor's kin didn't commit criminal offenses,
No one would dare give Their Highnesses a beating.

He strangled and killed a student and also his son,
And abducted his wife in order to make her his lady.
Three months after he had taken her to Zhengzhou,
You ordered him in a private letter to have her killed.

But somebody saved the life of this beautiful woman,
Who then came to the Eastern Capital to seek revenge.
When lady Zhang arrived here in the Eastern Capital,
She mistakenly appealed to your other son for justice.

He had her given a beating and then left her for dead,
He also robbed her of ten ounces of snow-white silver.
Fortunately there was one person with a decent heart,
Who saved the life of this woman in hairpins and skirt.

She has lodged an accusation in Kaifeng Prefecture,
And the corpses are also here in the prefectural office.
Your sons break the law and commit a capital crime,
And yet you dare curse us here in Kaifeng Prefecture?"

Her Ladyship did not know how to answer to all this,
And in a panic she hurried back to her own mansion.

包相燒太郡夫人官誥

Fig. 6.2
Minister Bao burns Her Ladyship's patents of nobility.

Having seen her sons, the emperor's close relatives,
Beaten with thorny cudgels and all covered with blood,
She wailed and wept till she arrived at the mansion,
Where the whole household shed tears in profusion.

Considering the case in detail she saw no solution,
But to view there in the hall their patents of nobility.
"The fourth lord, the Humane Ancestor, ennobled me,
And granted us this lofty mansion with its plaque.

The eldest of the highest rank, the second of the next:
We are the emperor's relatives and the emperor's kin.
To judge by their functions, we are the most revered
Of all the imperial relatives by birth and by marriage.

I will go back once again to that Kaifeng Prefecture
And there in the hall explain this to His Excellency.
If he sees their appointments and patents of nobility,
That Judge Bao will not dare beat the emperor's kin."

When His Excellency saw her, he was very pleased,
And loudly ordered his police officers to take action.
He told them to grab these official patents of nobility,
And to burn them all to ashes right there in the hall.

Her Ladyship thereupon addressed him as follows:
"Judge Bao, you too are a person who breaks the rules!
You have burned all our official patents of nobility,
Which carried the seal of the fourth lord, the emperor!"

His Excellency Judge Bao was overcome by rage,
And loudly he cursed her: "You old slut of the Caos!

Your patents of nobility should stay in your house,
Just as my letters of appointment are at my house.
His Sagely Majesty gave you these patents of nobility,
But who told you to parade them out on the streets?

If you behave in such a brazen manner, I'm afraid,
You must have broken the law, committed a crime!
I've burned your appointments and patents of nobility,
So please feel free to lodge an accusation against me!"

Her Ladyship thereupon returned to her own house,
And wondered in her mind how she should proceed.
After careful consideration she saw no other solution
But to go as fast as possible to the Chaoyang Palace.

Having left her own Without Sycophancy Mansion,
She came to the Eastern Floriate Dragon and Phoenix Gate.
And when she next had entered the Zhengyang Gate,
Palace maidens announced her arrival to the empress.

Her Majesty the empress came out to greet her, and
Hastily came out a long way to welcome her mother.
When she had greeted her mother and each sat down,
She made four times two, eight bows to her mother.

Dragon-Phoenix wax tea was offered by maids,
But Her Ladyship did not even drink a single drop.

Her Majesty the empress then asked her the question:
"My dear mother, please be so kind as to let me know:
What's the cause your brow remains locked in a frown?
What is the reason that you are so depressed and down?"

Her Ladyship, awash in tears, said to her daughter:
"Your Majesty, please be so kind as to listen to me.
Without a good reason I would not dare come here;
But there's some business I must bother you with.

Your brothers committed an act that breaks the law,
And have fallen into the claws of that pure Judge Bao.
Locked in a heavy cangue they languish in prison;
Beaten by thorny cudgels they're covered with blood.

By all means I beseech you, if only for my sake,
To save your brothers from the misery they suffer."

When the empress heard her mother's tale, she said:
"My dear mother, please listen to what I will say.
Other officials all are easy to deal with, but this Bao
Is really a man bereft of feeling and common sense."

Her Ladyship, awash in tears, said to her daughter:
"Your Majesty, please be so kind as to listen to me.
He is only a servant and slave and you are the master,
So how come you fear such an insignificant official?"

The empress then answered her mother as follows:
"Because he is proper and straight, without partiality!
When I mistakenly lent my carriage to Concubine Liu,
I was fined a lot of money by him here in the court.

Once the emperor laid out a banquet below the gate,
But he was chased away from Zhengyang Gate by Bao.

When he participated in the audience at break of dawn,
He fined his lord a hundred thousand in notes and gold.
    His lord and king handed him the gold and the money,
And he distributed it as a reward to the army soldiers.
    Minister Bao is so incorruptible, proper and straight,
That even the ghosts and the gods all fear that person.
When the emperor saw how pure and proper he was,
He gave him a golden plaque with this inscription:
    'With the exception of the emperor personally,
All imperial relatives and all the emperor's kin,
And the many civil officials and military officers,
Will be treated equally when committing a crime.'"
    The empress and concubines and prime ministers,
Each and every one feared that man surnamed Bao!
    "I do not see what can be done now my brothers
Have committed these crimes that break the law.
At present it's really impossible for me to save them;
Upon careful consideration I see no solution at all."
    "Now if I cannot even save my own darling sons,
On whom will I be able today to rely in my old age?"
When the empress heard this, she cried hot tears:
"My dear mother, please listen to what I have to say.
    Now you make sure to go safely back home today,
And I will wait till tomorrow, till break of dawn,
To sneak out of the palace, visit Kaifeng Prefecture,
And save my brothers from the misery they suffer."

Her Ladyship thereupon returned to her own house,
So let's tell about Her Imperial Majesty the empress.
In the third quarter of the fifth watch the emperor
Left the rear apartments to ascend the court hall.
    The empress then ascended her room, sat down,
Combed her hair, applied her make-up, got dressed,
And then issued an order with all her authority
To the eunuchs who served her inside the palace:
    "In my Dragon-Phoenix chair carried by eight men,
And accompanied by a few hundred palace ladies,
I will on my own initiative visit Kaifeng Prefecture
To save the lives of the imperial brothers-in-law."

She mounted the Dragon-Phoenix sedan chair, and
Imperial concubines and pretty maids formed rows.
With one half of a formal cortege she left the court;
Golden cudgels and large fans to her left and right.

A yellow gauze parasol was raised high above her;
Eight pairs of banners were arranged on both sides.
Three thousand pretty girls followed her carriage;
Eight hundred charming maids surrounded the empress.

She resembled Chang'e leaving the moon palace;
On all streets and markets people burned incense.
In front of wineshops the flag was pulled down;
Those walking all stopped, those seated all rose.

When the cortege arrived at the Prefectural Bridge,
Zhang Qian and Ma Wan came running like clouds.

When they arrived at the Kaifeng prefectural office,
They informed His Excellency: "Please listen to us.
Her Majesty the empress is coming here in person,
So you must go and welcome her outside the gate."

His Excellency thereupon hastened to dress himself,
He dressed himself formally to welcome the empress.
He welcomed Her Majesty, who sat down in the hall,
And he showed his respects with twenty-four bows.

His Excellency immediately gave out the order
To go and fetch the two imperial brothers-in-law.
From the Eastern Prison they fetched the younger;
From the Western Prison they fetched the eldest.

They were strung up there high in that hall,
And fifty strokes of the rod served as an appetizer.
Each and every stroke drew out new fresh blood;
Their tortured bodies were all covered with blood.

Her Majesty the empress was pained at heart, so
She promptly addressed that one man Judge Bao:
"Now even if these relatives of the emperor indeed
Have committed acts that break the rules and laws,

You should show some consideration for the sake
Of your lord and king and also of me, his consort!
Can't you, out of consideration for the emperor,
Pardon and free these imperial brothers-in-law?"

Hearing this, His Excellency was filled with rage:
"Your Majesty, now please listen to what I will say.
If these imperial relatives had committed no crime,
This humble official would not dare point at them.

But who told your brother to strangle a student,
And also to murder his little child of only three?
He abducted the wife, a woman in hairpins and skirt,
And forced her with violence to become his lady.

He had her with him in Zhengzhou for three months,
But after one letter from home he wanted to kill her.
Fortunately she was saved by somebody else, and
She came to the Eastern Capital to seek her revenge.

On the street she mistakenly appealed to his brother;
After a beating with iron whips, he left her for dead.
Again she had the good fortune of being saved, and
She lodged her accusation with me here in Kaifeng.

At present, the two corpses have both been located,
And the aggrieved party, the wife, has come to me.
Tell me, how on earth can I pardon and free people
Who have committed capital crimes such as these?

If all such people would be set free in this manner,
How can the world and empire achieve Great Peace?
Now Your Majesty is Empress Cao of the Main Palace,
So how can you leave the palace without any reason?

Your brothers have committed acts that break the law,
And now you again stealthily leave the palace at will.
If I would report this matter fully to our lord and king,
He would have you locked up in a cold palace prison."

Her Majesty the empress did not know how to answer,
And as fast as fire she hastened back to the palace gate.
Seated in her eight-man Dragon-Phoenix sedan chair,
She arrived at the Eastern Floriate Dragon and Phoenix Gate.

Just as she had arrived in the palace and sat down,
Her Ladyship her mother also arrived at the palace.
She promptly asked her: "My daughter, my dear child,
Did you manage to save the imperial brothers-in-law?"

Her Majesty the empress addressed her as follows:
"My dear mother, please listen to what I will say.

He truly is a pure official, that Dragon-Design Bao!
When you tell him the truth, he gives a true verdict.
    It's too bad for sure that my two dear brothers
Have fallen into his claws, but who is to blame?
What punishment does one deserve for a murder?
It's no minor crime to use force to abduct a wife!
    Ever since I've become empress here in the palace,
I've heard the stories about my brothers, that couple:
Again and again they get into trouble on the streets,
And without any good reason they beat good people.
    I earlier sent people over to discuss this with you,
But you only took my warnings as a passing breeze.
At home they have a wife and many concubines,
And serving maids and women without number.
    Why did he desire the wife of somebody else?
So who is to blame now you fell into his claws?
I stealthily went to Kaifeng Prefecture in person,
And now I almost got implicated in this mess myself!
    He said that I was in charge of the Chaoyang Hall,
And could not on my own authority leave the palace.
If he were to report this matter to our lord and king,
He would have me locked up in a cold palace prison!
    Upon careful consideration they cannot be saved,
And I here in the palace am wearied out by worry!"
    Her Ladyship her mother wailed, wailed and wept,
Continued to appeal most piteously to the empress,
And Her Majesty the empress was awash in tears,
As mother and daughter both wept most piteously.
    "Do not piteously appeal to me here in the palace,
But appeal to Our Sagely Ruler in the audience hall!
Tell him to go and persuade Dragon-Design Bao
To pardon the two imperial relatives, set them free!"

Her Ladyship thereupon returned to her own house,
And she eagerly waited for the next day, for dawn.
Late in the fifth watch the king ascended the hall;
Civil officials and military officers entered the gate.
    As soon as their lord and king had taken his seat,
The gatekeepers reported to the enlightened ruler

That Her Ladyship his mother-in-law had arrived,
For a reason as yet unknown, at the court's gate.
    When the emperor heard this, he hastily ordered
That Her Ladyship be summoned to enter the hall.
Three ushers brought her to before the golden steps,
And four escorts assisted her in greeting her lord.
    The emperor got up from his seat to welcome her,
And granted her permission to sit down on a stool.
She was given a cup of Dragon-Phoenix wax tea,
But Her Ladyship did not even drink a single drop.
    The emperor thereupon addressed her with a question,
Asking her: "Your Ladyship, dear mother-in-law,
What is the reason your brow is locked in a frown?
What is the cause of your vexations and sorrow?"
    Her Ladyship stood up from her seat and replied:
"Your Majesty, please kindly listen to what I say.
    Without a reason I would not dare come to court —
I am here on behalf of your two brothers-in-law.
They have fallen into the claws of Minister Bao;
Locked in a heavy cangue, they languish in prison.
    Because they have committed a criminal offense,
They've suffered such beatings they don't look human.
I beseech Your Majesty to show some compassion
And save the life of my children, my two dear sons!"
    The emperor thereupon addressed her as follows:
"Your Ladyship, please listen to what I will say.
    Other officials would present no problem at all, but
Minister Bao is bereft of feelings and common sense.
If the imperial brothers-in-law committed a crime,
I have no clever trick by which I could save them."
    Her Ladyship thereupon answered him as follows:
"Your Majesty is giving far too much credit to him.
He is your servant and slave, you are the master —
Why then be so afraid of that man surnamed Bao?"
    The emperor thereupon answered her as follows:
"Your Ladyship, please listen to what I will say.
It's not so that I am afraid of His Excellency Bao,
But he is proper and straight, shows no partiality.

Intelligent, proper and straight, without partiality:
At daytime he judges the living, at night the dead.
Whether you are imperial kin or a prime minister —
Whoever breaks the law, he treats them the same."

Her Ladyship once again appealed to the emperor:
"Your Majesty, please listen to what I will say.

In whatever way, please show some consideration,
Conceive of a plan to save my children, my sons.
If you cannot save imperial relatives by marriage,
On whom can I rely now at present, in my old age?"

Speak:

Her Ladyship repeatedly piteously appealed to the emperor: "Your Majesty,
if you do not save your own relatives, who will — I am advanced in
years — conduct my funeral upon my death? Who will offer sacrifice in
spring and autumn, and who will burn paper money for my benefit?" She
wept most piteously. The emperor said: "Your Ladyship, do not worry and
fret. Let's ask the ten officials who originally acted as guarantors for Judge
Bao to go and persuade him to pardon and free the imperial relatives."

Sing:

Having heard this, Her Ladyship was filled with joy.
Who were these ten officials who were his guarantors?
East of the hall the Dragon-Phoenix Drum was struck,
And west of the hall the Bright Light Bell resounded:
    Fast-footed imperial messengers were dispatched to
Urgently summon the ten guarantors of Minister Bao.
When these high officials learned they were summoned,
They all hastened to court to meet with the emperor.
    The first guarantor was His Excellency Chancellor Han;
The second guarantor was His Excellency Secretary Kou.
The third guarantor was His Excellency Chancellor Wang;
The fourth guarantor was His Excellency Marshal Di.
    The fifth guarantor was His Excellency Secretary Li;
The sixth guarantor the emperor's uncle, the Sixth Prince.
The seventh guarantor was Commandant-Escort Cai, and
The eighth guarantor was His Excellency Chancellor Tao.

The ninth guarantor was His Excellency Censor Tian, and
The tenth guarantor was His Excellency Chancellor Miao.
These ten court officials all arrived in the audience hall
To listen at the golden steps to the emperor's instructions.
　　The Humane Ancestor thereupon gave his instructions:
"You officials, please listen to what We will tell you.
The imperial brothers-in-law have committed a crime,
And have fallen into the claws of that pure official Bao.
　　Today We have summoned you here to the palace only
To bother you to walk all the way to Kaifeng Prefecture,
And to persuade that pure official, His Excellency Bao,
To pardon and free this couple of imperial relatives.
　　First of all, it would reflect Our edict and instruction,
Secondly, he would do the empress a favor this way.
And in the third place he would honor his guarantors
By pardoning and releasing these imperial relatives."

The ten guarantors accepted the emperor's command,
And Her Ladyship promptly returned to her mansion.
　　Once there she dispatched ten uniformed soldiers
To go to their offices and invite these ten guarantors.
The ten guarantors all came to her mansion together,
To have a few drinks there, in the Cao family home.
　　The officials all drank till they were drunk as a skunk,
But Her Ladyship did not drink one drop of the wine.
When the banquet was over, the last cup was downed,
The old woman implored the officials in this manner:
　　"Because they committed this single capital crime,
I must bother you gentlemen to persuade that person.
But if you manage to save my sons, my darling boys,
I will never forget that favor till the day of my death."

When she had spoken, the officials mounted their horses,
And each, surrounded by guards, rode through the city.
Without making a stop they came to Kaifeng Prefecture,
And the gatekeeper, informed, announced their arrival.
　　"Your Excellency, right now there are ten high officials,
Who have arrived outside the gate of Kaifeng Prefecture."
His Excellency wasted no moment to leave the hall, and
Hastened to go out a very long way to welcome them.

The ten officials all dismounted from their horses, and
Each of them greeted him in a most appropriate manner.
They took their places in the hall, the host and his guests;
When they had finished their tea, the issue was raised.

Speak:

Chancellor Wang rose from his seat and said to His Excellency: "We ten
officials have come here for no other reason than for the two imperial
brothers-in-law. First of all, there is the emperor's edict, secondly it is the
intention of the empress, and thirdly you would do it out of consideration
for the ten of us: we very much hope that Your Excellency will pardon and
free the imperial brothers-in-law!" When Judge Bao heard this, he was
overcome by a towering rage, and he told Zhang Qian and Ma Wan to
go inside, fetch the sword for beheading the highest nobles and the golden
tablet inscribed by the emperor, and hang them in the hall. When the
ten court officials saw this, they realized they would be unable to
persuade him.

Sing:

The golden plaque and the magic sword were displayed,
And the inscribed golden characters were clearly shown.
The ten high ministers all saw the objects and messages,
And each and every one of them was bereft of his energy.
   The civil officials all lowered their heads, and
The military officers all stuck out their tongues.
Judge Bao loudly told his officers to waste no moment,
And fetch the two imperial relatives from their prison.
   When he had them strung up high in that lofty hall,
The high officials flew into a rage upon seeing this sight.
When the officials saw this, they cursed him in his face,
They loudly cursed Judge Bao as a man without scruples!
   Judge Bao immediately addressed them in this manner,
"My guarantors, how come you now want to curse me?
   In ordinary times you never visited Kaifeng Prefecture,
So what kind of business now brings you to my office?
But once you see that I have arrested those Cao brothers,
You all come to this place and want to put in a word."

He loudly ordered his policemen and personal servants,
And the warden under his command and the prison guards:
"Close the gate of the Southern Office, Kaifeng Prefecture,
And I will first cut off the heads of these ten guarantors!"

Hearing this, these officials did not know how to reply,
And they hurriedly left Kaifeng Prefecture. Surrounded
By their cortege they all returned — scurrying through
Major streets and minor lanes they all fled like clouds.
    Without stopping they arrived in Little Chicken Lane;
Her Ladyship came out of the gate to welcome them,
But when the old woman carefully looked at the crowd,
She failed to see her sons, her two precious dear boys!
    She promptly asked these ten officials the question:
"Have you been able to save the life of my two babies?"
Chancellor Wang then answered her in this manner:
"Your Ladyship, please listen to what I have to say.
    We failed to save the two imperial brothers-in-law,
And we almost lost our lives because of this matter.
He said that we all have our own offices and tasks,
So why did we come without reason to his Kaifeng?
    But now you have seen I've arrested the Cao brothers,
You all have to come here and want to put in a word.
These imperial brothers-in-law committed a crime —
All who enter this office are men who break the law!
    If we had not managed to run and flee for our lives,
We would now suffer torture in Kaifeng Prefecture!
If we have failed to save the imperial brothers-in-law,
Your Ladyship, please don't blame it on us officials!"

When he had given this speech, the officials dispersed,
Leaving Her Ladyship in the throes of great suffering.
    She saw no solution but to go to the palace once again,
And enter the Eastern Floriate Dragon and Phoenix Gate.
As soon as the empress saw Her Ladyship had come,
She hastily came forward to welcome her dear mother.
    After she had bowed to her mother and taken her seat,
The empress addressed her in the following manner:
"Have you indeed appealed to His Imperial Majesty?
Have you succeeded in saving His brothers-in-law?"

Her Ladyship was awash in tears as she answered:
"Your Majesty, please listen to what I have to say.
This morning at dawn I visited His Imperial Majesty,
And I appealed to our lord and king, Our Sagely Ruler.

    He invited the ten officials who were his guarantors,
Who all had served as the guarantors of Judge Bao,
And he told them to go and persuade Minister Bao
To pardon and release those two imperial relatives.

    But not only did these men fail to save your brothers,
But they also almost lost their lives over this matter!
In each and every way it's impossible to save them —
That's why I piteously appeal to you, my daughter.

    I beseech you, my child, to show some compassion
And come up with some way to save your brothers.
If you cannot even save your own darling brothers,
To whom can I, this old woman, lift up my eyes?"

    Her Majesty the empress shed many tears, thinking:
"Closely considered, they can only blame themselves.
Not destined for a life of luxury, they had evil hearts,
So whom can they fault now they have been caught?"

    Her Ladyship her mother most piteously wept, and
Again and again implored the imperial consort to help.
So Her Majesty the empress told her the following:
"My dear mother, you should go back to your home.

    I will wait till our lord and king returns to the palace,
And then I will piteously implore our imperial lord,
Asking him to friendly persuade that Minister Bao
And save the lives of my two brothers, that couple!"

Her Ladyship her mother returned to her own place,
So now to the fourth emperor, the Humane Ancestor.

    Late at night our lord and king returned to the palace,
And there he directed his steps to the Zhengyang Hall.
When the empress heard that the emperor was arriving,
She hastily went outside to welcome her lord and king.

    Once she had welcomed him into the Zhengyang Hall,
The emperor sat down on his golden folding chair.
Her Majesty the empress sat down at his side, and
Palace ladies and pretty maids stood at both sides.

Her Majesty the empress was overcome by worries,
And her lord and king promptly asked for the reason.
"My darling wife, what is the cause of your worries?
Please tell your worries to Us, from the very beginning!"
　　Her Majesty hurriedly rose from her seat, and said
A number of times: "A myriad years to Your Majesty!
　　The only thing that is bothering me is nothing else
But the matter of the two imperial brothers-in-law.
They have committed an act that breaks laws and rules,
And have fallen into the claws of Dragon-Design Bao.
　　Locked in a heavy cangue they languish in prison;
Tortured by rods they do not look like human beings.
I, as empress in the palace, enjoy every pleasure, but
My brothers in prison endure every kind of suffering.
　　They are my full brothers, born of the same mother —
If I think of my vexations, my tears flow in profusion.
I beseech Your Majesty to show some compassion,
And to save the lives of my brothers, of that couple!"
　　Her lord and king immediately replied as follows:
"My dear wife, what's the need to be filled with grief?
Tomorrow morning I will have my cortege drawn up,
And I will personally go and visit Kaifeng Prefecture."
　　Her Majesty the empress then was overcome by joy
And expressed her gratitude for the emperor's grace.

The fifth watch, third quarter: the court horses moved;
The fifth watch, fourth quarter: the officials assembled.
The nine ministers and four chancellors had all arrived
In front of the golden steps, so as to greet His Majesty.
　　The whip was cracked thrice: the king ascended the hall;
When the large fans were taken away, they saw their lord.
The civil officials and military officers all knelt down,
Repeatedly wishing His Majesty a myriad of years.
　　When their lord and king saw them arranged in rows,
He summoned Chancellor Wang at the eastern side.
　　"Yesterday I dispatched you and other court officials
To the Southern Office to persuade that Judge Bao.
Did you all manage to save Our two brothers-in-law?
Report to Us everything in detail, from the beginning!"

Prime Minister Wang stepped forward and reported:
"Your Majesty the Son of Heaven, please kindly listen.
Once Your Majesty had given us Your sagely instructions,
All of us ten officials went off to Kaifeng Prefecture.

Repeatedly we kindly spoke to Dragon-Design Bao,
But his response to our pleas would scare one to death.
He said that we officials all had our own pure offices,
Why did we come to Kaifeng Prefecture for no cause?

He loudly ordered his police officers to take action,
And told them to arrest all these many court officials!
If it had not been for our ability to run for our lives,
We would be suffering misery in Kaifeng Prefecture!"

His emperor the Humane Ancestor declared an edict,
Ordering both his military officers and civil officials,
All the officials arranged on both sides, not to go home
"As We Ourselves will proceed to Kaifeng Prefecture!"

As soon as the emperor had pronounced this edict,
All officials lined up in two rows at the palace gate.

Compressed ten-syllable lines:

The chancellors on the left
    And chancellors on the right
        Following the imperial carriage;
The ten ministers
    And nine governors
        Supporting the enlightened ruler.
Hundred-flower gowns,
    Wrapped in jade belts:
        The commanders before the hall;
Helmets with face-pads,
    Dressed in gold armor:
        The generals guarding the hall.
Golden ball-cudgels,
    Silver ball-cudgels,
        Lances, daggers, axes and swords;
Golden lance units,
    Silver lance units:
        Generals guarding His Majesty.

Three large units,
    Two small units,
        On both sides leading the way;
Officers before the hall,
    Officers behind the hall,
        Following behind the entire road.
Dragon-Phoenix banners,
    And sun and moon banners,
        Paraded in front of the emperor;
Bronze gongs beaten,
    Moving drums resounding,
        Marching ahead way in front.
The guards to the left
    And the guards to the right
        Clearing the road for the emperor;
Civil officials in front,
    Military commanders following,
        With the ministers debating policy.
When the carriage moves forward,
    Highly raised aloft:
        The yellow gauze great parasol;
His throne the gold-encrusted
    Dragon-wheel conveyance,
        Which carries the enlightened ruler!

Sing:

When our lord and king had left the Chaoyang Hall,
He headed straight for the gate of Kaifeng Prefecture.
He arrived in one stretch at the Prefectural Bridge —
The gatekeeper promptly informed His Excellency.
    "Presently His Majesty has arrived, with his train
Of civil officials and military officers, at Kaifeng."
When His Excellency heard the emperor had come,
He prepared an incense table to welcome his ruler.

Speak:

Lord Bao walked up to the jade conveyance and bit three times in the jade belt around the waist of the emperor. The Son of Heaven was greatly surprised, and asked: "Minister Bao, what's the meaning of this?" Judge Bao replied: "Your Majesty, today is not a day for sacrificing to Heaven, sacrificing to Earth, or encouraging farming, so how can you leave the court without good reason? This will result in a great drought of three years in all-under-heaven! This humble servant is the white tiger, and Your Majesty is the green dragon. If the white tiger bites the green dragon, this great drought of three years can be avoided."

Sing:

His Excellency Minister Bao then said to the emperor:
"May Your Majesty live a myriad of years, but listen.
It's not the Sacrifice to Heaven or the Sacrifice to Earth,
So why did you leave the palace without any reason?"
    The Son of Heaven the Humane Ancestor answered:
"Dear Minister Bao, please listen to what We will say.
    We certainly did not come for some idle entertainment,
As We only came for the two imperial brothers-in-law.
Now We have come today to Kaifeng Prefecture, please
Pardon and free these imperial relatives, these two men."
    His Excellency Minister Bao then said to the emperor:
"Your Majesty, please kindly listen to what I will say.
This place is your humble servant's Kaifeng Prefecture,
And I did not invite my lord and master to come here.
    The imperial brothers-in-law have committed a crime;
According to the rules they deserve the death penalty.
In my administration of Kaifeng Prefecture, I only rely
On the laws of the king in pronouncing clear verdicts.
    If Your Majesty wishes to save these imperial relatives,
All you have to do is to promulgate a decree of pardon.
As soon as such an act of pardon arrives at this place,
The two imperial relatives will be released from prison.
    Why would Your Majesty have to draw up this cortege
And bother all these civil officials and military officers?
And then Your Majesty attempts to kindly persuade me,
Making himself ridiculous in the eyes of the people!
    If Your Majesty right now releases the Cao brothers,
I do not want to govern Kaifeng Prefecture anymore.
I will return to Your Majesty my plaque and my tablet,
Leave the bureaucratic service, and practice religion."

When His Majesty heard him speak like this, he said,
"Minister, sentence imperial kin according to the law."
    Judge Bao stepped forward and said to the emperor,
"Your Majesty, please kindly listen to what I will say.
You should not leave your palace without good reason,
So you will have to pay me a fine of gold and silver."

The Humane Ancestor returned to the imperial palace,
And brought out precious goods from the storage room.
He paid a fine of thirty thousand strings of ready cash
And a hundred ounces of gold and silver to Judge Bao.
    When His Excellency had received the cash and gold,
He expressed his gratitude with twenty-four bows.
He then went to the exercise grounds, took his seat,
And distributed the money to the government troops.
    After rewarding the troops, he returned to his home;
He took his seat in the hall, and spoke to his staff.
He ordered them to take out the documents, and fetch
The younger imperial brother-in-law from his prison.
    He had signed a full confession and brief summary:
The life of this imperial relative could not be spared.
He was stripped of all his inner and undergarments;
Locked in a heavy cangue he left through the gate.
    When they arrived at the market's execution place,
They waited for the right hour to cut off his head.
When his mother saw her son was to be beheaded,
She went to the court fast as fire to see the emperor.
    "The prefect of Kaifeng Prefecture, Minister Bao
Is about to execute my darling sons, both of them!
Your Majesty, please kindly issue an act of pardon,
To save your two relatives on the execution grounds."
    In accordance with her request the emperor promptly
In greatest haste issued and promulgated a pardon,
And messengers on fast horses left like shooting stars
For the market to save the lives of the emperor's kin.
    Zhang Long and Zhao Hu hastily came to report:
"Your Excellency, please listen to what we will say.
Imperial messengers are coming here with a pardon,
Prepare an altar to welcome the emperor's grace."

As His Excellency Minister Bao bowed his head,
A student, a presented scholar, recited the decree.
  "Within the Eastern Capital everyone is pardoned;
Also pardoned are the two imperial brothers-in-law.
All condemned criminals are covered by this pardon,
But people outside the Eastern Capital are excluded."
  Hearing this decree, Judge Bao was filled with rage,
"This emperor, the fourth Zhao King, is intolerable!
He only wants to pardon the two imperial relatives;
The world outside the Eastern Capital is ignored!"
  He tore the act of pardon to little shreds of paper,
And ordered the execution of the youngest brother.
  The executioner lifted his sword and said to him,
Said clearly to the younger imperial brother-in-law:
"Tonight you will appear before the Eastern Peak,[10]
And tomorrow you'll be received by King Yama!"
  As his body fell down, his head hit the ground —
The young master of the Cao family was beheaded!
This only left the elder imperial brother-in-law Cao,
As they waited for the arrival of the hour of noon.
  The old woman saw that her son was beheaded,
And she loudly cried out to Heaven to complain.

The fast messengers returned to the court and reported:
"Your Majesty, please be so kind as to listen to us.
  He said that Your Majesty's pardon was all wrong:
How can He rule the empire, treating it in different ways?
Inside the city it's the flowery world of His Majesty,
But outside the Eastern Capital it's a different world!
  Tearing the act of pardon into the tiniest shreds of paper,
He had the youngest imperial brother-in-law beheaded.
The elder imperial brother-in-law has still been spared,
But only because they are waiting for the hour of noon."
  The emperor the Humane Ancestor issued an edict,
By which he summoned the civil and military officials.

---

[10] The Eastern Peak is Mt. Tai in Shandong. It is also referred to as the Eastern Marchmount.
The Great Thearch of the Eastern Marchmount rules the realm of the dead.

He wrote it in his own calligraphy, with his own brush,
And twenty-four copies were dispatched by the court.

This act of pardon was first sent to the Criminal Court,
And next it was sent to the Western Terrace Censorate.
Once it had passed through the offices of the Six Boards,
Messengers on fast horses left the gate of the palace.

Once it had passed through offices large and small,
Messengers fast as fire took it to Kaifeng Prefecture.
His Excellency Minister Bao set out an incense table,
And hastily went out to welcome this act of pardon.

A student, a presented scholar, opened and read it,
And each word and each line was written correctly.
"As We rejoice in days of Great Peace, without war,
We widely pardon all criminals throughout the world.

Whether the crime was murder or arson or robbery,
The killing of innocent men, the abduction of women,
The Ten Heinous Acts, or even the Five Perversities,
Such people are pardoned and banished to the border.

Abducting by force the wives and daughters of others
And committing murder out of greed are pardoned too.
Stealing and selling a plowing buffalo is also pardoned;
The Sprout Tax this year will be lowered by a third.

All outstanding debts of money or grain are remitted;
Once this edict has arrived, they cannot be reclaimed."

"May prefectures and districts all prepare incense tables!"
Now this really pleased this one man, that Minister Bao!
When the act of pardon had been recited, he most happily
Ordered the release of the elder imperial brother-in-law.

When the elder imperial brother-in-law was released,
He felt relieved and expressed his thanks to Judge Bao.
"I did indeed commit an act that broke rules and laws,
So I am grateful to the emperor for this act of pardon."

His Excellency Minister Bao then answered him,
And said to the elder son and heir of the Cao family:
"You indeed committed a crime that broke the law,
But the emperor pardoned you so you can go home.

If you hold any office at court at some later date,
Make sure you never commit any crime or offense."

The imperial brother-in-law then went back home:
The whole family, old and young, were all weeping.
After he had greeted his mother, he thereupon said:
"My dear mother, please listen to what I will say.

While in prison I experienced such bitter suffering,
That it seems as if I had died and come back to life.
At present I do not want to be an official anymore:
I will leave for the mountains to practice religion."

Her Ladyship then answered her son by saying:
"My son, my dear little boy, now don't be so silly!"

The imperial brother-in-law didn't obey his mother,
But he went to the court to say adieu to the emperor.
After he had taken his leave of his own elder sister,
He returned home and said goodbye to all relatives.

His purple gown and golden belt he both burned,
As he had lost all desire for luxury and high status.
Combing his hair he bound it up as a pair of buns,
And, dressed as Daoist priest, he left for the wilds.

Around his waist he carried a few empty gourds,
And in his hand he also held a bamboo skimmer.
When he was hungry, he ate the mountain pine nuts,
When thirsty, he drank spring water — so he survived.

During the day, tigers and wolves were his companions,
And at night, the moon accompanied this lonely man.
After many days of practice, he achieved immortality,
And later he managed to join the crowd of immortals.

Among the Eight Immortals he takes third position,
He is that imperial brother-in-law surnamed Cao!

Let's not sing of the imperial relative as an immortal,
Let's change the subject and sing again of Judge Bao.
Now all criminals of the empire had been pardoned,
He went on the third day to court to thank the emperor.

After he had expressed his gratitude, he came home,
And ordered the men under his command in his train
To take out the bodies of both the father and the son
And to promptly cremate them without leaving a trace.

His Excellency said to the woman surnamed Zhang:
"Now the time has come for you to safely go home.

I'll provide you with travel money, gold and treasure,
[So you will have no financial worries] as you return."
     Lady Zhang immediately knelt down and bowed;
In the hall she expressed her gratitude to Judge Bao.
"[You exacted revenge] for my husband and son —
Till the day of my death I will not forget this favor!"

These many cases of injustice throughout the world:
The verdicts of Judge Bao were both equal and fair.
Above he accorded with Heaven — without partiality;
Below he accorded with Earth — never shortchanging.
     In between he accorded with men — without mistake:
In each and every case he pronounced a clear sentence.
Who kills a man repays with his life — the old rule;
Who owes a debt repays the money — it is like this.
     Done is the tale of the imperial brothers-in-law Cao —
Because they were evil, they fell into the claws of Judge Bao.
I now have performed this ballad to the very last line,
As I presented it to you all for your entertainment.

> *Blue Heaven, transparent and clear, cannot be deceived:*
> *Even before you conceive an intention, it already knows.*
> *So I urge you, you gentlemen, never to commit any evil:*
> *Who in past and present has ever escaped from the law?*

Newly Printed, in Prose and in Verse: The Case of Dragon-Design Bao Sentencing the Imperial Brothers-in-law Cao, The End.

Zhu Yixuan (ed.) (1997). *Ming Chenghua shuochang cihua congkan*, Zhengzhou: Zhongzhou guji chubanshe, pp. 188–222.

The Tale of Zhang Wengui.
Part One
A Ballad-Story of a Court Case
of Dragon-Design Bao

Newly Printed, Completely Illustrated, in Prose and in Verse

The Great Progenitor, the Great Ancestor, the True Ancestor —
The fourth emperor, the Humane Ancestor, abided by the Way.
For forty-[two years a lord in possession of the Mandate:]
Repeatedly he offered sacrifice to Heaven in the suburbs.

Ten times he offered sacrifice in the suburbs — for thirty years;
Four times [he sacrificed in the Bright Hall — for twelve springs.]
When a king abides by the Way, the ministers possess virtue,
To this very day his court produced many men who are wise.

The civil officials [protected the country like a golden screen],
The military officers guarded the realm like a marble gate.
The whole world had been pacified, the people were at peace,
Each and every family, [commoners and soldiers, were happy].

Let's wish our lord and king a thousand, a ten-thousand years,
May his sons and grandsons succeed him in the dragon-court!
The Humane Ancestor …
The hundred surnames sang for joy, celebrating a Great Peace.

The horses had been sent to pasture as there was no more war,
The three armies …
The four hundred civil and military officials in front of the hall
All were heavenly officials, astral gods who had come down.

Among the civil officials [we only mention His Excellency Bao],
During daytime a judge in this world, at night in the other.
Thirty-six criminal cases that offered no clue or lead, and
Seventy-two criminal cases of people who suffered injustice:
　　One hundred and eight cases that were misty and murky —
Each and every one was correctly solved and sentenced.
When people committed a crime and ended up in his hands,
He pulled out the tree with its branches to get at the roots.
　　He feared neither the emperor's kin nor the empress' relatives,
He had no fear for people like golden branches or jade leaves.
He was a lamp that when lighted above water shows the very bottom,
A wax candle lighting up heaven, here in the Eastern Capital!
　　Among military officers there was that fine Yang Wenguang,
Who truly was one to be called a pillar that supports heaven.
He subdued the nine river valleys and the eighteen ravines,
Annihilating the Southern Barbarians, turning them into dust.
　　It was only because our lord and king abided by the Way,
That men supporting heaven, guarding the throne were born.
One did not see scions of red gates end up as starving beggars;
All naturally, undistinguished families produced great men.

Listen as I sing of Xishui District in the Western Capital Region,
Of a well-known man who lived in the city of Xizhou.
　　For generations the family was known as Millionaire Zhang,
He was easily by far the richest person in all of Xizhou.
Husband and wife were both filial and compliant by nature,
But the couple had only one son to continue the family line.

Speak:

If one leisurely expounds the origin, one will understand the core of an ancient book. So I first talked about the emperor's virtue, and only then came to talk of past and present. Now let me tell that the fourth emperor, the Humane Ancestor, abided by the Way, and because of this the winds were mild and the rains came timely; the state prospered and the people were at peace; the common people happily pursued their occupations, and the five kinds of grains provided bounteous harvests. Let me not tell about loyal ministers and valorous officers, but let me tell of a man from Xishui District in the Western Capital Region, who was called Millionaire Zhang. His family was rich and noble and possessed large quantities of gold and silver. When a boy was born to him, the child seemed to be kneaded out of rouge and to have been formed out of powder. Millionaire's wife cherished the baby like the beat of her own heart and loved him like a pearl in her hand!

Sing:

Listen as I sing of the well-known Millionaire Zhang,
He loved and cherished his son like a pearl in his hand.

    He turned one, he turned two, and then he turned three;
He turned four, then five and six — that speaks for itself.
Eventually the boy had reached the age of seven years,
So a teacher was hired to provide instruction to our man.

    The young gentleman at this time entered the school,
In the study in the western courtyard he read the Classics.
His teacher selected a name for him at his first lesson,
And the young gentleman's school name was Wengui.

    If you want to tell how smart and intelligent he was —
Whatever the teacher taught him, he promptly understood.
He had read all of the Nine Classics and Three Strategies,
And the three scrolls of Ge Hong were stored in his belly.[1]

    The zither and go, calligraphy and painting he mastered,
He could paint pine trees in color and in black and white.

Light and shadow urge one on to age, fast like an arrow,
Sun and moon spur young men on, quick like a shuttle.
All of a sudden he had reached the age of fifteen years,
And the essays filling his belly resembled a full moon.

    On top of that, he was a very smart and handsome boy,
Clear brows and sparkling eyes — he cut a dashing figure.
With a flat crown, wide forehead, and full Storehouse,[2]
And red cheeks and white teeth he was quite attractive.

    Let's not sing of his parents, how much they loved him;
Let's change the subject as I will sing of the young man.

    It happened to be Cold Food Festival — no fire is lit,[3]
And each and every family went out to enjoy spring.

---

[1] Ge Hong (284–364) is best known as the author of the *Baopuzi*.
[2] The Heavenly Storehouse refers to the middle of the forehead.
[3] The Cold Food Festival was celebrated on the one hundred and fifth day following the shortest day. From the Song dynasty on, the festival was often identified with Clear and Bright, and celebrated in the early days of the Third Month.

When Wengui had given the matter some thought,
He came before the hall to ask his parents' permission.
　　Once Wengui had dressed himself for the occasion,
He went as fast as he could to the hall, and once there,
He greeted his father and mother with a light bow, saying:
"Dear father and mother, please listen to what I will say.
　　The only reason why I, your young son, have come here,
Is because, dear parents, I want to ask your permission.
Today happens to be Cold Food Festival — no fire is lit,
And each and every family goes out to enjoy spring.
　　I, your son, would also like to go out and enjoy spring,
So I would like to know whether I have your permission."
His parents addressed him then in the following manner:
"My dear son, make sure to be careful wherever you go!"
　　When the young man had heard this, joy filled his heart,
He said goodbye to his parents and left to enjoy spring.
From the back stable was brought his red-mane horse;
Servants followed behind him as he set out on the road.

Let's not sing at all of the many stretches of his road —
In due time he arrived at the district capital of Xizhou.
Inside the walls he saw a scene of wealth and splendor,
A luxury, wealth and splendor that are rarely seen.
　　Shops offering pearls faced shops for gold and silver,
Teashops faced establishments offering one wine:
Teashops catering to visitors of the Three Mountains,[4]
Wineshops inviting guests from all four directions.
　　The Eastern Market went on until the Western Market,
The Northern Street could hear Southern Street songs.
The young man, riding his horse, was filled with joy
At the sight of all these traders and buyers and sellers.
　　When he passed a crossing of two commercial streets,
He looked up, and then suddenly saw a crowd of people.
Wengui thereupon hastily dismounted from his horse,
And walked through the crowd to see what was going on.

---

[4] The Three Mountains are the three floating islands inhabited by immortals in the Eastern Ocean.

He saw that a placard had been posted, quite high,
But the imperial writing on the placard was very clear:
"On the third day of the Third Month We hold an exam,
For which We invite students from all over the world."
    As soon as Wengui saw this, he was filled with joy,
He immediately mounted his horse and went back home.

When he arrived back home without making one stop,
He dismounted from his horse, and went straight inside.
Arriving in front of the hall, he greeted his parents, saying:
"My dear parents, please listen to what I have to tell you.
    When I was having a good time going through the streets,
The imperial writing on the yellow placard was very clear.
'On the third day of the Third Month We hold an exam
For which We invite students from all over the world.'
    For some years your son has devoted himself to study,
And I would like to present my writings to His Majesty.
If I succeed and obtain an office or half a function,
That will change our status — we'll be people of rank!"
    When his parents heard this, they were very annoyed:
"My son, what you are saying makes no sense at all!
You have neither an elder brother nor a younger brother,
You don't even have any elder sister or younger sister.
    Who will manage the money and riches in our house?
Really the only one who can do so is you, our son!
In case you will leave us in search of fame and profit,
On whom are we, your parents, to rely in old age?"
    Wengui folded his hands and stepped forward, saying:
"My dear parents, there is something you may not know.
I once read the ancient authors, and they said it well;
They have left two lines of language that say it right.
    'If, while young, one studies the civil and military arts,
One is bound to seek to sell them to the imperial house.'
'For ten years by the window you are known by none;
Through one exam your name becomes famous all over.'"
    When his mother heard this, she was filled with thought,
And all of a sudden tears coursed down her cheeks.
"I cannot let you go, my son, in search of fame and profit!
Those many mountains and rivers — when will you return?"

Millionaire Zhang addressed his son in the following way:
"My dear son, there is something you have to understand."

Speak:

Zhang Wengui wanted to leave to seek office, and repeatedly he implored
his parents: "For many years I've suffered no end of misery by the lamp-lit
window. If today I don't go and seek office, I will miss my opportunity."
When his mother heard him say this, she was awash in tears: "My son,
I cannot let you go on that trip!"

Sing:

When the young man heard them talk in this manner,
He uttered not a single sound for even half an hour.
    Then he addressed his parents in the following way:
"I'll hang myself in my chamber, see the Lord of Shade."
When his parents heard their son speak in this way,
They replied: "Be sure to be careful wherever you go."
    His father and mother were unable to make him stay,
So they made arrangements to fit out the young man.
In front of the hall a banquet was promptly laid out,
He was treated royally to a most sumptuous banquet.
    A painting of divine immortals was hung up to the east,
"A phoenix returning to the wood" hung up to the west.
The china was placed in order on a black-lacquer table,
Rhino-hide folding chairs were arranged on both sides.
    Golden cups on golden plates and on golden trays;
Golden spoons and golden chopsticks in jugs of gold.
All kinds of delicacies and all flavors were provided,
Together with fruits of all seasons and seasonal treats.
    Millionaire Zhang was seated on the eastern side,
The lady, his wife, was seated on the western side,
And Wengui was seated next to the lady his mother,
Because it was just the three of them and no one else.
    Pair upon pair of serving maids poured them wine,
And couple upon couple of beautiful girls sang songs.
After each three cups of wine came one course of food,
And all of them drank till they were drunk as a skunk.

When they had had their fill, the banquet was over,
And each of them went off to his or her own room.

There is no need to sing of the five watches of the night —
The Golden Rooster was heard as it announced dawn.
 Wengui thereupon got out of bed and rose on his feet,
He dressed himself properly, putting on a formal gown.
Having finished breakfast, he hastily packed his luggage,
He bundled his zither and books to set out on the road.
 Millionaire Zhang came and gave him his instructions:
"My son, I have arranged for travel money for your trip.
Melon-seed scattered silver, all together thirty ounces;
And then you also get a thousand strings of green bats.
 On top of that you get ten horse-hoof silver ingots —
That money should be enough for going to the capital.
From the back stable we'll bring your red-mane horse,
And then two capable servants will accompany you."
 Wengui bowed to take his leave of both his parents,
Said goodbye to relatives and neighbors and set out.
His father and mother gave him the following advice:
"My dear son, please listen to what we have to say.
 When traveling on the road, you have to be careful,
Always be prepared against the evil of strangers.
Most important: stop early for the night, leave only late;
Do not travel by night because you want to make haste.
 When you get to the capital, don't waste your time,
But return home as soon as you obtain some office.
While in the imperial city, be prudent and cautious,
Always cede the way to others and lower your head.
 You cannot act without restraint like here at home,
Arrogance and pride are bound to result in disaster.
 Once inside the examination ground to take the test,
Write a skillful essay that will surpass all others.
My son, we hope you will pass in your first attempt,
So the linen gown will be replaced by one of silk."
 Again and again they urged their son to return home
As soon as he had succeeded in obtaining an office.
"You are the only child your father and mother have,
You have here no elder brother or younger brother."

When Wengui heard this, he made a bow, saying:
"Your words of wisdom I will store in my heart.
I hope you will continue to enjoy peace and happiness,
After the three years of exams, I'll promptly return."

Millionaire Zhang once more offered his advice,
But this time he urgently addressed the servants.

"If you are going to wait on the young master,
You have to be careful in everything you will do.
If the young master succeeds in passing the exam,
You'll get a handsome reward when you get home."

The servants answered him: "That's no problem,
You have no care or worry at all, so please relax!
We two will serve and wait on the young master,
So you, the old master, can put your mind at ease."

Millionaire Zhang then once again said to his son:
"My dear son, please listen to what I have to say.
If you obtain an office and pass the examinations,
Make sure to find a messenger to send us a letter."

The young master stepped forward, folding his hands,
And said: "Dear parents, please listen to my words.
Now your son goes off in search of fame and profit,
Much depends on the job the emperor will give me.

If he appoints me to another or a distant prefecture,
I'll return once the three years of the job are done.
My dear parents, please do not think about me —
There is bound to be a day when I will greet you."

When his parents heard him utter these words,
Tears coursed down from their eyes in profusion.

The young master now said goodbye with a bow,
He mounted his horse and set out on the journey.
He carried his zither and go game, books and sword,
And the two servants followed him from behind.

The five-mile marker they reached in a flash
Then the ten-mile marker appeared before them.
After thirty-six miles: Peach Blossom Station;
After forty-two miles: Apricot Blossom Village.

They journeyed on in the Third Month of spring,
So the weather was pleasant and perfect for travel.

Pair upon pair of busy bees was gathering honey,
Couples of butterflies teased the heart of flowers.
Orioles sang their lovely lays in the green willows,
Fishes splashed, popping up through the duckweed.
 The young master on horseback was filled with joy;
When he had covered one stretch, he did one more.
The willows were green on all hills, in each village;
At nightfall in a lonely inn, guests called each other.
 Tea was for sale by the roadside as well as wine,
So one stretch was easily turned into two stretches.
They ate when hungry, drank when thirsty — the usual way;
Leaving at dawn and resting at night — that's the old story.

When they had been on the road for a number of days,
They saw in the distance a large wooded mountain.
They also saw that this mountain was high and broad,
Its steep ridge a huge barrier to all coming and going.
 When the young master saw this, he grew apprehensive,
And asked other travelers for the name of the mountain.
When these travelers were asked this question, they said:
"Young master, please listen to what we have to say.
 The name by which it is known is Taihang Mountain,
If we tell you more, you are bound to be scared."
The travelers did not dare tell him in a loud voice,
They were afraid they might alert the lord of Jingshan.
 "In front of this mountain, pheasants always engage in fights,
Its creeks and the Heavenly Stream flow from one place.
Your ears hear golden lads convey messages to jade maidens,
You can listen to the conversation of Chang'e in the moon.[5]
 We've roamed the edges of heaven and corners of the earth,
But who of us has ever seen such a terrifying mountain?
The robbers on this mountain are counted in myriads,
The only way to cross this mountain is by flying on clouds."
 When the young master heard this, he was very annoyed —
How would he be able to cross this mountain forest?

---

[5] In other words, the mountain is so high that on top of it, one is close to heaven and can overhear its inhabitants.

Speak:

Wengui said, "Servants, these people tell a terrifying story. If we run into
these robbers, we'll probably lose our lives. But against my parents' wishes,
I insisted on going to the Eastern Capital in search of an office. If I go
back now, what kind of face will I have? — I will be a laughingstock! The
ancients said, 'Life and death depend on fate; wealth and status are
determined by Heaven.' Whether one succeeds or finds favor all depends
on the moment. If we don't encounter these robbers, we'll cross this
mountain. But if we run into these robbers, it will be due to Heaven and
Fate." Together with the servants, he promptly set out on the journey.

Sing:

"Life and death are determined by an earlier existence —
What kind of men are we if fearing death we cling to life?"
    When the two servants heard him say these words,
They set out on the journey, their brows furrowed by fear.
When they had traveled on for about some thirty miles,
They suddenly heard the din of gongs shaking the earth.
    The leaping flames of red banners torched the mountain,
Black banners resembled the clouds covering the ridge.
White banners were as white as the snow in late winter,
Green banners disturbed the hearts of the hundred flowers.
    Yellow banners had been planted in the central location;
The five-colored flags, once unfurled, outshone the sun.
There were something like thirty bandits or thereabouts,
Who stopped our threesome, which did not dare move.
    They shouted as with one voice: "Where are you going?
You have to pay gold to buy the right to use this road!"
    When the young master looked up to have a good look,
The large characters on the banners wrote very clearly
"The Great King of Jingshan, Grand Guardian Zhao —
Here on this mountain I am the most honored person.
    If there are any travelers who want to travel this road,
They must pay gold or silver and we will let them go.
But if they lack the yellow gold to buy use of the road,
We will take them to our lair as stuffing for dumplings."
    Zhang Wengui dismounted from his horse, bowed deeply,
And said: "Great Guardian, please be so kind as to listen.

This humble student lives in the capital city of Xizhou,
I was born and also grew up in the district of Xixian.
    I had heard the Humane Ancestor announced an exam,
So I left for the Eastern Capital in search of an office.
Because I've been traveling on the road for many days,
We have used up all our money and don't have a cent.
    So I beg Your Majesty to display some compassion,
Please grant us our life so we may cross this mountain.
In case you're kind enough to spare our pitiable lives,
We will not forget your grace till the day of our death!"
    When the Great King heard this, he grew very annoyed:
"Such a student is bound to carry treasure and money!"
He shouted to his bandits to arrest them immediately:
"Bring them to our lair to take out their livers and hearts!"

Just like a brown buzzard nabbing a swallow or sparrow —
They led them a long way deep into Taihang Mountain.
    The Great King sat down on his folding chair of gold,
And ordered them searched for treasure and money.
Their search revealed the ten horse-hoof silver ingots,
And the thirty ounces or more of small silver flakes.
    When the Great King saw this, he started to curse him,
"I told you ever so kindly to buy your use of the road.
A moment ago you said you had no money or treasure,
So where is all this gold and silver now coming from?"
    He then ordered his executioners to waste not a moment,
But to behead them this very moment, leave no one alive!
They first beheaded the servants, the two of them together:
The heads fell down below the blade — they lost their lives.
    When the student saw this, tears coursed down his eyes,
Weeping and crying he begged the Great King for mercy.
"I implore Your Majesty to show some compassion,
Please be so magnanimous as to spare my life and soul!"
    The Great King thereupon gave the executive order
To have the student tied up in the Flaying Pavilion.
"We'll wait for tomorrow, till dawn, and then take out
His liver and heart as a snack to chase down our wine."

The red disk of the sun was sinking in the west at evening,
In the skies over the eastern seas the moon became bright.

Fig. 7.1
Zhang Wengui runs into the Great King while crossing Taihang Mountain.

The country of Leaning Mulberries[6] was dyed in rouge,
Whereas the side of the eastern seas was made of amber.

The farmers stopped working and returned to their homes,
The quays of the river ferries stopped transporting people.
Travelers on the road at the end of the day found an inn,
And the ugly women of village and farm lit their lamps.

Our student at this time was overcome by suffering,
Tears coursed down his cheeks without him knowing.
On all sides the speckled pheasants were calling out,
Were calling: "A good and noble man will lose his life!"

When Wengui then lifted his head to have a good look,
Fireflies were flitting about on all sides in great profusion.
Upon seeing this, the student was overcome by vexation:
"How will I be able to escape with my life and my soul?

I did not pay heed to the words of my father and mother —
Could I have known that today I'm bound to lose my life?
If they had killed me, it would have been a minor matter,
But I also caused the death of those two servants."

Throughout the five watches of the night he did not sleep,
Then suddenly he heard the Golden Rooster's wake-up call.

The lord of Heaven chewed a red rock to smithereens,
And in a westerly direction he spit out a whole mouthful.
The red disk of a myriad of meters rose up from the east,
So people no longer would have to walk in darkness.

On seeing this, the student was overcome by suffering:
"This morning I am inescapably bound to lose my life!"
But Wengui was not yet meant to leave this world of light:
From an earlier life his fate provided for a saving star!

The Great King was just about ready to dispatch a man
To take out his heart and liver to serve as a wine snack.

But as the Great King was calling for one of the bandits,
He was unexpectedly visited by some minor officer,
Who told him he came from Taihang's northern slope,
On behalf of his colleague, the Great King of Fengdu.[7]

As this day was the birthday of the king of Fengdu,
He had written a letter to invite the lord of Jingshan.

---

[6] Leaning Mulberries or Fusang is usually located in the east, but here it refers to the western sky.
[7] Fengdu is one of the names of the underworld.

He also invited his lady to come along to the feast,
If she did not deign it below her to visit his house.
    Seeing this, the Great King was very happy indeed,
And he promptly gave orders to tens of his bandits.
"There is no need at all to moll this student now,
Let me wait till I get back and then I'll kill that guy."
    Once his wife had been provided with a car to ride,
They left all together to celebrate the birthday party.
Thirty bandits all on horseback accompanied them,
Lustily singing songs while descending the mountain.
    Their banners in all colors were without number —
They very much resembled a picture of divinities.
But let's not sing of the Great King's dazzling style —
Listen as our ballad-story sings of a fine marriage!

Let's resume the story of that student Zhang Wengui,
Who was desperately looking for some saving star.
He would like to flee to heaven, but to heaven there is no road;
He would like to enter the earth, but earth did not offer a gate.
    "Here on this mountain I had to run into these bandits —
They've already killed my servants, both of them.
Originally they had intended to kill me too on this day —
I was saved, I think, by that man who delivered a letter."
    Indeed, if this messenger had arrived only one step later,
Wengui's life and his fate would not have been saved.
Tears gushed from his eyes, falling like a shower of rain.
"Nowhere in this transparently clear sky is a saving star!
    As I look towards my hometown, thousands of miles away,
How can my parents at home have an idea of my situation?
They only know I have left in search of fame and profit,
Have no idea that I will die here in this mountain forest."
    Let's not sing about the student and his bitter pains —
Let's change the subject and sing of — who do you think?

The Great King of Jingshan happened to have a daughter,
And the name of this daughter was Princess Blue Lotus.
    When she heard that her parents had left to go to a party,
She went for a walk outside the palace to cheer her up.
Eight hundred royal concubines were waiting on her,
Three thousand comely maidens were following her.

After she had fetched the three-sided mirror of bronze,
She dressed herself — one big mirror right in the middle.
Inside, she hurriedly combed her hair and washed her face;
Dressed in all her finery, she emerged from the palace.

Her dark tresses tied into a coiled-dragon chignon;
Her locks on both sides combed into clouds of black.
The phoenix-heads of her belt made of seven jewels;
Strings of precious pearls fastened to her headdress.

In her ears she carried a pair of rings of eight pearls,
Each and every flower of pearls in the latest fashion.
The outer gown she wore was a 'Without Flattery' Dress,
While dangling jade pendants hung down from her belt.

Her triple-waisted embroidered pants tied high and low,
On top of that a skirt with its Xiang River water-waves.
Before she even moved a step, a fragrant breeze arose —
She resembled an immortal fairy descending to earth.

The curved shoes on her feet were three inches long,
Her breast-flattener was made of red silk from Shu.
Her fingers were long and tapered like bamboo sprouts —
Where on earth could one find such a one-span waist?

She was exactly Chang'e leaving the moon's palace;
She resembled Guanyin, only lacking her pure vase![8]

Her cheeks resembled the peach blossoms of spring,
Her mouth resembled the one dot of red of a cherry.
Her eyebrows resembled new willow leaves in spring,
Her eyes the clear blue waters of the autumn waves.

Neither too long nor too short, the right proportions;
Neither too fat nor too slim — she surpassed all others.
As she walked slowly her gait was that of a fairy;
Whenever she moved fragrance bowled one over.

Her smile turned the world into a world of flowers;
Her joy turned the world into a world of brocade.
She was surrounded all around by palace maidens:
A thousand flowers surrounding the peony's heart.

The princess sat down in her easy-roaming carriage,
In her easy-roaming conveyance she took her seat.

---

[8] Chang'e is the beautiful goddess of the moon. The bodhisattva Guanyin was widely venerated in the shape of a charming young girl.

Three thousand comely maidens marched in front,
And eight hundred palace beauties made up the rear.
    For her first stop she arrived at the Changchao Hall:
The princess lifted her head to have a good look.
She observed the marvelous sights outside the hall,
The golden steps, so wide and broad, were rarely seen!
    Golden pillars, golden beams, and pegs made of gold;
The floor covered by tiles of gold as flat as a mirror.
The painted beams and brackets done in the latest style;
And the embroidered stools arranged on both sides.
    The princess then went on in an easterly direction, and
Over there she arrived at the Pavilion of Rich Spring.
The three-drip water-eaves invaded the Cloudy Stream;
The balustrades on all four sides were new and stylish.
    Every pavilion-hall was supported by forty pillars,
Which were wrapped in pure gold from top to base.
The roofs were covered with flowery glazed tiles,
The floors were smoothly paved with bricks of gold.
    After passing this pavilion, she continued her trip,
And so arrived at the Pavilion of a Hundred Flowers.
The four seasons' finest flowers here never wilted,
And bamboos swayed their green on both its sides.
    Parasol trees were planted on the pavilion's eastside;
Weeping willows grew on the pavilion's westside.
A shed formed by climbing roses faced a rose frame,
There the red of apricots appeared in a bamboo grove.
    A tree peony fence faced a bed of herbaceous peonies,
Red crabapples blossomed in front of marble steps.
The gold-grain osmanthus spread its rich fragrance
In a garden filled by hibiscus and chrysanthemum.
    Having passed the Pavilion of a Hundred Flowers,
She next arrived at the Multiple Fragrance Pavilion.
A high artificial hill invaded the Heavenly Stream,
Ancient acacias and lofty pines resembled dragons.
    The blooming lilies in the pond spread their fragrance,
The goldfish in the tank nibbled at the duckweed.
The brocade balustrades all around: a riot of flowers;
Facing treasures on both sides: windscreens of jade.
    Having passed the Multiple Fragrance Pavilion,
She next arrived at the Pavilion of Pressed Peaks.

Here a refreshing fairy breeze was always blowing,
And the creek in the ravine below murmured coolly.
　　The speckled and dotted rocks resembled agate;
The dark stone resembled bronze spotted with green.
A lion made of pure gold rose twelve meters high;
Brandishing its claws, baring its fangs — quite scary!
　　The wealth and status and luxury were indescribable,
Outperforming the immortals in their grotto-heavens.
The concubines and comely maidens said, "Wonderful!
Let's go on and find some more fine scenes to watch."
　　When they arrived in front of the Eaglewood Pavilion,
They were overwhelmed by the fragrance it emitted.
On the white wall the Three Purities[9] were venerated —
Golden lads and jade maidens arranged on both sides.
　　A curtain of speckled bamboo, hung from gold hooks;
A balustrade wrapped in gold, producing a shimmer.
The Old Lord was grandly enthroned in his hall,[10] and
The Great Thearch, before the altar, produced an aura.
　　Never an end to the incense calling down the Perfected;[11]
As soon as the lute stopped playing, one heard the zither.
Once the princess at this time had burned her incense,
She left the Three Purities behind and went on ahead.
　　The princess then ascended her free-roaming carriage,
And went in all directions to find out the state of affairs.
When she arrived at the Pavilion of Rest and Coolness,
She was overwhelmed by the cool wind from all sides.
　　It happened to be the Sixth Month, the height of summer,
But the breeze was so cool it made one shiver from cold.
There were ten folding chairs made of water crystal —
As soon as one sat down, one felt cool and refreshed.
　　"Let's not stay here for too long, but go on again!"
They next arrived at the Warm and Cozy Pavilion.
A golden brazier had been placed in the very middle;
In that brazier a fire was burning that never stopped.

---

[9] The Three Purities are the highest deities in the Daoist pantheon.
[10] The Old Lord refers to the deified Laozi (the Old Master), best known as the author of the *Book of the Way and its Virtue*.
[11] The Perfected is another designation for the immortals.

Warm benches for all four seasons covered with plaids;
Good wine for all four seasons arranged on both sides.
The wine vessels were all the height of riches and status,
If you would come to this pavilion in time of winter.

When Princess Blue Lotus lifted her head and looked,
She immediately noticed a very handsome young man.
"For what crime has he been tied up in this place?
Tied to a bronze pillar — tears coursing down his eyes!"
　　Princess Blue Lotus addressed him in the following way:
"From which prefecture do you hail? From which district?
What kind of crime did you commit, breaking the rules?
Why have you been tied up, here in the Flaying Pavilion?"
　　Confronted with these questions, the student replied:
"Dear Princess, please be so kind as to listen to me.
If I have to tell you my family's background and lineage,
I can tell you we live in the city of Xizhou. But because
　　I went to the Eastern Capital in search of fame and profit,
I unexpectedly ran into the men of the lord of Jingshan.
My two servants have both already been killed,
And I was tied up and left here, in this Flaying Pavilion.
　　If the Great King had not gone elsewhere this morning,
I would already have lost my life earlier on in the day."
　　When the princess at this time heard his story,
She thought to herself: "My daddy is really too evil!
My daddy is too evil, acting without rhyme or reason,
Without any cause, out of the blue, he wants to kill him!"
　　She promptly ordered the concubines to waste no time,
She promptly ordered them to release the student's body.
The concubines and comely maidens implored her:
"Your Highness, dear princess, please listen to us.
　　If the student succeeds in being released, our crime
Will not be a light one if the Great King is informed.
We, royal concubines, don't dare untie his shackles —
Dismemberment by a thousand slices being the least."
　　Hearing this, the princess was very much annoyed,
And she stepped down from her easy-roaming carriage.
The princess at this time wasted not a moment, and
Her slender jade-white fingers untied the hemp cords.

When Wengui had been released, he made a deep bow,
While the princess questioned him about everything.
　"From which prefecture do you hail? From which district?
What is your name and surname? Where are you from?
You must tell me everything, from the very beginning,
Tell me the truth in all its details, as I want to know."
　Questioned like this, the student told her everything:
"Your Highness the princess, please kindly listen.
We live in Xizhou, in the Western Capital Region,
And I was born and also raised in Xishui District.
　My father is Millionaire Zhang, who has some money:
For generations our family has had gold and silver.
I am the only child my father and mother have had;
I have no elder or younger brother, it's just me alone.
　Since my youth I've read the books, studied hard;
Ever since my youth my school name was Wengui.
When I heard the Humane Ancestor announced an exam,
I left for the Eastern Capital in search of fame and profit.
　When yesterday the three of us passed by this mountain,
We unexpectedly ran into the Great King in person.
My two servants have both already been killed, but
I was tied to a pole here in the Flaying Pavilion.
　As soon as the Great King comes back, he will
Take out my liver and heart — a snack with his wine.
I am deeply grateful to Your Highness for releasing me,
I'll burn my flesh as incense to express my gratitude!
　I implore Your Highness to kindly pardon my crime,
Please grant me my life, allow me to leave the forest!
If today you will be so good as to spare my life,
I'll never forget your grace till the day that I die!"

When the princess heard this, she was filled with joy;
As she observed him closely, he was a handsome man.
So the Princess Blue Lotus ruminated in her heart;
Not saying a word, she debated the matter with herself.
　"Here in the palace I may live the life of a princess,
But I do not yet have a fitting partner of equal status.
Today I see that this student really has a fine figure;
As I think of it secretly, I've fallen in love with him.

His impressive body measures a full five feet, and
Whether lucky or unlucky, he's a handsome devil.
A broad crown, a flat brow, and a full Storehouse;
His earlobes touching his shoulders — a fine person.

His eyebrows clearly divided like the word 'eight,'[12]
A physique that is quite imposing: a minister's body!
On top of that, his belly is filled with fine essays, so
He's bound to be a gold branch, jade-leaf person."

So Princess Blue Lotus questioned the student again:
"Dear student, now listen to what I will have to say.
May I ask you how old you are? When were you born?
In which year? In which month? During which hour?"

The student addressed her in the following manner:
"Your Highness, the princess, please kindly listen.

I am very grateful, Your Highness, for your question:
I am an only child and I have not yet been engaged.
This year I have reached the age of eighteen years;
I was born on the fifteenth of the First Month at *zi*."[13]

Hearing this, the princess was overcome with joy:
"This is rarely found in this world, it is too strange!
You were born on the fifteenth of the First Month,
While I was born on First Night,[14] right in the middle.

The same year, the same month, and the same day too,
And we were also born at the same hour of the day.
Once in the past I made this vow that I would marry
The man who was born in the same year and month.

This means that we must have met in an earlier life;
This was fated some five hundred years in the past.
If you don't reject me for being too ugly of face,
Let's go to the palace to become man and wife."

When Wengui heard this, he hastily found an excuse,
Saying: "Dear Princess, please listen to my words.
I am a man who reads the books, a true gentleman,
I am not a guy to cross the rules or break the law."

---

[12] That is to say, like the Chinese character for the word eight (*ba*).

[13] The hour of *zi* is the hour of midnight (11pm–1am).

[14] First Night refers to the first night with a full moon, so the fifteenth day of the First Month.

When the princess heard this, she replied as follows:
"Dear student, you are not very quick to understand.
  Becoming husband and wife is not based on the present,
A prior karma determines who will be marriage partners.
By lucky accident you were on your way to the exam,
And Heaven saw to it that you ran into my daddy.
  And if my daddy had not been called away to a party,
Could I in this mess have been able to save your life?
Those who have karma will meet despite any distance,
Those without karma will miss each other face to face."
  When Wengui heard her speak in this way, he replied:
"Your Highness, please be so kind as to listen to me.
  As you are so kind as not to reject me as too lowly,
Let's wait until I've passed the exam to get married.
When I have obtained an office or half a function,
I'll ask the King for permission to come and fetch you."
  When Princess Blue Lotus heard this, she was very annoyed,
"Dear student, what you are saying is not very smart.
You go to the Eastern Capital in search of some office,
And vainly attempt to scare me with your fancy words.
  My dear student, if you are not too eager and willing,
You'll be tied to the pillar again in the Flaying Pavilion.
And when my daddy himself returns to this place,
He will bring you out and have your liver and heart!"

The student then pondered his situation in his heart:
"In this crisis it is best to adapt and follow her whim!
If I observe that Princess Blue Lotus in greater detail,
I find her more tender and charming than a painting.
  She resembles Chang'e who leaves the moon palace,
She looks like an immortal fairy descending to earth.
She is a Xi Shi who has been reborn in this world, and
She looks like a Da Ji who has come back to life again.[15]
  Palace beauties crowd around her, in front and behind:
A thousand flowers surrounding the peony's heart.

---

[15] Xi Shi and Da Ji are fabled beauties of ancient times. Xi Shi caused the downfall of King
Fucha (d. 473 BC) of Wu, whereas King You (d. 771 BC) of the Zhou dynasty lost his life
because of his infatuation with Da Ji.

Her physical appearance and her youth: a fine woman;
She surpasses even that Consort Yang of the Tang![16]
    If I say that I refuse to marry her as man and wife,
I will be robbed by her of my life and also of my soul.
I'm filled with gratitude because she has saved me,
So there is nothing I can do but to humor this girl!"
    The student thereupon addressed her as follows:
"I'll be happy to obey your order to be man and wife."
At this, Princess Blue Lotus was overcome with joy,
And with her master and man she entered the palace.

When they arrived in the palace, a banquet was spread,
A banquet was laid out to entertain her new husband.
Golden cups on golden plates and on golden trays;
Golden spoons and golden chopsticks in jugs of gold.
    Musicians played their music while dancers danced,
Pipes and songs and instrumental music resounded.
At the banquet the rarest fruits were in ample supply,
They only lacked dragon liver and phoenix heart.
    Pair upon pair of palace girls presented their songs,
Couples of beauties poured wine from jugs of gold.
Their first dish was the soup of a hundred treasures,
Made of the meat of elephant, dragon, and unicorn.
    Twenty-four rounds of drinks: the banquet was done;
Flowers and candles were set out in the nuptial chamber.
When our student lifted his head and looked around,
The wealth and splendor was something rarely seen.
    Wave upon wave of strong fragrance wafted in his face;
The heavy smell of musk and orchid pierced his heart.
The floor was paved with golden tiles, flat as a mirror,
While each and every rafter was made of gold.
    The bed-curtains were made of brocade from Sichuan;
The upper side of the head-rest was inlaid with gold.

---

[16] Precious Consort Yang was the favorite concubine of Emperor Xuanzong (reg. 713–756) of the Tang. Traditionally she was blamed for the rebellion of An Lushan, which cost the old emperor his throne.

The weights of the coverlet were made of pure gold,
And every weight, shaped like a baby, weighed a pound.
    The coverlet filled the bed with its riot of flowers;
The fine mat of dragon-whiskers was equally new.[17]
On both sides of the bed golden steps were arranged;
Their rails were skillfully adorned with seven jewels.
    On the bed were also placed a pair of golden lions,
The pupils of their eyes made of night-shining pearls:
There was no need to light a lamp throughout the night,
As the brilliance they produced brightened the room.
    And to their sides hung a pair of incense strings —
As soon as one touched them, fragrance was emitted.
The screens had been completely made up of pearls,
And a dressing pavilion faced an undressing pavilion.
    As soon as Wengui saw this, he expressed his surprise:
"Such luxury, wealth and splendor are rarely found!"
The two of them thereupon ascended the golden steps —
A scene of wealth and splendor rarely to be seen!
    At this point in time the princess wasted no moment,
Together with him she arrived at the ivory couch.
On that couch the two of them became man and wife,
On the mandarin-duck cushion they became a couple.
    The two of them called on the sun to be their witness,
On the sun, the moon and the stars to be their witnesses,
And while in bed they pronounced a thousand vows —
A shared couch while alive, a shared grave once dead!
    Their love was as heavy as a mountain, nay heavier!
Their passion was as deep as the sea, nay still deeper!
Like mandarin ducks with necks entwined, such love!
But all of a sudden the end of the night was announced.

The two of them thereupon did rise from their bed,
Ready for combing and wrapping and getting dressed.
    And when breakfast was finished and tea had arrived,
Our student wasted no moment and rose to his feet.
Wengui addressed the princess, speaking as follows:
"I want to go to the Eastern Capital to take the exam."

---

[17] Dragon-whiskers is the name of a plant, the stems of which were woven into mats.

When Princess Blue Lotus heard what he said,
She did not say a single word, but pondered the matter.
"I would like to keep my husband here for a few days,
But I'm afraid that my parents may come back home."
　Blue Lotus provided him with gold and with treasure,
She opened her boxes to take out both gold and silver.
She took out three priceless treasures, magical objects,
Which she brought over and entrusted to her husband.
　The first of these was a belt of black silk and blue jade;
It was a most exceptional and truly priceless treasure.
　If a dead person would wear this belt around the waist,
The three souls and six spirits all returned to the body.
If a sick person would wear this belt around the waist,
All four hundred and four diseases would be fully eradicated.
　If an old person would wear this belt around the waist,
He would promptly look like an eighteen-year-old boy.
And if an ugly person would wear this belt around the waist,
His physical appearance would truly surpass all others.
　The second object was an equally priceless treasure,
And it was called the easy-roaming never-ending jug.
As soon as one would tap this jug only once, it would
Be completely filled with wine, right to the very top.
　You could drink from it from early morning till noon,
You could drink from it from noon till evening dusk.
Even when you had drunk till the end of the banquet,
All you had drunk at that time was less than one drop!
　The third object was a warm and cold drinking cup:
In the world of man this treasure was truly priceless!
As long as you did not drink any wine, all was fine,
But as soon as you would drink, music would resound.
　All kinds of instrumental music would be played,
And all kinds of musical instruments could be heard.
Put the cup back on the tray, and you did see no drop —
At the banquet the sound of music has disappeared.
　"My husband, take these with you to the emperor,
And you'll be appointed to the high office of minister.
I also have here ten horse-hoof ingots of silver,
Together with ten thousand strings of green bats.

I will also provide you with a dragon-colt horse,
For you to ride on your journey to the Eastern Capital.
My husband, when you have obtained a high office,
Don't become one of those who betray their first love!"

Blue Lotus addressed the young master as follows:
"Please consider these three men of earlier times.

When Bojie had betrayed the Chaste Maiden Zhao,
She sold her hair and personally buried his parents.[18]
When Wang Kui betrayed his girlfriend Guiying,
She dragged him to the God of the Sea to stand trial.[19]

When Wenlong betrayed his wife the lady Xiao,
She recited the sutras for a full twenty-one years.[20]
In this world there are too many faithless fellows,
All guys have the gall to betray their first love!"

Wengui then pronounced a vow, facing Heaven;
Facing Heaven, he swore an oath to his wife:
"If I do not come and fetch you once I have an office,
I may sink for eternity into the three roads of hell!"

When he had sworn this oath, he mounted his horse,
And the princess came along to see her husband off.
When the young master and the princess said goodbye,
Both of them were awash in tears, weeping profusely.

---

[18] Cai Bojie and Zhao Wuniang are the main characters in one of the earliest southern plays (*xiwen*), later rewritten by Gao Ming (ca. 1307–ca. 1370) as *Pipa ji* (The Story of the Lute). Cai Bojie leaves home soon after marrying Zhao Wuniang in order to sit for the exams. When he has passed the examinations as top-of-the-list, he marries the daughter of the prime minister. In the meantime, his hometown is stricken by famine. Zhao Wuniang takes care of his parents, and when they die, she buries them with her own hands and sells her beautiful hair to pay the expenses. In the earliest version of this tale, Cai Bojie is killed by lightning for his betrayal, but Gao Ming contrived a happy ending.

[19] The student Wang Kui and the courtesan Guiying were the main characters in a once very popular but now lost early southern play. The poor student Wang Kui is enabled by the courtesan Guiying to prepare for the examinations. Before his departure he vows her eternal loyalty in the temple of the God of the Sea. Once he has passed the examinations, however, he refuses to recognize her. She lodges an accusation against him with the God of the Sea, and Wang Kui commits suicide in a fit of madness.

[20] Liu Wenlong and lady Xiao are the main characters in yet another early southern play, entitled *Jinchai ji* (The Story of the Golden Hairpin). Liu Wenlong leaves his young wife immediately after their marriage, not to return for many years. During his absence, lady Xiao withstands all pressure to remarry from the side of her husband's parents, who believe their son to have died.

When the student had mounted his dragon-colt horse,
He repeatedly turned his head to look back, again and again.
The princess gazed after her man till he had disappeared,
And then she returned to the palace, overcome by grief.
    "Today my husband has left for the Eastern Capital,
And I don't know how long it will take till his return!"

But let's not sing of Blue Lotus once back in the palace,
But listen to me as I sing of the man surnamed Zhang.
    After he had been traveling on the road for some days,
He had arrived in the neighborhood of the Phoenix City.[21]
From a distance he saw the royal walls rising dimly,
A suitable wind brought the sounds of pipes and strings.
    The dragon-colt horse raced on like a flying arrow, so
He promptly arrived at the gate of the emperor's city.
    The young master went into the city to have a look
At the six commercial streets and the three markets.
This was a flowery world that was woven of brocade,
A mild breeze had laid out this universe of brocade.
    High lofts, layer upon layer, hid inside the noble lords;
Painted pavilions, floor upon floor, housed immortals.
The Eastern Market went on until the Western Market,
The Northern Street could hear Southern Street songs.
    And whenever he passed in front of a winehouse,
Its banner was hung so high it reached to the clouds.
"Wine made for spring, summer, fall, and winter:
Sold to travelers from east, west, south, and north."
    The beauties who poured the wine were seductive;
The pretty girls who took your money bewitching.
Their bodies were dressed in a long shift of red gauze,
Their waists girdled by a gold-speckled orchid belt;
    In their hair they wore a sprig of fresh flowers, and
Their curved shoes were embroidered with clouds.
The cups and trays were all made of gold or silver;
The tea cups and table china were inlaid with gold.
    He passed in front of the gate of marionette theaters,
And in the playhouses virtuous men were the subject.

---

[21] Phoenix City is a designation for the imperial capital.

Shops of uncured herbs faced shops of cured herbs;
Crowds clamored at the shops for gold and silver.
Jade carvers were located next to shops of pearls,
And teahouses faced winehouses across the street.
    This was the best of all the four hundred garrisons,
Of the two thousand districts it carried the prize.
Indeed, the wealth and splendor of the Eastern Capital
Was nowhere else to be found but in heaven's halls!
    When the young master saw this, he very happily
Concluded: "This is quite rightly the emperor's city."
But as our student was drawn to the sights of the city,
All of a sudden the sun was setting on the western hills.

Travelers on the road were looking for an inn to stay,
The fisherman on the river laid down his fishing rod.
The beauty lit a lamp as she returned to her room,
And the farmer stopped working and went back home.
    The student had to find a place where he might stay,
So he looked for an inn where he could settle down.
When he arrived down the road at Bamboo Stave Lane,
He noticed an advertisement written neatly and clearly.
    On the white-washed wall was written in large signs:
"Residential rooms available for visitors and travelers."
The young master then entered the innkeeper's place,
And the innkeeper immediately welcomed his guest.
    He welcomed the student, and led him inside the inn;
After some conversation they sat down as host and guest.
He then asked the student: "Sir, where do you live?
What is your name and surname? Where are you from?"
    The young master then told the innkeeper everything:
"My dear sir, please listen to what I will tell you.
    We live in Xizhou, in the Western Capital Region,
And my family has always been rich and wealthy.
My father is Millionaire Zhang, who has lots of cash,
And I, this student Wengui, am one who reads books.
    As I heard that the emperor holds an examination,
I came to the capital in search of fame and profit.
Now tonight I have come to your inn to seek lodging,
And tomorrow I will go to the examination grounds."

When the innkeeper heard him speak in this manner,
He promptly ordered his servants: "Listen carefully!
Hurry up and immediately get us three cups of wine,
And prepare an evening meal to entertain the guest!"
He also ordered them to give him the finest room,
And to sweep and clean that room without any delay.
The young master then went upstairs to his room,
And lifted his eyes to look around the whole place.
The upstairs room, he saw, offered many fairy scenes;
Zither and go board, calligraphies and paintings too.
The cups and plates were laid out on a table of agate,
Folding chairs of rhino-hide were placed on both sides.
Calligraphies in all styles hung on opposing walls,
With landscapes by Zhang Sengyou in the middle.[22]
The one sleeping couch was very flat and clean;
The two layers of bed-curtains were equally new.
The couch was covered by a coverlet of brocade,
And the hundred flowers on the head-rest were new.
When he had finished his dinner and tea was poured,
The servants also placed lighted candles in his room.
Seeing this, Wengui exclaimed: "This is exceptional!
This innkeeper knows how to treat his guests well!"

The young master then was very much depressed
As he remembered the sorry fate of his two servants.
"And if my life had not been saved by Blue Lotus,
I would not have been able to stay here tonight.
She was so kind as to save my miserable life, but
Tonight here in this chilly room I'm feeling lonely.
She not only gave me these three priceless treasures,
But she also became my wife, there in the palace."
At this time the student said, speaking to himself:
"Let me get them and try them out, put them to the test.
Let me get them out right now to have a good look,
I have to see whether these objects really work!"

---

[22] Zhang Sengyou is a famous painter of the sixth century.

The young master thereupon hastily took them out,
And he took out the easy-roaming, never-ending jug.
When the young master held the jug to have a look,
It was a scene of wealth and splendor rarely seen!

He felt that the jug was very heavy indeed, because
It was completely filled with wine, to the very rim.
At this sight, the young master was filled with joy:
"Such a precious object is rare to find in this world!"

The young master took out the warm and cold cup;
As soon as he had found it, he tried it out for once.
He immediately poured out the wine into the cup,
And thereupon he promptly put the cup to his lips.

As long as he had not drunk yet, everything was fine,
But as soon as he drank, the sound of music blared!
The five notes and six halftones created a hubbub;
All kinds of musical instruments resounded loudly.

The young master had only wanted to have a look,
But unintentionally he had startled innkeeper Yang.
The man was so scared he was covered in sweat;
His whole family, old and young, was terrified.

Mr. Yang immediately went up to the second floor,
And the young master got on his feet as he saw him.
The innkeeper questioned the young master, saying:
"Why do we hear this hubbub here on your floor?

You are a true gentleman, who studies the books,
How can you startle people late at night, at midnight?"

Speak:

This innkeeper immediately went upstairs to his room and asked: "Dear sir, how can these musical instruments resound so loudly?" Questioned in this way, the young master hastily showed him the three magic treasures, and allowed the innkeeper to inspect them closely. The innkeeper then asked: "What do these treasures do?"

Sing:

The young master could only tell him everything:
"Dear Mr. Innkeeper, please listen to what I will say.

The first object is a belt of black silk and blue jade;
If a dead man ties it on, his soul returns to his body.
If a sick person would tie this belt around his waist,
The four hundred four diseases would be eradicated.

If an old man would tie this belt around his waist,
His white hairs would turn into his old black clouds.
If a hunchback would tie this belt around his waist,
He would immediately be turned into a fine fellow.

If a deaf person would tie this belt around his waist,
He would hear each and every word very clearly.
And if a dumb person would tie it around his waist,
He could pronounce each and every word clearly.

The second object is this easy-roaming wine jug:
As soon as you tap it once, it is completely filled.
The third object is this warm and cold drinking cup,
Whenever you drink wine from it, music resounds!"

The innkeeper, hearing this, could not believe it at all:
"Give them to me to try them out and to have a look!"
Wengui immediately handed them over to the man,
And, holding them, the innkeeper was very pleased.

First he lightly tapped the jug, which was promptly
Completely filled with wine, right to the very rim.
Seeing this, the innkeeper was filled with great joy:
"This is a treasure rarely to be found in this world!"

When he also tried out the young master's cup,
The house was filled with the hubbub of music!
When the innkeeper saw this, he exclaimed:
"Sir, your objects are precious treasures indeed!"

At this time the innkeeper thought to himself: "Why
Should I have to be an innkeeper toadying to guests?
The best would be to get my hands on these objects
And live my life for some years in happy idleness!"

He promptly ordered the serving girl to make haste,
They would try out the easy-roaming never-ending jug.

All kinds of seasonal fruits were laid out on the table,
With fried chicken, geese and duck, and fresh fish.

Pears and pine seeds together with peaches and dates,
Delicacies of the four seasons, a hundred flavors!
 The whole family, old and young, had all arrived,
They were drinking to happy songs, in a merry mood.
Before one cup was finished, another cup followed;
Before one glass was emptied, it was filled again!
 It is not the wine that makes us drunk but the drinking —
People sank into a drunken stupor there in that room.
The young master did not realize it had been a trick,
To get him so drunk that he would be drunk as a skunk.
 Once he was drunk he did not know north from south,
And all energy and strength had fled from his body.
That very moment the innkeeper rose to his feet, and
Tripped him up, so he stumbled and fell on the floor.
 That very night the innkeeper set out to kill him —
In his hands he held two meters of white gauze silk.
He called for his wife to help him out with his scheme,
But his wife refused to participate in this foul act.
 The innkeeper thereupon flew into a terrible rage
And wrapped the silk around the throat of Wengui.
He then got a straight flute with nine holes, and
Strangled the young master there on the ground.
 The red blood flowed from his nose and his ears,
And his life left him to see the Lord of Shade.
 Yang ordered his servants to waste no moment, and
Bury the body in the garden behind the house,
And to plant a banana tree at the grave's head-end,
So he would not be able to turn over for all eternity.
 In this way the student Wengui was cruelly killed,
Only because he tested the treasures out in his room.
While no one knows where his souls may have gone,
The innkeeper laid his hands on his precious treasures.
 On top of that, he obtained the dragon-colt horse,
Together with the ten horse-hoof ingots of silver.
On top of that, he got the ten thousand green bats,
So Mr. Yang was secretly very pleased in his heart.

How sad that Wengui suffered such a cruel death —
How would his father and mother learn about it?
I've reached the end of the first half of this ballad —
The second part will teach what happened next!

A poem goes:

> *When meeting strangers, tell them only one-third,*
> *You cannot bare to them the secrets in your heart.*

The Tale of Zhang Wengui, Part One, Newly Printed, Completely Illustrated, in Prose and in Verse, The End.

The Tale of Zhang Wengui.
Part Two

Newly Printed, Completely Illustrated, in Prose and in Verse

From that time onwards Mr. Yang rose in the world,
And he did no longer operate an inn at his home.
Each day a rich banquet was laid out in a high loft,
And he spent the whole day having a merry time.

   On a certain day Mr. Yang conceived of the idea
To roam the streets in order to cheer himself up.
The red-mane horse was brought out from the stable,
And surrounded by servants he set out on his way.

   He rode through the main streets and little lanes:
The world a riot of flowers, a universe of brocade!
And when he passed in front of the Palace Main Gate,
A yellow placard clearly posted the imperial writing.

   The poster read: "Her Imperial Majesty is seriously ill,
And it looks as if she may leave this world any moment.
If anyone can save her and restore her to her health,
We will give him one-half of eight superior districts!"

   When the innkeeper saw this, he was filled with joy:
"I'm destined to rise in the world and become an official!"
He returned with all speed back to his own house,
Dismounted from his horse, and then entered the gate.

   Once he was inside, he addressed his wife, saying:
"My dear wife, it is your fortune to become a Lady!"

Speak:

When this Mr. Yang came back home, he said to his wife: "When I was riding through the streets this morning, I saw a poster in front of the

309

palace, which read: 'Her Imperial Majesty the empress-dowager is gravely ill and may die any moment. If there is anyone who is able to save the empress-dowager, he will be raised to the rank of a marquis of eight superior provinces, and receive one-half of these prefectures.' Here at home we have this belt of black silk and blue jade, which can cure the four hundred and four diseases. If I can succeed in saving Her Imperial Majesty, the office to which I will be appointed will not be small!" When his wife heard this, she was overcome by joy. He got the three precious objects out with all speed and went off to present them, and entered the court to be received in audience by His Majesty.

Sing:

Mr. Yang mounted his horse, took his seat on the saddle,
And he arrived in one stretch at the Palace Main Gate.
Once there, he promptly took away the yellow poster,
Wanting to save Her Majesty, the emperor's mother.
　　The officer guarding the poster questioned him, saying:
"From which prefecture do you hail? Which district?"
　　Mr. Yang replied that he lived in the Eastern Capital,
That he was surnamed Yang, and born as a second son.
"I have a belt made of black silk and blue jade:
If a dead person ties it around his waist, he revives!"
　　The officer guarding the poster registered his words,
And entered the court to report this to His Majesty.
With twenty-four bows — a longevity like mountains:
Wishing him a myriad of years, he said: "Your servant."
　　"This humble servant was ordered to guard the poster.
Now there has come a local man of the Eastern Capital.
Living on Bamboo Stave Lane, called Yang the Second,
He possesses a priceless treasure made of black silk.
　　This can cure each of the four hundred four diseases;
If a dead person wears it around his waist, he recovers.
At present he has taken away the yellow poster outside,
He'll save Her Imperial Majesty, the empress-dowager.
　　Not yet having received the command of the emperor,
He does not dare enter and appear before Your Majesty."
Learning this, the Humane Ancestor was overjoyed,
And he ordered him summoned, without any delay!

Thrice summoned, he was led before the gold steps,
And four ushers showed him in, to see His Majesty.
With twenty-four bows — a longevity like a mountain:
Wishing him a myriad of years, he said, "Your servant."

The sun and moon, however high, are seen by all, but
It is rare for a mean fellow to see the Enlightened Ruler.
Today he had the luck to see the face of the emperor —
Likely because he burned fine incense in an earlier life.
  The emperor, having seen the report, summoned him:
"Please do not execute the ritual but get on your feet!"
He gifted him a brocade stool to sit down facing him
For one cup of imperial tea and three rounds of wine.
  The emperor thereupon addressed him as follows:
"Dear Sir, approach and listen to what I will say.
  In which prefecture do you live? In which district?
What is your surname and name? Are you the eldest?
You, Sir, have a precious treasure you want to present,
So how did you obtain this treasure to begin with?"
  Mr. Yang thereupon reported in the following way:
"Your Majesty, please be so kind as to listen to me.
  We hail from the Eastern Capital, Kaifeng Prefecture,
And I was born and grew up on Bamboo Stave Lane.
Since my youth I have been known as Yang the Second,
And for generations my family has been innkeepers.
  My father upheld the methods of divine immortals,
And they gifted him with three priceless treasures.
Then I learned that Our King had posted a placard,
In which he told of Her Imperial Majesty's disease.
  So I have come to present these three priceless objects
To save Her Imperial Majesty, the empress-dowager!
The first object is a belt of black silk and blue jade;
This treasure is a most unique and priceless object.
  As soon as a sick person ties it around his waist,
The four hundred and four diseases are all eradicated.
As soon as a dead person ties it around his waist,
The three souls and seven spirits return to the body.
  The second object is a single easy-roaming jug:
As soon as one taps the jug, it is filled with wine.

The third object is a single warm and cold cup:
This treasure is really priceless in the world of man.
As long as you don't drink, everything is fine,
But as soon as you start to drink, music resounds!"

Hearing this report, the emperor was very pleased,
And ordered these precious treasures to be shown.
The guard officers on duty wasted no moment,
And showed these objects to the Enlightened Ruler.

When the emperor opened the box to have a look,
A multicolored light brightly filled the palace hall.
The emperor immediately rose from his throne, and
Ordered the palace ladies to carry this tray inside.

Promptly sending these treasures to the Rear Palace,
He asked Her Imperial Majesty how she was feeling.

The emperor inquired of Her Imperial Majesty
How the situation of her illness had developed.
The empress-dowager answered the emperor thusly:
"Today my illness has only worsened once again!"

The emperor then asked for the belt of black silk,
Which he personally fastened around her body.
When he tied the belt around Her Majesty's waist,
Her illness indeed receded and she felt much better.

Before one hour had passed, the empress-dowager
Was completely cured, and was as healthy as before.
Her Imperial Majesty thereupon asked the following:
"Who is the man who offered such rare treasures?"

The emperor answered the empress-dowager, saying:
"A man surnamed Yang from the Eastern Capital."
Seeing that the empress-dowager was recovered,
The emperor left the Rear Palace, filled with joy.

The emperor thereupon had a banquet laid out
To entertain Mr. Yang in a most sumptuous way.
Golden cups on golden plates and on golden trays;
Golden spoons and golden chopsticks in jugs of gold.

Twenty-four rounds of wine: the dinner was finished,
And the emperor wrote out Yang's appointment himself.

On five meters of red gauze he wrote his function;
He appointed him to high office, not to a minor job.

Commander-in-chief of the eighty-four prefectures
And a liegeman of eight provinces, equally divided:
His monthly salary was seven thousand strings —
Mount your horse, it is gold; dismount, it is silver!

Yang's wife was raised to the rank of Lady, and
Gifted too with a phoenix cap and a roseate cape.
Her monthly salary was three thousand strings —
Ride your sedan chair: gold! Dismount: it is silver!

Having received this office Mr. Yang was pleased,
But while he did not say a word, he thought to himself:

"Three hundred officials and two hundred officers —
The only one I have to fear is the man named Bao.
If I am appointed to office I will need guarantors,
Because I lack the qualifications to be an official."

Having reached this conclusion the innkeeper,
Bowing before the golden steps, refused to rise.

The emperor thereupon had this order transmitted,
Saying: "Minister Yang, please listen to my words.
We have appointed you to one of the highest offices,
So how come you do not thank Us for Our grace?"

The innkeeper thereupon expressed his gratitude:
"Your Majesty, please be so kind as to listen to me.
I'm only a common citizen of the Eastern Capital,
And lack all qualifications to become an official."

When the emperor saw him express this concern,
He promptly selected men to serve as his guarantors.

The first of the guarantors was Chancellor Wang,
The second of them was none else but Minister Kou.
As the third he selected His Excellency Bao Zheng,
And as the fourth he selected the man surnamed Chai.

The story tells that Judge Bao of the Southern Office
Stepped forward to carefully observe this Mr. Yang.
His Excellency raised his three-cornered eyes, and
Scrupulously scrutinized his facial physiognomy.

The three lines through his cheeks lacked all feeling:
This was a traitorous man without any gratitude.

If this man was going to be a commander-in-chief,
He was bound to greedily bring harm to the people.
    His Storehouse was not full, defective on both sides:
Despite his glory today, he would be executed later.
So Judge Bao stepped forward and formally declared:
"I refuse to serve as guarantor for that person Yang."

Hearing this, the emperor was very much annoyed,
And he went to the Rear Palace to see his dear mother.
He then told her: "I made Yang commander-in-chief,
I appointed the man to an important position indeed.
    Commander-in-chief of the eighty-four prefectures
And a liegeman of eight provinces, equally divided!
But when I had appointed the man to this high post,
He did not dare to accept the imperial grace at court.
    He reported he lacked the required qualifications,
And that he needed officials at court as his guarantors.
We promptly acted in accordance with his request, and
Immediately selected four prominent officials at court.
    But that awful Judge Bao of the Southern Office had
The cheek to refuse to serve as the man's guarantor.
He said the commander was a man without morals,
Who was destined to be executed at some later date."
    When Her Majesty heard this, she was very annoyed:
"This man called Bao is really becoming too much!
If that Bao guy is refusing to serve as his guarantor,
I myself will act, right here and now, as his guarantor!"
    When the emperor heard this, he was filled with joy;
Re-emerging from the Rear Palace, he informed Yang.
"Her Majesty the empress-dowager will be a guarantor,
And here at court recommends you for your office."
    The emperor assigned three thousand men to him
To build a palatial compound for him in the capital.
All kinds of craftsmen were assembled for the job,
Within a month the construction was to be completed.
    The gates in the imperial palace were ten *zhang* high;
Those in his house would be nine *zhang* or even more.[23]

---

[23] One *zhang* equals 10 feet.

While the doors of the emperor had only nails of gold,
In his house the doors would have nails made of silver.
    Three hundred men were assigned to him as guards,
And two executioners would follow him at all times.
Grand marshal of the realm, commander-in-chief,
In charge of executions at court — that would be him!
    As he surpassed the four hundred officials at court,
All officials treated Mr. Yang with utmost respect.
The commander thanked His Majesty for his grace,
Wishing him a myriad of years on the dragon-throne.
    Having expressed his gratitude, he promptly retired,
"His Excellency" left the court through the palace gate.
As he arrived at the Main Gate and mounted his horse,
He was surrounded by runners cracking their whips!
    Three sets of ceremonial cudgels, six sets of whips;
A folding chair, a silver jug, and a clean handkerchief.
In front of the train banners displayed on both sides;
The executioners and servants arranged in two rows.
    One shouted "The commander-in-chief is here!" and
Those walking stopped, those seated rose to their feet;
The wineshops pulled down the flag before their gate,
And the teashops lowered the blinds in front of the door!
    On their way they arrived at the prefecture of Kaifeng:
Three times they shouted their cry as they passed by.
Earlier people only talked about Chancellor Bao, but
Now people only talked about the man named Yang!
    Straightaway the train arrived at Bamboo Stave Lane,
Where he dismounted from his horse and went inside.
The neighbors on all sides were all equally scared;
Each and every one who had seen it was stupefied:
    That innkeeper they all knew, little Yang the Second,
Had all of a sudden been raised to the highest clouds!

As the commander-in-chief leads a life of pleasure,
Let's sing of the good deed of the dragon-colt horse.
    Ever since Zhang Wengui was strangled and killed,
It was always shedding its tears in great profusion.
In the garden it continuously whinnied and snorted,
And nobody understood what the cause might be.

Everyday in the garden the horse shed hot tears,
As with each and every sound it wept for Wengui.
"You suffered here in this place a most cruel death;
And now back home they wait in vain for your return."

From the eastern garden it ran to the western garden;
From the southern garden it ran to the northern garden.
Each and every day it so complained of this crime,
And so the Jade Emperor up above soon was alerted.

The Jade Emperor then dispatched an astral official,
Who found the murdered body buried in the garden.

"This is Zhang Wengui of the Western Capital, who
Half a year ago was murdered, suffering great pain.
This is the reason why the horse always whinnies —
It may be an animal, but it still feels outraged!"

The Jade Emperor, the Great Thearch, gave his orders
And summoned all divine soldiers of the world above.
The assembled gods then received his commandment
To descend to earth to save the man surnamed Zhang.

The earl of wind and master of rain descended to earth,
The master of thunder and mother of lightning set out.
They called up a black storm and a black rain, which
Scraped the earth, raised dust, and blew people over.

Big mountains suffered such impact they were shaking,
Little mountains were completely flattened by the wind.
The tiles on the roofs flew through the air like swallows,
And big trees with all their branches were ripped out.

That huge storm and heavy rain never came to an end,
Scaring the wits out of the people of the Eastern Capital.
After they had continued for three days and three nights,
They brought to light the corpse of Zhang Wengui.

When they had brought to light the murdered Wengui,
The rains stopped, clouds cleared — a bright sky again!

Let's not sing of the gods returning to the world above;
Let's sing again of the deeds of the dragon-colt horse.

When it saw that the skies once again shone brightly,
It came to the rear garden gate as it used to do before.
And when it saw the exposed body of Zhang Wengui,
Large tears gushed from its eyes, in great profusion.

"While you already have lost your life in these parts,
Your parents back home are waiting for your return!"
Grabbing his clothes with its mouth — in one swing:
It carried the corpse on its back and set out on a trip.

That very moment it jumped across the garden wall,
And galloped like a cloud through the main streets.
All men and women crowded together to have a look;
Each and every one who saw this sight was stupefied.

"This animal is utterly bereft of rhyme and reason,
Why is it carrying the corpse of someone dead?"
Without ever halting it came to Kaifeng Prefecture,
And entered straightaway through the gate of the hall.

The runners in the hall all tried to scare it away:
"Stupid animal, why are you carrying a corpse?"
But for all their beating, they could not chase it away:
And it straightaway entered the hall of Judge Bao.

When it had dumped the corpse in front of his desk,
It knelt down before the hall and refused to rise.
His Excellency thereupon addressed it as follows:
"You horse, now come forward for questioning!

In which prefecture do you live? In which district?
What is your name and surname? Where are you from?
On what business did you come to the Eastern Capital?
And who is the man who murdered this lifeless corpse?"

When the horse was questioned, it could not answer,
Big tears coursed down its cheeks, in great profusion.
Judge Bao, upon pondering the matter in his mind,
Addressed the runners thereupon in the following way:

"Carry the corpse to the western corridor for storage,
And take good care of the horse, have it properly fed."

His Excellency thereupon left the hall and went inside,
Where he was welcomed that very moment by his wife.

When his wife had welcomed Judge Bao in her room,
She perceived that Dragon-Design Bao was not happy.
So his wife opened the conversation by asking him:
"My dear husband, what is the reason you are unhappy?"

Judge Bao then answered her in the following way:
"My dear wife, something happened you do not know.

Ever since I served as the prefect of Kaifeng Prefecture,
My fame has spread through the Eastern Capital Region.
  This is not because I'm so exceptionally pure and straight,
It is all thanks to Heaven and Earth and the divine gods.
Today, as I was sitting in court for the morning session,
A curious criminal case has presented itself to me there.
  This was because a dragon-colt horse, carrying a corpse,
Ran straightaway into the hall of the prefecture's building.
I questioned the horse as to where it was living, and
Who had been killed and departed for the Lord of Shade.
  I posed the questions repeatedly, but I got no answer,
While the horse shed tears, which fell in great profusion.
This is the reason why I am now so unhappy at heart —
How on earth am I going to solve this criminal case?"

Speak:

His wife replied: "My dear husband, this case cannot be solved. You don't know the name or surname of that person and you also don't know his place of registration and his place of residence. And this dragon-colt horse cannot speak. You also don't know who killed the man. If you want to solve this case, the dead will have to come back to life — only then can you come up with a clear sentence. There is nothing you can do."

Sing:

His Excellency that very moment came up with a plan,
And he addressed his dear wife in the following way:
"Yang the Second had presented three magical treasures,
And in this way he has saved the life of Her Majesty.
  One of these is a belt made of black silk and blue jade:
If a dead person wears it, he comes back to life again!
I have to come up with a plan to dredge up the dragon,
So I can borrow that precious treasure from the palace!"
  When his wife heard this, a smile appeared on her face:
"My dear husband, what you say makes no sense at all!
You refused to serve as guarantor for Commander Yang,
So how would they be willing to lend you that treasure?"
  Hearing these words, Judge Bao was not amused at all:
"My dear wife, please listen to what I have to tell you.

Fig. 7.2
Carrying Wengui's corpse, the horse appears before Minister Bao.

If I am not allowed now to borrow that belt of black silk,
Then what is the point of putting that corpse in storage?
  My wife, you'll have to go to the court, claim I am ill,
And so borrow that treasure from His Imperial Majesty."
As his wife had no excuse and had to make the journey,
She got ready to go by dressing herself in all her finery.
  On her head she wore the phoenix headdress of her rank,
And she also wore the roseate cape speckled with gold.
Serving maids accompanied her, in front and behind,
And eight lamps were arranged in rows on both sides.
  At the first shout of "Her Ladyship is here, make way!"
Those walking stopped, those seated rose to their feet.
At the Main Gate, she dismounted from her sedan chair,
And stormed into the Throne Hall to see His Majesty.
  When the emperor lifted his eyes to scrutinize her,
He promptly recognized the supplicant as Lady Li.
The emperor ordered her to dispense with all ritual —
"What brings you here without having been summoned?"
  Lady Li stepped forward and addressed the emperor:
"Your Majesty, please be so kind as to listen to me.
The only reason is I have to fear for my husband's life,
So I have come to the court to borrow that treasure.
  My husband's illness has grown extremely serious;
Now shivering, now feverish, he may die any moment.
I implore Your Majesty to display some compassion,
To take pity on him, and to save my husband's life."
  When the emperor heard this, he was very displeased,
Rising to his feet, he got up from his throne, saying:
"Lady, please be so kind as to wait here for a while,
And I will go to the Rear Palace and ask my mother."
  Because it was Minister Bao's life that was in danger,
He went to the Rear Palace to consult with his mother.
Straightaway he arrived in her Rear Palace apartment
In order to visit his mother, the empress-dowager.
  When he had greeted Her Majesty, he addressed her:
"My dear mother, please be so kind as to listen to me.
The life of Minister Bao of the Southern Office is in danger,
And his wife is now here, asking to borrow the treasure."

Hearing this, Her Majesty thought, "I'll be damned!
He still has the cheek to borrow that magical treasure!"
    Her Majesty thereupon addressed her son as follows:
"Lord and king, please listen to what I have to say.
There are plenty of other officials to serve in Kaifeng:
No way today will I lend it to that man surnamed Bao!"
    Hearing this, the Humane Ancestor turned around,
And back at court informed Lady Li of the outcome.
    "Your husband refused to guarantee Commander Yang:
No way today will she lend him this magical treasure.
We will dispatch some imperial physicians to his place;
These fine physicians are able to save your husband."

When Lady Li received this answer to her request,
She took her leave of the emperor, and exited the gate.
At the Palace Main Gate, she mounted her sedan chair,
And returned straightaway to the prefectural building.
    Upon arrival, she dismounted from her sedan chair;
Judge Bao promptly asked her how things had been.
In answer to that question she burst out in loud laughter:
"My dear husband, how can you be so utterly stupid!
    Because you refused to guarantee Commander Yang,
They of course refuse to let you borrow that treasure.
So, when I went there today, they refused to help out,
And even worse, a disaster is ready to strike us!
    A couple of imperial physicians soon will arrive,
Dispatched to feel your pulse and diagnose your case.
As soon as these physicians will return and report,
Your punishment, my man, will be no laughing matter."
    When His Excellency heard this, he could only smile:
"There is no need to be worried over such a trifle.
When these two physicians arrive here in person,
I've a cunning trick prepared to dredge up the dragon."
    He tied up his upper arm with a length of white silk,
And as a result his pulse did not show any movement.
"My dear wife, you take your seat here in the room,
And then you tell these fine physicians the following:
    You tell them that since your dear husband fell ill,
No food or drink has touched his lips for three days.

If some unknown person suddenly crashes into him,
He is bound to die and depart for the Lord of Shade.
    Let them feel my pulse on the other side of the bars —
In that way these men will not be able to tell the truth."

Speak:

Judge Bao said: "My dear wife, I will tie a white silk handkerchief around
my arm so the blood will be unable to flow. For all they may feel my pulse,
there just will be no movement. I will lie down on my bed, and stretch my
hand through an opening between the window bars, so they can feel my
pulse, and you will say to those physicians, 'My husband has not taken any
food or drink for three days — he has not even drunk any water! If he is
confronted with an unknown person, he is bound to die!'"

Sing:

When she heard this, Lady Li was filled with joy,
Her husband was indeed a smart and cunning man!
The couple had barely finished their conversation,
When two imperial physicians arrived at the gate.
    Lady Li at that time went out to welcome the two,
She led them into the hall, and offered them tea.
    Lady Li then addressed them in the following way:
"Gentlemen, please listen to what I have to say.
My husband has been ill now for three full days,
And, I'm afraid, soon will join the Lord of Shade."
    The imperial physicians answered her as follows:
"Your Ladyship, please listen to what we tell you.
Because His Excellency is suffering from a disease,
We will have to feel his pulse to diagnose his case."
    Lady Li once again addressed them, as follows:
"Gentlemen, please listen to what I have to say.
No unknown person can confront him at this time,
So please feel his pulse from outside the window."
    The imperial physicians had to do as she told them,
And immediately walked over to outside his room.
His Excellency thereupon stretched out his hand,
So they could feel his pulse and diagnose his case.

In both his arms they detected no pulse at all, so
The imperial physicians were covered in sweat.
The two of them thereupon reported to Lady Li:
"His Lordship's condition is grave — beyond cure!"
    The two imperial physicians returned in all haste,
And back at court they reported to His Majesty.
Twenty-four bows — longevity like a mountain:
Wishing him a myriad of years, saying, "Your servant!"
    "We were personally dispatched by Your Majesty
To Kaifeng Prefecture to diagnose the patient Bao.
The two of us immediately went and felt his pulse —
His Excellency had no pulse whatsoever anymore!"
    Hearing this report the emperor was very annoyed,
And quite unhappy at heart he sank into a depression.

Let's not talk about the goings-on at Dragon-Design Bao's,
But let's sing for a while about that Commander Yang.
Everyday at home a rich banquet was spread out,
Each and every day he merrily downed his wine.
    Think of clothes — his body was wrapped in silks;
As to food — delicacies of a hundred new flavors.
When thirsty he only drank the wine from the palace,
When hungry the hundred flavors were ready to be served.

But let's not sing of the merry life of the commander,
Listen as I sing of the stable boys back in the garden.
Suddenly one day when they came to feed the horses,
They did not see the dragon-colt horse there anymore.
    Zhang Xing and Li Wang were at a loss what to do,
And searched throughout the garden, from east to west.
The neighbors on all sides had not seen a thing either —
How were they going to avert this looming disaster?

Speak:

The establishment of Commander-in-Chief Yang had thirty fine horses, and two men each day had the duty of feeding these horses. When Zhang Xing and Li Wang went to the stable to feed the horses their hay, they did not see the dragon-colt horse. After the two of them had searched for the horse all day, they still had not found a single trace. The two of them were very anxious, "What to do if the commander finds out? When some days ago one of the horses died of a disease, it was said that it had died of starvation because it had received insufficient food, and those two men were killed. Now today this horse has disappeared, our lives are in danger too!" That very night they sneaked away and fled the city, and we will hear no more of them. But then one day, when Commander Yang had to attend the morning audience at court, he ordered his underlings to bring him this dragon-colt horse because he wanted to ride it to court. When his underlings came to the stable, the dragon-colt horse had disappeared, and they reported to their master that the dragon-colt horse was not to be found. The commander promptly called for a roll-call of the grooms, and Zhang Xing and Li Wang were found to be missing. So this horse must have been stolen by these two, who then fled! The commander thereupon dispatched men in all directions to track them down and arrest them.

Sing:

The commander-in-chief immediately issued an order,
Ordering for a roll-call of the grooms from the garden.
His underlings thereupon promptly reported to him
That both Zhang Xing and Li Wang had disappeared.
    As the men and the horse had disappeared on this day,
His Excellency immediately flew into a towering rage.
"It must have been these fellows who stole the horse —
Have posters put up for their arrest at all city gates!"

But let's not sing in our tale of the commander-in-chief,
Let's sing of the upright minister Dragon-Design Bao.
    He once again told his wife to go to the imperial court,
And ask to borrow the precious treasure like before.
Lady Li could do little else but go there once again,
And straightaway she arrived at the Palace Main Gate.
    With twenty-four bows — a longevity like a mountain;
Wishing a myriad of years, calling herself, "Your servant."
Her lord and king graciously allowed her to be seated:
"Dear lady, how has your husband's illness developed?"
    Lady Li fell down on her knees before the golden steps:
"May Your Majesty be so kind as to listen to my words.

If I come to talk about the disease of my dear husband,
I am afraid that very soon he'll join the Lord of Shade.
    So I have come here once again to report on this matter,
And I hope that Your Majesty will deign to listen to me.
If Your Majesty will save my husband's life from danger,
We will never forget your kind grace till the day we die."
    Hearing this, the emperor left and entered the Rear Palace,
Where he visited Her Majesty, the empress-dowager.
The emperor promptly addressed her in the following way:
"My dear mother, please listen to what I have to say.
    I've been told that Minister Bao of the Southern Office
Very soon, it is to be feared, will join the Lord of Shade.
So please be so kind for this one time, for my sake,
To let him borrow for a while that belt made of black silk."
    Her Majesty the empress-dowager said she was unwilling,
On no account would she save that man surnamed Bao.
When the emperor was told so, he was very much annoyed,
And he said to the empress-dowager: "Now please listen.
    In case His Excellency Bao will not be with us anymore,
On whom will this one country, this one realm, then rely?
If this man ever dies, we will have to give this empire
With all its fine mountains and streams to somebody else!"
    When the empress-dowager heard him talk in this manner,
She gave in and promptly produced the precious treasure.
Observing this, the emperor was overcome with joy, and
Promptly went back, carrying the belt in a golden tray.
    Straightaway he returned to the main hall of the palace,
And there he entrusted the magical object to Lady Li.
When Lady Li had received this belt made of black silk,
She took her leave of the emperor, and left the palace hall.
    Arriving at the Main Gate, she mounted her sedan chair,
Straightaway returning to the prefectural office of Kaifeng.

When Lady Li dismounted from her sedan chair and entered,
His Excellency greeted her, and asked how things had gone.
Lady Li thereupon produced the belt made of black silk,
And she immediately presented the belt to His Excellency.
    When Judge Bao took it in his hands and had a good look,
A ray of light rose up and penetrated the clouds of heaven.

Seeing this, Judge Bao exclaimed: "How extraordinary!
This object is truly exceptional, a true priceless treasure!"
   He thereupon ordered his officers to waste no moment,
But to fetch him the dead body from the western corridor.
He then told them to wash it with fragrant warm water,
And to dress the body in a complete set of new clothes.
   Even though the corpse had been buried for half a year,
The body had not changed in even the slightest detail.
They thereupon tied the black silk belt around his waist,
And Judge Bao sat down to see how things would develop.
   After all together roughly a full hour had passed,
The three souls and seven spirits returned to the body.
Thirty officers all hurried over to come and see this,
And each and every one who saw this was stupefied!
   He exactly resembled one who revives from a stupor,
He looked like one who wakes up from a deep sleep.
   He widely opened his eyes to observe his surroundings,
And recognized Dragon-Design Bao, the prefectural judge.
The latter once had judged a case in the Western Capital;
Today he saw that star that brightens the night again.
   Zhang Wengui hastened to get on his feet and bow down,
While tears coursed down his cheeks in great profusion.
Judge Bao thereupon immediately gave his orders:
"Let me hear all details of the case, from the beginning.
   In which prefecture do you live? And in which district?
What is your surname and name? Where are you from?
For what reason did you come to the Eastern Capital?
Who killed you, so you had to join the Lord of Shade?"
   The student Wengui bowed down with lowered head,
"Revered Judge, please listen to what I have to say.
I lack the energy and strength to tell you everything,
So allow me to present this statement for your perusal.

Speak:

The person who presents this statement, Zhang Wengui, who is without disease, and hails from Xishui District in Xizhou Prefecture, states as follows:
   In the Second Month of the twelfth year of the reign period Taiping a yellow placard was posted in our district, which widely summoned all

excellent gentlemen who studied books. I therefore left in search
of fame and profit, and when I passed through the Taihang Mountain,
I unexpectedly ran into the Great King of Jingshan, who arrested me in
front of the mountain, and tied me to a pillar. After he had first killed my
two servants, I begged the Great King: 'I am a student in the school of
Confucius, so please spare my life!' It happened that the Prince of Fengdu
on the other side of the mountain was celebrating his birthday and invited
the Great King and his wife to the party. Now the Great King had a
daughter who was called Blue Lotus, who came out to walk about and
enjoy the mountain scenery, and when she saw me tied to a pillar, she set
me free, and asked me for my background. It turned out that she and I
had been born in the same year, in the same month, on the same day, and
at the same hour. This maiden became my wife of her own free will, and
gave me three magical objects: a belt of blue jade, a free-roaming never-
ending jug, and a warm and cold cup, so I could offer them to the court.
When I arrived at the Eastern Capital, I took a room at the establishment
of the innkeeper Yang on Bamboo Stave Lane. When Yang the Second
noticed my three magical treasures, he was overcome by desire, so he set
out a banquet at midnight, forced me to drink till I was drunk, strangled
me with a piece of white silk of one *zhang* and two feet and a bamboo
flute with nine nodes, and then buried me in the back garden. He also got
his hands on my dragon-colt horse, ten-thousand green bats, one hundred
ounces of yellow gold, and ten horse-shoe ingots of silver.

    Yang the Second committed murder wanting my wealth, and this cruel
wrong and blatant injustice has not yet been undone. I therefore have
drawn up this statement, in order to report this matter to His Excellency
the prefectural judge, so he may scrutinize the situation and act
accordingly.

    Drawn up on a day of the Second Month of the twelfth year of the
reign period Taiping.

Sing:

As soon as Judge Bao had read this person's statement,
He exclaimed: "This man surnamed Yang is intolerable!
In this universe which is at peace, in this world so pure,
We have a murderer right here in the emperor's capital!"
    Judge Bao then addressed Wengui in the following way:
"My dear student, please listen to what I have to tell you.

Know that Yang by donating these treasures to the court
Was able to save Her Majesty the empress-dowager's life.
The imperial court appointed him to a very high office,
So he has risen to an exceedingly high position and status.

He is the commander-in-chief of eighty-four prefectures,
Has been given the income of one-half of eight provinces.
When he passes in front of my prefectural office building,
His guards give three shouts as they pass before the gate.

One day as my court was in session here in this hall,
A horse walked in, carrying your corpse on its back.
I questioned the horse, but the horse could not speak,
So I had to do a lot of thinking to deal with this case.

I feigned to be ill while hiding here in the office, and
In this manner I borrowed this treasure from the court.
Only by borrowing this belt of black silk and blue jade
Was I able to save you and bring you back to life again."

Hearing this, Wengui bowed while lowering his head:
"By burning my flesh as incense I could not repay you!
I humbly pray that Your Excellency will on my behalf
See that justice is done in this case — out of pity for me!"

Judge Bao instructed some of his underlings, saying:
"Now tell them to bring out that horse, and get it here."
These two underlings thereupon wasted no moment
And brought the dragon-colt horse to the judge's hall.

When it arrived in front of the steps of the judge's hall,
It widely opened its eyes and then looked all around.
And when the dragon-colt horse had seen Zhang Wengui,
It knelt down with lowered head, weeping profusely.

When Wengui saw this, he too burst out in tears —
For half a year he had not seen this dragon-colt horse.
"If you, my horse, had not carried me to this place,
How could my life have been saved, my soul restored?"

When His Excellency saw this, he too heaved a sigh:
"It may be an animal, but still has such a noble heart!"

Dragon-Design Bao thereupon ordered that a banquet
Should be spread out to feast the man surnamed Zhang.
Serving girls with young faces poured him his wine,
And handsome singers sang songs to please his mind.

Before one cup was finished, another cup followed;
Before one glass was emptied, another one was filled.
When the wine reached the third bowl and fifth cup,
His Excellency pondered this matter most carefully.
    "If one comes to speak of Commander-in-Chief Yang,
He is the most revered of all four hundred court officials.
His guards at all times consist of three hundred people,
So who would dare to arrest this man out on the streets?"
    His Excellency then came up with some clever scheme,
Capable to dredge up a dragon, a report to the Throne.
He thereupon ordered the western study to be prepared
For Wengui, so he could stay there for the time being.

Let's not sing in our tale of what happened that night —
Let's just wait for the bright sky of the next morning.
    When the Golden Rooster cried out in Fusang country,
And when bells of bronze dismissed the stars in the sky,
His Excellency rose to his feet in his official mansion,
And put on his court gown in order to see the emperor.
    The fifth watch's third quarter: the King ascended the hall,
And the civil and military officials all entered the gate.
With twenty-four bows — longevity like a mountain;
Wishing him ten thousand years, they said, "Your servants!"
    On his throne the Humane Ancestor ordered his officials:
"You, civil officials and military officers, all listen to Us.
If there is any business, may some high official report on it;
If there is no business, all ranks are allowed to exit the gate."
    Before the emperor had even finished giving his order,
One minister rushed forward, leaving his place in the ranks.
A purple gown, an ivory tablet, and a belt made of gold —
Holding his tablet before his breast, he addressed the king.
    When the emperor with his dragon eyes observed him,
It turned out to be that upright minister Dragon-Design Bao.
    Judge Bao at this moment had hastened to kneel down,
So the Sagely Ruler helped the man surnamed Bao to rise.
He first allowed him to take a seat on a brocaded stool,
And then addressed him with the following question:

"Ever since you, dear minister, suffered from that illness,
We have been deeply worried, right to our heart and liver!
Only today, now you are healthy again, fully recovered,
Are we able to be at ease once again for the first time!"

Judge Bao rose from his seat and expressed his gratitude:
"I'm deeply grateful for the grace bestowed on my person.
The only thing is that my wife in her lack of discernment
Had made a vow that I personally would wear a cangue.

As today I want to fulfill this vow of wearing a cangue,
I would like that Your Majesty would order all officials,
Both the two hundred officials and two hundred officers,
To come to Kaifeng Prefecture to drink a round of wine."

When the emperor heard this, he agreed to this proposal,
And there in court he gave the order to all his officials:
"Because today Dragon-Design Bao will fulfill his vow,
All you officials should go to his place to have a drink!"

Judge Bao expressed his gratitude and returned to his office —
Let's sing of that other man, Commander-in-Chief Yang!
When he returned to his mansion, he was not happy at all:
His face was clouded by worries and bereft of all pleasure.

Speak:

When Commander-in-Chief Yang returned to his mansion and was
welcomed by his wife, the latter saw that his face had a worried expression,
so she asked him: "My husband, today your office is high and your
position grand — much better than when you were an innkeeper! So why
are you so annoyed?" Her husband replied: "My dear wife, of course you
don't know why! Today Minister Bao wants to fulfill his vow of wearing a
cangue, and His Majesty has ordered all four hundred civil and military
officials to go to his mansion and have a drink!

Sing:

Of the four hundred civil and military officials at court,
The only one I have to fear is that man surnamed Bao!"
His wife answered her husband in the following way:
"You should be ashamed to call yourself a man, a guy!

You have the highest office of all officials at court,
So why should you fear someone with a lower office?
If that man called Bao acts without any rhyme or reason,
Have him beheaded first, and then report to the Throne!"
  When her husband heard this, he was filled with joy:
"My dear wife, what you say hits the nail on its head!"
The commander-in-chief then hastily mounted his horse,
And went off to the mansion of the prefect of Kaifeng.

The four hundred officials all arrived at Bao's mansion,
Leading goats and carrying wine they arrived at the gate.
Judge Bao at this time had made all required preparations,
And the paraphernalia were all set out at the entrance.
  A heavy wooden cangue was placed before the steps,
Goalkeepers and policemen were arranged in two rows.
Large bands of musicians all day faced small bands;
All civil and military officials walked the whole way.
  The common people of the whole town came to watch,
And it brought the population of the whole town together.
Straightaway they came to the prefectural office of Kaifeng,
And they only left after the cangue had been put down.[24]
  The officials then returned to Kaifeng Prefecture,
Where a banquet had been set out in the main hall, and
Judge Bao then invited all officials to take their seats,
To take their seats according to their rank, high or low.
  Those whose offices were high were seated in the hall,
Those whose offices were lower were all seated outside.
His Excellency Judge Bao was seated in the host's seat,
And throughout the hall the music resounded of drums.

---

[24] The description of the ritual is so short it hardly makes sense, but we most likely have to assume that Judge Bao as an act of penance, thanking the gods for his miraculous recovery, carries a heavy cangue from the prefectural office to the temple of the Great Thearch of the Eastern Marchmount, and there donates the cangue to the god. On his long walk he will have been preceded by musicians and followed by the officials on foot. Wu Zimu's *Mengliang lu* (Millet Dream Record) of 1334, in its description of the celebration of the birthday of the Great Thearch of the Eastern Marchmount on the 28th day of the Third Month in the Southern Song Capital of Hangzhou, mentions "groups of people wearing cangues like heavy criminals." See Meng Yuanlao et al. *Dongjing meng Hua lu (wai sizhong)*, Beijing: Zhonghua shuju, 1962, p. 151.

All kinds of entertainers and musicians had arrived,
Performing their plays to reed-organs, flutes and lutes.
After many bowls of wine, when the cups fell down,
Dragon-Design Bao raised himself from his seat.

Speak:

While Commander-in-Chief Yang and the other officials were drinking,
Judge Bao rose from his seat and went out, where he told the three
hundred officers under his command: "When the party is over, you will all
arrest Commander-in-Chief Yang. Each of you will be rewarded with one
jug of wine and one pound of lamb." Hearing this, the officers were filled
with joy, and replied they would act on his orders!

Sing:

Judge Bao thereupon turned around and went back,
He went back to the banquet and drank some wine.
He offered some wine to the commander-in-chief:
"Many thanks for taking the trouble to come here!"
    Dragon-Design Bao addressed the commander-in-chief:
"Tonight I had a dream which was very clear indeed!
Someone from the Western Capital suffered a wrong;
Here in the Eastern Capital a murder was committed.
    Let me tell you the story of a certain Zhang Wengui,
Who was carrying three priceless magical objects.
He intended to present these treasures to the court,
And rented a room at your place, commander-in-chief.
    You, commander-in-chief, strangled Zhang Wengui,
Because you wanted to lay your hands on his treasures.
Then you presented these magical objects to the court:
By robbing him of his merits, you obtained your rank!"
    Hearing this, the commander-in-chief, highly upset,
Loudly cursed Judge Bao: "You cheating bastard!
Tomorrow at court I will report you to His Majesty.
You can count on it that you'll be cut at the waist!"
    As he heard this, Judge Bao could only smile faintly,
And he promptly called for Zhang Wengui to appear.
When he was called, Wengui hurriedly came out, and
In the hall he recognized that man surnamed Yang.

Walking up to him, he grasped Commander Yang,
Crying: "Why did you strangle me, causing my death?"
When Yang the Second heard this, he was scared to death —
Caught like a swallow or sparrow grabbed by a hawk!
    The other four hundred court officials lost their color,
And each of them thanked for the wine and went off.
Once outside Kaifeng Prefecture, they said: "Luckily
We could escape from the hell of Kaifeng Prefecture!"

Let's not sing of the officials who went back home —
Let's sing of the upright minister, Dragon-Design Bao!
He promptly ordered the wardens and prison guards
To drag the man surnamed Yang before the office hall.
    More than a hundred strokes of the yellow-thorn cudgel:
His skin and flesh were beaten — he was bleeding all over.
One enormous cangue was locked around his neck —
Weigh it on a balance, and it came to a hundred pounds!
    "Now confess the full truth, according to the facts,
And I will sentence you lightly — a light punishment!
But if you still refuse to confess to the facts here today,
We will apply one more torture and get a confession."
    Tears coursed down from the eyes of Yang the Second,
And while he did not say a word, he thought to himself:
"Of course I would not want to confess here today, but
How could I bear yet another questioning and beating?
    But if I now suddenly would confess to the murder,
I would involve all the members of my whole family.
Too bad I did not think this through wisely at the time!
Now I feel remorse, there is no way to flee anymore!"
    So Yang the Second could do nothing but draft a confession:
"Your Excellency Bao, please listen to what I will say.
    I've always been an inhabitant of the Eastern Capital;
I'm the second among my brothers, my surname is Yang.
All through my life my family has been running an inn,
On Bamboo Stave Lane, where I was born and grew up.
    One day a student came and wanted to rent a room;
This man informed us that his surname was Zhang.
With him he carried three priceless magical objects,
And he came to our place, staying on the second floor.

At midnight or thereabouts he tried out his treasures,
And instrumental music resounded through the house.
I was startled awake by this loud noise and ruckus,
And I went upstairs to ask him what was going on.
 The young man then showed me his three treasures,
Which were truly exceptional and priceless objects.
As soon as I saw them, I harbored an evil desire,
And I set out a banquet to entertain him with wine.
 And when I had made sure that he was quite drunk,
I strangled him with white silk, so he passed away.
I obtained the belt of black silk and blue jade,
And secondly the free-roaming, never-ending jug.
 Thirdly I also obtained the warm and cold cup,
Together with ten thousand or more green bats.
On top of that there was his dragon-colt horse, and
Gold and silver and other goods, and his clothes."
 Each and every detail he confessed that very day,
And he wrote out his confession in a very clear way.
When His Excellency saw it, he exclaimed: "Alas!
In the Imperial Capital a murder has been committed!"

He ordered to have him taken to the Western Prison,
And Judge Bao went to court to meet with the emperor.
He straightaway entered, and reported to the Throne:
"Your Majesty, please be so kind as to listen to me."
 He then reported to the Throne about Commander Yang:
"This man has been a criminal who breaks the law!
He strangled Zhang Wengui of the Western Capital,
And in this devious way obtained his magical objects.
 I invited that man to the office of Kaifeng Prefecture,
And then immediately arrested that man named Yang.
At present he is locked up in the Western Prison, and
I have come on purpose to report to Your Majesty."
 When he heard this report the emperor was annoyed:
"This Judge Bao is really a quite detestable creature!
He has barely recovered from a life-threatening illness,
And here he comes again, making enemies at court!"
 [And he said:] "Now go back to Kaifeng Prefecture
And release that man surnamed Yang from his prison.

If Her Majesty my mother comes to learn of this matter,
You, Judge Bao, will have committed a serious crime!"
    Judge Bao stepped forward and reported once more:
"The confession he has written spells it out very clearly.
This is the confession which Yang the Second has signed.
Please allow me to present it Your Sagely Majesty!"
    When the emperor had finished reading the confession,
He summoned Judge Bao and questioned him as follows:
"Who may have been the person to lodge an accusation?
And what kind of evidence was presented in your hall?"
    Dragon-Design Bao reported to the emperor, saying:
"A horse carried the corpse to the gate of my hall!"

Speak:

Judge Bao then rose to his feet and reported: "Your Majesty, one day when
I was holding court, I suddenly saw a dragon-colt horse which carried a
corpse arriving before my hall, where it knelt down on the earth. Your
servant questioned the horse, but the horse could not speak. I concluded
that this must be a case of grave injustice, and overcome by frustration I fell
ill. Therefore I borrowed the belt of black silk and blue jade from Your
Majesty, not only in order to save my own life, but also in order to bring that
man back to life. Only after he had given me a clear statement, did I dare
arrest Yang the Second. If Your Majesty does not believe me, that man is still
staying at my office." When His Majesty heard this report, he was stupefied.

Sing:

When the emperor saw this report, he ordered a summons,
And so summoned to court the man surnamed Zhang.
When Wengui saw that he was summoned by the emperor,
He came to court as fast as fire to meet with His Majesty.
    The emperor raised himself from his dragon-throne,
And questioned him while leaning on the golden railing.
    "In which prefecture do you live? And in which district?
What is your name and surname? Where do you live?
For what reason did you come to the Eastern Capital?
Who killed you so you had to join the Lord of Shade?"
    Before the golden steps Wengui answered the emperor:
"Your Majesty, please be so kind as to listen to me.

Your humble servant is domiciled in Henan Prefecture,
And it was in Xishui District that I was born and grew up.
My father there is Millionaire Zhang who has lots of cash,
And I am the only, really the very only son he has sired.
    Since my youth I've studied the books, practiced letters,
And my school name was Wengui as I read the books.
When I heard that Your Majesty would hold an exam,
I left for the Eastern Capital in search of fame and profit.
    When I had been on the road for a number of days,
I arrived at the foot of a forested mountain range.
The name of the mountain was Taihang Mountain,
And while traveling I ran into the Lord of Jingshan there.
    Having arrested your servant, he took me to his lair,
At that time his intention was to kill my humble person.
And after he had first done away with my two servants,
He had me tied to a pillar in his Flaying Pavilion.
    But when he was invited by the Great King of Fengdu,
The Lord of Jingshan left to have a few drinks there.
Now it happened that this princeling had a daughter,
Who went by the name of Princess Blue Lotus.
    On this day she left the palace to go for a walk,
And in this way she ended up discovering my person.
When the princess had seen me, she questioned me,
And I replied fully in all detail to her many queries.
    She also asked me how old your humble servant was,
In what year I was born, in what month, at which hour?
It turned out we were born in the same year and month,
And on top of that on the same day, at the same hour!
    Hearing this, the princess was overcome with joy,
And she and I tied the knot and became man and wife.
The princess also gave me the three precious treasures,
In order that I should present them to Your Majesty.
    The first of these was a belt of black silk and blue jade,
And the second was a free-roaming, never-ending jug.
The third of these objects was a warm and cold cup —
Carrying these with me I arrived at the Eastern Capital.
    I took a room at the inn of the innkeeper Yang the Second,
And when it was almost midnight, in the third watch,
Your humble servant made a test of the magical objects,
And in this way I aroused the innkeeper, Mr. Yang.

He climbed the stairs to the second floor and asked me
For what reason musical instruments made such noise?
Because he questioned me so insistently, your servant
Eventually showed him these three priceless treasures.

Seeing these, Yang the Second harbored an evil desire,
And spread a banquet, pouring me drinks till I was drunk.
And after he had killed me by strangling my person,
He had me buried in the garden behind his house.

But thanks to High Heaven I was saved in the end,
Because my body was removed from the garden.
Now I today am allowed to gaze on Your Majesty,
I'm an old mirror polished again, regaining its light."

Hearing this report, His Majesty was very pleased,
And he allowed Minister Zhang to sit down on a stool.
He ordered an imperial banquet for his entertainment,
And with the imperial brush he wrote out his title.

On a piece of red silk of one *zhang* and two feet
He wrote out the high office to which he was appointed:
Commander-in-chief of eighty-four prefectures,
And one-half of the income of eight provinces!
His monthly income was to be more than three thousand —
The most honored one of the four hundred court officials!

The emperor also dispatched messengers in all haste
To write a letter and deliver it to the Lord of Jingshan,
And also to the man's daughter, Princess Blue Lotus —
Those two imperial messengers immediately set out.

Let's not sing of the messengers trekking by day and night,
Let's sing of the emperor holding the true mandate at court.

He promptly issued an order to Judge Bao which stated
That the whole family of Yang the Second was to be killed.
Commander-in-Chief Yang was taken from his prison
And taken to court to appear before His Sagely Majesty.

When the emperor saw him, he loudly cursed him as
A thief and a murderer, a criminal without conscience!
He then ordered the executioners to waste no moment
In taking him to the execution grounds for his beheading!

As soon as the executioners had received this instruction,
They promptly took hold of Yang the Second and set out.

And when the latter arrived at the execution grounds,
He was overcome by remorse for his earlier desire.

    The two executioners were truly most brave and fierce,
The supervising official resembled the god Huge Spirit.[25]
After waiting for the third quarter of the noon hour,
The executioners raised their swords as they told him:

    "We act by order of the emperor, and not on our own,
So do not lodge an accusation against us down below!"
And when they loudly shouted the single word "Hit!"
His head fell to the ground as the swords came down.

    The emperor also issued yet another edict, ordering
The beheading of all members of the Yang household.
Also his mansion was to be immediately taken down,
And his property was to be confiscated to the last cent.

    The emperor thereupon also issued an edict ordering
The construction of a new mansion for Minister Zhang.
For this purpose he made available ten thousand strings,
And in the Eastern Capital the mansion was constructed.

    Each and every kind of artisan joined the construction,
And within a month the new mansion had been built.
When other officials passed in front of his mansion,
They dismounted from their horses in front of his gate.

    Before the golden steps Wengui thanked the emperor,
With twenty-four bows for the emperor's many favors.

    But let's not sing of Commander-in-Chief Zhang Wengui,
Let's change the subject, sing of the imperial messengers!
As the relay horses never stopped, they went very fast,
Traveling by night and day they soon reached the borders.

    And when they arrived at the Taihang mountainrange,
The soldiers who were on duty asked them who they were.
"Give us your yellow gold if you want to buy your way,
We will spare your life, allow you to cross the mountain!"

    The imperial messengers addressed them as follows:
"You soldiers, please listen to what we have to say.

---

[25] Huge Spirit (Juling) is a giant divinity who with one stroke of his ax separated Mt. Hua from Taihang Mountain, providing the Yellow River a passage to the sea.

We are messengers dispatched by the imperial court,
We have been dispatched to invite the Lord of Jingshan."
    The bandit soldiers immediately wasted no moment,
But took them to their mountain lair for questioning.
In front of the hall the generalissimo asked them:
"From which prefecture are you? From which district?"
    The two messengers replied in the following words:
"Your Princely Majesty, please listen to what we'll say.
We are messengers sent here by the Humane Ancestor,
For summoning Your Majesty to His imperial court."

Speak:

When these two imperial messengers arrived at the foot of Taihang
Mountain, the extensive scenery was extraordinary. They were escorted by
bandit soldiers, and when they arrived in front of the great hall, the
generalissimo asked them: "Where are you from?" The two men replied:
"Your Majesty, we are imperial messengers of the emperor, the Humane
Ancestor. We have arrived here bearing an imperial edict which summons
Your Majesty to join the court, which allows for no delays." The Great
King set up incense and an altar, and after he had received the edict, he
saw that it read:

> "We, the Son of Heaven of the state of Song, transmit these
> words to the Prince of Jingshan. When recently the student
> Zhang Wengui from Henan Prefecture in the Western Capital
> Region passed in front of your mountain because he was going
> to the capital in search of an office, he was taken by you,
> Generalissimo, to your mountain lair, but just when you were
> about to kill him, you were invited by the Prince of Fengdu to
> have some drinks. Your Majesty has one daughter, named
> Princess Blue Lotus, and she agreed to become his wife. At
> present, Zhang Wengui is at Our court, where he has been
> appointed commander-in-chief of eighty-four prefectures. So We
> invite Your Majesty and Princess Blue Lotus so she may be
> united in wedlock with Zhang Wengui. Upon arrival at court
> you will be appointed to office."

Sing:

When the Great King had seen this, he was taken aback,
Sunken in thought for a while, he said not a single word.
He reconsidered his thoughts of the last few months —
Indeed, there had been that student he had captured.

"Just when I was about to have that student beheaded,
The Prince of Fengdu invited me to have some wine.
My wife and I left together to go to that party over there,
And I tied that student to a pillar in my Flaying Pavilion.

The Prince of Fengdu kept us with him at his place,
And we have only now returned after six months or so.
This morning for the first time I remembered that man,
And I was just about to inquire what happened to him.

It must be, I am sure, that during our absence from here
Blue Lotus became intimate with that young student!"
The Great King hit the table and roared in a fit of rage,
"Damn you, you rotten cheap slut with no morals at all!
While I am here on this mountain the king of the hill,
You have shamed me today and robbed me of my honor!"

He then ordered his bandit soldiers to waste no moment
But to enter the palace and there arrest his own daughter.
These bandit soldiers immediately entered the Rear Palace,
And they told her everything they knew in great detail.

"Messengers from the emperor arrived with a summons,
And they claimed that you have married Zhang Wengui.
In the hall our lord and king told us to summon you —
We don't know why, but he is gnashing his teeth in rage!"

When Princess Blue Lotus had considered this matter,
She went to the Changyang Hall to appeal to her mother.
She told her what had happened, from the very beginning,
And when her mother had heard this, she was stupefied.

"My daughter, you have acted in a most reckless manner
By giving yourself to some man on your own initiative!"
Blue Lotus again and again beseeched her dear mother:
"Please save my life, please save me from a certain death!"

As soon as her mother saw her child speaking like this,
She considered that this was her own darling daughter.
Mother and daughter thereupon both raised themselves,
And straightaway they arrived in front of the great hall.

When they arrived there, they both deeply bowed down,
But, seeing them, the Great King was filled with rage.
He immediately loudly cursed his own darling daughter:
"Cheap slut without any morals, you slept with a man!"
    Blue Lotus had to reply to his words, and she said:
"My father and king, please calm your towering rage!
This happened not because my body desired a husband,
But this was determined by karma from an earlier life.
    When I went out for a walk on that one particular day,
I discovered that student as I pursued my promenade.
And when I addressed him with a number of questions,
His answers made our karmic affinity quite obvious.
    He was born in the same year and month as I was,
And that is the reason why we became man and wife.
But because I was afraid that you two would come back,
I only kept him for one night, then sent him on his way!"
    Hearing this, the Great King was very much annoyed:
"Damn you, you rotten cheap slut with no morals at all!"
He loudly ordered the bandit soldiers to promptly kill her,
He ordered her beheaded — she was not allowed to live!
    Her mother thereupon tried to talk him around, saying:
"Your Majesty, please listen to what I have to tell you.
    Husband and wife is not a matter decided in the present,
These people were joined together five hundred years ago.
Throughout our married life we only had this daughter,
So how can you bear to discard her life and her soul?"
    As the Great King was talked to by his own wife,
He was mulling the matter over in his heart, and thought:
"Even though I may be a king here on top of my hill,
My title is only that of a robber hiding in the brush."
    The Great King thereupon promptly changed his mind:
"It would be unbearable to discard the life of this child!
I must conclude that this marriage was destined to be,
And my daughter's husband has become an official.
    She too must be destined to rise to a high rank later!"
So he pardoned his daughter's life in front of the hall.
The Great King also ordered a banquet to be laid out
To entertain the imperial messengers from the court.

The Great King instructed his bandit soldiers as follows:
"Prepare a sedan chair and a horse for a trip to the capital!"
When he had finished his wine, he mounted his horse,
And with Princess Blue Lotus he set out on the journey.

Generalissimo Zhao rode a horse with red manes, and
Princess Blue Lotus rode a brightly painted sedan chair.
The two imperial messengers hastily mounted their horses,
They traveled as fast as clouds that are blown by the wind.

Let's not sing at all about what happened on the road —
Eventually they arrived at the emperor's capital city.
They entered the city wall, and saw wealth and splendor;
Then entered the court to stay at the imperial guest house.

They waited till the fifth watch, when dawn clears the sky,
And then entered the palace yard to meet with His Majesty.
The third quarter of the fifth watch: the king entered the hall,
And the civil and military officials entered the inner gate.

The two messengers wasted no moment, but went in,
According to their rank, in order to see His Majesty.
With twenty-four bows — longevity like a mountain;
Wishing him ten thousand years, they said: "Your servant."

Their lord and king immediately issued an edict,
And the civil and military officials listened to his edict:
"If there is any business, may some high official report;
If there is no business, may all you officials exit again."

Even before the Son of Heaven had finished speaking,
The two messengers came forward to report to the king.

"Bearing the edict of Your Majesty, the two of us
Went to Taihang Mountain to invite the Lord of Jingshan.
Currently he and his daughter, Princess Blue Lotus,
Are awaiting Your orders outside the gate of the court."

Hearing this, the Humane Ancestor was filled with joy:
"Summon him with a golden plaque, no delay is allowed!"
And when the Great King now received this summons,
He straightaway entered to see the His Sagely Majesty.

In front of the hall, the Great King deeply bowed down;
The Humane Ancestor helped him to rise from the dust.
He granted him a brocade stool to sit down facing him —
One cup of imperial tea, and then three rounds of wine.

The emperor thereupon issued yet another edict,
By which he summoned to court Princess Blue Lotus.
When Blue Lotus was summoned she entered the court,
And in front of the jade steps she greeted His Majesty.

With twenty-four bows — longevity like a mountain;
Wishing the king a myriad of years on the dragon-throne!
"The sun and the moon may be high, yet are easily seen;
It is a rare opportunity now for me to see Your Majesty!

If today I am allowed to see the face of my lord and king,
It must be because of the karma of burning good incense."
The emperor then addressed them in the following words:
"Generalissimo, please listen to what I have to tell you.

This spring there was a certain student, Zhang Wengui,
Who passed by your mountain on his way to the capital.
However, he was arrested by you, Great King, and then
Taken to your mountain lair for further questioning.

Just as you were about to have that student killed,
The King of Fengdu invited you to have some drinks.
This had to be so in order for Princess Blue Lotus
To tie the knot as man and wife with Zhang Wengui.

Your daughter gave the student three magical objects
To take with him and to present to Us, the emperor.
But when he arrived in this city of the Eastern Capital,
He took a room in an inn on Bamboo Stave Lane.

The innkeeper of that inn, one Yang Little Second,
Strangled the student in the third watch of the night.
And when Her Majesty the empress-dowager fell ill,
It was he who presented these three priceless treasures.

Because We did not realize the injustice involved,
We appointed that man surnamed Yang to high office.
Now Wengui was also the owner of a dragon-colt horse,
Which was kept in the rear garden of the Yang mansion.

The horse carried the corpse to Kaifeng Prefecture,
Where the animal was questioned by Dragon-Design Bao.
By borrowing the true treasure he restored him to life,
And Zhang Wengui provided a full account of the facts.

Yang the Second and his whole family have been killed;
Minister Zhang has been appointed to very high office:
He is commander-in-chief of eighty-four prefectures,
And receives as income one-half of eight provinces.

When some time ago Minister Zhang reported to Us,
He told Us the whole story, from the very beginning.
Great King, you have a daughter, called Blue Lotus,
Who is meant to be the wife of our Minister Zhang."

In the hall the Humane Ancestor then rose to his feet,
And urgently summoned all civil and military officials.
When the officials learned they were summoned again,
They hastily returned to the court to see the emperor.
  The officials and officers greeted His Imperial Majesty,
Who issued the following edict to his asscmbled officials:
  "At present the King of Jingshan is staying at court,
And with him he has brought his daughter Blue Lotus.
We now have summoned you officials to deliberate
Which office and title should be given to these persons."
  Even before the emperor had finished these words,
The man surnamed Bao came forward from the ranks.
Judge Bao stepped forward and proposed as follows:
"Your Majesty, please be so kind as to listen to me!
  If Your Majesty would consider my humble suggestion,
You should ennoble him as the Prince of No Worry.
Your Majesty should also ennoble the prince's wife,
And ennoble her as a High Lady Protecting the Country.
  Thirdly, Your Majesty should ennoble Blue Lotus,
Ennoble her as the High Lady who Presented Treasure."
  The emperor then addressed him in the following way:
"Generalissimo, please listen to what I have to tell you.
Do not continue your life as a thief and highway bandit,
But just enjoy your emoluments for the rest of your life."
  The Great King immediately answered the emperor:
"Your Majesty, allow me to express my deep gratitude!"
Thereupon a banquet was laid out in front of the hall,
And the Great King was feasted most sumptuously.
  When the banquet was finished, he rose to his feet;
The Great King thanked the emperor, and went back.

His Imperial Majesty then issued yet one more edict,
And by this edict he summoned the man named Zhang.
The emperor summoned his minister Zhang Wengui,
And Wengui hastened to court to meet with the emperor.

The emperor thereupon addressed him as follows:
"We hereby order the celebration of your wedding.
The wedding will be celebrated in Kaifeng Prefecture,
And We will in person serve as your matchmaker."

He also ordered the four hundred officials at court
All to go to Kaifeng Prefecture to have some drinks.
Judge Bao immediately put the office in good order,
And a banquet was laid out in the prefectural hall.

On the eastern wall a landscape painting was hung;
On the western side drunken immortals were hung.
The china was all set out on tables of eaglewood,
And the brocade stools were all made of finest silks.

Let's not sing of the banquet at Judge Bao's place,
Let's only sing how the emperor left the palace.
Accompanied by civil officials and military men,
The imperial cortege departed through the gate.

Two hundred civil officials, two hundred officers,
Together with the Lord of Jingshan of Mt. Taihang.
Banners and insignia in all colors were carried ahead,
And all families along the road burned incense.

Straightaway he arrived at Kaifeng Prefecture,
Where a banquet had been laid out in the hall.
Facing south, the emperor took his seat, and
The Lord of Jingshan sat on his eastern side.

The civil and military officials all arrived, and
Were ordered to take their seats according to rank.
Twenty-four glasses of wine [...]
All officials bowed [...]

The imperial cortege then returned to the palace,
And the officials all returned to their own mansions.

Let me admonish you never to commit any evil deed:
Heaven and Earth and the gods will all be witnesses.
If a man does good deeds, Heaven will send blessing;
If you commit devious deeds, disasters will follow.

People of this world, do not imitate Yang the Second,
He ruined his heart out of desire for another man's goods.
But if you in your life will always practice good deeds,
Heaven and Earth will have fortune's star shine on you.

But only in the case of the student Zhang Wengui,
A man was brought back to life following his death.
Today I have sung his book and I've reached the end,
Presenting it to you gentlemen as entertainment.

Newly Printed, Completely Illustrated, in Prose and in Verse: The Tale of Zhang Wengui. Part Two, The End.

Zhu Yixuan (ed.) (1997). *Ming Chenghua shuochang cihua congkan*, Zhengzhou: Zhongzhou guji chubanshe, pp. 223–251.

The Story of How Shi Guanshou's Wife Liu Dusai on the Night of the Fifteenth, on Superior Prime, Watched the Lanterns. Part One

Completely Illustrated, in Prose and in Verse

After the moment Pangu had divided all-under-heaven,
The Three Lords and Five Thearchs ruled the cosmos.
The virtuous emperors will be renowned for eternity,
Those bereft of the Way create disorder in their court.

With one sentence we raise the subject of the emperor,
Secondly I mention the eternal spring of ancient books.
But let's not sing of the earlier lords and later thearchs —
Our story sings of a lord of the Great Song of China.

One virtuous emperor was that Great Progenitor Zhao;
When he died, the throne passed to the Great Ancestor.
The Great Progenitor, the Great Ancestor, the True Ancestor —
The fourth emperor, the Humane Ancestor, abided by the Way.

The Humane Ancestor was a true arhat of the seven jewels;
Assisted by buddhas, dispatched by devas, ruling the people.
The sun in the southeast shone on the thousand-year palace;
A northwesterly breeze scented the myriad-year pavilion.

Green grasses grew atop the border's high lookout towers;
Nowhere in the eight directions any smoke and dust of war!
The double rings of the sword in its scabbard grew rusty;
The moldy strings snapped on the curved bows put away.

The horses had been set free in the woods to roam at will,
[Along the borders] peace reigned: no troops marched forth.
Fishermen present treasures found [in the Eastern Ocean],
And hunters present a unicorn caught in the mountains.
  What other proof was there of the virtue of this lord and king?
The officials and officers before his throne were immortals!
The astral lord of the civil arts turned into Chancellor Bao;
The astral lord of the martial arts became Generalissimo Di.

Let's not tell about the affairs at the court of the emperor,
Let's tell about a man from a small district in the provinces.
Listen as I sing of a man surnamed Shi from Go Board Lane
In the Western Capital, the capital city of Henan Prefecture.
  The name of this Mister Shi was "the man who is loaded,"
Because his family was wealthy, they had gold and silver.
That's why the neighbors all called him Millionaire Shi,
And that's why they called his old lady "Her Ladyship."
  On the banks he operated shops selling gauze and silk;
On the rivers his boats and ships never stopped sailing.
  The grand halls one after another numbered ten in total;
The gate buildings were so high that people were scared!
[His granaries] were stocked with the five kinds of grain;
Gold and silver filled his storerooms, new silk and brocade.
  A high wall had been constructed all around his mansion;
From the outside you could not see the people inside.
The water lodge on the east was built of carved rafters,
The horse-racing pavilion was decorated in all five colors.
  In front of the mansion one rice hall had been erected,
In which rice was provided to assist poor people all day.
Everything others lacked could be found in his place;
When you came for a loan, you were not thrown out.
  Half of the city used the notes issued by the Shi family,
And the Shi family could feed half the city's population.
Leaving and entering the servants all rode saddled horses;
The young maids they employed all wore golden earrings.
  Ever since Mister Shi had left for the Western Paradise,[1]
The only persons to be left behind were his two dear sons.

---

[1] In other words, since his death.

His eldest son went by the name of Shi Guanshou;
The second son was called Shi Ma — they were those two.
    The wife of the eldest son was called Liu Dusai,
She had been brought home as his bride five years ago.
She was the mother of a boy who had just turned three,
And this one and only child was called Shi Jinbao.

Because it was the night of the fifteenth, Superior Prime,[2]
Every prefecture, every district hung out red lanterns.
Each and every family went out to watch the lanterns
And celebrate the Sagely Divine Lord Equal to Heaven.[3]
    The Turtle Mountain Monastery in the Western Capital
Constructed its Easy Roaming Precious Lantern Frame.[4]
Once in three years they built the Easy Roaming Frame,
And this was a unique and priceless sight to behold.
    Thirteen tall poles were placed in the ground, so tall
The dazzling red lanterns hung halfway to the clouds.
When all three hundred and sixty oil lamps were lit,
All heaven and earth turned red by their light.
    People from all over the world came to watch the sight,
So the Western Capital was filled with crowds of visitors.
    Our story goes that this woman named Liu Dusai
At this time was just sitting in her own private room.
Her two young maids, their hands tucked into their sleeves,
[Said:] "Mylady, please be so kind as to listen to us today!"

Speak:

Her two young maids, their hands tucked into their sleeves in front of their breasts, stepped forward and said: "Mylady, we think we should inform you that at present the Turtle Mountain Monastery in this city has constructed its Easy Roaming Precious Lantern Frame, which is said to be unique in

---

[2] Superior Prime designates the fifteenth of the First Month, the first night of the year of a full moon.

[3] The god of Taishan, the Great Thearch of the Eastern Marchmount.

[4] The "turtle mountains" are the floating islands in the Eastern Ocean that are supported by giant turtles. As the islands are the abode of the immortals, they offer a world of plenty and happiness. But the expression "turtle mountain" was also used for the elaborate displays of lanterns that replicated this world of the immortals. "Free and easy roaming" is a quality of the immortals.

the cosmos, without peer in this world! People from every prefecture, garrison, county and district throughout the world come here to watch these lanterns — so why don't you have some fun and go and watch them?" When their mistress heard this, she was very pleased, and said to her maids: "These lanterns must be truly exceptional. Let me tell my mother-in-law we are going, and get dressed to go out."

Sing:

The young maids, their hands tucked into their sleeves,
Stepped forward and said: "My lady, please listen to us.
   The Turtle Mountain Monastery displays its red lanterns,
And every house and family goes to watch these lanterns.
As soon as an [old] man sees this Easy Roaming Frame,
He looks like a young man again of eighteen years of age.
   As soon as a young man sees this Easy Roaming Frame,
He is as handsome as the Divine Second Son of Guankou.[5]
And as soon as a woman sees this Easy Roaming Frame,
She is as beautiful as Guanshiyin of the Southern Sea."[6]
   When this woman heard this, she was pleased at heart,
And she started to comb her hair and put on new clothes.
   On her head she placed a hundred flowers headdress;
A chain of rings hung down from the lobes of her ears.
She wore a musk-scented jacket, and around her waist
She tied a skirt with large flowers decorated with jewels.
   The embroidered shoes on her feet were extremely small:
She looked like Guanyin and only lacked her pure vase.
   As soon as this woman had finished dressing like this,
She lightly moved her lotus steps and left her room.
In one stretch she arrived at the high hall, and called
"A myriad of blessings!" two or three times in a row.
   Her mother-in-law was seated there in the high hall,
And this woman deeply bowed down before her mother.
When she bowed, she looked like a red peony flower,
Like a slender willow swaying in the breeze of spring.

---

[5] Guankou Erlang was widely venerated in the shape of a dashing young man.

[6] The text reads *namo* (hail) instead of *nanhai* (Southern Sea). The bodhisattva Guanyin (or Guanshiyin) was widely venerated in the shape of a beautiful maiden. The small island Putuo in the ocean off the Ningbo coast was identified as her mythical abode Mt. Potalaka and became a major center of pilgrimage.

In the hall her mother-in-law asked her as follows:
"My daughter-in-law, please be so kind as to listen.
Today is not the winter festival of the shortest day,
So for what reason have you come here to this hall?"
    This woman had her hands tucked into her sleeves,
And stepped forward, saying: "Dear mother-in-law,
    The Turtle Mountain Monastery shows its red lanterns,
That wonderful Easy Roaming Precious Lantern Frame.
I would like to go to the Turtle Mountain Monastery,
So I have come to ask my mother-in-law's permission."
    Hearing this, her mother-in-law was highly upset,
And loudly cursed her daughter-in-law: "You lowlife!
If you mention the name and surname of this family,
We are not to be compared to ordinary or lower folks.
    It would be fine for you to go and watch the lanterns,
But I am afraid that people will humiliate our family.
It would be a minor matter if they humiliated only you,
But such a stain on our reputation affects descendants."
    When she was cursed in this way, she had no answer,
She blushed even behind her ears and said not a word!

Speak:

This woman wanted to go to the Turtle Mountain Monastery to watch the lanterns, so she dressed herself up and went to the hall, where she bowed to her mother-in-law and told her about the lantern viewing. When her mother-in-law heard this, she cursed her in the following words: "You rotten lowlife, you humiliate our family!" When the woman was cursed like this, she kept her silence and said not a word. An hour later, she again stepped forward with her hands tucked into her sleeves, and addressed her as follows: "Mother-in-law, if you do not allow me to watch the lanterns, then that is fine — no problem at all. But three years ago, when I gave birth to Shi Jinbao, it was a very difficult delivery, and I prayed to the Eastern Marchmount and mentally made a vow that I would visit his temple, but until today I have not fulfilled that vow. Let me avail myself of tonight's lantern viewing and go and fulfill this mental vow." When her mother-in-law heard this, she gave her permission, and also ordered the household servant uncle Zhang and four young maids to accompany her daughter-in-law.

Sing:

The mother-in-law then and there spoke as follows
As she instructed the old household servant Zhang:
"You will all go to the temple of the Eastern Marchmount,
And you shall return as soon as she has fulfilled her vow.
    I allow her to go to the temple and burn her incense,
But don't let her go and watch the lanterns on display.
If you accompany her and go and watch the lanterns,
Don't enter the gate of my house when you return!"

Upon these words the woman returned to her room,
And she dressed herself up in her finest new clothes.
She got out her boxes with powder for her make-up,
In front of the bright mirror made of green bronze.
    Her raven tresses she did up in a coiled-dragon bun —
Some ten or more golden hairpins in the latest fashion.
Let me add three characters to the seven-character line,
And in lines ten characters long I'll tell how she looked!

Ten-character lines:

Speaking of skirts and hairpins —
    Once she had done up her hair,
        She went on to dress herself up.
Rouge and powder she equally
    Applied to her fragrant cheeks:
        Her whole appearance was great!
On red embroidered shoes,
    That wrapped her golden lotuses,
        She firmly walked on fragrant streets;
Tied around her waist was
    A plaited skirt made of seven widths,
        Which was fully speckled with gold.
She wore fragrant gauze
    Which clung to her jade body,
        Doubling her attraction and allure;
Her brocade incense sachets
    Were embroidered in all colors,
        And each and every pattern was new.

Her coiled-dragon bun
    Was as black as the clouds,
        And a golden chaplet kept it in place;
The ten hairpins
    She had inserted in front
        Were all made of solid yellow gold.
...
    ...
        Had been inserted aslant on both sides;
A comb made of ivory
    And inserted at the back
        Resembled the crescent of a new moon.
From her fragrant shoulders
    Pearls hung down
        Like the long necklaces of bodhisattvas,
And with a charm of their own
    Golden earrings
        Dangled with each of her movements.
Her two eyebrows
    Were barely emerging
        Willow leaves, cut out with scissors,
And her pair of eyes
    Resembled autumn waves,
        Shaded by the jet of her eyebrows.
On the red gauze
    She used as a waist band,
        Mandarin-ducks sported in pairs;
Moving her lotus feet,
    She left her inner apartment,
        Stepping slowly, walking at ease.

Once she had left the mansion through its triple gates,
She pressed on ahead on the main streets of the city.
Soon the sun would go down and evening would fall:
The red disk sank in the west, the moon rose in the east.
    Single-mindedly to the Eastern Marchmount's temple,
As a nine-curved Yellow River filled the sky with stars.[7]

---

[7] The Yellow River and the Heavenly River (the Milky Way) are believed to be one waterway.

Fig. 8.1
Liu Dusai views the lanterns at Turtle Mountain Monastery.

Each and every family had lit its own red lanterns,
Each and every house hung lanterns in front of the gate.
    Passing through the main streets and the narrow alleys,
She walked as fast as if she were transported by storms.
So before she had had to walk for quite some time,
She had arrived in front of the Deity Equal to Heaven.
    When she arrived at the Eastern Marchmount's temple,
Tapering tender jade sprouts held the burning incense.[8]
A cloud of auspicious smoke rose up into the sky, and
The incense's fragrance straightaway pierced the clouds.
    The woman then and there knelt down and bowed,
Praying to the Sagely Divine Lord Equal to Heaven:
    "Because I gave birth to my little son Shi Jinbao,
I have now come here as one who offers you incense.
May the two brothers never experience any strife, and
May sons and grandsons never be divided forever!"
    As soon as she had finished her prayers to the deity,
She turned around and left through the temple's gate.
As soon as she was outside, back on the main street,
She addressed the family servant surnamed Zhang.

Speak:

When the woman had burned incense, she said to the household servant uncle Zhang: "Come here, there's something we have to talk about. My mother-in-law told me not to go and watch the lanterns, but don't think I'm not going to go and watch them. My mother-in-law at present is seventy-two years old, and once her life is over, I will be the lady of the house, and I will be in charge of the family capital of millions and the chests filled with silver. Let's keep my mother-in-law in the dark, and quickly go and have a look." Uncle Zhang said: "My lady, I'm afraid that that will take too much time!" But the woman said: "That will not take too much time. I'll have one look over there, and then immediately go back!"

Sing:

When uncle Zhang was told this, he said it was fine,
And the six of them set out to watch the lanterns.

---

[8] "Jade sprouts" are a conventional image for a woman's fingers.

The household servant uncle Zhang walked in front,
And as he did so, he held a large staff in his hands.
    The four young maids walked on both her sides —
Bees congregating on the heart of a peony flower.
No need to talk of main streets and narrow alleys:
There they arrived at Turtle Mountain Monastery!
    As they lifted their heads as they were walking in,
They saw the Four Diamond Kings on both sides.[9]
They straightaway went to the Main Hall to watch,
To watch the Easy Roaming Precious Lantern Frame.
    The red lanterns dazzled you with their bright light:
All heaven and earth turned red by their glare.
The thirty-three lanterns at the very top represented
The Three Purities, the Jade Emperor, and immortals.
    In the middle the Nine Palaces and Eight Trigrams,
The Five Planets and the five regions of earth below.
At the bottom King Yama ascended his hall in hell;
The dragon kings of the four seas were clearly shown.
    When the woman then and there looked around,
She saw thousands and ten thousands of people.
Tall people were standing in front to have a look;
Short people piled up bricks to support their feet.
    Fat people were so squeezed they could hardly breathe,
Skinny people were so squeezed their bones snapped.
There were also high officials with [their underlings],
There were also patriarchs of high and mighty families.
    There were military men as well as common citizens,
There were shopkeepers there as well as peddlers.
There were young men there in the prime of spring,
But you also had monks and nuns and Daoist priests.
    The people watching the lanterns were millions,
But where were the people with her a little while ago?
Initially she had said that she would return quickly,
But seduced by the lanterns she had not gone back.
    When the woman turned her head to look around,
She failed to see the family servant surnamed Zhang.

---

[9] The fearsome Four Diamond Kings are portrayed at the entrance of Buddhist monasteries as they are protective deities.

The four maids had gone off in different directions:
She was left all alone, a woman — hairpins and skirt!
　As soon as she realized this, she was filled with fear —
How would she, she wondered, talk herself out of this?

Soon the first quarter of the first watch had arrived;
No need to mention the second quarter of the second watch.
But when the third watch arrived and midnight came,
A terrible disaster took place, deeper than the ocean!
　Initially a bright moon had been shining in a clear sky,
But all of a sudden black clouds arose from all directions,
And out of the blue a mighty storm had started to blow
That sent bricks and stones flying in a terrifying manner.
　It ripped the tiles of the roofs of the houses of people,
And the snow-capped waves in the river rose up to heaven.
Big trees were blown over with all their branches attached,
Smaller trees were torn from the ground with their roots!
　Then suddenly she heard a thunderous roaring crash
As the Easy Roaming Precious Frame was blown down,
[Shattering to] smithereens the three hundred glass lamps,
Scattering the terrified crowd in all possible directions.
　Those who were strong fled in front of all others, and
The people who were weaker fell down on the ground.
In that frantic flight at midnight, during the third watch,
Thousands and tens of thousands were trampled to death.
　When the woman had fled and stood outside the gate,
She found herself standing there on the main street.

While she did not say a word, she pondered her plight,
And in her mind she became more and more convinced
That she should have done as uncle Zhang had said —
How was she going to find the way back to her house?
　"This is all because I didn't believe my mother-in-law,
And wanted to see the Easy Roaming Precious Frame.
If I had followed my mother-in-law's advice,
I'd not have to suffer her biting words, sharp like knives!"
　This was what that woman was thinking to herself,
But how could she understand the extent of the disaster?
Four large gauze lanterns carried in front led the way, and
With them came a pair of men shouting: "Clear the road!"

Their loud shouts told all people to quickly make way,
And the crowd of people on the road divided into two.
A group of twenty government runners followed behind,
In their middle on horseback one high and mighty official!
    The woman was so scared that she was dumbfounded,
And she walked on ahead to avoid this mighty prince.
But when this great prince on horseback lifted his head,
He saw on the road ahead this woman — hairpins and skirt.
    Her proportions were perfect, not too tall, not too short;
Not too fat and not too skinny she was a perfect beauty.
Three buckets of rouge as well as two buckets of powder:
She had been sculpted from rouge, formed from powder!
    Seeing how well her hairpins and skirt were proportioned,
He did not say a word, but he evaluated her as follows:
"If I only would be able to get this person to be my wife,
I would be happy, even if it would mean I'd have to die!"

Speak:

This woman Liu Dusai was by birth sculpted out of rouge and formed out
of powder; her proportions were neither too tall nor too short, neither too
skinny nor too fat. The white of her body resembled silver, the red of her
body resembled brocade. She was a red flower wrapped in raw silk: outside
and inside supported each other. Romantically inclined gentlemen could
never watch her enough, because from her crown to her toes she was
without any blemish: her eyebrows resembled the new moon, her eyes
looked like autumn waves, her fingers resembled jade bamboo sprouts, and
her feet appeared to be golden lotuses. While still on horseback that high
official promptly asked her: "You, skirt and hairpins, whose daughter are
you? Or whose wife? Why are you here out on the street at midnight, in
the third watch?" When this skirt and hairpins was asked this question, she
promptly conceived of a plan, so she did not tell him she belonged to a
family of the Western Capital, but she said: "I hail from the Eastern
Capital, and my husband is a traveling merchant who sells brocade,
pushing a wheelbarrow. When we heard how beautiful the lanterns were in
the Western Capital, my husband and I both came here to view the red
lanterns, but unexpectedly we saw how the Easy Roaming Precious Frame
was blown over, and I was separated from my husband. As I have no idea
where he may have gone, I am standing here, waiting for him." When the

great prince heard this, he promptly said: "At this time late at night when nobody is around, you will not be able to find him, so you'd better come along with me, and stay at my place for one night. Tomorrow is still early enough to go and look for your husband."

Sing:

As soon as the great prince had spoken, those behind him
Carried her with them, a woman — hairpins and skirt.
The woman could do nothing but go along with them,
Both worried and happy — very much wounded at heart.
  When he arrived at his mansion, he quickly dismounted;
He stepped down from his horse and entered the mansion.
His silver folding chair with its tiger skin was set down,
And then he ordered a magnificent banquet to be prepared.
  Seven bright lamps represented the Northern Dipper,
And six candles of wax stood in for the Southern Star.
When the tea had been served, a cup of wine followed,
And then he called over that skirt and hairpins, the woman.
  "I am a member of the imperial family, I am one of those
Who are commonly called golden branches and jade leaves.
I am a full younger brother of the current emperor,
Prefect and lord of the Western Capital, Prince Zhao!
  At the present moment I have thirteen lovely wives,
But I still lack a lover who really pleases my heart.
As I have seen how beautiful you are, I want you
To be the one who will share my couch and cushion.
  If you here today act in conformity with my proposal,
I will raise you to the rank of my one and only wife.
But as soon as you say a single word of opposition,
A blade of finest steel will make you lose your life."
  When the steel sword he had came out of its scabbard,
It was as sharp as a wind-blown fire, as white as silver!
The woman was so scared that she was dumbfounded,
With lowered head she did not speak as tears flowed.
  "Had I known this, I'd have listened to my mother-in-law,
But why did I have to run into such a disaster today?
But if I would not obey this prefect, this Prince Zhao,
One stroke of his blade of fine steel will finish my life!"

She seemed to have swallowed a needle and thread:
Her innards were troubled and her heart was pierced!
She was not allowed to say anything in her defense
But taken away to an inner apartment — her prison.
    The woman had no other possibility but to comply,
He made her the one who shared his couch and cushion.

But let's not sing how the woman became his victim,
Let's sing of the millionaire who was her husband.
    As he was seated in the high hall, facing southward,
The household servant uncle Zhang told him the story.
He came on purpose to inform the millionaire, saying:
"This disaster is even deeper than the deepest ocean!
    Mylady went and watched the Easy Roaming Frame,
Which earned her many biting words, sharp as knives.
A sudden twister destroyed the Easy Roaming Frame,
And the terrified crowds scurried off in all directions.
    The four young maids had been divided and scattered,
And I had no clue to where Mylady might have gone.
I looked for her on the streets, in the alleys, but to no avail,
And I have no idea at all where Mylady now may be."
    Even before uncle Zhang had finished with his tale,
Millionaire Shi was very much upset. In that very hall
He repeatedly gave expression to his bitter suffering,
And he plucked a basin of blazing fire from his heart.
    "For you to watch the lanterns may not be a big deal,
But you've ruined our reputation, people despise us.
Alas, you low caste slut, you were devoid of reason,
Why on earth did you have to behave like a whore?
    Now our three-year-old son has heard you are lost,
He weeps, cries at the top of his voice for his mother.
Come to think of it, you as a mother acted foolishly:
Why did you join the crowd that views the lanterns?
    A man of ancient times, I learned, expressed it well:
Governing a family and a state require the same skill."
    He ordered thirty young servants to scour the streets
In order to locate that woman — hairpins and skirt.
On all gates of the city he posted a notice and placard
In order to retrieve that woman — hairpins and skirt.

For anyone who found Liu Dusai there would be
A thousand ounces of gold, ten thousand of silver!
But if anyone had kidnapped this woman Liu Dusai,
He would go off to Kaifeng and lodge a complaint.
    If the case would be heard by Dragon-Design Bao,
The criminal and his family would die by the sword!

Let's not talk about Millionaire Shi, that man so rich —
Listen as I sing of that one woman, that Liu Dusai.
That skirt and hairpins was seated in her inner apartment,
And pearly tears flowed from her eyes in great profusion.
    She was filled with longing for her baby Shi Jinbao,
She also longed for her husband and his enduring love.
"When will I be able to see my husband face to face?
When will he be the one who takes revenge for me?"
    All of a sudden four days had passed by in a flash,
And with her hand supporting her cheek, she thought:
"I'm afraid I'll never be able to see my dear husband,
And I'll not be able to take care of my baby Jinbao!"
    Eventually three months had passed by in sequence,
And the air of her rage penetrated the gate of heaven.
When the Metal Star of Great White observed this,
He descended to earth to save the one surnamed Shi.
    After giving three shouts he transformed his body,
Transforming himself into an insect called the moth.
He promptly flew into her fragrant apartment, and,
Straightaway rushed to the clothes hung on the rack.
    He chewed her skirt and her jacket full of holes,
Then the Golden Star bodhisattva returned to heaven.

After a full night, five watches, the sky turned bright;
As the sun rose in the east, the whole sky turned red.
    Liu Dusai had just gotten up, when the Golden Rooster
By crowing thrice announced the bright light of dawn.
When she had combed her hair, applied her make-up,
Only then did the woman want to put on new clothes.
    When she picked up her jacket, it was holes all over,
And the skirt also was so moth-eaten it was all holes.
Now her clothes and garments were all so moth-eaten,
She was filled with longing for her earlier loving man.

All day long she was longing for Millionaire Shi —
Her heart and liver, cut by a knife, were burned in fire!
Tears of desolation flowed down from her eyes, and
Tears coursed down her cheeks of rouge and powder!
     When the prefect Prince Zhao heard this, [he asked:]
"My wife, why are you crying and weeping like this?
If you want clothes, I've a thousand boxes of brocade;
A hundred kinds of delicacies, each and every one new.
     Are you longing for your father and for your mother?
Is it the memory of your former husband and brothers?
My wife, what is it that is causing you such distress?
Please tell me the full story, from its very beginning!"

Speak:

This imperial prince said: "My wife, what is the reason for your crying and weeping? If you want clothes, there are a hundred boxes of silk and satin; if you want food, there are a hundred kinds of delicacies. Is it the memory of your parents and mother-in-law, or are you longing for your former husband?" Dusai said: "Your Majesty, it is not the memory of my parents or my mother-in-law and former husband." The great prince said: "My wife, such a merchant has one dime as capital, and considers the second dime his profit. I am a prefect and prince, a golden branch and jade leaf, and would I not measure up to your husband?" Dusai replied: "The only reason is that moths have ruined my clothes and skirt. They had a woven pattern of the Five Directions and the Five Planets, the myriad phenomena of highest heaven, the five lakes and the four oceans, and the blue rivers and dark mountains, and that's why I loved them so much." The great prince said: "Then don't be so upset! You can have not only one trunk, but ten trunks of those!"

Sing:

The great prince ascended the high hall of his office,
And an order summoning craftsmen was sent out:
All craftsmen of the Western Capital working the loom
Had to report for duty at the high hall of his office!
     Millionaire Shi, this rich man of the Western Capital,
Was the third generation in his family to be a weaver.
His technique was superior, a true master in his craft —
He had been appointed as the empire's head weaver.

Riding his proud and spirited steed the millionaire
Arrived at the gate of the prefectural office building.
As soon as the prefect saw him, he was very pleased,
And ordered to invite Mr. Shi to enter into the hall.
    After greeting each other, they both took their seats,
And only after tea had been served he told the story.
The great prince addressed him in the following way:
"Dear Mr. Millionaire, be so kind as to listen to me."

Speak:

The great prince said: "Dear Mr. Millionaire, you have been officially appointed as the head weaver of the empire. How many weavers are there in the Western Capital?" The millionaire replied: "There are a hundred craftsmen. But at present a hundred men are engaged in the weaving factory of the Eastern Capital, because of the pressing demand for satin. For two years they have not been able to return home, and the roster of circulation is not observed. So there are only thirty men, but their technique is negligible, and they work very slowly, so they cannot weave [such fabrics]." The millionaire said: "Your Majesty, it cannot be done, there is no one who can weave [such fabrics]." The great prince said: "Then you must weave them for me!" The millionaire beseeched the great prince: "I have only one brother who works as a weaver in Yangzhou, and he has not been back for twenty years, so there is only me. My possessions are quite extensive, and I would not feel at ease." The great prince said: "That is no problem. I will dispatch twenty-four guards to protect your house. But you have to weave these garments." When the millionaire heard this, he did not dare refuse and could only comply.

Sing:

At that moment the great prince was very pleased, and
Ordered to pour him three goblets of wine as a reward.

(Page 9 of the original is missing. From the following text it would appear that the weaver is summoned to the establishment of the prince together with four other weavers. When his wife learns that he has arrived, she plies the prince with alcohol till he is drunk, and then sneaks away so as to meet with her husband.)

The weavers were so scared they were soaked in sweat.
When the prefect awoke from his stupor and looked
Around, he nowhere saw the one person Liu Dusai.
    He promptly threw open the double door of the room,
And walked out of the room to see what had happened.
In one stretch he arrived at the hall out in front,
And there he saw husband and wife, the two together.
    "That damned Millionaire Shi, loaded with money,
Worked the loom but now has committed a crime.
Seducing my wife he deserves capital punishment,
The punishment he has earned today won't be light!"
    Liu Dusai was so scared she was dumbfounded,
And in a flutter she scurried back again to her room.
When the prefect saw this, he was greatly angered,
And he shouted to his underlings there in the hall
    To arrest Millionaire Shi, a man loaded with money,
Together with the four other weavers present there,
And to take them to the crowded place for executions,
To be beheaded there and turned into headless ghosts!
    The great prince hastily mounted his spirited horse,
And rode through the streets at the head of his train.
When he arrived at the market, the place of execution,
He ordered them beheaded — and no one was spared!
    When these five weavers had all been beheaded,
The high official mounted his horse and returned.
When he had returned to his high hall in one stretch,
He thought to himself, his hand supporting his cheek:
    "Rip out weeds and roots — if the roots still remain,
Sprouts will flourish in spring and display their green.
Let's just wait till the fifth watch, till the break of dawn —
Then we'll go and kill the Shis, the whole mansion!"

Let's not sing of the thoughts harbored by the prince —
Dawn was about to break, and the skies turned bright.
Listen as I sing of [the heir of] the Shis, Shi Jinbao:
The little boy was three years old and living at home.
    Because the little boy did not see his mother's face,
He cried all through the night till the early morning.
When uncle Zhang saw that he did not stop weeping,
He took him in his arms and went out to buy cakes.

When he got to the bridge, cakes were not yet on sale,
So let me now tell of the prefect, Imperial Prince Zhao.
    He called up five hundred headsmen and executioners,
And he went off to kill the Shis, the whole mansion!
The main gates in the front and the back were closed;
Not a breeze could pass through the tight encirclement.
    Long lances pierced open the mandarin-duck curtains;
Short swords pried open the gates made of large planks.
They captured the lovely girls still so young of years,
They grabbed the young boys with their handsome looks.
    The old men they had arrested were killed on the spot,
And even none of the young boys or girls was spared.
A hook pulled down the head, and a sword cut it off:
The women in skirt and hairpins lost their three souls.
    The dogs they found in the rooms were cut into three;
Spotted cats on the steps were castrated with scissors.
The men and the women were equally destined to die;
Not a cat or a dog in the house escaped with its life.
    They killed from the eastern side to the western side;
They killed from the southern side to the northern gate:
Corpses were strewn all around like bundles of hay,
And covered with blood the floor had all turned red.
    After a single engagement, everyone had been killed,
They had murdered all the Shis, the whole mansion.
The fine family possessions had all been carried off, and
Pavilions and halls, rooms and sheds were burned down.
    Pigs and goats, cattle and horses were all led away,
Silks and satins, gold and silver placed in storerooms.
The cruel fire was started where it would catch the wind,
And the red glare of the fire lit up Heaven and Earth.
    Uncle Zhang returned and came back to the mansion
Only after the prince was done killing and had gone off.
When he arrived in front of the gate and looked around,
Corpses were strewn all around like a herd of sheep.
    The gold and jade of the family had been carried off,
Rooms and sheds had all been burned down by the fire.
Uncle Zhang was overcome by vexation at this sight:
"What kind of crime had this family ever committed?"

The neighbors on both sides spoke to him as follows,
This they told the household servant surnamed Zhang:
"It is all because you went out and viewed the lanterns,
That they exterminated the Shis, the whole mansion!"
    Hearing this, uncle Zhang reached the conclusion
That he should quickly flee in order to save his life.
"I should not tarry here in this place any longer, but
Go off to Yangzhou and inform the second master."

Let me not tell you of the travels of uncle Zhang—
Let's change the subject and return to Prince Zhao.
The great prince was seated in his high hall, his mind
Occupied by these many thoughts and considerations:
    "I have killed these one hundred and three people,
But in Yangzhou his younger brother is still alive.
If Second Master Shi Ma comes to know of this,
That man will definitely set out to seek revenge."
    After considering hundreds and thousands of plans,
He all of a sudden conceived of one particular scheme.
    With both hands he brought out his Dongque inkstone,
And filled a container with water from a clear spring.
He spread out a sheet of paper (Cai Lun's invention),[10]
And in his hand he held a brush made in Xuanzhou.
    Lightly, lightly he rubbed the raven-black, oily ink,
Then dipped in the tip of the brush for one-third.
On his black-rhinoceros desk he started to write;
Each character and each line was written very clearly.
    In his letter he did not write about any other matter,
He only discussed the Shis, the whole mansion.
He wrote: "From the prefectural office of Henan
Prince Zhao writes to his friend surnamed Sun.
    At present I have acquired Liu Dusai by force,
And I have killed off the Shis, not leaving one!
But in Yangzhou you still have Master Shi Ma,
And I fear very much that he will seek revenge.

---

[10] The eunuch Cai Lun reported the invention of paper in 105 AD, but archaeological discoveries show that the production of paper had been slowly perfected in the preceding decades.

Patrol the streets three or five times each day,
Have the second son of the Shi family arrested.
And if you would beat Master Shi Ma to death,
You and I will equally share the family's fortune."
　When he had described the full course of events,
He tightly sealed the envelope, layer upon layer.
He entrusted the letter to two of his guardsmen;
Sent to the Eastern Capital, they took the letter.
　Each person was awarded three jugs of wine,
Ten ounces of yellow gold, ten ounces of silver.
When the two had said goodbye to the prince,
They dressed themselves for the trip and set out.
　On their heads a black felt hat with curling brim;
Dressed in a brocade jacket with a short apron.
When the stables had readied their proud horses,
They took out carved saddles, completely new.
　When the belly-bands were securely fastened,
They mounted the thoroughbreds in one move.
Once outside the walls of the Western Capital,
It seemed as if they were carried by the winds.
　Going slowly they overtook the low-flying geese,
And running fast they overtook even falling stars.
They resembled the currents below Luoyang's bridge,
And looked like an arrow that has left the bowstring.
　Having gone one mile, they longed for the next one;
Having gone one stretch, they hastened to do the next.
When they were going fast, they were truly going fast;
When they put in effort, they really put in great effort.

Just as these guardsmen were making great haste,
They saw from afar the beautiful Eastern Capital.
Seen from afar, the peach blossoms shimmered red;
Coming up closer, the willow leaves were green.
　They had no desire to go and see the city's sights,
But quickly entered the triple iron-covered gates.
　Once they had entered the triple gates of the city,
The Eastern Capital presented a different world.
The Eastern Street: playboys vied with young nobles;
The Western Street: young nobles and fighting quails.

Without listening to what the people were saying,
They arrived at the gate of the Sun family mansion.
The guardsmen then and there promptly dismounted,
Dismounted from their horses to enter the mansion.
    When they arrived at the high hall and looked up,
They promptly reported to the man surnamed Sun.
When Mr. Sun lifted his head to have a good look,
[He saw the two guardsmen] in front of the high hall.
    The guardsmen stepped forward, hands in their sleeves,
And reported: "We have been sent here by Prince Zhao.
We lack the eloquence to explain the matter at hand,
But we have with us a letter that provides information."
    They quickly took the private letter from their bosom,
And handed it there in the hall to the man surnamed Sun.
The latter opened the letter in order to read the message,
He opened the envelope in order to read what it said.
    The letter read: "The prefect of the Western Capital
Writes the following to this friend Sun Wenyi.
At present I have acquired Liu Dusai by force,
And I've killed off the Shis, the whole mansion!
    But in Yangzhou there still is Master Shi Ma,
And I fear very much that he will seek revenge.
It is my desire that you will beat him to death —
You and I will equally share the family's fortune."
    When he had read this, a very happy Mr. Sun
Ordered to tip the men who had brought the letter.
Their spirited horses were taken to the stable,
While they went outside to learn about Mr. Shi.

The line of our story now bifurcates into two,
As a single narrative now divides into two lines.
    Listen as I sing to you of Mr. Shi Ma in Yangzhou,
Who at midnight had a dream that was all too clear:
He dreamed that his whole family met with disaster,
That the whole family, old and young, was wiped out.
    He slept till the fifth watch, till the break of dawn,
Until the sun emerged in the east, reddening the skies.
Filled with foreboding the Second Master, Shi Ma,
Invited a soothsayer, one who reads the hexagrams.

Speak:

The Second Master Shi Ma at midnight had a dream in which his whole family, old and young, met with disaster. At break of dawn the next day he invited a master and had him read a hexagram. The master replied: "This hexagram is 'fire under earth, light before dawn,'[11] and means great misfortune. Your whole family will meet with disaster, and you too will find it impossible to escape."

Sing:

Second Master Shi Ma was very troubled and upset,
And after paying the soothsayer, he set out on his trip.
Leaving the Southern Capital, Yangzhou Prefecture,[12]
He mounted his horse, and went off on his journey.
    Once outside the walls of the city of Yangzhou,
He traveled his road as fast as a wind-blown cloud.
Do not sing how he rested at night, departed at dawn —
His horse seemed to fly, running with greatest speed.
    When he came to a place called Horse Ridge Village,
He suddenly noticed their servant surnamed Zhang.
Uncle Zhang was carrying the darling little toddler,
And weeping and wailing he told what had happened.
    Second Master Shi Ma was very troubled and upset,
So he shouted at the top of his voice at uncle Zhang:
    "What did my family do to deserve this from you —
You abandoned your lord and ran away to this place!
It would still be a minor matter if you had run off,
But why did you have to carry this infant with you?"
    Uncle Zhang put Shi Jinbao down on the ground,
Tucked his hands into his sleeves, and stepped forward,
Saying: "The disaster that befell us is beyond words,
The whole family was wiped out in that misfortune!
    It all happened because on the night of the fifteenth
People view the lanterns at Turtle Mountain Monastery.
It was too bad but your elder brother's wife Liu Dusai
Left the house and joined the crowd watching lanterns.

---

[11] The reference is to hexagram No. 38 in the *Book of Changes*.
[12] The text reads "Eastern Capital," which must be a mistake.

When a twister broke down the Easy Roaming Frame,
The millions watching the lanterns scattered in fright.
At that moment I also lost sight of lady Liu Dusai,
And the four young maids had fled in all directions.
    I had no idea at all to where Liu Dusai had gone off,
But somewhere on the streets she ran into Prince Zhao.
Because he wanted to acquire that woman Liu Dusai,
He came and killed off all the Shis, the whole mansion.
    But because this little boy had been crying all night,
I had taken him with me to go and buy some cakes.
If we two had not been able to escape with our lives,
He would have extirpated the whole family, leaves and roots!"
    When he had heard this, Shi Ma was dumbfounded;
He fainted and fell down from his thoroughbred horse.
But if a man is not hurt in the heart, he cannot just die,
So after half an hour Shi Ma regained consciousness.
    Shi Ma thereupon gave the following instructions
To the household servant, the man surnamed Zhang:
"We will go to the Eastern Capital now all together,
And in Kaifeng Prefecture we will lodge an accusation."
    Uncle Zhang also mounted a proud and spirited horse,
And in his arms he carried the precious little toddler.

Let me not sing of the stretches of the road traveled —
From afar they espied the walls of the Eastern Capital.
Once they had entered the triple gates of the city,
The three of them dismounted at an inn for the night.
    Shi Ma at this time recalled everything from the start,
And he felt as if his heart were pierced by a sharp knife.
He did not drink any tea and he also did not eat any rice:
Wounded at heart, overcome by sorrow, not his own self.
    He only said: "Tomorrow morning at break of dawn —"
Eventually the sun began to sink and dusk approached.
One clear lamp had the position of the Northern Dipper;
A candle of wax stood in the place of the Southern Star.
    He took out a sheet of paper made of mulberry bark,
And lightly rubbed the fine ink like raven-black clouds.
Holding a brush made with Xuanzhou hairs in his hand,
He wrote out an account, clearly, from the very start.

When the full statement had been written by midnight,
Soon the drums sounded the arrival of the fourth watch.
Intently he waited for the next morning's break of dawn,
With craned neck he watched for the morning star's rise.
　　Three years had been put together to make for one night;
Five days had been put together to make for one watch.
The sun had got stuck in the eastern country of Fusang;
The morning star had grown roots below the earth.
　　The very moment he was about to give in to depression,
Unexpectedly the Golden Rooster gave out its first cry.
The Golden Rooster told the sun to emerge from Fusang,
And the bronze bell's sound dispersed the stars in the sky.
　　Second Master Shi Ma gave the following instructions
To the old household servant, the man surnamed Zhang:

(Page 14 is missing from the original. From the following it appears that
Shi Ma early in the morning on the streets of Kaifeng submits his
accusation to Sun Wenyi, whom he mistakes for Judge Bao. Sun Wenyi
orders him beaten to death, and then orders that the body be taken to the
river on a door leaf and covered by cabbage, in order to be dumped into
the waves. When some time later Judge Bao arrives at that spot of the
beating, his horse refuses to move despite all prodding.)

Speak:

Chancellor Bao called his guards on both sides: "This horse has a very
strong and stubborn character. There are three conditions under which it
refuses to move. It will not move when the emperor and his train come
through the streets; it will not move when the empress or the crown
prince come through the streets; and it will not move when there is the
wronged ghost of someone who died unjustly." So he told Zhang Long
and Zhao Hu to go and visit the teashops and winehouses along the main
street and hear these people out. When Zhang Long and Zhao Hu
received this order, [they replied:] "Your Excellency, there's no wronged
ghost of someone who died unjustly here. But in the first little side lane
four guardsmen are carrying a [door leaf full] of yellow cabbage leaves."
His Excellency said: "Quickly call them over!" The two men went out
on the main street and called those guardsmen. These four guardsmen
were so scared their souls flew off and their spirits scattered. Chancellor
Bao questioned them, saying: "Under whose command do you serve?

And where are you carrying this?" The guardsmen replied: "We are guardsmen under the command of Sun Wenyi. Because the sellers of yellow cabbage leaves had piled these up in the street, each was given forty strokes, and the four of us were told to take these cabbage leaves to the city moat and dump them there." Chancellor Bao said: "This is Sun Wenyi's fault." Then he conceived of a plan: "My wife at home a few days ago caught a cold and she wants to eat yellow cabbage leaves, so take these to my mansion."

Sing:

When Judge Bao had said this, he turned around,
And the four guardsmen followed him to his house.
The guardsmen were filled with fear at this moment:
"Today we are bound to end up being thrown in jail.
    The disaster that has struck us is as big as heaven —
How are we going to talk ourselves out of this mess?"
At the Department of State Affairs' Executive Office
Judge Bao dismounted from his thoroughbred horse.

Speak:

Chancellor Bao told the four guardsmen to take the yellow cabbage leaves to the Western Prison, and he gave each of them fifty coins, saying: "You four guardsmen, tell nobody that you took these to my office, because I am afraid that people will make fun of me, telling everywhere that I was born a peasant and love to eat yellow cabbage leaves!"

Sing:

The guardsmen were happy once they had been released:
They had escaped with their lives from King Yama's hall!
    Let's not sing of the guardsmen who quickly disappeared,
But let's only sing of His Excellency Chancellor Bao.
He told his men to put these cabbage leaves to one side
To see whether something was hidden under the leaves.
    The soldiers under his command wasted no moment,
And went to the Western Prison to see what was there.
As soon as they pushed the cabbage leaves to one side,
They did find the mortal remains of a human being!

Speak:

When Chancellor Bao saw the corpse, he found its features most impressive. As the face showed no change at all,[13] this man was definitely murdered by Sun Wenyi. But what was the name of this man? And from where did this man come? He instructed the wardens in the Western Prison to keep a close eye on the corpse.

Sing:

The body was taken to the Western Prison, waiting
For someone to report a murder and seek justice.
Let's not sing of Judge Bao of the Southern Office,
Let's sing of the household servant surnamed Zhang.
    From the early morning he waited till meal time,
And from meal time he waited till the hour of noon.
When eventually he had waited for quite a while,
He went to Kaifeng Prefecture to lodge a complaint.
    While carrying the little Shi Jinbao in his arms,
He was walking ahead, there on the main street.
On both sides the office gates were without number,
But which of them was that of Kaifeng Prefecture?
    As he was walking he lifted his head, and saw
The Department of State Affairs' Executive Office.
All other offices opened towards the south, but not
Fierce Judge Bao: his office opened towards the north.
    On the gate were written three lines of characters,
And each character and each line was written clearly.
    All men who came to the gate to lodge a complaint,
Should thrice beat the drum of injustice at the gate;
All women who came to the gate to lodge a complaint,
Should thrice beat the bronze gong to get attention.
    So when uncle Zhang looked around him, he saw
The bronze gong and leather drum each to one side.
When uncle Zhang saw these, he wasted no moment,
But quickly grasped the drum sticks in his two hands.

---

[13] A common belief held that in the case of murder, decomposition would only set in once the murder had been avenged.

He promptly beat the drum of injustice three times;
Three times the claim for justice resounded loudly.

His Excellency was seated in the high hall, and he
Dispatched guardsmen under his command, saying:
"Go and look immediately in front of this office
Who the person is who so loudly clamors for justice.

Perhaps it is an elderly person advanced in years,
Perhaps it is a young girl in the prime of her spring.
Make sure you don't frighten them or scare them off
So they will not submit their accusation to Kaifeng."

The soldiers, hearing this order, came outside to look,
And found an elderly person there, advanced in years.
"His Excellency dispatched us to come and ask you in,
So you may be questioned in front of the high hall."

When uncle Zhang arrived in front of the high hall,
He tucked his hands into his sleeves to tell his story.
He prostrated himself in front of the steps of the hall,
And repeatedly cried out: "Murder! Murder most foul!"

Uncle Zhang then and there spoke in the following way:
"This disaster that befell us is as deep as the ocean!"

The Story of How Shi Guanshou's Wife Liu Dusai on the Night of the Fifteenth, on Superior Prime, Watched the Lanterns, Part One, Completely Illustrated, in Prose and in Verse.

The Story of the Judgment of Dragon-Design Bao in the Case of Prince Zhao and Sun Wenyi. Part Two

Completely Illustrated, in Prose and in Verse

As he heard this, Judge Bao addressed him as follows,
Asking the question: "Uncle, you are advanced in years.
What is your surname and name? Where do you live?
And what may be your original place of registration?

Do you live in the Eastern Capital or in the Western?
Are you from the Southern Capital or the Northern?
Do you live in the countryside or perhaps in the city?
Do you carry on your trade in a town or in a market?

Are you surnamed Zhang or are you surnamed Li?
Or are you perhaps surnamed Wang, Liu, Ma or Sun?
Which of the hundred plants or roots is your surname?
Tell me the truth from the very beginning, in detail!

Did a buffalo eat your grain or a horse eat your beans?
Did you get into a violent fight and was somebody hurt?
Could it be that the local official was not pure and righteous?
Could it be that the village head has been harming you?

Or is this a dispute over fields and their boundary lines?
Or was perhaps the sprouts tax unevenly apportioned?
If you have a single sentence to say, then speak up now;
If you have a single word to say, then say that one word!

If what you say is right, the verdict too will be right;
If what you say is true, the verdict too will turn out true.
But if what you say is mistaken or if it makes no sense,
It's your own fault if the verdict turns out to be wrong.

Make sure today that your statement follows the facts,
And do not make a false accusation against a good man.
Other officials may perhaps be open to interventions,
But I, Judge Bao, will not take relations into account."

Questioned like this, uncle Zhang answered as follows:
"Your Excellency, please be so kind as to listen to me.
I lack the eloquence to explain this case in all details,
But I've brought a statement which spells it out clearly."

He held the statement seeking redress of injustice,
And handed it to His Excellency, Chancellor Bao.
When the latter received it and opened it, he saw
That each character and line had been written clearly.

"The person submitting this statement is Shi Ma,
Who was both born and raised in the Western Capital.
Settled in the Western Capital, the prefecture of Henan,
We are the Shi family that resides on Go Board Lane.

We have been listed as weavers for three generations,
And we have been appointed as superior head craftsmen.
My elder brother went by the name of Shi Guanshou,
And the name of my elder brother's wife is Liu Dusai.

On the night of the fifteenth, the day of Superior Prime,
The Turtle Mountain Monastery displayed its red lanterns.
My elder brother's wife went there that night to watch —
She was twenty-four years old, in the prime of her spring!

She was accompanied by a total of four young maids,
And they went together to view the monastery's lanterns.
A mad twister broke in a flash the Easy Roaming Frame,
And the terrified maids scattered and fled in all directions.

That intolerable Prefect Zhao of the Western Capital,
A man who is one of the golden branches and jade leaves,
Acquired my elder brother's wife Liu Dusai by force
And went on to kill all the Shis, the whole mansion!

The only person able to escape was the servant Zhang,
And he carried away my brother's little son Shi Jinbao.
All together one hundred and three people were killed,
Including twenty young maids employed in our house.

Including thirty male servants employed by our family —
Even the cats and the dogs in our house were not spared.

Fig. 8.2
Servant Zhang lodges an accusation with Prime Minister Bao.

The undersigned was working as a weaver in Yangzhou;
The three of us together now submit this statement!
　　In principle one cannot accuse an imperial relative,
But he murdered the Shi family, the whole mansion!
Lofts, terraces, rooms and sheds — burned to the ground;
Our family's possessions were all lost to the flames!
　　The gold and silver and treasure were all carried off,
So thoroughly not even half a hair was left behind.
We pray that Your Excellency will show some pity,
Lift up His clear mirror and pronounce a fair verdict!"
　　Once he heard this, Judge Bao was very much annoyed,
And the skin on his face was suffused with a deep red color.
He angrily stamped his feet then and there in the hall,
And he gnashed his teeth, filled with a towering rage!

Speak:

Chancellor Bao spoke: "You must be uncle Zhang?" The latter replied:
"Your Excellency, indeed I am." Judge Bao said: "How could this three-
year-old infant flee?" Uncle Zhang said: "We could escape with our lives
because I was going to buy some cake for the boy." Judge Bao asked:
"Where is Second Master Shi Ma?" Uncle Zhang said: "He left early to
lodge this accusation." Judge Bao said: "He never arrived to lodge an
accusation." He then ordered a soldier to take the household servant uncle
Zhang to the Western Prison to identify the body, to see whether it might
be Second Master Shi Ma.

Sing:

In the high hall Judge Bao called his underlings,
Shouted an order to the soldiers under his command,
Telling them to escort him to the Western Prison
In order to ascertain the identity of the deceased.
　　When he thereupon arrived at the Western Prison,
He identified him as Shi Ma, the Second Master.
As soon as uncle Zhang saw him, he fell to wailing:
"How come you have died and now are found here?"
　　Straightaway they returned once again to the hall,
And he repeatedly cried: "Murder! Murder most foul!

The corpse that is stretched out in the Western Prison,
Is none other than that of Second Master Shi Ma!
Today he left early to go and lodge his accusation,
So how come he has suddenly died in this manner?"
  When Judge Bao heard this, he was very pleased,
And said to the household servant surnamed Zhang:
"Don't go out onto the street for the time being,
But wait here patiently, and I'll catch the murderer!"

With both his hands he got a donkey-hoof inkstone,
And lightly rubbed the fine ink to write an account:
"I, Chancellor Bao of the Southern Office, respectfully
Greet this prefecture's main god of Wall and Moat.
  If an act of injustice occurs in the Eastern Capital,
You urge the victims to appeal for justice with me.
You are the lord of this region in the realm of shade,
While I in the world of light support Our Sagely Lord.
  You, in the realm of shade, are as clear as a mirror,
While I in the world of light resemble pure water.
At present a certain Sun Wenyi of this walled city
Has beaten to death one Second Master Shi Ma.
  I order you to send back this Second Master Shi Ma
Before we reach the third watch, the midnight hour.
If you are only a little bit late in this commission,
Your Majesty's punishment will not be negligible."
  When he had written this report, he sealed it tightly,
And also told his soldiers not to waste any moment:
"Go out to the street and buy wine and meats,[14]
We cannot tarry any moment, we have to go now!"

Judge Bao mounted a proud and spirited horse,
And he was followed by a train of fifty soldiers.
He straightaway arrived at the City God's temple,
Where he dismounted and then entered the gate.
  As he lit one stick of priceless, precious incense,
He told the prefecture's main god of Wall and Moat:
  "That Shi Ma who has been killed by Sun Wenyi
Has to be released and returned to life by midnight!

---

[14] The wine and meats are part of the sacrifice to the City God.

I have already unlocked the gate of this temple —
I'll have it burned to the ground if you are too slow!"
    When he said this, he burned the sheet of paper,
And the ashes rose up in the rising smoke of the fire.
Judge Bao thereupon turned around and went back —
Quickly the evening fell as the sun sank in the west.

Boats on the river moored at the bank for the night;
Ferries on the river did not accept any passengers.
Travelers on the road looked for an inn for the night,
Farmers ended their work and returned to the village.
    On the drum in the tower the watches were sounded,
And soon the bronze bell also announced the watches.
On the southern tower the drum told the first watch,
The second watch was told by the drum very clearly.
    With the third watch the drum announced midnight:
Shi Ma returned to life, and regained consciousness.
His mouth released three long mouthfuls of breath,
But his eyes were still hazy, so he recognized none.
    First he was given to eat some soul-stabilizing soup,
And then he swallowed the cinnabar miracle medicine.
The soldiers reported this to Chancellor Bao, saying:
"At midnight this man has regained consciousness."
    When he heard this, Judge Bao was very pleased,
He raised his hands up high and so thanked Heaven.
When Shi Ma, helped by others, arrived in the hall,
His Excellency in his seat asked him what had happened.
    "Who is the person by whom you were beaten to death?
What injustice did you suffer here in the Eastern Capital?"
As his tears flowed down, Second Master Shi Ma replied:
"Your Excellency, please be so kind as to listen to me!
    Because an imperial prince had kidnapped Liu Dusai,
I wanted to lodge an accusation against him in Kaifeng,
But on the street I ran into a certain Sun Wenyi, and,
Beaten by him to death, my life went to the shades."
    Chancellor Bao was very much upset and annoyed:
"That Sun Wenyi is truly intolerable! Most likely
Heaven and Earth must have urged on King Yama
To check his records and have ghosts grab his soul!"

His Excellency spoke to Shi Ma in the following way:
"You should not go out on the street for the moment.
Just stay here at this place and practice some patience.
Wait here tomorrow as I go and arrest the murderer."

In the fifth watch of the night, as the sky turned bright,
A cleverly thought-out scheme emerged in his heart.
He washed his face in a decoction of scholar-tree buds,[15]
So his face turned yellow and wasted, bereft of spirit.
    As soon as Judge Bao had dressed for the audience,
He hastily mounted his horse and entered the palace.
When at court he arrived in front of the golden steps,
He shouted: "A myriad of years to Our Sagely Ruler!"
    But before he was done with the twenty-four bows,
He collapsed on the ground on that self-same spot.
The emperor on his throne opened his golden mouth,
Asking: "Who collapsed in front of the golden steps?"

Speak:

Chancellor Bao performed the twenty-four bows, but before he had
finished them, he collapsed on the golden steps [leading up to the Throne
Hall]. When the emperor asked who had collapsed, Chancellor Wang
stepped forward and reported: "It was Chancellor Bao who collapsed."
The emperor said: "Support him and let him approach the throne."
    When Judge Bao received this command, he ascended the hall, saying:
"Forgive your servant for this breach of protocol." The emperor said:
"What happened to you?" Judge Bao reported: "Since last night at
midnight I am suffering from this disease. My skull seems [cleaved] by an
axe, my eyes seem gouged out by knives, and [my tongue] seems to be cut
off by a sword; my whole body is hot as if burning in a fire, my two legs
are wracked with pain, and all my limbs have lost their strength." The
emperor hastily wanted to summon the imperial physicians to come and
cure him, but Judge Bao said: "Your Majesty, I am only two-thirds ill,"
and he also said: "Your Majesty, I will not be able to attend the audiences
in the early morning." The emperor said: "You are excused from
participating in the audience." Judge Bao then left the palace.

---

[15] The buds of the Chinese scholar tree (also known as the parasol tree) were used to make
a yellow dye.

Sing:

Judge Bao mounted his proud and spirited horse
And returned straightaway to his office buildings.
Suddenly he [went off] to the shades for five days,
[His body was cold, but for one spot] in his heart.

    Zhang Long and Zhao Hu were then dispatched,
And they arrived in front of the palace main gate.
[The gatekeepers went inside] to report their arrival,
And they were told to invite these two soldiers in.

    The summoned soldiers came to the golden steps,
[And the emperor on his throne] said to them:
"The chancellor recently suffered an illness,
We haven't heard about his condition till now."

    [The soldiers knelt down,] shouting: "A myriad years!
May Your Majesty be so kind as to lend us your ear.

    Because the chancellor has been suffering from this disease,
[His condition has worsened,] become very serious!"
He does not drink any tea nor does he eat any rice;
[He has abandoned] his body, has left for the shades."

    The emperor was immediately very much upset,
And summoned for consultation officials and officers.

    "The disease of Chancellor Bao is extremely serious,
So what to do in this case? How to proceed now?

    For days on end We have been bereft of all energy
Only because this man is suffering from a disease.
On whom can We rely of the officials in this court
In case death would rob Us of Chancellor Bao?"

    Chancellor Wang then stepped forward and said:
"Your Majesty, please listen to what I will propose.
Quickly dispatch imperial physicians to visit him,
So they may save him by some miracle medicine!"

    The emperor on his throne opened his golden mouth,
Hastily ordering his imperial physicians to save him.
Receiving this order, the physicians wasted no time,
And arrived at the gate of the Kaifeng Prefecture.

    When they had dismounted from their proud horses,
The two of them were received into the front hall.
Her Ladyship wasted no moment at their arrival,
But came out to welcome them in the prefecture.

Following a fragrant brew to rinse their mouths,
They had a cup of tea and three drinks of wine.
As soon as they had finished these three drinks,
The two physicians inquired about the situation.

Speak:[16]

These two imperial physicians said: "Mylady, we have been ordered by His Majesty to diagnose the chancellor." Her Ladyship said: "Please sit here for a while, as I report your presence to the chancellor." Her Ladyship went to the bedroom, [and said:] "Two imperial physicians who have been sent by the emperor are here to diagnose you." The chancellor said: "Mylady, go and tell them that I borrowed a lion from the temple of the Eastern Thearch to guard the door and that no stranger is allowed to enter the room."[17] Her Ladyship hastily returned to the hall in front and replied to the physicians: "He has borrowed a lion from the temple of the Eastern Thearch to guard the door, and no stranger is allowed to enter." The physicians replied: "We wouldn't dare enter the room. But from outside the gauze window we will pass him a golden needle with thread through the gauze window. If the golden needle is inserted in the chancellor's upper arm, we can read his pulse outside the window." But when Her Ladyship had taken the needle from them, she stuck it in a folding screen.

[*Sing:*]

Once the golden needle had been stuck in the screen,
The two imperial physicians set out to read the pulse.
In the left-side pulse there was no movement at all,
And the right-side pulse did not show any movement!
　　The two physicians then addressed her as follows:
"Mylady, please listen to the conclusion we've reached.
There's no notable pulse at all in either of his two arms,
There's not the slightest movement in his four limbs.
　　His whole body from head to toe is as cold as ice:
To our eyes, he exactly resembles a man of wood.

---

[16] The second character *shuo* 說 (speak) in the original is most likely a mistake.
[17] The guardian lion of the temple of the Great Thearch of the Eastern Marchmount has most likely been borrowed to protect Judge Bao's bedroom from the entry of any evil miasma.

If this condition is going to last any longer at all,
He is bound to join the Lord of Shade very soon."
　　Having said this, the imperial physicians returned,
They mounted their horses and set out on their trip.
Straightaway they arrived at the gate of the palace,
And they hastily dismounted, then entered the gate.
　　When they arrived in front of the golden steps,
They shouted: "A myriad of years to the emperor!
Judge Bao has no noticeable pulse at all anymore,
To our eyes, he exactly resembles a man of wood."
　　Having heard this, the emperor was very anxious:
"How can I do without this one man, Chancellor Bao?"

But let's not sing of the emperor's anxious thoughts —
Let's change the subject and talk about Judge Bao.

Speak:

Chancellor Bao called his wife and said to her: "Come here, there's
something I must discuss with you. Tell the soldiers to find a fine
craftsman. Let him split fine bamboo into strips, and let him make a
mannequin of bamboo strips. Dress that in my clothes, and place it on my
ivory bed. When tomorrow the sky turns bright in the fifth watch, go to
the palace, dressed in full mourning and accompanied by my servants and
soldiers, carrying the thirty magical objects, and also the sword for the
execution of imperial relatives, to return the seals of my office and to weep
at the golden steps in the precious hall. When the emperor asks you:
'When did your husband die?' you only say: 'He died in the third quarter
of the hour of midnight.' When the emperor then asks you: 'Did he leave
me any words of advice when he was about to die?' you reply: 'My
husband didn't say anything special. He only said: 'Time and again
I feigned illness, but this disease now is only all too true, so I haven't been
able to bid adieu to my lord. There's only one thing that I failed to report
to my ruler!' He said that after his death nobody would be fit to serve as
prefect of Kaifeng. If a pure official had to be in charge of the seal, the
four hundred civil officials and military officers at court were all to the very
last man greedy lovers of money and treasure, and there was not a single
good, loyal servant to be found among them. The only one fit to serve as
prefect of Kaifeng was the prefect of the Western Capital, who not only
was an imperial relative, but also was as clear as the water of a bottomless

well and as clear as the light of the full moon. He only passed away after he had said that. So I now report it to Your Majesty."

Sing:

Judge Bao had come up with a very clever scheme,
And with his wife he discussed the plan in all detail.
She promptly ordered two of her husband's soldiers
To go out on the street and find a skilled craftsman.
   When the soldiers had found a bamboo-strip worker,
They brought him to the high hall of the prefecture.
They ordered the craftsman to make bamboo strips,
And to construct a mannequin in the shape of a corpse.
   They then covered the mannequin with papier-mâché,
And dressed it in the clothes of His Excellency Bao.
They laid the mannequin down on top of his ivory bed,
And it looked exactly like Chancellor Bao in person!
   When eventually everything had been properly done,
The red sun had already started to sink in the west.
And when in the fifth watch the sky became brighter,
Her Ladyship dressed herself up to go to the palace.

There's no need to tell the full story of that one night —
Unexpectedly the Golden Rooster gave out its first cry!
   Her Ladyship quickly made sure everything was ready;
When she had dressed herself up, she set out on the trip.
She was dressed in full mourning from head to toe, and
Carried those magical objects with her on her person.
   She straightaway arrived outside the gate of the palace,
Where she waited as the court officials entered inside.
The commissioner of the gates reported her presence,
And he was told to summon her to enter the palace.
   Once she had been summoned inside, Her Ladyship
Walked on, until she arrived before the golden steps.
   As she was standing at the foot of the golden steps
She shouted: "A myriad of years to Our Sagely Ruler!"
While she made the many bows, she wept and wailed,
And tears coursed down her cheeks in great profusion.
   "You civil officials and military officers are still alive,
But where on earth is my dear husband now to be found?

This time he is not standing before the golden steps,
Only in a future life will he again display his loyalty!"
    The emperor on his throne addressed her as follows:
"Why on earth are you weeping and crying like that?
What has happened? What may be the reason for this,
That you create such a disturbance here in the palace?"
    When questioned, Her Ladyship came forward, saying:
"Your Majesty, please be so kind as to listen to me.
My husband has died tonight, as in the third quarter
Of the midnight hour he joined the Lord of Shade."
    The emperor was so startled he was dumbfounded,
And the officials and officers at court were alarmed.
The then-ruling Son of Heaven was awash in tears,
Which soaked his dragon robe and streaked his cheeks.
    "If indeed We have lost Chancellor Bao by his death,
On whom of all the officials at court will We rely?"

Speak:

The emperor said: "Mylady, . . .

(Page 23 is missing in the original. Judge Bao's wife reports his
recommendation of the current prefect of the Western Capital for
appointment as prefect of Kaifeng Prefecture. After some discussion, the
emperor follows the proposal and summons his younger brother from the
Western Capital, who decides to leave for Kaifeng as soon as he receives
the summons.)

[*Sing:*]

...

He completely fell into the trap that had been set!
"I want to get everything ready as soon as possible,
To enter the Eastern Floriate Dragon and Phoenix Gate!"
    He commandeered thirty large ships for the transport
Of his private property back to the Eastern Capital.
The imperial prince rode a proud and spirited horse,
And was followed by a train of boys and servants.

The imperial prince, the story tells, made great haste;
He overtook the winds, he even overtook the clouds!

After he had traveled on the road for a number of days,
He saw from afar the Eastern Capital, city of brocade.
  He had no desire to view the sights inside the city,
Heading to the Eastern Floriate Dragon and Phoenix Gate.
  The commissioner of the gate reported his presence:
"Your Majesty, please be so kind as to listen to me.
The prince-prefect of the Western Capital has arrived.
Your Majesty, please let us know how to proceed."
  Once the prince was summoned to the golden steps,
He greeted the emperor, the lord of a myriad of years.
When he knelt down, his knees touched the ground;
But when he rose up, his feet walked the middle steps.
  The emperor on his throne rose from his own seat,
Inviting him with his own hand to sit down on a stool.
First they drank one cup of Dragon-Phoenix wax tea;
Then they had three drinks of imperially-sealed wine.
  The emperor thereupon rose once again to his feet,
Saying: "My younger brother, please listen to Us.
  In the Southern Office Chancellor Bao has died,
And We are looking for an honest and capable man.
Here at court Sun Wenyi has recommended you,
So We want you to become the prefect of Kaifeng."

Speak:

The emperor said: "My dear younger brother, Chancellor Bao has died, and We have summoned you to be prefect of Kaifeng!" The prince said: "Your Majesty, Judge Bao was pure and incorruptible and served as a champion of the people. He did not accept the world's riches, and was as pure as the water in a pool, as bright as the moon in the sky. I am still too young and lack the qualifications for this appointment — how could I be prefect of Kaifeng?" The emperor said: "No problem! I will appoint you to multiple offices, just as in the case of Judge Bao." He got a piece of yellow gauze of twelve feet long, thickly rubbed the fragrant ink, deeply dipped in the hare-hair brush, and writing in his own hand appointed him as the army's golden pupil great prince, sixth great prince, silver pupil great prince, palace front grand master for urging on the ranks, palace rear grand master for urging on the ranks, western terrace censor-in-chief, and prefect in the Southern Office, holding in a single hand the two seals as commander of the troops and governor of the people.

Sing:

"We appoint you to exactly the same ranks and offices
As those held here before in the past by Chancellor Bao.
The big yellowwood cangue and the yellowwood cudgel
Are for judging imperial relatives by birth and marriage.
    The big paulownia cangue and the paulownia cudgel
Are for judging the people of prefectures and districts.
The big purplewood cangue and the purplewood cudgel
Are for judging the crimes of well-connected bullies.
    The big pinewood cangue and the pinewood cudgel
Are for judging military families and common people.
The big blackwood cangue and the blackwood cudgel
Are for judging the people on the roadside at the palace.
    The big peachwood cangue and the peachwood cudgel
Are for judging this world by day, the shades at night.
There is also this golden plaque of one foot two inches,
And three court officials will serve as your guarantors."
    The first of these sponsoring officials was Sun Wenyi,
The second was Incorruptible and Straight General Fan;
The third official who sponsored him: Chancellor Wang!
In front of the golden steps they sponsored Prince Zhao.
    When the prince had received this imperial appointment,
He thanked the emperor for his grace before his throne.
Once he had exited the nine-bay lofty palace hall, he left
To celebrate his appointment by a conspicuous parade.

Our story sings that the sponsoring official Sun Wenyi
Accompanied the new prefect, the Imperial Prince Zhao.
The thirteen magical objects were carried behind him,
And so he set out on the street with his armed escort.
    In front went two criers who shouted to clear the road;
As cudgels applied the law, people moved to the sides.
A pale yellow banner formed the head of the procession,
With twelve lances with tips as pointed as willow leaves.
    Pairs of soldiers with shields cleared the road ahead,
And these soldiers were dressed up in a startling way.
A silver-[ringed] rattan staff they held in their hands,
While their body was covered by one purple garment.

The soldiers in front and behind numbered hundreds,
While their official rode high in the saddle on horseback.
When up front the soldiers shouted: "The prince arrives,"
All families, rich or poor, tightly closed their doors.

The great prince on his horse cursed them as follows,
Loudly cursing the people of the streets and markets:
"In the past you relied for protection on Judge Bao,
But on whom will you rely for protection at present?

My troops have been away from home for a while,
They are short on traveling money, cash for the road.
If people do not come up with their satin and brocade,
I will steal it from them to reward my many troops!"

Each and every family cursed the prince as follows:
"What a good-for-nothing is that prefect Prince Zhao!
It is all the bad luck of us here in the Eastern Capital
That Judge Bao had to die and join the Lord of Shade!"

The Eastern Capital had an extra trouble-brewing lord,
The Western Capital was freed of a murderous monster:
When the prince arrived before the Executive Office,
He observed a long banner fluttering high in the sky.

Speak:

The prince said: "What kind of place is this to have erected such a long
banner?" The soldiers explained: "The prefect of Kaifeng is lying in state in
the hall and has not yet been buried." Hearing this, the prince flew into a
rage: "I selected a good hour and a lucky day to assume office, so how come
the coffin has not yet been removed? Until when do they want to wait?"

Our story now tells that Zhang Long and Zhao Hu reported to His
Excellency: "Prince Zhao and Sun Wenyi have arrived with their parade
celebrating the new appointment of the prince." When Judge Bao heard
this, he was secretly pleased, and he instructed them as follows: "Take that
fake body of bamboo strips away, but bring out the coffin, and let Lady Li
wear heavy mourning. When they ask her: 'When will the coffin be
removed?' she should say: 'Only after more than half a month!'"

Sing:

His Excellency had come up with a dragon-catching scheme,
He patiently waited for the arrival of the prince and his cronies.

Her Ladyship was leaning on the coffin, crying and weeping,
When the prince and his retinue arrived at the gate of the hall.
    After dismounting from his horse, he ascended the hall, and,
Loudly shouting, started to abuse and swear at Her Ladyship.
"I took care to select a good hour and also a lucky day —
Until what time is this rotten coffin going to stay here?"
    As tears profusely coursed down her cheeks, Her Ladyship
Answered him as follows, her arms crossed before her breast:
    "We have managed to identify a good year and a good month,
But we've not yet been able to find a good day and good hour.
    If you want the coffin of my late husband removed for burial,
You will have to wait, I guess, for half a month or even more."
When the great prince heard this, he was very much annoyed,
And loudly shouted his curses at his underlings there with him.
    But thirty of his soldiers were unable to move the coffin,
They definitely could not move it even the tiniest little bit.
Even forty of his soldiers could not move the coffin at all,
Fifty of his soldiers could not move the coffin a fraction.
    At this time the imperial prince was very much annoyed,
And started to vilify His Excellency Bao himself, by name:
"From now on I will call you silly fool Bao, and this corpse
Is that of that silly old fool who carried the surname Bao!"
    But before he had cursed him three times in this manner,
A certain person walked up to him from one of the sides.

His Excellency immediately started to loudly curse him,
Curse this lord of a prefecture, this Imperial Prince Zhao.
    "Do you recognize me, Your Highness, or perhaps not?
Who is it you curse so brazenly, at the top of your voice?"
He shouted a single order to his soldiers to take action,
And numerous troops emerged as if out of the blue!
    These fierce and violent troops [numbered a hundred],
And all were men who captured dragons, caught tigers.
The gates in the front and in the back were all locked,
Leaving no way for the prince and his servants to flee.
    His Excellency gave out an executive order, and
Two-thirds of his "teeth and claws" promptly acted.
They ignored each and every protest and complaint,
But arrested the imperial prince and threw him into jail!

Sun Wenyi was locked up in the Eastern Prison, and
Imperial Prince Zhao was locked up in the Western Jail.

His Excellency thereupon spoke in the following way,
Instructing Zhang Long and also Zhao Hu as follows:
"Take that coffin apart and beat it into small pieces,
And take it out of the high hall, out of the office gate!"
   The silver folding chair with its tiger skin was set out,
And that man surnamed Bao took his seat in the hall.
He was surrounded by twenty-four merciless soldiers,
And twelve "gods of doom" were on duty that day.
   The thirty magical objects were all brought out, and
Were put on display in front of the steps to the hall.
The Seeking-Life Cord was laid out before him, and
The three-foot golden plaque was hung above the gate.
   Sun Wenyi was fetched from the Eastern Prison, and
Imperial Prince Zhao was taken from the Western Jail.
Their outer and undergarments were all taken away,
Their whole bodies stripped till they were stark naked!
   His Excellency Prime Minister Bao spoke as follows,
Questioning the imperial prince in the following way:
   "For what reason did you come to the Eastern Capital?
What kind of business took you to the Eastern Capital?
You are a younger brother of His Imperial Majesty, so
How did you become a criminal who crosses the law?"
   The imperial prince could only answer as follows:
"Your Excellency, please be so kind as to listen to me.
   I came here because I was summoned by His Majesty,
But I had no idea for what reason I was summoned.
I have never committed any act that crosses the law,
I'm one of those called a golden branch, a jade leaf."
   Having heard this, Judge Bao displayed a faint smile,
But his whole face turned to the deepest color of red.
He loudly ordered his soldiers to take action together
For a thorough interrogation of Imperial Prince Zhao.
   Before His Excellency had finished giving his order,
The soldiers at his command displayed their violence.
From the left side appeared ten men or more, and
From the right side appeared twenty men or more!

They resembled a black eagle catching a rabbit,
And also looked like a falcon that captures a quail.
Those on the left tied him up with a triple cord, and
Those on the right tied him up with a hempen cord!

His Excellency feared they did not tie him tightly,
So he ordered his soldiers to drench him in water.
Scaring Heaven and Earth he thrice loudly ordered
That he be beaten with cudgels and thorny sticks.

The cudgels came down on him like drops of rain,
And all over his beaten body red clouds appeared.
When he had been administered a full forty strokes,
Judge Bao again questioned Imperial Prince Zhao:

"Quickly confess to your crime to escape punishment,
So you will not suffer further torture here in the hall.
Other officials may be receptive to intercessions,
But I, this old Bao, will show no consideration at all!"

The imperial prince again addressed him as follows:
"Your Excellency, please be so kind as to listen to me.

I am a full younger brother of His Imperial Majesty,
So how could I be a criminal who crosses the law?
I have always been told that you are as clear as water,
But on this occasion you are the one who is unclear!"

His Excellency Prime Minister Bao was annoyed,
And addressed the Imperial Prince Zhao as follows:
"We've eight types of cudgel, thirteen rules for use:
We never beat an innocent man with a false cudgel."

Just now he was beaten with a thorny cudgel, but
Next he was beaten with a mulberry wood staff.
The first rule: the iron cudgel is as bright as water,
The second category is strung up with a hemp cord.

For the third category a big cangue is standing by,
And the fourth rule foresees a cudgel as big as a man.
The five finger presses are all inlaid with silver, and
The three pairs of burning irons are quite terrifying.

The eight bronze cudgels are used according to rule:
From all directions they will soften up even a prince!
Nine: the Eastern Marchmount grabbing evil ghosts;
Ten: just like King Yama's Gate of Life and Death!

The prince had been beaten till he lost consciousness,
And then Judge Bao questioned the prince once again:
"In the Western Capital you kidnapped one Liu Dusai,
And then murdered all the Shis, the whole mansion!"

Awash in tears, the prince then addressed Judge Bao:
"Your Excellency, you really got everything wrong!
I have no less than thirteen lovely wives all together,
So how could I be a criminal who crosses the law?"

His Excellency Prime Minister Bao loudly ordered
That he be questioned once again, from the beginning.
The hair on his head was tied to the ends of his cangue,
And one large cudgel was left in both his hands.

His hands and feet were tied together with a cord,
So how could he still refuse to confess to his crimes?
The prince was beaten till he lost consciousness, and
When his three souls were revived, two were lacking.

When he had not yet come to after more than an hour,
The soldiers on duty sprinkled cold water in his face.
A man cannot die unless he has been hurt in his heart,
So from Ghost Gate Pass this man came back to life.

"If you refuse to talk during this round of torture,
You will talk following the next round of torture!"

Needles were spread out in front of the steps to the hall,
And Imperial Prince Zhao was placed on top of them.
From the eastern side he was pushed to the western side,
So he resembled a fish, pared of its scales by a knife.

"I will rather die by the sword in front of this hall —
I never kidnapped any woman with the surname Liu!
I am a full younger brother of His Imperial Majesty,
So how could I be a criminal who crosses the law?"

His Excellency Judge Bao displayed a faint smile:
"So you still refuse to confess? You still will not talk?"

Three pints and three pecks of iron water chestnuts
Were spread out in front of the steps to the high hall,
And Imperial Prince Zhao was placed on top of them —
The points of the iron chestnuts stood out very clearly.

Walking back and forth he was pushed in all directions,
So he resembled a fish, pared of its scales by a knife.
As he refused to talk during the first round of torture,
He also refused to talk during this round of torture!

Judge Bao immediately flew into a towering rage,
And he loudly ordered the soldiers under his command
To insert bronze nails under the nails of his ten fingers
And on top of them to bind them with a hempen cord.
    "If a rabbit burrows a hole, as a rule it's two feet deep,
But this time around the holes have to be three feet deep!"
All other kinds of torture he had been able to withstand,
But these rabbit holes he found impossible to endure.
    The imperial prince succumbed to this kind of torture,
He fainted but then later regained consciousness again.
In front of the hall he could only confess to his crimes
And admit he was a criminal who had crossed the law.
    He told the whole story from the beginning in all details,
He told the whole story in detail in accord with the truth.
    "It was indeed me who had kidnapped that Liu Dusai,
And I also murdered all the Shis, the whole mansion.
I also murdered four other weavers in that connection,
Today I make a full confession, so as to leave no doubt."
    Upon hearing this, Judge Bao was very much pleased,
And the bronze nails were all taken out and put away.
The bronze nails under his ten nails were all taken out —
All of his body was covered in blood from head to toe.
    Judge Bao immediately ordered the clerks of his staff
To bring paper and brush so as to write down the truth.
The clerks who served on his staff wasted no moment,
They presented the paper and brush they were holding.
    The paper was spread out in front of the steps of the hall,
And each and every character was written out correctly:
"I confess: on the festival night of the First Month this year,
On the day of First Night, I went out to view the lanterns.
    By accident I came across Liu Dusai on the main street,
A seductive and beautiful woman — in hairpins and skirt.
I fell in love with her because she was so seductive,
And I kidnapped her to make her one of my concubines.
    But because I ordered the weaving of satins and silks,
It turned out that Master Shi was the head craftsman, and
Because I was afraid that he might want to seek revenge,
I murdered the family, removing both weeds and roots."

When Judge Bao had seen this written confession,
He ordered him taken down to the prison for criminals.
One big cangue made of yellowwood was brought out,
And locked around the neck of the Imperial Prince Zhao.
 At the end of the cangue was inserted a merciless piece,
And the Daoist priest's opening was divided into two.
Now the imperial prince had made a full confession,
His accomplice Sun Wenyi was fetched from prison.
 When he had been stripped of clothes and garments,
Judge Bao started to interrogate the man surnamed Sun.
"Why did you have Shi Ma beaten to death? Quickly
Confess to the facts and admit you committed a crime!"
 The hemp cords may be soft but the cudgels are hard:
Loudly he thrice gave the order to have the man beaten.
When he was beaten slowly, he still refused to talk,
So this greatly angered His Excellency, Judge Bao!
 He loudly ordered his runners to string him up highly,
And beat him with yellow thorns as he was strung up.
That Sun immediately could not withstand the torture,
And told he was a criminal who had crossed the law.

Speak:

His Excellency Bao asked him: "Sun Wenyi, why did you beat Second
Master Shi Ma to death? Quickly tell me the truth so you'll avoid being
tortured in front of the hall." Sun Wenyi said: "Your Excellency, I murdered
this man because of my desire for money and treasure." Judge Bao asked:
"How did you come to desire his money and treasure?" Wenyi replied:
"Prefect Zhao, the imperial prince, sent me a letter, instructing [me to
make sure] to beat Second Master Shi Ma to death. He would then equally
divide the family's possessions with me."

Sing:

Hearing this, His Excellency Bao was very pleased:
Sun Wenyi had made a full confession of his crimes.
Once a large cangue had been locked around his neck,
He [and the imperial prince were taken back] to jail.
 The five planets do not shine into true prison cells,
Which only take in criminals who crossed the law.

The two of them [were secured] by cangue and cord,
And the prison guards left the gate like falling stars.
   Once they got their triple beating on entering jail,
They were locked up in prison to suffer its torture.

Let's not sing of the many sufferings of the prince —
His soldiers were released from the Western Prison.
When these soldiers had been released, they returned:
Lotus flowers in a raging fire again had grown roots.
   Once they had left the walls of the Eastern Capital,
They went and told the woman of hairpins and skirt:
   "At present the imperial prince, the Prefect Zhao,
As well as his accomplice in crime Sun Wenyi,
Have both been arrested by His Excellency Bao;
Thrown into prison they suffer its many tortures.
   Because he had kidnapped the woman Liu Dusai,
And murdered all the Shis, the whole mansion,
He unexpectedly ran afoul of His Excellency Bao
And became a criminal who had crossed the law."
   When Dusai heard this, she was very pleased:
"Who restored justice on behalf of our family?
   I should not stay any longer here in this place!
Let me go to Kaifeng and lodge an accusation.
I've suffered in silence till Heaven opened its eye,
How can I go on living if I don't seek revenge?"
   She wore a musk-scented jacket of red satin
On top of a skirt of ten kinds of Sichuan silk.
And as soon as Dusai had finished dressing up,
She lightly moved her lotus steps to go outside.
   When she had entered the Eastern Capital's walls,
This spirited woman could not be stopped by anyone:
At the Department of State Affairs' Executive Office
She rushed straightaway into the hall of Judge Bao!
   When she hastily knelt down in front of the steps,
His Excellency loudly asked: "Who is this person?"
Her hands tucked into her sleeves she came forward:
"Your Excellency, please listen to what I will say.
   I hail from the Western Capital, Henan Prefecture;
I was both born and raised in the Western Capital.

The name that was chosen for me was Liu Dusai,
And my parents married me to a man surnamed Shi.
   My husband's family lived on Go Board Lane,
And for three generations they had been weavers.
   When I had been with the Shi family for five years,
I gave birth to a little baby boy. The infant's name
By which we called him was Shi Jinbao, and we,
Husband and wife, cherished him like a treasure.
   On the night of the fifteenth day, Superior Prime,
I viewed the lanterns in Turtle Mountain Monastery.
A mad twister broke down the Easy Roaming Frame,
And my scared maids scattered in all four directions.
   At that time I, this simple woman, lost my way,
And on the street I ran into a man inclined to evil.
That intolerable Prefect Zhao of the Western Capital
Abducted me with force, not listening to any reason!
   That very night he took me with him to his home,
And there he forced me to become his wedded wife.
If I'd said only a single word to express my refusal,
One stroke of his steel sword would have finished my life.
   His sword of steel he had drawn from its scabbard,
So I, this poor woman, could only do as he wanted.
After he had murdered my husband, Shi Guanshou,
He also murdered all the other Shis, the whole mansion!
   Day and night my tears flowed down in profusion,
But I didn't dare loudly appeal to other people.
Please show pity for me because of my misery —
My husband has left me behind, separated forever!"
   Judge Bao told her in all details from the beginning
How someone had lodged an accusation with him.
Shi Ma was called from the back part of the hall,
And he appeared, holding her darling in his arms!
   When Dusai lifted her head to have a good look,
She promptly recognized Second Master Shi Ma,
And when she had seen [her own baby], her son,
Tears burst from her eyes like pearls falling down.
   Master Shi Ma abused her at the top of his voice,
Loudly shouting: "[Liu Dusai, you] lowlife slut,
Because you had to go out and view the lanterns,
All of the Shis, the whole mansion, were murdered!"

His Excellency Prime Minister Bao gave the order
To fetch that pair of criminals from their prison.
When the two men had arrived at his high hall,
He loudly pronounced his verdict in both cases.

The imperial prince had kidnapped Liu Dusai,
And also murdered the Shis, the whole mansion.
Their numerous satins and silks, gold and silver
[He had carried off and taken away to his place.

For this crime the prince was to be beheaded,][18]
His body to be destroyed by a myriad of cuts.
His household was banished from the capital,
More than three hundred miles, as commoners.

His gold and silver and silks were confiscated,
And the servants in his service became soldiers.
Because of his greed for huge profit Sun Wenyi
Also was to be beheaded at the gate of the hall.

Once His Excellency had pronounced his verdict,
He ordered to saddle his thoroughbred horse, and
When Judge Bao had mounted his spirited horse,
He rode out onto the street with his full retinue.

He chose from many roads the one leading to
The bustling market place, to execute the prince.

A banner of black gauze was erected, as the sun
Shone on the golden plaque for the beheadings.
A single reed mat was laid out on the ground,
And three shovels of earth placed on top of it.

The executioners brandished their swords, and
Each held their magical objects in their hands.
A thousand short blades, one three-foot sword:
Golden rings behind the head reflecting the sun!

First they beheaded the Imperial Prince Zhao —
Crushed by a thousand blades nothing remained.
Next they beheaded his accomplice Sun Wenyi:
One stroke and his head fell down into the dust.

"Today you will visit the Eastern Marchmount,
Tomorrow you will see the judge in the shade.

---

[18] Two lines here seem to be missing from the original.

May one stroke take you to the realm of darkness,
And at Ghost Gate Pass [we will meet] again!"
    Cut into two by one stroke the bodies had died,
Turned into characters in a Southern Branch dream.
When the prince had been beheaded, Judge Bao
Turned around to go to court, to see His Majesty.

Now when he came to the court, he dismounted,
And the gatekeeper reported him to the emperor.
"His Excellency Prime Minister Bao has arrived,
He awaits Your summons at the appropriate place."
    When the emperor heard Judge Bao had arrived,
The news scared all high officials and dignitaries.
The emperor on his throne ordered him summoned,
And carrying this summons he greeted His Majesty.
    After he had bowed twenty-four times to his king,
The latter asked him to sit down on a brocade stool.
After he had had a cup of Dragon-Phoenix wax tea,
He was served three drinks of sealed imperial wine.

Speak:

The emperor asked: "Chancellor, why did you fake your own death?"
Judge Bao reported: "I had to take care of a case. On Go Board Lane of
Henan Prefecture, the Western Capital, there lived a weaver by the name of
Shi Guanshou. His wife Liu Dusai was very beautiful and seductive. When
she went out on the night of the fifteenth, Superior Prime, to view the
lanterns in Turtle Mountain Monastery, she ran into the prefect of the
Western Capital, Imperial Prince Zhao. Not only did he kidnap Liu Dusai,
but he also killed the one hundred and three members of her household,
old and young. He also murdered four other weavers. The household
servant uncle Zhang escaped, carrying the three-year-old infant in his arms.
Now there was Second Master Shi Ma, who worked as a weaver in Yangzhou.
Prefect Zhao wrote a letter to Sun Wenyi of this prefecture and had him
beat Second Master Shi Ma to death. They had wrapped him in yellow
cabbage leaves and were carrying him to the city moat, when they were
directed by me to Kaifeng Prefecture. The imperial prince abducted with
force the wife of someone else, murdered all members of the Shi family,
and also killed four weavers. Their silks and other textiles, gold and silver

are here at the golden steps. This was a crime deserving the punishment of a thousand cuts. Sun Wenyi killed one man, and paid back for that crime with his life. Both men have been beheaded, and the household members of the imperial prince have been banished beyond three hundred miles as commoners." When the emperor had heard this report, he offered him three cups of imperial wine with his own hands, [saying:] "These merits will be entered into the registers, and your name will be glorified in the Tower Rising Above the Clouds." Judge Bao also said to the emperor: "I recommend Second Master Shi Ma as the new prefect of the Western Capital." His Majesty accepted his proposal.

[*Sing:*]

The Son of Heaven, the Humane Ancestor, accepted
The proposal of this one man, His Excellency Bao.
"As he is honest and straight and free of corruption,
We don't have to worry he will not please Our will."
    He summoned Second Master Shi Ma in order to
Appoint him to a quite substantial official position.
"We appoint you as prefect of the Western Capital,
To be the lord and governor of the Western Capital.
    You alone will be in charge of Henan Prefecture;
You'll command the troops, you'll govern the people.
The gold and silver and silks will be returned to you,
And you will also take Liu Dusai along with you.
    [Also accompanied by Shi] Jinbao and uncle Zhang
The four of you will travel together on horseback.
And one hundred and twenty soldiers will be dispatched
To escort you on the way back to the Western Capital."
    When Master Shi received this imperial order,
He expressed his gratitude with twenty-four bows.
When he had finished his bows and exited the hall,
Judge Bao mounted his horse to go back to his office.
    Once Master Shi had left the Golden Phoenix Hall,
He repeatedly expressed his elation and surprise.
Before the Five Phoenix Loft he mounted his horse;
Once on the saddle he quickly left the imperial city.

Celebrating his high appointment he rode the streets,
Accompanied by Judge Bao and his body of guards.

Each and every family in the city cheered them on,
And nine out of ten thanked their ruler for his grace.
    Shi Ma dismounted from his proud and spirited horse
And he expressed his thanks to His Excellency Bao.
"I am really grateful to you, I'm really very grateful,
I am very grateful to Your Excellency for your help!"
    His Excellency Judge Bao addressed him as follows,
Speaking to Second Master Shi Ma in this manner:
    "As I am your sponsor and guarantor for this job,
You should not covet treasure or lust after money!
If you cross the rules, you'll run afoul of old Bao,
And this old Bao is not a man to show any mercy!
    I also want to express my respect for uncle Zhang:
This man really is not your common sort of fellow!
If uncle Zhang hadn't lodged an accusation with me,
Who would have redressed the wrongs done to you?"
    Having thanked His Excellency Dragon-Design Bao,
The four of them departed for the Western Capital.
"No one else but Judge Bao of the Southern Office
Could have managed to arrest Imperial Prince Zhao!"
    When Master Shi had mounted his spirited horse,
They left through the gates of the Eastern Capital.
[In each prefecture] local officials welcomed them,
In each district they were welcomed by its officials.
    There's no need to sing of the stretches they traveled:
[Soon they had arrived back in the] Western Capital.
Having selected a good hour and also a lucky day,
He took up his post, governing both army and people.

[Now I have written] this story in prose and verse,
I present this new tale to you, my noble audience!

The Story of the Judgment of Dragon-Design Bao in the Case of Prince Zhao and Sun Wenyi, Part Two, Completely Illustrated, in Prose and in Verse.

Zhu Yixuan (ed.) (1997). *Ming Chenghua Shuochang Cihua Congkan*, Zhengzhou: Zhongzhou guji chubanshe, pp. 264–288.

Glossary

ba 八
Bai (family) 白
Baijia gong'an 百家公案
Baitu ji 白兔記
Bao daizhi 包待制
Bao daizhi Chenzhou tiaomi ji 包待制陳州糶米記
"Bao daizhi chushen yuanliu" 包待制出身源流
Bao daizhi chushen zhuan 包待制出身傳
Bao daizhi duan wai wupen zhuan 包待制段歪烏盆傳
Bao gong 包公
Bao Longtu 包龍圖
Bao Longtu duan baihujing zhuan 包龍圖斷白虎精傳
Bao Longtu duan Cao guojiu zhuan 包龍圖斷曹國舅傳
"Bao nü de jia" 包女得嫁
Bao qingtian 包青天
Bao Wenzheng 包文正
Bao Zheng 包拯
Bao zhuanghe 抱粧盒
Baopuzi 抱樸子
bianwen 變文

Cai Bojie 蔡伯喈
Cai Lun 蔡倫
Cao (Empress) 曹
Cao Bin 曹彬
Cao Guojiu 曹國舅
Chenzhou tiaomi 陳州糶米
chuanqi 傳奇
Chuke pai'an jingqi 初刻拍案警奇
ci 詞

cihua 詞話
ciwen 詞文
Cui fujun 崔府君
Cui Hu 崔護

Da Ji 妲己
Di Qing 狄青
Dong Chao 董超
Dongyue dadi 東岳大帝

Fan Zhongyan 范仲淹
Feng Menglong 馮夢龍
Fengdu 豐都
Fuchai 夫差

Gao Ming 高明
Ge Hong 葛洪
Geng (potters) 耿
Gengzhi Zhang Qian tishaqi 鯁直張千替殺妻
Guankou Erlang 灌口二郎
Guanshiyin 觀世音
Guanyin 觀音
Guiying 桂英
Guo Huai 郭懷

Hetong wenzi 合同文字
Hetong wenzi ji 合同文字記
Hong Bian 洪楩
Hou Wenyi 侯文異
hu 斛
Hua Guan Suo 花關索
huaben 話本
Huai xi qu 淮西去
Hudie meng 蝴蝶夢
Huilan ji 灰闌記

Jin Chun 金春
Jin Ping Mei 金瓶梅

Jinchai ji 金釵記
Jindou 今斗
Jingshi tongyan 警世通言
juan 卷
Juling 巨靈

Kong (master) 孔

Laozi 老子
Li (Concubine) 李
Li (Lady) 李
Li Hu 李虎
Li Ji (criminal) 李吉
Li Ji (runner) 李吉
Li Wang 李旺
Li Xingdao 李行道
Lin Zhaode 林昭德
Ling Mengchu 凌蒙初
Liu (Empress-dowager) 劉
Liu Bei 劉備
Liu Dusai 劉都賽
Liu Wenlong 劉文龍
Liu yanei 劉衙內
Longtu erlu 龍圖耳錄
Longtu gong'an 龍圖公案
Lu (Lord) 魯
Lu Zhailang 魯齋郎

Ma Wan 馬萬
mao 卯
Mengliang lu 夢粱錄
Mingtang 明堂

namo 南無
Nanhai 南海
Nao Fanlou duoqing Zhou Shengxian 鬧樊樓多情周勝仙
Nong Zhigao 儂智高

Ouyang Xiu 歐陽修

Pan Cheng 潘成
Pangu 盤古
Pen'er gui 盆兒鬼
Peng Zu 彭祖
Pu Lin 蒲琳

Qian Chu 錢俶
Qian Hui 錢晦
Qian Weiyan 錢惟演
Qian Xuan 錢暄
Qin (Magistrate) 秦
Qingfengzha 清風閘
qingguan 清官
Qingping shantang huaben 清平山堂話本
Qixia wuyi 七俠五義

renchen 壬辰
Renzong 仁宗
Renzong renmu zhuan 仁宗認母傳
Ruan Ding 阮定

San Sui pingyao zhuan 三遂平妖傳
"San xianshen" 三現身
San xianshen Bao Longtu duan yuan 三現身包龍圖斷冤
Sanguo yanyi 三國演義
Sanhuang 三皇
Sanxia wuyi 三俠五義
Shen Yuanhua 沈元化
Shi Guanshou 師官受
Shi Guanshou qi Liu Dusai shangyuan shiwu ye kandeng zhuan
　師官受妻劉都賽上元十五夜看燈傳
Shi Jinbao 師金保
Shi Ma 師馬
Shi Yukun 石玉昆
shuochang cihua 說唱詞話
Song Qi 宋琪
Songshi 宋史
Sun Jiao 孫焦

Sun Wenyi 孫文儀
Sun Xiao'er 孫小二

Taiping xingguo 太平興國
Taizong 太宗
Taizu 太祖
Tang (old master) 唐
Tao (emperor's in-law) 陶
Tian Sanshu 田三叔
Tianpeng 天蓬

wai 外
Wan (Concubine) 萬
wanfu Bao daizhi 萬福包待制
Wang (censor) 王
Wang (innkeeper) 王
Wang Gongchen 王供辰
Wang Kui 王魁
Wang Liang 王梁
Wang Xing 王興
Wang Ze 王則
Wang Zeng 王曾
Wanhua lou 萬花樓
Wenqu xing 文曲星
Wu Kui 吳奎
Wudi 五帝
Wuhu pingnan 五虎平南
Wuhu pingxi 五虎平西
Wuqu xing 武曲星

Xi Shi 西施
Xiao (empress-dowager) 蕭
Xiao (lady) 蕭
Xiao Sun tu 小孫屠
"Xiaosu Baogong zhuan" 孝肅包公傳
Xiechai 獬豸
Xingshi hengyan 醒世恒言
Xinkan jingben tongsu yanyi zengxiang Bao Longtu pan Baijia gong'an
  新刊京本通俗演義增像包龍圖判百家公案

xiwen 戲文
Xixiang ji 西廂記
Xu (Palace Intendant) 徐
Xuanzong 玄宗
Xue Ba 薛霸
Xue Rengui kuahai zheng Liao gushi 薛仁貴跨海征遼故事
Xue Rengui zheng Liao shilüe 薛仁貴征遼事略

Yan Hui 嚴回
Yang (innkeeper) 楊
Yang (precious consort) 楊
Yang Wenguang 楊文廣
Yang Zhibao 楊知保
Yang Zongfu 楊宗富
Yingge xing xiaoyi zhuan 鶯哥行孝義傳
Yongle dadian 永樂大典
Yongshuntang 永順堂
You (king) 幽
Yu Yue 俞樾
Yuan Wenzheng 袁文正
Yuanqu xuan 元曲選

zaju 雜劇
Zang Maoxun 臧懋循
Zeng (imperial relative) 曾
Zeng Gong 曾鞏
zhang 丈
Zhang (abbot) 張
Zhang (Concubine) 張
Zhang (Top Courtesan) 張
Zhang Fangping 張方平
Zhang Long 張龍
Zhang Qian 張千
Zhang Qing (runner) 張清
Zhang Qing (servant) 張青
Zhang Qing (warden) 張青
Zhang Sengyou 張僧繇
Zhang Wengui zhuan 張文貴傳

"Zhang Yuanwai yifu minglingzi; Bao Longtu zhizhuan hetongwen"
張員外義撫螟蛉子; 包龍圖智賺合同文
Zhao Hu 趙虎
Zhao Sheng 趙省
Zhao Wanli 趙萬里
Zhao Wuniang 趙五娘
Zhao Yuanyan 趙元儼
Zhaonafu 招納府
Zhenzong 真宗
Zhong Kui 鐘馗
Zhuge Liang 諸葛亮
Zhuo Ji Bu zhuanwen 捉季布傳文
zi 子

Bibliography

Abe, Y. 阿部泰記 (2004). *Hōkō densetsu no keisei to tenkai* 包公傳說の形成と展開 [The Formation and Development of the Legend of Judge Bao]. Tokyo: Kyūko shoin.

Akamatsu, N. 赤松紀彦 (1991). *"Genkyoku sen ga mezashita mono"* 元曲選がめざしたもの [The Aim of the *Yuanqu xuan*], in *Tanaka Kenji hakase sōshū kinen Chūgoku koten gikyoku ronshū* 田中謙二博士頌壽記念中國古典戲曲論集 [Articles on Chinese Classical Drama for Dr. Tanaka Kenji on the Occasion of his Eightieth Birthday]. Tokyo: Kyūko shoin, pp. 161–186.

An Yushi 安遇時 (1999). *Baijia gong'an* 百家公案 [One Hundred Court Cases], ed. by Shi Lei 石雷. Beijing: Qunzhong chubanshe.

Baogong an 包公案 [The Cases of Judge Bao], ed. by Feng Buyi 冯不异 (1985). Beijing: Baowentang.

Baogong an cihua bazhong Shi lang fuma zhuan 包公案詞話八種石郎駙馬傳 [Eight Ballad-stories of Cases of Judge Bao; The Biography of Prince-consort Shi], in *Guben xiaoshuo congkan*, Ser. 22, Vol. 4 (1991). Beijing: Zhonghua shuju.

Bauer, W. (1974). "The Tradition of the 'Criminal Cases of Master Pao' *Pao-kung-an* (*Lung-t'u kung-an*)," *Oriens*, 23–24, 433–449.

Bauer, W. (trans.) (1992). *Die Leiche im Strom: Die seltsame kriminalfälle des Meister Bao* [The Corpse in the River: The Curious Cases of Judge Bao]. Freiburg: Herder.

Blader, S. (1977). "A Critical Study of *San-hsia wu-yi* and its Relationship to the *Lung-t'u kung-an* Songbook." PhD Dissertation, University of Pennsylvania.

Blader, S. (1978). "*San-hsia wu-yi* and its Link to Oral Literature," *Chinoperl Papers*, 8, 9–38.

Brook, T., Bourgon J. and Blue, G. (2008). *Death by a Thousand Cuts*. Cambridge MA: Harvard University Press.

Cass, V. (1982). "Revels of a Gaudy Night," *Chinese Literature Essays Articles Reviews*, 4(2), 213–231.

Chaffee, J. W. (1999). *Branches of Heaven: A History of the Imperial Clan of Song China*. Cambridge MA: Harvard University Asia Center.

Chen Guidi 陳貴棣 and Chun Tao 春桃 (2007). *Baogong yigu ji* 包公遺骨記 [The Remaining Bones of Judge Bao]. Taipei: Jiujing chubanshe.

Cheng Rufeng 程如峰 (1994). *Baogong zhuan* 包公传 [A Biography of Judge Bao]. Hefei: Huangshan shushe.

Chenghua xinbian Liu Zhiyuan huanxiang Baitu ji 成化新編劉知遠還鄉白兔記 [The Chenghua Reign Newly Compiled Story of the White Hare — How Liu Zhiyuan Returned Home]. (1980). Yangzhou: Jiangsu guangling guji keyinsuo.

Comber, L. (1964). *The Strange Cases of Magistrate Pao: Chinese Tales of Crime and Detection*. Rutland VT: Charles E. Tuttle.

Ding Chuanjing 丁傳靖 (1981). *Songren yishi huibian* 宋人轶事彙編 [Collected Anecdotes of Song Persons]. Beijing: Zhonghua shuju.

Ding Zhaoqin 丁照琴 (2000). *Suwenxue zhongde Baogong* 俗文學中的包公 [Judge Bao in Popular Literature]. Taipei: Wenjin chubanshe.

Fan Jiachen 范嘉晨 (ann.) (2006). *Yuan zaju Baogongxi pingzhu* 元杂剧包公戏评注 [An Annotated Edition of the Judge Bao Plays in Yuan *Zaju*]. Ji'nan: Qi Lu shushe.

Franke, H. (ed.) (1976). *Song Biographies*. Wiesbaden: Franz Steiner Verlag.

Ge Liangyan. "Narrative Affinities between *Shuihu zhuan* and the Judge Bao *cihua* Cluster: In Search of a Common Storehouse of Convention." Unpublished Paper.

von Glahn, R. (2004). *The Sinister Way: The Divine and the Demonic in Chinese Religious Culture*. Berkeley: University of California Press.

Hammond, C. E. (1991). "An Excursion into Tiger Lore," *Asia Major*, Third Series, 4(1), 87–100.

Hammond, C. E. (1992–1993)."Sacred Metamorphosis: The Weretiger and the Shaman," *Acta Orientalia*, 46, Fasc. 2–3, 235–255.

Hammond, C. E. (1995). "The Demonization of the Other: Women and Minorities as Weretigers," *Journal of Chinese Religions*, 23, 59–80.

Hammond, C. E. (1996). "The Righteous Tiger and the Grateful Lion," *Monumenta Serica*, 44, 191–211.

Hanan, P. (1973). *The Chinese Short Story: Studies in Dating, Authorship, and Composition*. Cambridge MA: Harvard University Press.

Hanan, P. (1980). "*Judge Bao's Hundred Cases* Reconstructed," *Harvard Journal of Asiatic Studies*, 40(2), 301–323.

Hayden, G. A. (1978). *Crime and Punishment in Medieval Chinese Drama*. Cambridge MA: Harvard University Press.

Hegel, R. E. and Carlitz, K. (eds.) (2007). *Writing and Law in Late Imperial China*. Seattle: University of Washington Press.

Hu Shi 胡适 (1980). "*Sanxia wuyi* xu" 三俠五義序 [Preface to *Three Heroes and Five Gallants*], reprinted in his *Zhongguo zhanghui xiaoshuo kaozheng* 中国章回小说考证 [Evidential Research on Traditional Chinese Novels]. Shanghai: Shanghai shudian, pp. 393–435.

Huang Bingze 黄秉泽 (2002). "Baogong xi yuanliu xulu zhi yi" 包公戏源流叙录之一 [A Systematic Account of the Interrelationships of Judge Bao Plays. Part One], *Ningbo zhiye jishu xueyuan xuebao*, 2(2), 41–54.

Huang Bingze (2002). "Baogong xi yuanliu xulu zhi er" 包公戏源流叙录之二 [A Systematic Account of the Interrelationships of Judge Bao Plays. Part Two], *Ningbo zhiye jishu xueyuan xuebao*, 2(3), 40–43.

Huang Bingze (2002). "Baogong xi yuanliu xulu san" 包公戏源流叙录三 [A Systematic Account of the Interrelationships of Judge Bao Plays. Three], *Ningbo zhiye jishu xueyuan xuebao*, 2(4), 37–42.

Idema, W. L. (1996). "Why You Never Have Read a Yuan Drama: The Transformation of *Zaju* at the Ming Court," in S.M. Carletti et al. (eds.), *Studi in onore di Lionello Lanciotti* [Studies in Honor of Lionello Lanciotti]. Napoli: Istituto Universitario Orientale, Vol. 2, pp. 765–791.

Idema, W. L. (1999). "Guanyin's Parrot: A Chinese Animal Tale and its International Context," in A. Cadonna (ed.), *India, Tibet, China, Genesis and Aspects of Traditional Narrative*. Firenze: Leo S. Olschki Editore, pp. 103–150.

Idema, W. L. (2006). "Something Rotten in the State of Song: The Frustrated Loyalty of the Generals of the Yang Family," *Journal of Song-Yuan Studies*, 36, 57–77.

Idema, W. L. (2007). "Fighting in Korea: Two Early Narratives of the Story of Xue Rengui," in R. E. Breuker (ed.), *Korea in the Middle: Korean Studies and Area Studies*. Leiden: CNWS, pp. 341–358.

Idema, W. L. (2008). *Heroines of Jiangyong: Traditional Narrative Ballads in the Women's Script*. Seattle: University of Washington Press.

Idema, W. L. (Forthcoming). "Prosimetric and Verse Narrative," in Kang-I Sun-Chang and S. Owen (eds.), *Cambridge History of Chinese Literature*. Cambridge: Cambridge University Press.

Inoue, T. 井上泰山 et al. (1989). *Ka Kan Saku den no kenkyū* 花關索傳の研究 [A Study of the Biography of Hua Guan Suo]. Tokyo: Kyūko shoin.

Julien, S. (trans.) (1832). *Hoei-lan-ki; ou l'Histoire du cercle de craie: Drame en prose et en vers* [*Huilan ji* or The Story of the Chalk Circle. A Play in Prose and in Verse]. London: Oriental Translation Fund.

King, G. O. (1989). *The Story of Hua Guan Suo*. Tempe: Center for Asian Studies, Arizona State University.

Kinkley, J. C. (2000). *Chinese Justice, The Fiction*. Stanford: Stanford University Press.

Komatsu, K. 小松謙 (1991). "Naifukei shohon kō" 内府系諸本考 [A Study of the Texts Originating from the Imperial Palace], in *Tanaka Kenji hakase sōshū kinen Chūgoku koten gikyoku ronshū*. Tokyo: Kyūko shoin, pp. 125–150.

Kong Fanmin 孔繁敏 (1986). *Bao Zheng nianpu* 包拯年谱 [A Year-by-Year Biography of Bao Zheng]. Hefei: Huangshan shushe.

Kong Fanmin (1998). *Bao Zheng yanjiu: Lishi yu yishu xingxiang zhongde Baogong* 包拯研究：历史与艺术形象中的包公 [Studies on Bao Zheng: Judge Bao in History and Artistic Imagination]. Beijing: Zhongguo shehui kexue chubanshe.

Lévy, A. (1971). "Le motif d'Amphitrion en Chine: 'Les cinq rats jouent mauvais tours à la capitale orientale'" [The Motif of Anphytrion in China: 'The Five Rats Create Havoc in the Eastern Capital'], in *Études sur le conte et le roman chinois* [Studies on the Short Story and Novel in China]. Paris: École Française d'Extrême Orient, pp. 115–146.

Li Hanqiu 李汉秋 and Zhu Wanshu 朱万曙 (1993). *Baogong xilie xiaoshuo* 包公系列小说 [The Judge Bao Novels]. Shenyang: Liaoning jiaoyu chubanshe.

Li Ping 李平 (1978). "Shilun qingguanxi de jiji yiyi" 试论清官戏的积极意义 [A Discussion of the Positive Meaning of Plays on Pure Officials], *Guangming ribao* November 14.

Li Shiren 李时人 (1986). "'Cihua' xinzheng" 词话新证 [New Materials on Ballad-stories], *Wenxue yichan*, 1, 72–78.

Li Yongping 李永平 (2007). *Baogong wenxue ji qi chuanbo* 包公文学及其传播 [Judge Bao Literature and its Dissemination]. Beijing: Zhongguo shehui kexue chubanshe.

Liu, J. T. C. (1973). "The Sung Emperors and the *Ming-t'ang* or Hall of Enlightenment," in F. Aubin (ed.), *Études Song: In Memoriam Étienne Balazs*. Paris: Mouton, Sér. 2, pp. 45–58.

Liu, X. (1986). "The Art of Gong'an Fiction: A Study of the Themes, Characterization and Narrative Structures of the *Longtu gong'an* and the *Sanxia wuyi*," *Stone Lion Review*, 14, 80–108.

Liu Yongnian 刘永年 and Shi Peiyi 施培毅 (1966). "Jianjue dangdi fengjian wenyi de wuzhuo. Ping Yuan zaju zhong jige 'Baogong xi' he dui ta de chuibang" 坚决荡涤封建文艺的污浊。 评元杂剧中的几个包公戏和对他的吹棒 [Firmly Clear Away that Stain of the Feudal Arts. A Criticism of Some Judge Bao Plays among the Yuan-Dynasty *Zaju* and their Supporters], *Guangming ribao* May 15, p. 4.

Lou Yao 樓鑰 (1981). *Beixing rilu* 北行日錄 [Diary of a Trip to the North], in Wang Minxin 王民信 (ed.), *Nan Song guoxin yulu sizhong* 南宋國信語錄四種 [Records of Four Southern Song Embassies]. Taipei: Wenhai chubanshe.

Luo Ye 羅燁 (1940). *Xinbian Zuiweng tanlu* 新編醉翁談錄 [Newly Compiled: Conversation Records of a Drunken Graybeard]. Tokyo: Bunkyudo.

Ma, Y. W. (1971). "The Pao-kung Tradition in Chinese Popular Literature." Dissertation, Yale.

Ma, Y. W. (1973). "Themes and Characterization in the *Lung-t'u kung-an*," *T'oung Pao*, 59, 179–202.

Ma, Y. W. (1975). "The Textual Tradition of Ming *Kung-an* Fiction: A Study of the *Long-t'u kung-an*," *Harvard Journal of Asiatic Studies*, 35, 190–220.

McGrath, M. (2009). "The Reigns of Jen-tsung (1022–1063) and Ying-tsung (1063–1067)," in D. Twitchett and P. J. Smith (eds.), *The Cambridge History of China*, Volume 5: *The Sung Dynasty and Its Precursors*. Cambridge: Cambridge University Press, pp. 279–346.

McLaren, A. E. (1990). "The Discovery of Chinese Chantefable Narratives from the Fifteenth Century: A Reassessment of their Likely Audience," *Ming Studies*, 29, 1–29.

McLaren, A. E. (1996). "Women's Voices and Textuality: Chastity and Abduction in Chinese *Nüshu* Writing," *Modern China*, 22(4), 382–416.

McLaren, A. E. (1998). *Chinese Popular Culture and Ming Chantefables*. Leiden: E. J. Brill.

Meng Yuanlao 孟元老 et al. (1962). *Dongjing meng Hua lu (wai sizhong)* 東京夢華錄外四種 [The Eastern Capital: A Record of a Dream of Hua, and Four Other Works]. Beijing: Zhonghua shuju.

Ming Chenghua shuochang cihua congkan 明成化说唱词话丛刊 [A Collected Edition of the Ballad-stories for Telling and Singing of the Chenghua Reign of the Ming Dynasty] (1973). Shanghai: Shanghai bowuguan.

Ming Chenghua shuochang cihua congkan 明成話說唱詞話叢刊 [A Collected Edition of the Ballad-stories for Telling and Singing of the Chenghua Reign of the Ming Dynasty] (1979). Taipei: Dingwen shuju.

Perng, Ching-Hsi (1978). *Double Jeopardy: A Critique of Seven Yüan Courtroom Dramas*. Ann Arbor: Center for Chinese Studies, University of Michigan.

Qu Chunshan 屈春山 and Li Liangxue 李良学 (1994). *Baogong zhengzhuan* 包公正传 [A Biography of Judge Bao]. Zhengzhou: Zhongzhou guji chubanshe.

Roy, D. T. (1981). "The Fifteenth-century *Shuo-ch'ang tz'u-hua* as an Example of Written Formulaic Composition," *Chinoperl Papers*, 10, 97–128.

St. André, J. (2002). "Picturing Judge Bao in Ming *Shangtu Xiawen* Fiction," *Chinese Literature Essays Articles Reviews*, 24, 43–74.

St. André, J. (2007). "Reading Court Cases from the Song and the Ming," in R. E. Hegel and K. Carlitz (eds.), *Writing and Law in Late Imperial China*. Seattle: University of Washington Press, pp. 189–214.

Schmoller, B. (1982). *Bao Zheng (999–1062) als Beamter und Staatsmann* [Bao Zheng as Official and Statesman]. Bochum: Brockmeyer.

Schommer, S. (1994). *Richter Bao — der chinesische Sherlock Holmes. Eine Untersuchung der Sammlung Kriminalfälle Bao Gongan* [Judge Bao — the Chinese Sherlock Holmes. A Study of the Collection of Court Cases *Baogong an*]. Bochum: Brockmeyer.

Shi Yukun and Yu Yue (1997). *The Seven Heroes and Five Gallants*, trans. Song Shouquan. Beijing: Panda Books.

Shih Yü-k'un (1998). *Tales of Magistrate Bao and his Valiant Lieutenants: Selections from* San-hsia wu-i, trans. S. Blader. Hong Kong: Chinese University Press.

Su Li 苏力 (2006). *Falü yu wenxue: Yi Zhongguo chuantong xiju wei cailiao* 法律与文学以中国传统戏剧为材料 [Law and Literature: On the Basis of Chinese Traditional Drama]. Beijing: Sanlian.

Sun Kaidi 孫楷第 (1953). *Yeshiyuan gujin zaju kao* 也是園古今雜劇考 [A Study of the *Yeshiyuan zaju*]. Shanghai: Shangza chubanshe.

Sun Kaidi (1985). "*Baogong an* yu *Baogong an* gushi" 包公案與包公案故事 [The *Baogong an* and the Stories in the *Baogong an*], reprinted in his *Cangzhou houji* 滄州後集 [Second Cangzhou Collection]. Beijing: Zhonghua shuju, pp. 67–150.

Tan Zhengbi 谭正璧 and Tan Xun 谭寻 (1985). *Pingtan tongkao* 评弹通考 [A Comprehensive Study of Prosimetrical Storytelling]. Beijing: Zhongguo quyi chubanshe.

Tu Xiuhong 涂秀虹 (1997). "Baogong xi yu Baogong xiaoshuo de guanxi shang" 包公戏与包公小说的关系上 [The Relation between Judge Bao Plays and Judge Bao Novels, Part I], *Fujian shifan daxue xuebao*, no. 2, 75–82, and Part II, idem, no. 3, 78–82.

Waltner, A. (1990). "From Casebook to Fiction: *Kung-an* in Late Imperial Fiction," *Journal of the American Oriental Society*, 110(2), 281–289.

Wang Jiaxin 王家歆 (2007). "Songshi Bao Zheng zhuan suzheng" 宋史包拯傳疏證 [Annotations to the "Biography of Bao Zheng" in the *History of the Song*], in his *Chang'e, Li Shangyin, Bao Zheng tanze* 嫦娥李商隱包整探賾 [Researches on

Chang'e, Li Shangyin, and Bao Zheng]. Taipei: Wenshizhe chubanshe, pp. 129–174.

West, S. H. (1991). "A Study in Appropriation: Zang Maoxun's Injustice to Dou E," *Journal of the American Oriental Society*, 101, 282–302.

West, S. H. (2003). "Text and Ideology: Ming Editors and Northern Drama," in P. J. Smith and R. von Glahn (eds.), *The Song-Yuan-Ming Transition in Chinese History*. Cambridge MA: Harvard University Press, pp. 329–373.

Xu Zhongmin 徐忠明 (2002). *Baogong gushi: Yige kaocha Zhongguo falü wenhua de shijiao* 包公故事一个考察中国法律文化的视角 [Judge Bao Stories: A Perspective from an Inquiry into Chinese Legal Culture]. Beijing: Zhongguo zhengfa daxue chubanshe.

Yang Guoyi 楊國宜 (ed.) (1989). *Bao Zheng ji biannian jiaobu* 包拯集編年校補 [A Critical and Expanded Edition, Chronologically Arranged, of the Collected Writings of Bao Zheng]. Hefei: Huangshan shushe.

Yang Guoyi 楊國宜 (ed.) (1999). *Bao Zheng ji jiaozhu* 包拯集校注 [A Critical and Annotated Edition of the Collected Works of Bao Zheng]. Hefei: Huangshan shushe.

Yang, Xianyi and Yang, G. (trans.) (1979). *Selected Plays of Guan Hanqing*. Beijing: Foreign Languages Press.

Yang Xurong 杨绪容 (2001). "Baogong zhi Bozhou haishi Haozhou" 包公知亳州还是濠州 [Did Judge Bao Administer Bozhou or Haozhou?], *Gudian wenxue zhishi*, 5, 120–122.

Yang Xurong (2005). *Baijia gong'an yanjiu* 百家公案研究 [A Study of *One Hundred Court Cases*]. Shanghai: Shanghai guji chubanshe.

Yang Zhihua 杨芷华 (1993). "Yan wei shuochang, jiwang kailai. Ming Chenghua kan Baogong gushi shuochang cihua bazhong shuping" 演为说唱继往开来明成化刊包公故事说唱词话八种述评 [Developed into Chantefables, Continuing the Past and Opening the Future — A Description of the Eight Ballad-stories for Telling and Singing on Judge Bao Printed during the Chenghua Reign of the Ming Dynasty], *Henan daxue xuebao*, 33(2), 75–80.

Yu Tieqiu 于铁丘 (2004). *Qingguan chongbai tan: Cong Bao Zheng dao Hai Rui* 清官崇拜谈从包拯到海瑞 [On the Veneration of Pure Officials: From Bao Zheng to Hai Rui]. Ji'nan: Ji'nan chubanshe.

Yuan Haowen 元好問 et al. (1986). *Xu Yi Jian zhi; Huhai xinwen Yi Jian xuzhi* 續夷堅志湖海新聞夷堅續志 [The Continued Record of the Listener and New Stories from Lakes and Seas: A Continued Record of the Listener], Chang Zhenguo 常振國 and Jin Xin 金心 (eds.). Beijing: Zhonghua shuju.

Zeng Yongyi 曾永義 (2003). *Suwenxue gailun* 俗文學概論 [A Survey of Popular Literature]. Taipei: Sanmin shuju.

Zhang Dengwen 张登文 (1986). "Lianxuti gong'an lei jiangchang wenxue de xianqu — Ming Chenghua ben 'Bao Longtu gong'an cihua' chutan" 连续体公案类讲唱文学的先驱明成化本包龙图公案词话初探 [A Forerunner of the Court-Case Type Prosimetrical Literature in Installments — A First Inquiry into the Court Case Ballad-stories of Dragon-Design Bao of the Chenghua Reign of the Ming Dynasty], *Dongyue luncong*, no. 5, pp. 71–74.

Zhang Huasheng 张华盛 and Fu Tengxiao 傅腾霄 (1985). *Bao Zheng* 包拯. Hefei: Anhui jiaoyu chubanshe.

Zhao Jingshen 趙景深 (1937). "Baogong chuanshuo" 包公傳說 [The Legend of Judge Bao], in Zhao Jingshen, *Xiaoshuo xianhua* 小說閒話. Shanghai: Beixin shuju, pp. 104–137.

Zhao Jingshen (1937). "Suoluomen yu Bao Zheng" 所羅門與包拯 [Solomon and Bao Zheng], in Zhao Jingshen, *Xiaoshuo xianhua*. Shanghai: Beixin shuju, pp. 138–152.

Zhao Jingshen (1972). "Tan Ming Chenghua kanben 'shuochang cihua'" 谈明成化刊本说唱词话 [On the Prosimetrical Ballad-stories Printed in the Chenghua Reign of the Ming Dynasty], *Wenwu* (November), 19–22.

Zheng Qian 鄭騫 (1972). "Zang Maoxun gaiding Yuan zaju pingyi" 藏懋循改訂元雜劇評議 [An Evaluation of Zang Maoxun's Revision of Yuan-dynasty *Zaju*], in his *Jingwu congbian* [Collected Writings of Jingwu]. Taipei: Taiwan Zhonghua shuju, Vol. 1, pp. 408–421.

Zhou Qifu 周启付 (1982). "Tan Ming Chenghua kanben 'shuochang cihua'" 谈明成化刊本说唱词话 [On the Ballad-stories for Telling and Singing Printed in the Chenghua Reign of the Ming Dynasty], *Wenxue yichan*, no. 2, 120–127.

Zhu Wanshu 朱万曙 (1995). *Baogong gushi yuanliu kaoshu* 包公故事源流考述 [A Study of the Development of the Judge Bao Story]. Hefei: Anhui wenyi chubanshe.

Zhu Yixuan 朱一玄 (ed.) (1997). *Ming Chenghua shuochang cihua congkan* 明成化说唱词话丛刊 [A Collected Edition of the Ballad-stories for Telling and Singing of the Chenghua Reign of the Ming Dynasty]. Zhengzhou: Zhongzhou guji chubanshe.